口適中菜譜

Chinese Kosher Cooking

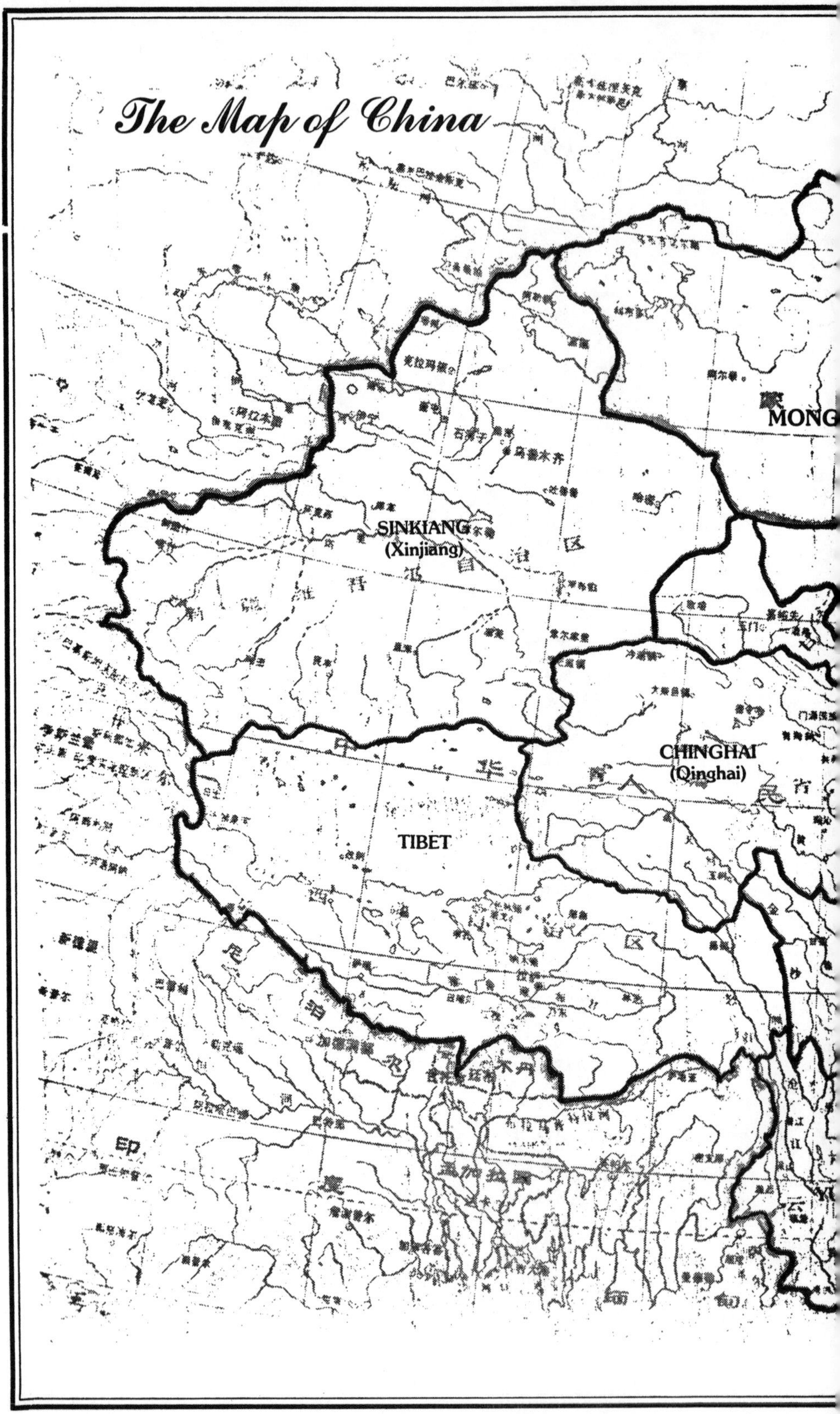
The Map of China
MONG
SINKIANG
(Xinjiang)
CHINGHAI
(Qinghai)
TIBET

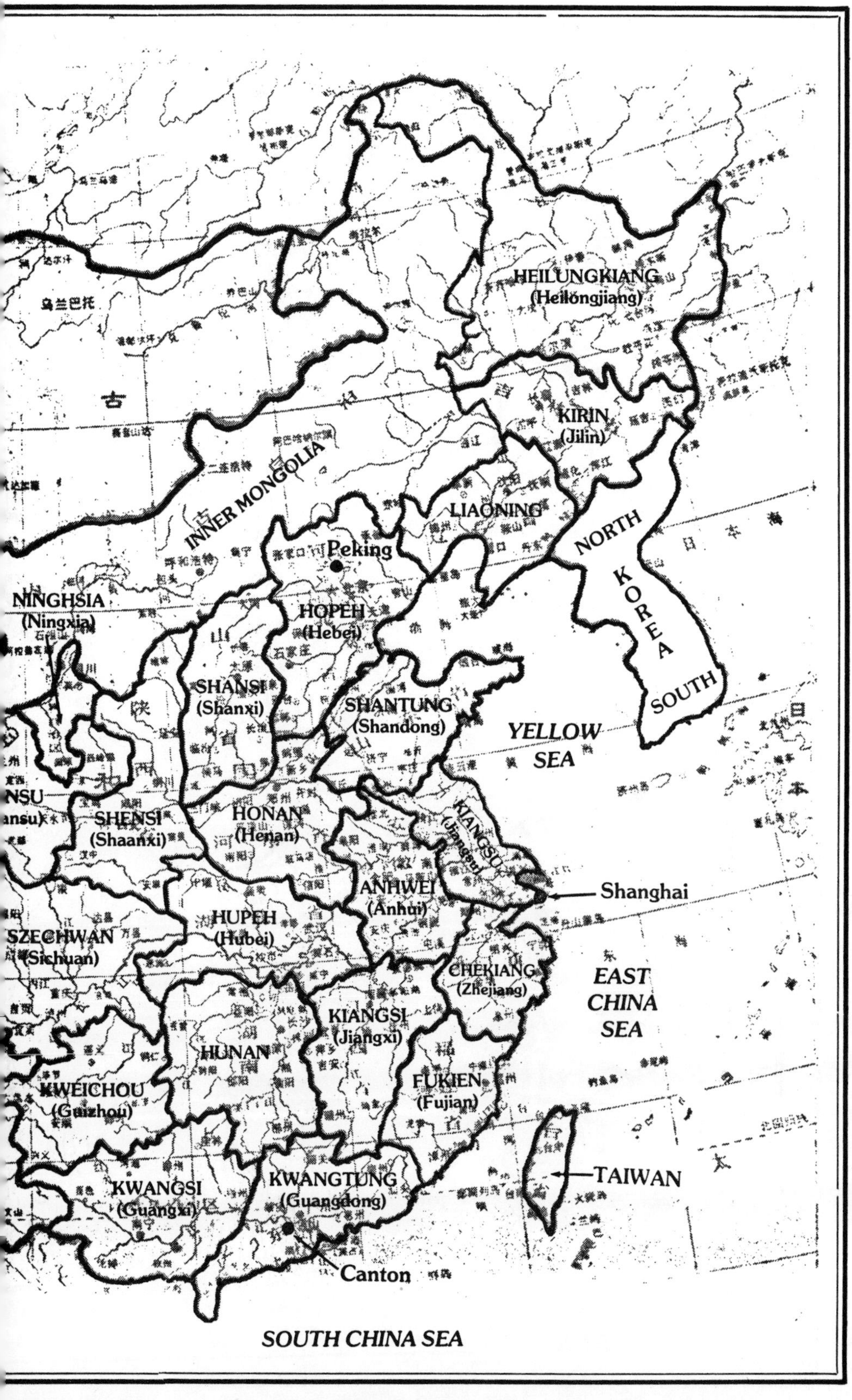
HEILUNGKIANG
(Heilongjiang)
KIRIN
(Jilin)
INNER MONGOLIA
LIAONING
NORTH
KOREA
SOUTH
Peking
NINGHSIA
(Ningxia)
HOPEH
(Hebei)
SHANSI
(Shanxi)
SHANTUNG
(Shandong)
YELLOW
SEA
SHENSI
(Shaanxi)
HONAN
(Henan)
KIANGSU
(Jiangsu)
Shanghai
ANHWEI
(Anhui)
HUPEH
(Hubei)
SZECHWAN
(Sichuan)
CHEKIANG
(Zhejiang)
EAST
CHINA
SEA
KIANGSI
(Jiangxi)
HUNAN
FUKIEN
(Fujian)
KWEICHOU
(Guizhou)
KWANGSI
(Guangxi)
KWANGTUNG
(Guangdong)
TAIWAN
Canton
SOUTH CHINA SEA

口適中菜譜

Chinese Kosher Cooking

Betty S. Goldberg

JD
Jonathan David Publishers, Inc.
Middle Village, New York 11379

CHINESE KOSHER COOKING

Jonathan David Publishers, Inc.
68-22 Eliot Avenue
Middle Village, New York 11379

Library of Congress Cataloging in Publication Data

Goldberg, Betty S.
Chinese kosher cooking.

Bibliography: p.
Includes index.
1. Cookery, Jewish. 2. Cookery, Chinese. I. Title.
TX724.G652 1984 641.5'676 83-5178

Chinese calligraphy by Anne Ho
Illustrations by Rima Grad
Layout by Arlene Schleifer Goldberg

Printed in the United States of America

To my human guinea pigs—
Josh, Aaron, Michael,
Benjamin and Nancy

Contents

Acknowledgments

For providing the encouragement I needed for this book, I would like to thank the following:

My publisher, Rabbi Alfred J. Kolatch, for saying yes; my editor, David Kolatch, for expanding my horizons and for teaching me the meaning of the word consistency; Alyce Chaikin Kleinman, my mentor by mail; the owners of China Trading Company, New Haven, Connecticut; and especially Monica Yu, for her interest, encouragement, the many hours she spent on the Chinese characters, and for the mini-lessons in the beautiful Chinese language.

Preface

For our first wedding anniversary my husband bought me *The Pleasures of Chinese Cooking,* by Grace Zia Chu, and it is to both Josh and Mme. Chu that I owe thanks for my introduction to Chinese cuisine. Josh and I both enjoy cooking, and we soon began experimenting with recipes from the cookbook. Before long we found ourselves planning elaborate Chinese dinners, and within a year we proudly prepared our first "big" dinner for friends who often frequented Chinese restaurants. The response was enthusiastic.

Within a few years Josh and I had held more than thirty of these special dinners, at which were featured anywhere from two to ten appetizers, a soup, one to six main dishes, and usually a very un-Chinese rich dessert (my style of serving). Most of the cooking was done at the dinner table, using one or two electric skillets for deep or stir-frying. Thus, although I might put in enormous amounts of time cutting, chopping, slicing, and measuring ingredients during the day, I could be with my friends most of the time after they arrived. A typical dinner would last as long as five hours.

After living in Swarthmore, Pennsylvania, for some time, I found I'd served Chinese dinners to just about everyone I knew. Taking the step from hostess to teacher, I organized a six-lesson course called "Advanced Chinese Cooking for the Beginner," drawing students first from my friends and then from the general community.

One day in the fall of 1974, one of my students and I sold over 100 Chinese luncheon platters at our town fair. We used our "right-before-your-eyes" method of cooking: Jody wrapped egg rolls while I fried them in my electric skillet. Those who didn't like Chinese food could at least watch the show.

The evening of the fair my knowledge of Chinese cuisine grew dramatically: we had a visit from nonkosher friends who over a dinner of Sloppy Joes and apple pie described some of the exotic appetizers they'd been served at one of their favorite teahouses in New York's Chinatown. The moment they left I consulted my ever-expanding collection of Chinese cookbooks and found virtually all the succulent foods they'd described. It took seven months of modifying recipes to make them kosher, and in April Josh and I invited our friends back for a "teahouse" dinner of eleven appetizers, fried rice, various sauces, and my customary dessert. At the end of the dinner they commented, "Do you know, these appetizers are virtually exactly what we get at the tea parlor!" Yes, Virginia (it really is Virginia), I worked at that.

Shortly after moving to Ridgefield, Connecticut, in 1975, we joined the local synagogue, and soon I found myself fixing tacos at the annual temple fair while I jealously watched the rabbi corner the market with his Chinese food booth. His "cold hot noodles" and *lo mien* were major attractions at the fair. As the rabbi watched the group clustered around his wok, waiting for the next batch (stir-frying as he watched, of course), he glanced over at me in the next booth and remarked, "You know, we're doing it wrong. What would really make money would be a whole Chinese dinner at the temple." I took the rabbi's suggestion from there, and our first fundraising "Chinese Banquet—Goldberg Style" was held in March 1976

When we moved to the New Haven area several years ago and joined a local synagogue, we brought our fundraising Chinese banquet with us. I also taught a series of Chinese cooking lessons as a sisterhood fundraiser. Writing a cookbook was the next logical step.

The recipes in *Chinese Kosher Cooking* draw on my experience teaching Chinese cooking and preparing hundreds of Chinese banquets and home dinners. The book is the result of eighteen years of delicious experimentation. Every recipe has been tested and retested to please the experts—my family and friends.

B.S.G.

Woodbridge, Connecticut
July 1984

口適中菜譜

Chinese Kosher Cooking

Part 1

Introduction to Chinese Cuisine

Regional Chinese Cooking

China has many styles of cooking within its borders. The recent proliferation of regional Chinese restaurants in the United States has helped teach the restaurant public that Chinese cooking is actually comprised of a number of individual cuisines. While it is true that a variety of cooking methods—including stir-frying, steaming, stewing, and simmering—are used in all parts of China, each area has developed its own characteristic dishes based on availability of principal ingredients, seasonings, and spices.

Americans are most familiar with the southeastern, or Cantonese, style of cooking, because it is from Canton that the first Chinese were able to emigrate in large numbers. Stir-fried dishes, in which individual ingredients retain their flavors and colors even as they blend to create a whole dish; light marinades of soy sauce, ginger, and wine; the use of chicken stock; and the liberal use of fresh produce, fish, and seafood are all characteristic of Cantonese cuisine.

Moving inland to the provinces of Hunan and Szechwan, we find that in home cooking liberal use is made of hot peppers. Interestingly, Szechwan *banquet* dishes are more often bland and light, reflecting the influence of northerners who migrated from Peking. This inland area of China gives us the intriguing Szechwan peppercorn, whose distinctive taste affects any dish it touches.

Shantung and Peking dishes, from northern China, are closely related. This is due to the active trade that has existed in that region and the resultant "borrowing" of dishes and "exchanging" of chefs. Northern cooking features garlic and scallions extensively, and is also well known for its use of wheat as a staple rather than rice. Peking duck and the pancakes served with *mu shu* dishes are from the North as well.

The cuisine of Honan Province, which is either included in discussions of northern Chinese cuisine or treated as a separate school of cooking, is most famous for its sweet-and-sour fish. However, Cantonese chefs readily welcomed the flavorful Honan sauces and sweet-and-sour dishes into their own repertories, and thus it is with the Cantonese that we generally associate sweet-and-sour preparations.

Many food authorities consider the culinary center of the coastal region of China to be the province of Fukien (although some focus on Shanghai cooking when discussing the East Coast). Fukien is famous for its red-cooked dishes (foods cooked in soy sauce) as well as for its seafood preparations and its clear, light soups.

Although no school of cooking has developed in sparsely populated Mongolia, that northern region has become known for its use of lamb, which is not often eaten in other parts of China.

Chinese restaurants in America may feature "Mandarin cooking" (often in neon lights), but there is no such area or province in China, nor are there typical Mandarin dishes. In America "Mandarin" has become a synonym for "Chinese," although a *mandarin*, literally, is an official. In China Mandarin dishes originally were those prepared for the aristocracy, and the term therefore became associated with Peking dishes. Mandarin cooking now refers to fine restaurant cooking in general, not to a regional type of cooking.

Regardless of where they live or how or what they cook, the Chinese consider the appearance and aroma of a finished dish as crucial as its taste. Color contrast, flavor balance, degree of spiciness, even serving temperatures are vital in a well-planned meal. In China, food is not just for eating—it is part of a total experience.

Chinese Cooking in the Kosher Kitchen

One of the chief characteristics of Chinese cooking is its adaptability. The chef's staff sent to market for a banquet buys the best ingredients available; the chef then plans the menu based on those ingredients. Because Chinese cooking is so very practical and flexible, it is not surprising that modifying Chinese recipes for the kosher kitchen is not so difficult as one might initially expect.

Pork is the principal meat used in China, but in the kosher home it is possible to substitute beef, veal, or lamb in Chinese preparations with excellent results. Red-cooked Whole Brisket, Veal Chao Mien, and Barbecued "Spareribs" (using breast of lamb) use cooking methods and seasonings typical of Chinese dishes cooked with pork, so they have a distinctive Chinese flavor. The kosher adaptations use meat cut from the forequarter because this is the meat most commonly available from kosher butchers. (The process of removing all the veins from the hindquarter is so expensive that it is unusual to see hindquarter cuts in the kosher kitchen.) Sometimes recipes can be used just as they appear in Chinese cookbooks, with the simple substitution of a kosher meat for the pork. Often the cooking time can be shortened, because pork requires a longer cooking time than many meats. Actually, some modifications for the kosher kitchen improve Chinese recipes. As you will discover in this book, the method of kashering chicken livers by broiling them makes the livers easier to use in stir-fried dishes.

Fresh shellfish are caught and eaten in the coastal regions of China, and classic dishes such as lobster Cantonese and shrimp toast are popular in Chinese-American restaurants. In this book fillets of flounder or sole are substituted for the shellfish. The fillets bring a delicacy to the Fillets of Flounder Cantonese and "Shrimp" Toast without compromising the flavor and textural interest of the authentic Chinese recipes from which they derive. Most of the sweet-and-sour, steamed, and fried fish dishes of China already use fish having fins and scales, and no modifications are necessary for the kosher kitchen. Although fish is *pareve*—that is, neither meat nor dairy—some Jews do not mix fish and meat in one preparation. A vegetable broth is an acceptable substitute for chicken broth in fish recipes.

Milk, butter, cheese, and other dairy products are rarely used in Chinese cooking (these products have never been readily available in China), so it is easy for the kosher cook to avoid mixing meat and dairy products in preparing a kosher Chinese meal. In this cookbook there are only four recipes that call for dairy products: one is a variation on congee; one a creamed Chinese cabbage; the third is a recipe for Almond Float (in which a nondairy substitute could be used); and the fourth is a rich dessert made with whipped cream and chestnuts. These dishes can be served as part of a vegetarian or a dairy meal.

One of the most versatile Chinese ingredients is *tofu,* a soybean curd which looks like a block of soft cream cheese. *Tofu* is neither a dairy nor a meat product, so it can be used in the kosher kitchen with any meal. Prepackaged *tofu* is now labeled *pareve* by some companies.

Lard, the rendered fat of a pig, is used extensively for stir-frying in China, but any vegetable shortening or oil can be substituted in the kosher home. Chicken fat, which is also used in China, adds a special flavor to stir-fried foods, and it can be used in preparing any of the meat or vegetarian recipes in this book. Unlike butter or margarine, chicken fat withstands the high temperatures necessary for stir-frying.

Lard is also used as the shortening in the steamed breads of northern China, and sometimes to flavor steamed desserts. In testing recipes, I experimented with oil, vegetable shortening, and chicken fat. Oil is used in the Steamed or Baked Buns, where ease of preparation is more important than adding a special taste to the dough. Chicken fat is a principal ingredient in Pan-fried Scallion Cakes, adding an identifiable flavor to the little breads.

The substitution of beef and other meats for pork, of fish fillets for shellfish, and of chicken fat for lard, the use of *tofu,* and the virtual absence of milk dishes in the Chinese cuisine make Chinese cooking in the kosher kitchen possible. The use of Chinese vegetables, seasonings, and other Chinese ingredients, as well as the Chinese cooking techniques which you will read about later, gives kosher Chinese recipes the delicious taste of authentic Chinese cuisine.

Home Cooking vs. the Chinese Banquet

Once a year, usually sometime in winter, the six of us go to Long Island, where we are joined by numerous cousins to be fattened up for the year by Aunt Sue and Uncle Irving. This means that Aunt Sue has spent no less than two months preparing mountains of chopped liver, at least two kinds of *knishes,* barbecued flanken, chopped eggs and onions, split pea-beef-and-bean soup (the only time my eldest son will eat onions is in Aunt Sue's wonderful soup—he knows the onions are there and not only does he eat the soup anyway, he asks for seconds!), roast chicken with stuffing, brisket with gravy, brisket without gravy, carrot and *knaidlach tsimmes,* potato *kugel,* bowls of vegetables, and a giant salad with six kinds of low-calorie dressing. Sometimes the neighbors send in their specialties because when they hear we're coming, they know Aunt Sue can't possibly have too much food. Aunt Sue and Uncle Irving never get to eat, of course. They are too busy serving and making sure no one goes hungry. Dessert—usually pastries, coffeecakes, fruitcakes, and chocolate cakes—comes hours and hours after dinner. Is this a typical kosher dinner in this country? No, it is a banquet. So it is with Chinese cooking. There are everyday home-cooked meals . . . and there are banquets.

A family meal in China is not composed of separate courses—appetizer, soup, main dish, dessert—nor is there a focus on any *one* main dish. Everything is set out on the table at once, and there is always more than one dish. China is a poor country, and everyday meals are for the most part basic. Thus, rice in southern China and noodles in the North are the predominant foods. Soup is served along with all the other foods. The soup may only be boiled water flavored with a few vegetables. Each person gets his own bowl of rice, while the other dishes are shared. The dishes will consist largely of vegetables. For protein, one will have bits of meat in it, another may contain small amounts of fish or chicken, and a third could be a bean curd dish, perhaps with strips of egg on top for color. The pieces of food must be small enough to handle with chopsticks, as each family member takes a small amount from a serving dish and eats the food directly, or first puts it in his own rice bowl. The food is tasty and simple, and although the meal may be meager by Western standards, there will always be a balance of color, flavor, and ingredients.

In the southern part of China, which includes Canton, as well as in Hong Kong, tea tends to be served throughout the meal. In other areas tea is generally served before and after the meal only. (Note that since most Chinese restaurants in the United States were opened by immigrants from southern China, it has become the general practice to serve tea throughout the meal in most Chinese-American restaurants.) If dessert is served at all, it consists of fresh fruit.

When you plan a Chinese family meal in your own home, you'll prepare a number of recipes, but no particular dish will stand out as the feature. For example, an egg drop soup, barbecued chicken wings, a beef and vegetable combination, a spicy vegetable, and plenty of rice make up a tasty family meal that can be coordinated to be served all at once.

Banquet meals, which in China are used by the wealthy for entertaining very special guests and business acquaintances, are more likely to be served at restaurants than in the home. They are expensive and elaborate and therefore out-of-reach for most Chinese. (There are festival meals served in Chinese homes on special holidays, but Americans who travel in China or frequent Chinese-American restaurants are more familiar with restaurant banquets than home festival meals.)

Unlike the everyday home-cooked meals described previously, the banquets of China do have separate courses, but these differ markedly from ours in sequence and content. First, the guests sample nuts and dried or fresh fruits, which are preset on the table. A selection of cold dish appetizers is either arranged on the table as well or brought out soon after the banquet commences. A warmed yellow rice wine is served with the appetizers and may be made available throughout the meal.

Now come the hot dishes, usually one by one. Like home-cooked food, banquet dishes are eaten with chopsticks (except for soup, of course, which is eaten with porcelain spoons). Somewhere in between the hot dishes, a heavy or thick soup will be served. There may be one dish that is considered the high point of the banquet, such as Peking duck. Such a dish will add prestige to the banquet either because it is so rare and expensive or because an inordinate amount of time has been spent on its preparation (or both).

Rice is served sometime during the meal for its blandness and digestibility: it helps to offset the rich foods. Toward the end of the meal, a light soup may be served to cleanse the palate. A whole fish, which can be prepared by any cooking method—frying, steaming, baking, etc.—is traditionally the last of the many "main" dishes served at a banquet. Tea is served between courses as a refresher. Small sweet pastries, which we would ordinarily consider dessert, are served between courses as a change of pace. Dessert proper is likely to consist of a thickened walnut "tea," a special rice pudding, and a selection of exotic fresh fruits. At a Chinese banquet, the emphasis is on the unusual, the exotic, and the expensive.

One of the best ways to prepare a Chinese banquet at home is to arrange to share the preparation and cost with friends who also like to cook and eat. You don't need to serve spectacular numbers of dishes to have a wonderful meal. The most important thing to remember in planning the banquet is the sequence: mixed nuts or fresh fruit, one cold appetizer, one hot meat or poultry and vegetable dish, a small tidbit, a thick or heavy soup, the featured dish, rice, and finally the whole fish followed by a colorful selection of sliced fresh fruits. This is a feasible meal for several people to put together. Once you have had experience with a variety of Chinese dishes, you may want to try to entertain a group of friends on your own, preparing a menu with more unusual and exotic ingredients than you would use in a family meal but on a smaller scale than the banquet meal. Since only one hot dish is served at a time, and the cold foods are prepared in advance, there is no frenzy of last-minute activity to pull everything together at once.

Not all restaurant meals in China are as elaborate as banquets. Teahouses, the informal restaurants popular in southern China, offer luncheon meals consisting of a grand assortment of small dumplings and snacks known collectively as *dim sum;* soups, noodle dishes, and many different teas are also served. Trays or carts of *dim sum* are brought to the table, and the diner makes his selection. Tea is served throughout the meal.

Teahouses began in China as gathering places where friends chatted over tea and snacks, and businessmen conducted luncheon meetings. They are now open mornings to catch the breakfast crowd, but they do the most business during the lunch hours, when patrons can grab a quick bite or sit over a leisurely lunch.

If you decide to prepare a teahouse meal, plan to serve a selection of appetizers, perhaps with a soup, rice, or noodle dish.

In addition to family, banquet, and teahouse meals, the Chinese have traditional foods associated with their major holidays, which are celebrated in part with festive family meals served at home. The most important holiday is the Chinese New Year, which falls in January or

February and receives wide attention in America because it is publicized in supermarkets and Chinese-American restaurants. A very good selection of Chinese ingredients is usually offered in American markets during the Chinese New Year, making it a particularly good time to experiment with Chinese recipes.

Some of the traditional ways of celebrating the Chinese New Year are reminiscent of Jewish holiday traditions. It is a time when all debts and quarrels are settled, corresponding to one aspect of Yom Kippur; the children receive gifts, as do our children during the Chanuka celebration; and as with so many of our Jewish holidays, special foods are eaten. In addition to festive home-cooked meals featuring at least one pork dish (even the poorest families want to show that they can afford meat at this time), the Chinese New Year features sweets and snacks. One of the treats served to visitors during the week-long New Year's celebration is spring rolls, thin sheets of dough wrapped around meats and vegetables and then fried. Another New Year's specialty is a dumpling filled with a sweetened red bean paste. Rice cakes are also eaten to celebrate the New Year.

Another Chinese holiday celebrated with special foods is the Moon Festival, which occurs during the eighth lunar month, when the moon is brightest. Just as we eat *hamantashen* during Purim to symbolize the triumph of the Jews over Haman, the Chinese eat moon cakes to celebrate the triumph of the Chinese over the Tartars centuries ago. It is said that the women baked messages into the cakes, enabling Chinese rebels to coordinate an attack that overthrew their rulers. Moon cakes, sold in bakeries, are sweet pastries filled with jam or fruits and nuts.

In China, birthday celebrations include parties and special family meals. Birthday dinners always include long, uncut noodles, a symbol of longevity.

Whether planning a home-cooked family meal, a teahouse meal, a more formal dinner, or a festival celebration, use the background information in this section to help you select recipes and menus appropriate to the occasion.

Selecting Ingredients

Chinese cooking depends more on what is done with what's available than on using exotic ingredients. Occasionally a dish relies on a very special ingredient for its interest, but often there are satisfactory alternatives. Even when a substitution changes the character of a dish, the variation may be as good as or better than the original, and a new recipe is created.

All the ingredients described below are used in Chinese cooking. Some are ingredients common to many cuisines, while others are uniquely Chinese. If you are unable to find a particular ingredient for a recipe, check this section to help determine what part that ingredient plays in the flavor, texture, color, or aroma of the dish. You are the chef, and like all Chinese chefs you will either make an appropriate substitution or omit the ingredient and change the name of the recipe.

Bamboo Shoots

Canned bamboo shoots, available in Asian (Oriental) groceries and many supermarkets, are pale yellow, slightly sweet, mildly flavored, with the consistency of undercooked carrots. They come sliced or in chunks in cans ranging from six ounces to many pounds for quantity cooking. The canned bamboo shoots do not require any cooking, but to help eliminate the "canned" taste drain the shoots and rinse them in cold water, then bring them to the boil in enough water to cover them completely. Drain the bamboo shoots and again rinse them in cold water, then store them in water in a clean jar or other covered container in the refrigerator, changing the water every few days. The shoots will keep for several weeks this way. Fresh bamboo shoots are available in some large cities. The fresh shoots require about fifteen minutes of boiling before they can be used in recipes.

Bean Sprouts

Mung bean sprouts, crisp and white, add more texture than taste to a dish. They are thinner and more delicate in both flavor and texture than soybean sprouts. In this book all recipes calling for bean sprouts were tested with fresh mung bean sprouts.

Fresh sprouts are recommended in all recipes, as they are used mainly for their crispness. Canned bean sprouts should be used only when the sprouts are a minor ingredient in a recipe. Once you've tasted fresh bean sprouts, you will never want to use the canned version. To restore some of the crunchiness of canned sprouts, drain the sprouts and rinse them in cold water, then soak them in ice water for an hour, or refrigerate the sprouts overnight in a container of cold water before using.

Fresh bean sprouts are available in many Asian groceries, some health food stores, and in large supermarkets. Before purchasing, make sure the sprouts are crisp and dry, for they are very perishable and will keep for only a few days in the refrigerator. Sprouts will sometimes keep a little longer if stored in a container of water in the refrigerator. Cover them completely with cold water, and change the water daily.

Growing Your Own Sprouts

Mung beans, sometimes called "mung peas," are small, round, hard green seeds which are available in small packages in Asian groceries and some health food stores. One tablespoon of mung beans grows into four to six tablespoons of sprouts.

To start the beans, soak them overnight in warm water, then drain. Place a piece of cheesecloth or screening over a pan (a layer cake pan or pie plate will do), spread the drained beans on the cheesecloth, cover them with a damp towel, and keep them in a dark place. Keep the towel moist but not wet by "watering" the towel daily with a watering can, or sprinkling water over the towel several times a day. In five to seven days the sprouts should be ready to use. When the thick white part of the sprout is between one and two inches long, transfer the sprouts to a bowl of cold water and swish them around to help remove any of the green shells that might remain. For banquet dishes and elegant home dinners, the thin brown root ends can be removed, but this is a time-consuming task.

In a simplified version of the above, the soaked and drained beans are placed directly in a pan, covered with foil, and rinsed and drained daily. Some people grow bean sprouts successfully in a jar. Select a jar that allows enough room for growth, put the soaked and drained beans in the jar, and cover the jar loosely. Keep the sprouts in a dark place, but don't forget about them. Rinse and drain daily. When the sprouts begin to grow, turn the jar on its side to give them more room.

I had one delightful student who couldn't understand why her sprouts grew those long tails and never gave her more than one set of green leaves. The part of the sprout that is eaten *is* that long white "tail." The sprouts should not grow to the point where they develop leaves.

Beef

Chinese cookbooks often recommend flank steak for stir-fried recipes because it slices easily into thin pieces of uniform size, holds up well under the constant tossing around, and is flavorful. London broil cut from the shoulder also works well, and it is used in the stir-fried recipes in this book because it is more commonly available from kosher butchers.

Once you have experienced cutting beef thinly (see Slicing, Cutting, Serving, Freezing, page 36), you can use any cut you desire. I remember telling one group that for a stir-fried dish just about any cut of beef could be used—except for brisket, which would be much too tough. I no sooner had the words out of my mouth than a student told me what a wonderfully tasty and tender steak and mushrooms she'd had, using brisket very thinly sliced at a 45-degree angle.

Brisket has its own distinctive texture and excellent flavor, and comes out marvelously well in the red-cooked dishes. The long, slow simmering in soy sauce gives the meat a lovely Chinese tinge. Leftover brisket can be turned into *wontons* just as easily as *kreplach*.

Bok Choy

This variety of Chinese cabbage, available in Asian groceries and some supermarkets, looks somewhat like Swiss chard with long, smooth white stalks and dark green leaves, but it is sold in a bunch like celery. The uncooked stalks are crisp and mild, with just a hint of a cabbage flavor. The leaves, though not as tender as most of our salad greens, have a flavor something like a tart romaine. Although romaine is sometimes suggested as a substitute for *bok choy,* the stems of cooked *bok choy* add more crunch to a dish, and the cooked leaves add a stronger flavor of their own. *Bok choy* is the kind of Chinese cabbage usually used in restaurants. Store *bok choy* in the refrigerator, and wash each stalk carefully before using. Freshen wilted *bok choy* in a bowl of cold water.

Celery Cabbage

Celery cabbage, often sold as "Chinese cabbage" in supermarkets, is different from the *bok choy* and *nappa* varieties. Of the three, celery cabbage is the most widely available; therefore, unless otherwise specified, that variety was used in testing the recipes in this book. *Bok choy* and *nappa* will make good substitutes, but green (regular) cabbage should never be used, for green cabbage is much stronger in flavor and might drown out the flavors of other ingredients. Romaine can be substituted successfully, but note that it requires less cooking than celery cabbage.

Unlike celery, the leaves of celery cabbage grow all along the stalk, not just at the top. The stalks are white, shading to a light to medium green at the leaves, and they are much broader and more tender than celery. Celery will not make an adequate substitute for celery cabbage in the recipes in this cookbook.

Refrigerate celery cabbage as you would any salad green, and wash it thoroughly before using. Use it uncooked in salads or stir-fried as a vegetable. If celery cabbage goes limp in the refrigerator, soak it in cold water.

Cellophane Noodles

Cellophane noodles, sometimes called "bean thread" or "Chinese vermicelli," are very long, thin, brittle, and white when dry, which is the way they are sold. They are available in Asian groceries and some specialty shops in packages of two, four, and eight ounces. They will keep on the pantry shelf as long as a year. Check the label: it should list mung beans or bean starch as an ingredient, not just wheat flour or wheat starch. There is another kind of dried noodle, also called "Chinese vermicelli," that looks like cellophane noodles but is made from wheat. Do not confuse the two—the wheat vermicelli is more like spaghetti and doesn't have the unusual texture of cellophane noodles.

Cellophane noodles are named for the way they look when soaked in water—that is, transparent. Because of their soft consistency, they partner well with meat, and they are known not for any flavor of their own but for their ability to absorb the flavor of the cooking liquid both in soups and in noodle-and-meat dishes. Cellophane noodles are almost always soaked in warm or hot water and then cut before being used in main dishes or soups.

Cellophane noodles have one other very interesting property. When cut or broken into pieces and then dropped into deep hot oil or shortening, they immediately puff up and become crisp and white. They are used this way in some appetizers and also as a garnish for meat and vegetable dishes. Rice noodles can be used in this manner also, but rice noodles are a little thicker and do have some flavor of their own. A word of caution: when cellophane noodles are to be fried in deep fat, don't soak them first. We tried this in one cooking session and were surprised to find that the soaked noodles disappeared completely. They were not just transparent and hard to find—they were *gone!*

Chinese Cabbage *See also* Bok Choy; Celery Cabbage; *and* Nappa

Three kinds of Chinese cabbage are described in this book. *Bok choy,* the one most commonly used by the Chinese, has the strongest taste and deepest coloring. Celery cabbage, more commonly available in American supermarkets, also works well in Chinese cooking. *Nappa* resembles celery cabbage more than *bok choy* in appearance and taste; it is occasionally available in supermarkets. All three Chinese cabbages can be purchased in Asian groceries. Although they do not taste exactly alike, they are similar enough to be used interchangeably in the recipes. Availability and personal taste will determine which Chinese cabbage you select.

Corn *See* Miniature Corn

Cornstarch

Small amounts of cornstarch are used to thicken and glaze. The cornstarch is always first mixed with cold water, broth, or other liquid until smooth, then it is stirred into the hot food during the final stage of cooking. If cornstarch is overcooked, it loses its thickening power. Cornstarch-thickened products do not freeze well, as the gravy tends to break down and lose its smoothness. Therefore, if you plan to freeze a dish, don't add the cornstarch until the food is reheated and ready to be served. Arrowroot is an acceptable substitute for cornstarch as a thickening agent, but flour is not. Flour will not work in smoothly in a stir-fried dish, it requires more cooking than cornstarch, and it does not make the lovely glaze of a cornstarch-thickened sauce.

Many Chinese chefs avoid the use of cornstarch or any thickener, maintaining that well-prepared dishes need no such addition. Others feel that the thickener enhances the texture and appearance of certain preparations. Dishes served in Chinese-American restaurants are likely to be glazed with a cornstarch-thickened sauce: the patrons expect the glaze. I take a position of convenience. For quick stir-fried family meals, I don't bother with the glaze; and when I'm doing a banquet for 120 people, it's difficult to have a cornstarch paste available for each batch of freshly cooked food. When I'm entertaining at home, however, and I cook each dish at the table at a leisurely pace, I often use a cornstarch thickener.

Cornstarch has other uses in Chinese cooking as well. Diced pieces of meat are coated with it before stir-frying. It makes a crispy coating for fish and deep-fried meat and poultry. It is an ingredient in batters. Flour can also be used for coating and in batters, but flour and cornstarch are not always interchangeable in recipes because they react differently with some ingredients.

Note: For all recipes in this book calling for either cornstarch or flour, unless otherwise specified neither the cornstarch nor the flour is sifted before measuring.

Dried Chinese Mushrooms

These have a unique taste (slightly smoky, somewhat earthy) and a completely different consistency (chewy) than fresh mushrooms. They are available in Asian groceries and some specialty shops, commonly in packages of two, four, and eight ounces. Although the dried mushrooms are expensive, generally only a few are required in any one recipe, and they keep well if stored in a tightly lidded jar on the pantry shelf.

Always soak dried Chinese mushrooms in hot or boiling water for about fifteen minutes, until softened, before using, then remove and discard the tough stems. Slice or chop the softened mushrooms as the recipe directs. Occasionally a dried mushroom won't soften after soaking. Try resoaking the mushroom in boiling water, and if that doesn't work, discard it.

Duck Sauce

There is no duck in this meatless condiment—the name is derived from the preparation's use as a dip or sauce for roast duck. Duck sauce is usually made from apricots or peaches, vinegar, sugar, and corn syrup; however, it is the sweet and pungent taste that comes through more than the fruity taste. In Chinese-American restaurants, this reddish-brown condiment is usually set out with hot mustard and fried noodles.

There are many brands of duck sauce on the market. Asian groceries and most supermarkets sell it in jars or containers ranging in size from six ounces to one gallon. Duck sauce keeps very well refrigerated.

Note that although some cookbooks refer to duck sauce and plum sauce as the same condiment, what I buy as plum sauce in Asian groceries is thicker, heavily laden with chunks of ginger, and similar to chutney.

Egg Roll Skins or Wrappers

In Asian groceries, these thin seven-inch squares of dough are sold fresh or frozen in one, two, and five-pound packages. There are generally from twelve to fifteen to a pound. They can be used to prepare egg rolls, *wontons,* dumplings, and fried noodles. When fried, they emerge golden and crisp. When boiled or steamed, they taste like a bland noodle, notable more for their use as convenient holders than for their taste.

Egg roll skins are made of flour, water, and usually a small amount of egg. Cornstarch is used to prevent the finished skins from sticking to each other. Wrap them well and refrigerate if they are to be used within a day or two, or freeze them for later use. Once frozen, they cannot be separated until thawed, so don't freeze a whole five-pound package in one unit unless you know you'll be needing sixty to seventy-five egg roll wrappers at one time. The skins dry out quickly when exposed to air, so unused ones must be kept covered while you're working. If some dry out, use them for fried noodles.

There are many different brands of prepackaged egg roll wrappers sold in supermarkets. Some contain more egg than the skins available in Asian food stores, making them more yellow in appearance and a little heavier when fried, but they are very tasty when used for soup *wontons.* The thickness of the skins varies from one brand to another, and the range is from twelve to more than twenty to a pound. The size ranges from six and one-half to seven inches square.

In this book, I've included two recipes for homemade egg roll wrappers. One is a flour-and-water dough that is similar to the commercially prepared egg roll skins. The other is a cooked shell, much like a *blintz.*

Fermented Black Beans (Salted Black Beans)

These soft, slightly chewy, and very salty small black beans are sold prepackaged in Asian groceries. In cooking, they are often used in combination with ginger root and scallions for both texture and saltiness, especially with steamed fish. Fermented black beans will keep for a very long time in a tightly covered jar at room temperature. To decrease the saltiness, soak the beans in warm water for fifteen minutes just before using.

Five-spice Powder

This combination of ground spices has the licorice-like star anise as its base, along with Szechwan peppercorns, anise seeds or fennel, cloves, and cinnamon. The spices found in the commercially prepared five-spice powders may vary, but the unmistakable fragrance of anise is always present. The powder is added sparingly to red-cooked dishes, and it is used as well to flavor roast duck and barbecued meats. Although allspice is sometimes suggested as a substitute for five-spice powder, the predominant flavor is different. It is not difficult to make up your own mixture using ground anise lightly spiced with ground fennel, cloves, and cinnamon. Five-spice powder is available in Asian groceries and some supermarkets. It should be stored, as any spice, in an airtight container away from heat and moisture.

Ginger Root

Fresh ginger root, pungent and tangy, is used in small quantities as a flavoring agent in numerous Chinese dishes. It adds spiciness and a special aroma to stir-fried dishes and a more subtle, gentle flavor to stews and red-cooked meats (foods cooked in soy sauce are described as "red cooked"). Ginger root is also used by the Chinese to counteract the fishiness of strongly flavored fish. Powdered ginger has neither the pungent aroma nor the taste of fresh ginger root and is therefore not an acceptable substitute.

Fresh ginger root, sold by the piece in Asian groceries and some supermarkets, resembles a small, gnarled tree root. The root has a light brown skin, which when peeled reveals a creamy yellow interior. The lighter and thinner the skin, the more likely it is that the root is young and fresh. The peeled root can be sliced, minced, or grated, or it can be forced through a garlic press.

Store fresh, unpeeled ginger root in the refrigerator, where it will keep from a few days to several weeks, depending on how old it was when purchased. To keep ginger root from becoming moldy, peel it with a vegetable peeler, put it in a clean jar, cover the ginger root with sherry, secure the lid, and refrigerate. The root retains its flavor well when wrapped airtight and frozen. The root can be grated successfully while still frozen, but when defrosted it tends to become soft. However, since the ginger is used mainly for its flavor, the change in consistency is not a problem.

Occasionally a piece of ginger root will turn out to be very woody. This indicates that the root has matured too much, and although it can be used in a chunk in stews and removed before serving, it should not be used in stir-fried dishes.

When a recipe in this cookbook calls for a slice of ginger root, the slice should be about one inch in diameter and one-eighth inch thick. The amount of ginger root used can be adjusted to suit personal taste. I tend to underuse ginger root because I find it often overpowering, but there are many people who consider no amount too much. Once, when I was doing a Chinese cooking demonstration at Waldbaum's supermarket in New Haven, Connecticut, my partner minced a two-inch piece of ginger and added it to the skillet when I wasn't looking. The effect was startling. People literally ran over from the other side of the store to sample what we were cooking—and they *loved* the samples.

Glutinous Rice

This chewy, starchy rice, also called "sticky rice" and sometimes "sweet rice" because it is used in desserts, is always an ingredient in the banquet dessert called Eight-treasure Pudding (see page 322 for recipe). It can also be used in meatballs, stuffings, and soups. As one of its alternate names implies, glutinous rice becomes sticky when cooked. It is used for that property and also because it takes on a pearly look when steamed. Glutinous rice can be purchased in Asian groceries. It will keep for very long periods of time in a covered container on the pantry shelf.

Golden Needles (Dried Tiger Lily Buds)

Offering more of an exotic quality than taste, these are brittle when dry, but when soaked in hot water they soften and become chewy with a woodsy flavor. Golden needles are about three inches long, have an orange to golden brown color, and are used in hot-and-sour soup and *mu shu* dishes. Sold prepackaged in Asian groceries, they will keep for years in a tightly closed jar on the pantry shelf, although they do darken after several years.

Hoisin Sauce

This thick, smooth, dark purplish-brown sauce has a soybean base with added flavorings of sugar, vinegar, garlic, and chili; flour is added to thicken. The exact spices depend on the brand, but *hoisin* sauce always has a strong, distinctive taste with both a sweetness and an afterbite. The sauce can be used as a dip or condiment, and it lends a unique flavor to dumplings and meat dishes.

Hoisin sauce, which is sometimes called "Peking sauce" because it is the sauce always served with Peking duck, is sold in cans in Asian groceries and some supermarkets. It will keep refrigerated for many weeks in a clean glass jar with a good lid, or it may be frozen. Note, however, that *hoisin* sauce does not freeze solidly, so it can be used directly from the freezer without thawing. Eventually there will be some loss of flavor, especially in frost-free freezers (placing the container in a plastic bag will eliminate the dehumidifying effect of the frost-free freezer). No matter how you store your *hoisin* sauce, be sure to label it clearly, because it can easily be mistaken for a rich fudge sauce (which my eldest son found out one afternoon when he nearly fixed himself a *hoisin* fudge sundae).

Hot Bean Sauce

A canned mixture of soy and kidney beans, spices and seasonings, this thick brown sauce is hot and spicy. Hot bean sauce, which is not smooth but actually contains pieces of bean, is used in Hunan dishes. Taste a very small amount before using, and adjust the amount called for in a recipe according to how hot and spicy you like foods. Hot bean sauce can be used to add color, spiciness, and texture to many meat, poultry, fish, and vegetable dishes. Sold in small cans in Asian groceries, the sauce should be refrigerated once opened.

Hot Chili Paste (Sauce) With Garlic

If you want to add fire to any dish, this red-hot-looking (and tasting) blend of finely chopped hot peppers, garlic, and oil will accomplish the task. The hot chili paste has a consistency something like bottled horse-radish, while the hot chili sauce, which contains vinegar, is thinner than the very thick paste. Both are available in small jars in Asian groceries and will keep almost indefinitely if refrigerated. Do not confuse hot chili sauce with the commercially available chili sauce (such as Heinz) that comes in bottles in the ketchup section of supermarkets. In a pinch, liquid hot pepper sauce can be used as a substitute to provide the zip of hot chili paste or sauce.

Hot Radish With Chili

Although not as fiery as the hot chili paste with garlic, this preparation will spice up any dish. Consisting of small pieces of Chinese radish and shreds of hot pepper in a little oil, it is used as a condiment or seasoning in Szechwan and Hunan dishes. The radish itself, with its soft chewiness, gives body to this relish, but it is the taste of the hot peppers that comes through. Hot radish with chili is available in various size cans in Asian groceries. Once opened, it should be refrigerated.

Hot Turnip (Szechwan Hot Turnip)

Available in cans in Asian groceries, hot turnip adds more of the "hot" than the "turnip" flavor, but it isn't as fiery as the hot chili paste or sauce with garlic. Hot turnip can be used interchangeably with hot radish with chili in the recipes in this book. If refrigerated after opening, it will keep for many weeks.

Lo Mien (Noodles)

Fresh *lo mien,* a type of noodle, is very long, round, and thin. It closely resembles freshly made spaghetti. Some *lo mien* is almost white, while other brands contain a lot more egg and look much like long, thin egg noodles. There is some variation in thickness and delicacy among the different brands. Unlike dried pasta, fresh *lo mien* must be refrigerated. Freeze it if you don't expect to use it within a few days of purchase.

Fresh *lo mien* cooks much more quickly than the dried Italian-style pasta we are used to buying in supermarkets. Taste it after only two or three minutes of cooking. Drain the *lo mien* as soon as it is done to your satisfaction, then mix the noodles with oil to keep them from sticking together.

Dried *lo mien* is available, but like any dried pasta it requires more cooking time than the fresh. If you make your own noodles, make them very long and cut them very thin; then use them exactly as you would fresh *lo mien*. Note that, if necessary, thin spaghetti, which resembles *lo mien* in shape and texture, can be substituted for it in recipes.

In China, *lo mien* (literally "tossed noodles") is one kind of *mien* purchased for the preparation of the same name. Another kind of noodle is used for *chao mien* (stir-fried noodles). The noodles sold as *lo mien* in Asian groceries can be used for all recipes in this book.

Miniature Corn

These two-inch-long baby ears of corn are sold in fifteen-ounce cans in Asian groceries and some supermarkets. They are used by the Chinese to add color to stir-fried preparations. The entire ear, including the cob, is eaten. Because miniature corn is tender, it is added toward the end of the stir-frying and tossed with the other ingredients for about thirty seconds, just long enough to heat the corn through. It is not necessary to use a whole can of corns for each preparation—slice four to six ears on the diagonal to use in any one dish. Each little ear of corn can be sliced into two or three pieces. Store the remaining miniature corn in the refrigerator in a covered container of water, changing the water every day. The corn will keep for several days and can be added to any stir-fried recipe.

Monosodium Glutamate (MSG)

The Chinese have been using MSG for years to bring out the natural flavors of foods. When Chinese restaurateurs in the United States began using this chemical compound in unreasonable quantities to cover up poor quality or poorly prepared food, the use of MSG became controversial. It was found that some people are allergic to the chemical and develop severe headaches after ingesting it.

Although in my opinion a pinch of monosodium glutamate does add a fine touch to stir-fried vegetable dishes, a well-prepared dish does not need MSG. Furthermore, I am extremely suspicious of any recipe that calls for as much as a teaspoon of MSG. A little goes a long way. Even when doubling or tripling a recipe, use the amount called for in the original.

Mushrooms, Dried *See* Dried Chinese Mushrooms

Mushrooms, Fresh

Fresh mushrooms are an ingredient in numerous recipes in this cookbook. Because they are usually stir-fried and cooked briefly, until just barely tender but not soft, canned mushrooms are not an appropriate substitute. "Fresh mushrooms" refers to cultivated, commercially available mushrooms, not to wild mushrooms (which might be poisonous).

Mushrooms are a product of the earth and as such need to be cleaned well before they are used. Although some cooks argue that mushrooms must be wiped clean with a damp cloth and should never be washed, I generally find it much easier to wash the mushrooms under cold running water. I loosen the dirt with my fingers, wash off each mushroom, drain the mushrooms, and pat them dry. I don't find that they add any more liquid to a dish than mushrooms that are just wiped clean. Either before or after cleaning the mushrooms, cut off the very end of each stem, that which is darkened and rough.

Nappa (Napa)

This Chinese cabbage is similar in taste and appearance to celery cabbage, but the leaves are broader, whiter, and more crinkly, and the head is more stout. It is sometimes impractical to buy *nappa* because it may not be possible to use up the large heads usually available. Celery cabbage is a good substitute. Store *nappa* in the refrigerator; soak limp leaves in cold water to restore freshness.

Oil for Deep-frying

Almost any vegetable oil—including a blended oil, soybean oil, corn oil, peanut oil, safflower oil, and sunflower oil—can be used for deep-frying. Olive oil is not used in Chinese cooking because of its strong flavor. Some people find that foods fried in peanut oil emerge lighter and more tasty, but it is also true that peanut oil has a lower burning temperature than corn oil and therefore needs to be watched a little more carefully. Peanut oil is very expensive to use in quantity, but I recommend it for special occasions. Soybean oil is the oil most widely used in China due to its availability.

In most cases, oil can be reused once or twice if strained properly. Heat the oil to 275 degrees F. if it has cooled down, then strain it through a paper towel fastened securely with a rubber band around a clean, empty metal can. Indent the paper towel, forming a cup into which the oil can be poured. To further clarify, fry a few pieces of raw potato in the oil when you next heat it. (Oil in which fish has cooked is best discarded as the flavor of the fish may come through when the oil is reused.) Note that if oil is reused too often, it begins to foam and can be hazardous.

All the recipes in this book were tested with oil rather than solid vegetable shortening. Shortening does not seem to clarify as well as oil, and it foams up more the second time around. Some people also find that oil gives a more delicate crust to deep fried foods. However, if you usually use shortening for deep-frying with good results, it is an acceptable substitute.

Oil for Stir-frying

Peanut, corn, safflower, sunflower, soy, blended—whatever oil you usually use—can be used for stir-frying. Peanut oil is often used in Chinese recipes, whereas olive oil would impart a strong flavor not characteristic of Chinese cooking. In China, lard is used for stir-frying, as it is readily available and adds a flavor which the Chinese like. Of course lard has no place in a kosher kitchen, but chicken fat does. The Chinese do use chicken fat in stir-frying, and it is a perfectly acceptable substitute for the oil required in stir-fried meat dishes, although it will impart its own flavor to the dish. Sesame oil is used to flavor dishes once they have been cooked; it is not used for stir-frying.

Oriental Vinegars

There are many different kinds and brands of Oriental rice vinegars. Some are used primarily in salads, others in sweet-and-sour sauces. Ask for help from Chinese storekeepers in selecting what is suitable. (I was once told that one particular vinegar was used in China for stimulating the production of breast milk.)

Red Bean Paste (Sweetened)

Red bean paste is very thick, with a bland but sweet taste. In small amounts it is used to add color (it is the color of kidney beans), body, and a sweet flavor to some dumplings and marinades, and in larger amounts it is used as a filling in Chinese desserts. A Chinese storekeeper told me that the *sweetened* paste is used in China only for desserts, never in dumplings or main dishes, but everything I've tested with sweetened red bean paste is delicious, so I continue to use it. The paste is available in cans in Asian groceries. Once opened, it will keep well if refrigerated in a tightly covered jar. It can also be frozen. Because red bean paste freezes solidly, freeze it in ice cube trays so you can defrost a small amount at a time.

Red bean paste, which is essentially a thick bean purée, is made from dried Chinese red beans which are available in packages in Asian groceries. You can make your own red bean paste by cooking the red beans until tender in enough water to cover. Purée the beans in a food processor or a blender with enough liquid to process them. You should end up with a thick, very smooth paste. To sweeten red bean paste, blend in half a cup of sugar for each uncooked cup of red beans. The sugar is not added until after the beans are cooked and puréed.

Red-cooked Starter Sauce (Master Sauce)

The first time you red-cook (that is, cook in soy sauce) a chicken, brisket, or stew and find yourself with a leftover cup or more of a rich, dark, flavorful gravy, you are on your way to keeping a red-cooked sauce on hand to start off your next chicken, brisket, or stew. Strain any whole spices out of the liquid, and refrigerate the gravy in a covered jar. This sauce, known in China as a master sauce, should keep for a week under refrigeration. Skim off the fat before using the sauce as the basis for your next red-cooked dish. If you know you won't be using the sauce for a while, freeze it. Each time the sauce is used as a starter, the new meat, spices, and other ingredients add additional richness to the flavor and aroma. (See the recipes for Red-cooked Sauces, page 140.)

Rice *See* Glutinous Rice

Rice Noodles

Rice noodles are similar to cellophane noodles in appearance and texture, but they have much more of their own flavor when cooked. Made of rice flour, they have a grainy taste reminiscent of rice. They are brittle when dry and become soft when soaked in warm or hot water. Rice noodles are used in stir-fried dishes and soups.

Like cellophane noodles, uncooked rice noodles puff up in hot oil and are used as a garnish. Do not soak rice noodles that are to be deep-fried, as they will become brittle. Rice noodles are related to rice sticks or rice stick noodles, which are considerably wider.

Salted Black Beans *See* Fermented Black Beans

Scallions (Green Onions, Spring Onions)

A scallion is an immature onion, with a long, thick green stem and a small white bulb at the root end. The stem branches out into a dark green top consisting of grasslike leaves. Raw scallions have a sharpness like uncooked onions, and they are used extensively in Chinese food preparation for their color, crisp texture, and sharp but fresh taste. In cooked dishes they taste similar to leeks but do not require as much cooking.

Although they do not have quite the same flavor as scallions, in cooked dishes regular onions may be used as a substitute. Fresh chives may substitute as an uncooked garnish.

To use scallions, cut off the root end, peel off any tough outer layers, and wash the scallions thoroughly. Cut off the very dark, wilted, or tough parts of the green tops, and use the crisper green section as well as the white part.

Sesame Oil (Oriental)

Oriental sesame oil, a golden brown oil made from roasted sesame seeds, is aromatic, with a strong, nutty, smoky taste. It is generally used to flavor dishes after they've been cooked, but use it sparingly at first: it tends to overwhelm. Buy a good-quality Oriental sesame oil, which is more concentrated and darker than Middle Eastern sesame oil. Sesame oil will keep for months on the pantry shelf.

Sherry

This cookbook calls for dry sherry for the tablespoon or two of wine used in some recipes. Cantonese cooking in particular often uses light marinades of soy sauce and wine. Rice wine is readily available in China and therefore is used there. Dry sherry is readily available here and works well in Chinese cooking. There are some people who find rice wine distinctive and essential. If Chinese rice wine is available, try it and see what you think. I am sure there are Chinese chefs who come here, discover dry sherry, and never want to go back to rice wine.

Snow Peas

Snow peas, sometimes called Chinese pea pods, are not "baby peas" that are picked before the peas develop in the pod. They are actually a special variety of pea resembling flat pea pods. The small, bright green pods are more tender and hence more desirable than the large ones. Fresh snow peas are seasonal, sometimes hard to come by, and often very expensive, but they have a crunchiness and taste, as well as a lovely color, that turn a plain dish into a special one. Their flavor is similar to that of the pods of very young green peas, but they do not have the tough fibers of regular green pea pods. Very fresh snow peas will keep for several days in the refrigerator. Wash the peas before using, then break off the tips and pull down along the seams to remove any "strings." If you hesitate, because of the expense, to buy the full quantity of snow peas called for in a recipe, do not despair. A few will go a long way.

Another variety of pea, the sugar snap pea, has well-developed pods, but they are not as fibrous as ordinary pea pods and are completely edible. They work well as a substitute for snow peas. Commercially packaged frozen snow peas tend to be watery. In the freezing they lose much of their texture and color and are therefore never a satisfactory substitute for fresh snow peas. If you have planned a dish requiring fresh snow peas but can't obtain them, select another green vegetable. Even frozen green peas would be a more desirable alternative than frozen snow peas. In fact, frozen green peas have been adopted by many Chinese chefs and cookbook authors in this country because they add color, sweetness, and a reasonably fresh taste to a dish; they also hold their shape and are readily available. Remember, though, that frozen green peas are to be used as a substitute only when fresh snow peas are not available, for they will change the texture and flavor of the dish.

Soy Sauce

Soy sauce is used for its saltiness, slightly fermented taste, and very dark brown color. There are many different kinds of soy sauce, with numerous flavors, but most of the standard brands readily available in supermarkets do not have the rich taste or color of the soy sauces sold in Asian food stores. (Some are not even made from soybeans.) There are light, dark, thin, thick, black, salty, sweet, and probably many more soys. Buy a small quantity until you find one you especially like. A good-quality Chinese soy sauce is recommended for all recipes. Soy sauce keeps well at room temperature.

Most Chinese cookbooks categorize soy sauces as light or thin versus dark or thick. Light soy sauces, which are lighter in color and thinner than the dark soys, are used in marinades and dips. Dark soy sauces, made with molasses, are used in slow cooking and simmering. My personal preference is for a combination of two soys which are imported from mainland China. One is simply called Soy Superior and lists as its ingredients "extract of soya beans, wheat flour, salt, and water." The other is called Mushroom Soy, and although I can detect no taste of mushrooms, its ingredients are "extract of soya beans, wheat flour, mushroom, salt, sugar, and watering." The Soy Superior is thin and salty, while the Mushroom Soy is darker and more flavorful but less salty—and more expensive. I buy a five-pound container of each and mix the two in a smaller bottle for use in all my Chinese cooking.

Many people tell me that they would like to cook Chinese food but that their low-sodium diets forbid the use of soy sauce. To them I point out that there are excellent Chinese dishes requiring no soy sauce, and others where the soy sauce may enhance the food but isn't vital. Except for the red-cooked dishes and some marinades, you can enjoy Chinese foods without soy sauce. If you are simply looking to reduce your sodium intake, as a compromise use the concentrated soy sauce known as tamari, which has a lower sodium content than regular soy sauce. Tamari is sold in health food stores, many Asian groceries, and some supermarkets.

Spring Roll Sheets

Spring roll sheets are larger, thinner, and more delicate than regular egg roll skins. They more closely resemble the egg roll wrappers used in China than the thicker wrappers more commonly available here. Use them for egg rolls and light fried noodles, and they are essential for Spring Chicken Packages (see page 71 for recipe). However, they do not work well for *wontons* and other dumplings.

Spring roll sheets, which taste more like edible paper than like a noodle dough, are sold in Asian groceries. Look for them in the refrigerator or freezer section, prepackaged under various names, including Spring Roll Sheets, Shanghai Egg Roll Wrappers, and Thin Egg Roll Skins. The packages weigh about one pound, and the wrappers come in squares or circles, usually twenty-five in a package.

Spring roll sheets will keep in the refrigerator for a few days, and they freeze well. They cannot be separated until thawed, so don't freeze an entire package unless you expect to be using all of the sheets at once. Roll up five or six sheets together, wrap well in foil, label clearly, and freeze. Spring roll sheets dry out very rapidly when exposed to air, so work quickly when you use them, and keep unused wrappers covered.

See page 70 for a recipe for homemade spring roll wrappers.

Star Anise

This spice, sold in packages in Asian groceries, earns its name from its shape: the whole pieces have a star shape. The licorice-like flavor of star anise is noticeable in any dish in which it is used. Pieces of the spice should be strained out of the sauce or gravy before serving. If star anise is not on hand, ground anise or five-spice powder, a blend of spices with an anise base, can be used. As any spice, star anise should be stored in a cool, dry place.

Sweet Bean Sauce

This thick brown sauce probably is named more to distinguish it from the hot bean sauce than for its taste, for it is truly more salty than sweet. In fact, it is too salty to be used directly from the can as a condiment; but when used in stir-fried dishes and stews, it adds body and color as well as a mild flavor. In Chinese cooking, sweet bean sauce can be used as a gravy enhancer, and it is marvelous in fish dishes.

Sweet bean sauce, sold in cans and jars in Asian groceries, must be refrigerated or frozen once opened. The sauce does not freeze firmly, and it can be used without any defrosting.

Szechwan Peppercorns

As an experiment, I asked my five human guinea pigs to sniff Szechwan peppercorns with their eyes closed. The responses were: yum (my husband); yuk (my eldest son); peppercorns (second son); choking reaction (third son); parsley (my daughter). Nathan, our dog, backed away from them. Aromatic, sweet, spicy, slightly reminiscent of black pepper but with a flavor all their own, these reddish-brown Szechwan peppercorns are crushed for use in marinades, sauces, and red-cooked dishes. They are sometimes one of the spices included in five-spice powder. Buy small quantities in Asian groceries, and store them in airtight containers. Crush the peppercorns slightly just before using to bring out their full flavor.

Tapioca Starch

This extract from the root of the cassava plant is used as a thickener much the same as cornstarch. In combination with wheat starch it is used for some *dim sum* doughs where a translucent appearance is desired.

Tofu (Soybean Curd)

Tofu (pronounced *dofu* in the Mandarin dialect and *fu juk* in Cantonese) is a relatively inexpensive protein source made from pressed soybeans. When the bean curd is fresh, it is creamy white, with the consistency of custard pie. It has little flavor of its own, but it picks up the flavors of other ingredients. Bean curd, widely used in China as a major source of protein, is said to resemble cheese, but it is a vegetable (nondairy) product.

Tofu is sold in small cakes about three inches square by three-fourths inch thick in Asian groceries and health food stores, and in one-pound packages in some supermarkets, usually in the produce department. The packages may be labeled "soft" or "firm." Use the firm style for the recipes in this book; it will hold up better when stir-fried or deep-fried. Large pieces of fresh *tofu* can be sliced (the small cakes don't need to be sliced), pressed between two sheets of waxed paper, and weighted down by large, heavy books for a few hours. Pressed *tofu* holds up especially well in stir-fried dishes and becomes slightly chewy.

Fresh *tofu* will keep in water in the refrigerator for a few days; the water should be changed daily. To freeze *tofu,* drain well and wrap in foil or freezer paper. Squeeze excess water from thawed *tofu* before proceeding with recipes. Canned *tofu* or bean curd can be used as a substitute for the fresh product.

Tree Ears (Tree Fungi)

These dried grey-black irregular-shaped pieces of fungus, sometimes called "cloud ears" or "wood ears," are sold in various weight packages in Asian groceries and some specialty shops. Called *mu-er* in Mandarin and *win yee* in Cantonese, they are used for their chewy texture and exotic quality in *mu shu* dishes and hot-and-sour soup.

Tree ears must be soaked in very hot water before being used. When soaked, their texture changes from brittle to rubbery, and they become easy to cut. Tree ears swell considerably when soaked, so don't be deceived by the small amount usually called for. They keep almost indefinitely at room temperature in tightly sealed glass jars.

Vinegar *See* Oriental Vinegars

Water Chestnut Powder

Water chestnuts are pulverized to make this product, which has the consistency of matzo meal. In China, water chestnut powder (or flour) and lotus root flour—both readily available and inexpensive—are used to thicken sauces and to coat items to be deep-fried. In the United States, cornstarch is much more easily obtained and is significantly less expen sive. Furthermore, cornstarch dissolves better than water chestnut powder, resulting in smoother sauces. In the United States, cornstarch is generally used in published recipes. If, however, you want to authentically duplicate the cooking of China, use water chestnut powder wherever cornstarch is called for. It is sold in small packages in Asian food stores.

Arrowroot, another substitute for cornstarch, is used both in China and in the United States as a thickening agent; it can be used interchangeably with cornstarch.

Water Chestnuts

Fresh water chestnuts are crisp and sweet, usually quite expensive, and often so hard to obtain that they can be considered a delicacy. Water chestnuts resemble regular chestnuts, but the skin is blacker and they are pointed on top. They need no cooking. Just peel them to reveal the white meat, cut out any blemishes, and use them whole or sliced as called for in recipes. Fresh water chestnuts should be firm, with no soft spots. They will keep in the refrigerator for as long as two weeks if very fresh when purchased.

Canned water chestnuts are readily available in supermarkets and Asian groceries in various size cans. Although almost tasteless, they do have some of the crispiness of fresh water chestnuts; and they are used for their texture in stir-fried dishes and some appetizers. In recipes, unless otherwise noted, canned water chestnuts are an acceptable substitute for the more succulent fresh ones. Once opened, drain the water chestnuts, rinse them with cold water, and keep them refrigerated in a jar of water, changing the water every few days. They can be kept for weeks if properly attended to.

Wheat Starch

Wheat starch, available in Asian groceries, is wheat flour from which the gluten has been removed. It is used in combination with tapioca starch to make a dough for certain *dim sum.* The dough becomes translucent when steamed; the texture is slightly gelatinous. Since it is the gluten in flour that becomes elastic and forms the structure of bread, the glutenless wheat starch will not rise and is therefore not used to make breads.

Wonton Wrappers or Skins

Sold fresh or frozen in one-pound packages in Asian groceries and some supermarkets, *wonton* wrappers are made from flour, water, and egg. They have a heavier taste than egg roll skins. The *wonton* wrappers come precut in the proper size, and they are sold in regular and thin versions, the latter being difficult to handle without tearing. Supermarket *wonton* and egg roll wrappers usually have identical ingredients and differ only in size.

Wonton wrappers must be refrigerated, or freeze them if they are not to be used within a few days. Once frozen, the wrappers can't be separated until thawed, so you may want to make up small packages to freeze. I have included two *wonton* wrapper recipes in this book (see pages 150 and 152), one of which is actually what I use for *kreplach*.

Where to Buy Chinese Ingredients

If there is a Chinatown or an Asian area in your vicinity, that's the first place to visit. If there are a number of Asian food stores, frequent them all; selection, prices, and quality may vary. Chinese groceries can be a source of information as well as supplies. Generally, store owners and personnel are knowledgeable, and often they are delighted to answer questions about Chinese cooking in general and specific ingredients in particular. Shop at Japanese and Korean groceries as well—the three cuisines use many of the same ingredients.

To locate the Asian food stores in your area, check the Yellow Pages under "Oriental Foods" or "Food—Oriental." (It should be noted that the Chinese prefer the term "Asian" to "Oriental," which has a somewhat negative connotation. Efforts are being made to convince telephone companies to change their listings.) Small-towners can take advantage of mail order services offered by some Asian groceries. Consult the Yellow Pages of your nearest large cities, and call or write for mail order information. Also look under the "Gourmet Food" and the "Health Food" listings. Remember, too, that many specialty stores carry Asian foods, and telephone shopping can save time. Many supermarkets offer a variety of Chinese ingredients, although these items are usually more reasonably priced in Chinese food stores.

HOW TO FIND KOSHER CHINESE INGREDIENTS

Looking for kosher Chinese ingredients can be a wonderful experience. I've had many pleasant conversations and exchanged letters with some lovely people during the course of my researching kosher Chinese food. In trying to find a source for kosher egg roll wrappers, I learned from the owner of a local kosher catering business that his company has in the past been supplied by his brother's certified kosher noodle company, but now he uses his own *kreplach* dough for the egg rolls as well. The manager of the supermarket with the most complete line of kosher foods in my area gave me a list of his kosher frozen food suppliers. That's how I came to talk with Pearl, from Quality Frozen Foods in Brooklyn, New York. After telling me something about her son who also loves to cook, Pearl assured me that she could supply my local supermarket with certified kosher egg roll wrappers. I received a handwritten note from the president of Tabatchnick referring me to companies that handle kosher Chinese products. And a beautiful letter, complete with a story about his personal interest in Chinese cooking, was sent me by a vice-president of Kineret Foods Corporation. He also directed me to a friend of his, a rabbi, who he thought would be able to offer assistance.

Here are some concrete suggestions for locating strictly kosher Chinese ingredients. I hope you'll meet some nice people in your search.

- Start with your supermarket shelves. They may already be stocked with kosher "chow mein" noodles, duck sauce, soy sauce, Chinese mustard, and the like. Write to the companies that manufacture these products and ask for a complete listing of their kosher Chinese ingredients. Some Asian groceries also carry certified kosher products.
- Ask the manager of the store that handles the kosher grocery items you buy to look into supplying you with kosher Chinese foods. Give him a list of what you need. Or, ask for the name of his suppliers of kosher foods, and call directly.
- Call your local kosher caterers to find out where they get their ingredients for Chinese dishes.
- Check the frozen foods department where you shop, and write to the companies that handle kosher frozen foods.
- Check the Yellow Pages for noodle companies and make some telephone calls. You may be lucky enough to find one that has kosher egg roll wrappers.
- There are kosher Chinese restaurants in many large cities in America. Some sell kosher Chinese products in addition to conducting their restaurant business. If you don't see such products on display, ask the manager if what you need is available for sale.

Is Special Equipment Necessary?

Invariably, when I tell someone of my interest in Chinese cooking, the immediate response is either "I have a wok" or "I'd like to cook Chinese food, but I don't have a wok." The assumption is that one *must* have a wok—the all-purpose metal cooking pan used by the Chinese—for authentic Chinese cooking. As you will see, although woks are versatile and especially useful for some Chinese dishes, satisfactory alternative cooking pans can be found in any American kitchen.

CHINESE COOKING EQUIPMENT

long cooking chopsticks

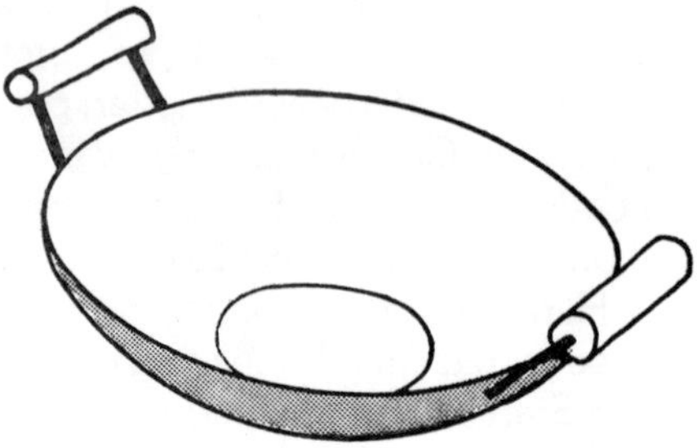

wok

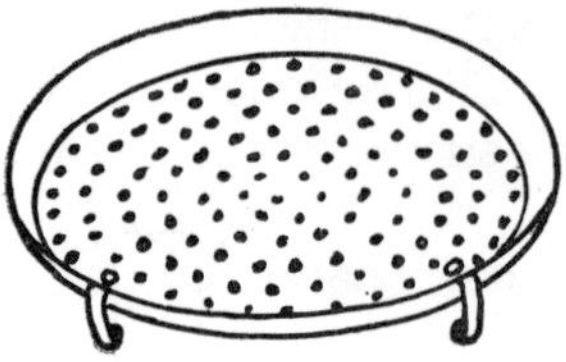

metal steaming tray

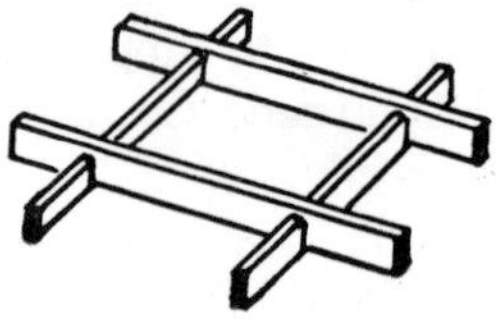

wood steaming rack

boning knife

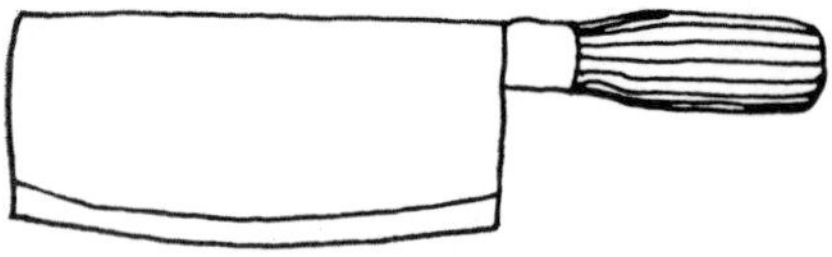

cleaver

Compared to other cuisines, Chinese cooking uses a minimum of special utensils. The wok, the Chinese cleaver (which replaces all other knives), and chopsticks are the basic utensils of the Chinese cook. Woks and chopsticks are available in department and houseware stores and some supermarkets, and all Chinese utensils can be purchased in Chinese hardware stores located in large American cities. Although they add to the pleasure of Chinese cooking, these utensils are not essential. On the next pages you will read about the role of woks, cleavers, and chopsticks in the preparation (and, for chopsticks, the eating) of Chinese food. Also included is a discussion on how to improvise a steamer.

Woks

Many people who use woks love them dearly, and perhaps some feel that Chinese food isn't authentic unless a wok is used. The wok has a large surface area and a shape that lends itself beautifully to stir-frying. Because of the wok's rounded bottom and flaring sides, food can be tossed constantly but won't be tossed out of the utensil. The Chinese use woks also for steaming, slow-cooking, pan-frying, and deep-frying.

In the United States, metal rings are sold with woks so the rounded bottoms will fit on gas stoves. On electric ranges woks conduct the heat best when they are set directly on the heating element. In Chinese homes, woks are set into small braziers so a large part of the wok is exposed to heat. This arrangement leads to quick and even heating, retention of heat, and—most important for the Chinese—use of less fuel than standard pots and pans require. Rolled steel (not stainless steel or aluminum) 14-inch woks with wooden handles are recommended by some experts because (1) they heat rapidly and conduct the heat well, (2) they are heavy enough not to tip over, (3) the size is suitable for most households, and (4) one can hold the handles without burning one's hands.

I began using a large electric skillet instead of a wok early in my experience with Chinese cooking, and I have always found it satisfactory. A major advantage of using an electric utensil is that it allows me to cook right in the dining room, where I can enjoy the company of my guests. When I demonstrate in a supermarket or school or before a Hadassah group, my electric skillet comes with me. When we do a banquet for 100 people, I take along three electric fry pans (while my husband takes along his voltmeter to make sure we don't overload the circuits). A second advantage is safety: I've heard stories of woks catching fire and flaring up, but I've never heard the same about electric skillets. The major disadvantage of using an electric skillet (or an electric wok) is that it never gets as hot as a wok set on the stove.

Wok, fry pan, electric skillet—use whatever you're comfortable with as long as it gives you good results.

Chinese Cleavers

I cooked Chinese food for about eight years before purchasing a cleaver. I bought one when I was about to give private lessons to someone who was accomplished in French cooking, and I wanted to give her the most impressive course possible. At lesson one I learned that she had a Chinese cleaver which she didn't like at all. I now have two Chinese cleavers. My friend has become an accomplished Chinese cook, and she manages very well without a cleaver. Meanwhile, I've learned to use a cleaver in preparing Chinese food and find it an asset when I have a lot of vegetables and meat to slice, chop, or mince.

The Chinese cleaver consists of a rectangular blade made of high carbon steel which is firmly attached to a wooden handle. The blade measures 3½ × 8 inches. Cleavers come in different weights. The lightweight cleaver does a good job slicing and chopping meats and vegetables, while the heavy cleaver is also used to chop through bones. The Chinese cleaver is particularly useful for slicing meat thinly as well as for mincing. Its wide blade is excellent for transferring chopped foods to the pan for cooking.

To prevent rusting, the Chinese cleaver must be washed and dried immediately after each use. And it should be kept sharp (we use an old-fashioned sharpening stone). When properly sharpened, it is frightfully sharp—*handle with awe.* Keep the fingers away from the blade, and never use the cleaver when young children are around.

Chopsticks

Although some Chinese chefs have an array of spoons and skimmers, most stirring and turning implements can be replaced by one pair of cooking chopsticks, which will be longer than chopsticks used for eating. In China, meals are always eaten with chopsticks, but the handling of these two long, thin bamboo sticks is elusive to many Americans.

Think of a pair of chopsticks as very long tweezers with only one movable arm. One arm of the tweezers rests in the "v" between the thumb and index finger, and is balanced on the side of the middle finger, and held in place by the thumb. The top arm is moved by the index finger, opening and closing the tweezers. When you first attempt to use chopsticks, pick up the biggest pieces of food on the plate; as you gain experience, small grains of rice won't be such a challenge.

Steamers

Many recipes in this book require the use of some kind of steamer. Inexpensive adjustable stainless steamer trays that fit into any size pot are available in many cookware departments; they are nice for steaming vegetables. The perforated flat-bottomed steamer trays sold in Asian groceries and some hardware stores are better for the dumplings and buns. A colander can be used if necessary, but because of the colander's shape the foods tend to all fall toward the bottom and may not therefore cook evenly. A heatproof plate works well for steaming fish, and duck can be steamed in a large bowl. Woks often come with wood strips which form a rack onto which a plate, a tray, or a bamboo steamer can be set for steaming. A large electric skillet with a dome lid will often accommodate a steaming tray or plate.

A steamer can be improvised if you have on hand a large pot with a good lid and several heatproof jars or a heatproof bowl that will be stable enough to support a plate or steamer tray. Fill the jars (or bowl) with water above the level of the water in the pot or they'll tip over. For the steaming tray, use a flat-bottomed perforated tray, an aluminum pie or cake pan with holes poked in the bottom, or a piece of perforated aluminum (available in hardware stores) with the edges bent up (be careful of sharp edges). Or use any heatproof plate that will fit into the pot; it must be large enough to hold the food but small enough to allow the steam to circulate around the plate.

In the recipes for steamed breads and dumplings, it is preferable to use a perforated steaming tray so the water doesn't condense back on the food being cooked. If you want to collect the juices when steaming fish, meat, and poultry, use a plate or bowl without holes.

Clam steamers and bamboo steamers can be expensive, but of course they can be used in any recipes calling for steaming. The bamboo steamers used by the Chinese can be stacked, enabling the cook to steam many different foods at once, but they are difficult to clean.

Cooking food in the top half of a double boiler is not an acceptable substitute for steaming.

Steaming as a cooking method is discussed in the Techniques section, which follows.

Chinese Cooking Techniques

Because fuel has always been in short supply, the Chinese have developed special cooking techniques that use a minimum of energy. Stir-frying, probably the most well-known method of Chinese cooking, requires high heat but a very short cooking time. This contrasts with the French technique of sautéing, in which foods are cooked in a small quantity of fat, generally over moderate heat, over a longer period of time. Even when the Chinese deep-fry dumplings and batter-coated food, the pieces of food are small enough to cook quickly. For dishes such as home-style duck, the whole duck is first steamed until tender then deep-fried just to crisp the skin.

In another fuel-saving measure, the heat is turned off when the food is only partially cooked. The heat remaining from the turned-off burner, the cooking utensil, and the food itself is sufficient to complete the cooking. Rice and white-cut chicken are cooked in this manner.

Chinese homes have only top-of-the-range cooking, and the technique of steaming replaces baking for such foods as breads, puddings, and cakes. Stews are important in many cuisines as a way of tenderizing fibrous cuts of meat; the Chinese version of stewing is called red-cooking (red-stewing). Meat, poultry, or fish cooks over low heat for a long period of time in water and soy sauce, taking on a red color.

In the following pages, the cooking techniques of stir-frying, steaming, red-cooking, and deep-frying are explained more fully.

Stir-frying

This is the all-important method of cooking food quickly in a small amount of oil by stirring it continuously over high heat. Meat that is to be stir-fried is sliced into very thin pieces of uniform size. Vegetables, which are also sliced into uniformly small pieces, are cooked only until crisp-tender. If the food sticks to the cooking utensil, more oil is required. The temperature of the oil should be kept between 375 and 400 degrees F. for vegetables and between 350 and 375 degrees F. for meats. If the oil temperature is too low, the food will not cook quickly enough; if it is too high, the food will burn. As a general rule, a drop of water sprinkled carefully into the oil should spatter instantly, but the oil should not be smoking.

In some of the recipes requiring stir-frying, I have not specified the amount of oil to be used. This quantity will vary with the size of the skillet or wok being used and the kind and amount of food being cooked. Your goal should be to cook in the minimum amount of oil necessary to prevent the food from sticking. In the recipe instructions, the words "coat the wok or skillet" mean that you should use enough oil to cover the cooking surface with a thin film. "Coat liberally or generously" means that you should be able to swish the oil, which will be to a depth of about one-eighth inch. If half an inch or more of oil is called for in a recipe, the food cooked in it can no longer be said to have been stir-fried.

It is possible to stir-fry without adding oil at all, especially if a nonstick pan is used. Even when a wok or skillet with an untreated surface is used, almost no oil is necessary if onions are the first ingredient put into the hot pan. The onions can be stir-fried at high heat in a dry pan without burning, and they will give off a small amount of liquid which will keep the next vegetable added from being burned. Eventually you may have to add a small amount of oil to prevent sticking. If so, pour the oil down the sides of the wok or pan instead of sprinkling it over the vegetables so it has a chance to become hot before being mixed with the vegetables. Adding a little broth will also help prevent sticking, but then you are no longer stir-frying. Omitting oil completely from stir-fried dishes sacrifices some of the flavor, but you can compensate by adding other flavors, such as soy sauce or *hoisin* sauce.

Steaming

Steaming is another important energy-conserving cooking method used in China. Foods can be steamed over a pot of food already cooking, and stacks of bamboo steamers can be set over just one wok, so that a small amount of fuel is used to cook many foods.

In steaming, food is placed on a rack, tray, plate, or bowl that is set above water in a pot. The water boils and thereby creates the steam that does the cooking. The pot of water must be covered so the steam does not escape. To use a steamer (see the discussion on steaming in the section Is Special Equipment Necessary?), place an inch or two of water in the bottom of a large pot, pan, or wok. Place the steaming rack or tray or plate in the pot, making sure the bottom of the tray is at least an inch above the water. Adjust the amount of water to the length of time the food will be steaming (of course, a dumpling requiring ten minutes of cooking doesn't need as much water as a bread requiring thirty minutes). Cover the pot and bring the water to the boil. The pot must have a good lid so all the steam doesn't escape, but it shouldn't be so tight that pressure builds up. In a pinch, use aluminum foil to cover the pot.

Red-cooking

Red-cooking, or red-stewing, involves cooking large cuts of meat, poultry, and sometimes fish in soy sauce. The meat is simmered for a long period of time, becoming so tender that small pieces can be pulled off with chopsticks. The resulting gravy is a reddish-brown color, with a very rich flavor. Leftover gravy can be refrigerated or frozen and used as the base for the next red-cooked dish.

Deep-frying

Many recipes for appetizers call for as little as one-half inch to one inch of oil for frying. These appetizers can be deep-fried in more oil, but that isn't necessary. Fry the food on one side until golden, then turn each piece with a large spoon, tongs, or long chopsticks and fry the other side. As you remove each piece of food, hold it above the oil, shake off excess oil, and drain the food well on paper towels. Serve deep-fried food immediately, while still crispy. If you must wait, keep the food in a 300-degree F. oven, where it should stay crisp for at least fifteen minutes without drying out.

The recommended temperature for deep-frying is 375 degrees F., which will brown the food without burning it. Never crowd the cooking utensil. If you put too much food in the pan all at once, the temperature of the oil will drop and the food will not brown properly.

Be careful when using oil in quantity, as spattering or spilling can cause fire. Food can be deep-fried in a wok, a four to eight-quart pot, an electric deep fryer, or an electric skillet. A pan or skillet with sides only a few inches high is not recommended because of the danger of spattering or spilling.

Slicing, Cutting, Serving, Freezing

Boning Chicken Breasts Yourself

Boning raw chicken breasts is reasonably easy if you have the right implement. A boning knife, which has a narrow blade that tapers toward the tip, is the tool to use. Many restaurants and kitchen supply stores carry these knives, and occasionally butchers will sell their old boning knives when they are replaced with new ones. The boning knife must be kept sharp to be useful.

The first step in separating the chicken breast meat from the bone is to press down hard enough on the breastbone to crack it. If pressing down hard doesn't work, grasp one-half of the chicken breast in each hand, with the skin against your hands and the bone facing you, then snap your hands back toward each other **(illustration 1).** Put the chicken down and

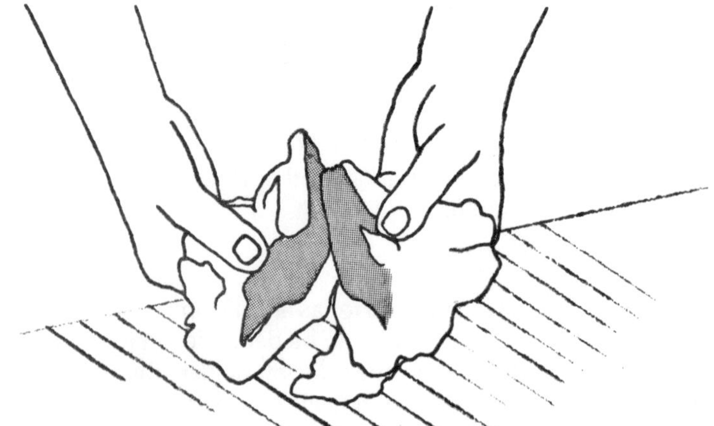

1

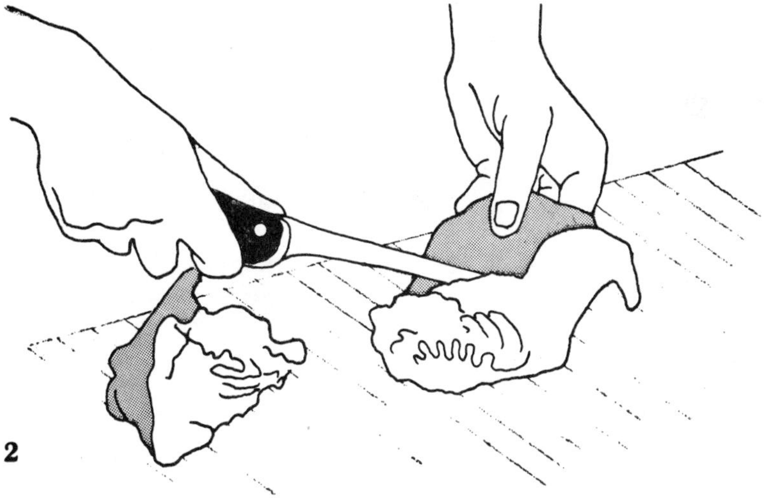

2

use the knife to help crack the center bone if necessary. Then slip the knife into the crack to cut the meat through. Pull off the skin. Half the chicken breast will probably have an extra piece of breastbone attached; the other half may not have this piece and will be easier to work with. Start with the easier half.

Insert the knife between the meat and bone near the breastbone, where the meat is the thickest, and work your way toward the ribs. The knife blade should face the bone, not the meat **(2).** Free the entire piece of chicken from the bones, pulling the meat gently with one hand while cutting with the other **(3).** You'll be constantly touching the meat and bone to get a sense of where to cut and what to extricate. Make sure there are no small bones left attached to the meat. Don't worry about leaving pieces of chicken on the bones. Use the skins and bones for chicken broth; the extra pieces of meat will help flavor the broth.

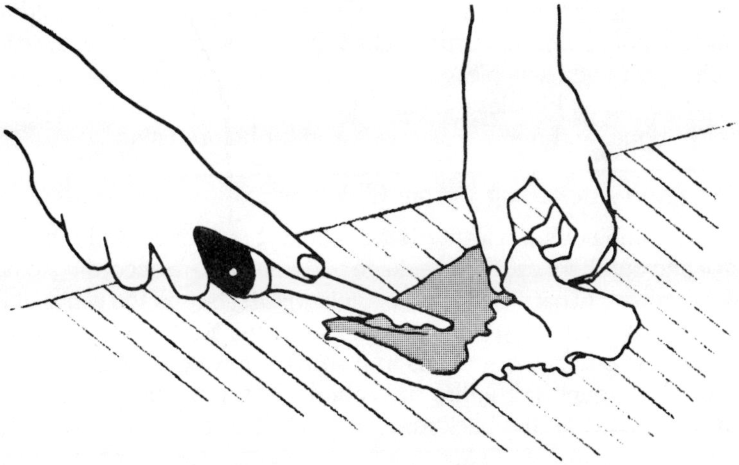

3

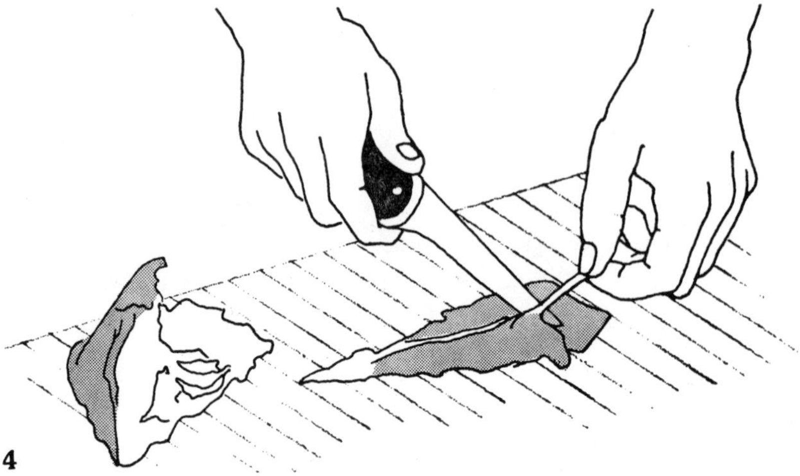
4

When working with the other half of the chicken breast, which has that extra piece of bone attached near the thickest part of the meat, it may be easier to insert the knife at the thinner part, toward the ribs. The procedure is the same. Always keep the knife blade facing the bone so you don't make gashes in the meat, and cut slowly until the entire piece is free.

After the chicken breasts are boned, look for a long white tendon on the underside of each half. To remove it, wet your fingers for an easier grip, then grasp the tip of the tendon with the wet fingers while scraping against the tendon gently with the boning knife **(4).** Continue until the tendon is free from the meat. Trim off all fat from the chicken breasts. A one-pound chicken breast with bone yields about one-half pound of boned meat.

Chicken thighs can be boned also, but you won't be able to free the meat as neatly as in the breasts. However, thigh meat tends to be juicier than white meat, and some people find it tastier. To bone, cut down the length of the thigh until you reach the bone, then slip the knife between the meat and bone until all meat is free. Cut away fat, gristle, and tendons. Boning uncooked chicken drumsticks is not recommended because it is difficult to get even-size pieces.

If you purchase boneless chicken breasts or thighs, check for small pieces of bone, and remove all gristle and fat before using.

Cutting and Packaging Whole Chickens

If you're ambitious and want to save money, buy a lot of whole chickens on sale and cut them up, then package and freeze them according to how you'll use them. (This takes some planning.) First cut off the wings at the joint, then cut each wing into three pieces at the joints. Use the tips for soup and the other two sections in the chicken wing recipes.

Now cut through the entire breastbone. Lay the chicken open, and press down hard on the backbone until you hear a crack. Next, with a sharp knife or cleaver, cut off the backbone on both sides. Package the backbones, gizzards, necks, and wing tips together for soup.

Cut each half of the chicken in half, separating the breast from the thigh. Bone the breasts and package them as they will be needed in cooking. Recipes most often call for one pound of uncooked chicken, or sometimes two or three whole uncooked chicken breasts. Package four legs and thighs together for Very Tasty Cold Chicken (page 109). Or, for the same dish, package twelve legs per batch and bone the thigh meat for use in stir-fried dishes. Freeze the livers for one of the chicken liver recipes.

Mincing Beef

To mince beef, freeze the beef partially, slice it as thin as possible, then chop the beef into smaller and smaller pieces. A sharp knife or cleaver is a must. Heap the meat on top of itself and slice or chop down the middle. Continue heaping and slicing, heaping and chopping. You're aiming for tiny pieces, but the actual size isn't as important as uniformity. Put the knife aside and run through the beef with your hands to make sure there are no large pieces. Remove and discard any gristle or fat.

Many food processors do a good job of mincing beef. Cut out and discard gristle and fat before placing the beef in the processor. Follow the instructions in the food processor booklet, and be careful not to grind the beef into a paste! After processing, again go through the minced beef with your fingers, searching for gristle and fat.

The major advantage of minced beef over ground beef is that the fat can be removed from the former. Minced beef also offers a different texture, holds together better, and tends to be more tender than ground beef.

Cutting Paper-thin Beef Slices

To slice beef very thin, use a good, sharp ten- or twelve-inch knife or cleaver. Freeze the meat until it is quite firm but not so hard that you can't cut any slices at all. If the beef is already frozen, defrost it just until it can be sliced.

5

London broil (or flank steak if your kosher butcher carries that cut) is the easiest cut to slice uniformly. Both should be sliced at a 45-degree angle against the grain of the meat (usually the narrower side) for maximum tenderness **(5)**. Chuck steak is less tender but very flavorful; try it once you've learned to slice very thinly. Roasts are more economical than steaks; they can be sliced uniformly with practice.

Serving a Whole Fish

Serving boneless portions of an unboned cooked whole fish is something of an art. Here's how: lay the fish on its side on a platter. Using two spoons, take off serving-size pieces from the top side, then feel your way down to the bones with the spoons. Be careful not to include any bones in the serving **(6)**. Eventually the entire spine and the attached bones will be

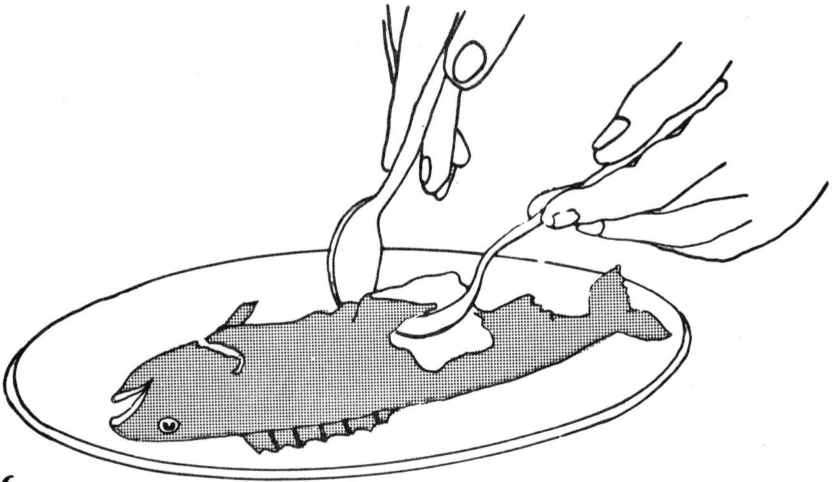

6

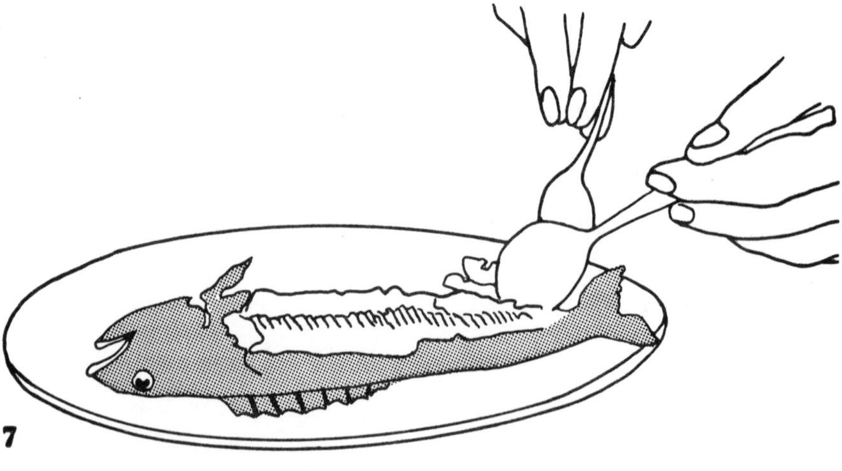

7

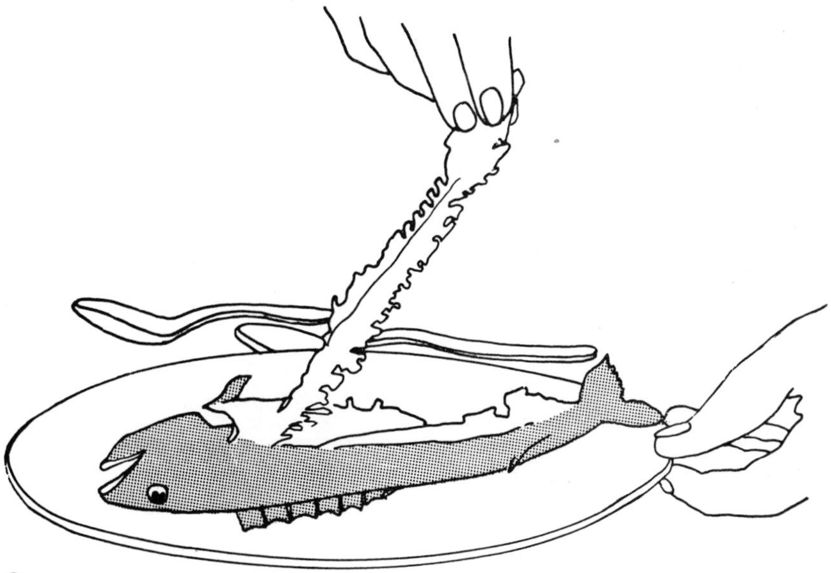

8

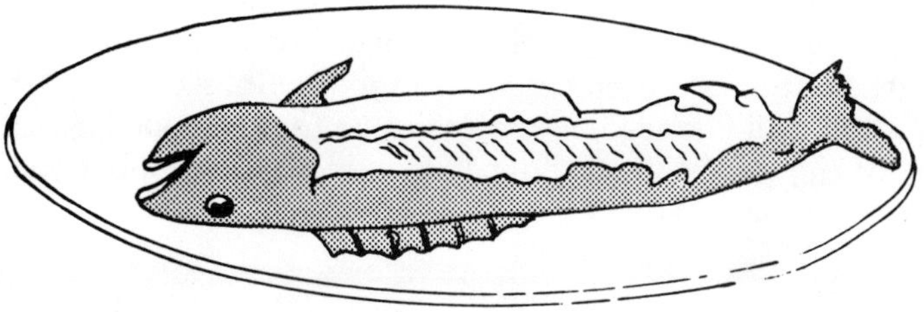

9

exposed **(7)**. Remove the spine in one piece if possible **(8)**, and continue serving the bottom side of the fish **(9)**.

An alternate way of serving portions of a whole fish is to bring the fish to the table so it rests on its belly. Then use two spoons to break off servings of fish from each side, again taking care to avoid serving bones. To serve whole fish family-style, each diner simply takes pieces off the whole fish with his chopsticks.

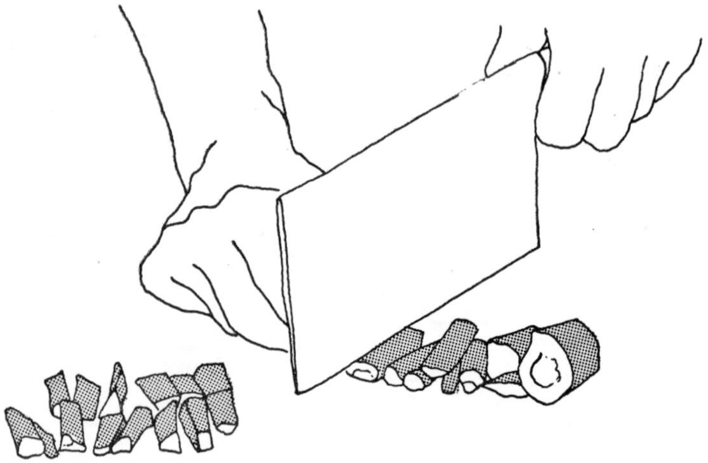

10

Slicing Vegetables

It is important that vegetables be sliced uniformly, both for even cooking and for attractiveness **(10)**. Many vegetables look especially nice sliced on the diagonal **(11)**, and they cook more quickly because more surface area is exposed. Some food processors do a good job of slicing vegetables. Large quantities of chopped vegetables to be used in appetizer fillings (such as for egg rolls) can be chopped in food processors, but you will almost certainly get a more even cut by hand.

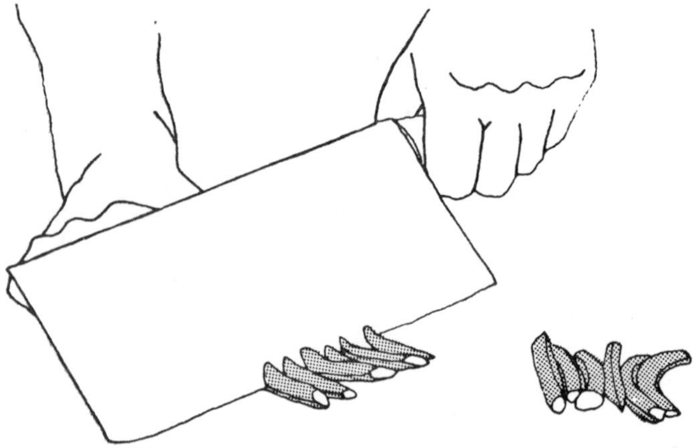

11

Freezing Rice Dishes

Plain cooked rice and many rice dishes can be frozen and then reheated by steaming without first defrosting. It's a good idea to freeze the rice in the approximate shape of the steaming tray or plate to be used, so it will fit right in and can be steamed while still frozen. Line the steaming tray or plate with foil or freezer paper, pack the cool rice into the foil in the shape of the tray, wrap well, and freeze.

Freezing Soups and Broths

Liquids expand as they freeze, so allow an inch of head space in the container when freezing soups and broths. Because of the danger of cracking, do not freeze in glass containers. When dumplings and *wontons* are frozen directly in the soup, gentle heating is advised to keep the dumplings and *wontons* from falling apart.

Tray-freezing

This method enables you to freeze many appetizers in quantity and take out only the amount you need at one time. Grease a cookie sheet or large tray that will fit into your freezer. Several cake tins will do if space is a problem. Or, line the tray with greased wax paper. Place the items to be frozen on the greased surface, making sure the sides do not touch each other. Freeze the food solidly. Quickly place the frozen items in freezer containers or freezer bags, label them, and return them to the freezer.

Planning a Chinese Dinner

Confucius didn't say this, but the wise Jewish cook will experiment with Chinese cooking one dish at a time rather than immediately preparing an elaborate Chinese dinner. Perhaps first serve a Chinese dish as part of an everyday meal. As you familiarize yourself with Chinese ingredients and cooking techniques, you will become comfortable enough to try a complete dinner. The dinner could be served American style (the way we are usually served in Chinese restaurants), with appetizers, soup, main dish(es) and accompaniments, and dessert. Or, serve the meal the way a Chinese family does, putting out soup and a variety of dishes all at once. If it is more convenient, serve the dinner as a banquet, bringing out one dish at a time. Regardless of what kind of Chinese dinner you plan, the suggestions and ideas in this section will help you execute it smoothly.

General Considerations

A well-planned Chinese dinner will have variety, balance, and contrast in tastes, textures, and color. The fundamental Chinese philosophy of living in harmony pervades every aspect of life, including the very basic experience of eating, making balance vitally important in meal preparation. The Chinese rely on combinations of ingredients to make their foods appealing, therefore textural and color contrasts are more important than they are in other cuisines where the attraction may be a large slab of beef or an elaborate sauce. Because most Chinese dishes are mixtures, and most meals consist of several different preparations, it is particularly important to pay attention to how each dish fits into the whole meal.

Serve one dish that has been stir-fried, one that has been steamed, and one boiled, pan-fried, or roasted—that is, use a variety of cooking methods. Serve some unusual dishes and some more familiar ones. A variety will please everyone.

Contrast a mildly flavored soup with a spicy meat or vegetable dish, and a hot dish with a cold one. Serve steamed fish with crisp stir-fried vegetables and a red-cooked beef. If serving a dish such as Spicy Eggplant and Tofu (page 260), be sure to balance it by also offering something crisp for texture, at least one colorful dish, and one bland or lightly seasoned dish that will blend in with everything. Plan your menu with an eye toward making substitutions if necessary. If you're planning to serve steak, mushrooms, and snow peas but find that fresh mushrooms or snow peas are unavailable, be prepared to make a last-minute switch to a stir-fried steak-and-green-bean dish.

Special Considerations for Large Gatherings

When planning a menu for a large group, ask yourself whether the dishes under consideration can be handled in quantity. Egg rolls, for example, can be fried in a large electric skillet over a period of time to serve a crowd informally, but steamed fish as a main course might be difficult to cook and serve. Anything requiring a great deal of last-minute preparation should be avoided. Peking duck takes a long time to slice attractively, and it must be cut at the last minute. It would be difficult for the amateur cook with an amateur staff to handle a number of ducks.

Another consideration is whether the dishes are easy to serve and eat. Chicken prepared and served wrapped in wax paper or foil would not be practical for the cocktail hour, for there is no convenient way to unwrap and dispose of the inedible wrappings. Spring Chicken Packages, however, with their edible wrappers, are ideal.

Suggested Quantities of Food

The president of our synagogue confided to me that he's not sure his wife is really Jewish because she's always concerned that she'll have too *much* food. I almost always have leftovers, and my children would be very disappointed if there weren't any snacks left at the end of a Chinese dinner.

The amount to prepare depends on the kind of Chinese dinner being served. When I'm planning a Chinese dinner with typical American courses, I like to serve two to five different kinds of appetizers, allowing two or three pieces of each kind of appetizer per person. I usually serve one appetizer at a time, and soup is served somewhere with the appetizers. Then comes a long break for ping-pong or air hockey or running around the block. Next, I cook one or two main dishes at the table. If one of these dishes doesn't contain either noodles or rice, then rice is served also. We take another break, and then dessert is served.

Sometimes I serve a teahouse meal consisting of appetizers only. There might be eight appetizers along with a number of dips and sauces and also a soup and dessert. The food is cooked as we go along, and this kind of meal is enjoyed over a long period of time.

The Chinese family dinner is perhaps the kindest way to feed a guest, because all the food is set out at once and there are no groans of "Oh, no, not another dish." Plan to serve soup, rice, and four dishes for six people. Add one dish for each additional two diners. These four dishes should not all be heavy meat dishes. One can be a stir-fried chicken and vegetables, another a stew, one a steamed fish, and the fourth an extra vegetable. If you know that your guests have starved themselves for two days waiting for this feast, you may feel more comfortable beginning the meal with pineapple boats or melon wedges to take the edge off these appetites, which certainly won't need any whetting.

For a banquet you will want to also serve *dim sum* and other tasty morsels either as appetizers, in the American fashion, or here and there throughout the meal between courses, as the Chinese do. Because a banquet lasts longer than a family-style meal, more food can be consumed. You might serve a heavy soup toward the beginning of the meal and add a light broth toward the end. Plan to have many different foods, but small servings of each one.

Shopping List for Ingredients

Unless you have a phenomenal memory, a complete shopping list is your insurance that you'll remember everything. Make up the list well in advance if you want to take advantage of sales or quantity price breaks. List what can be bought ahead and frozen or stored and what is perishable and can only be purchased a day or two ahead. Package meats and egg roll, spring roll and *wonton* wrappers in the quantities in which they'll be used for each recipe. Go through the recipes and prepare a chart listing every ingredient. A partial list looks like this:

Ingredients	**Egg Rolls**	**Dumplings**	**Beef Buns**	**Total**
Egg Roll Skins	1 pound	¾ pound		1¾ pounds
Beef	½ pound	½ pound	¾ pound	1¾ pounds
Bean Sprouts	1 cup			1 cup

From here divide the ingredients into a "supermarket" list and "Asian (Oriental)" store list. On some Chinese ingredients—such as canned water chestnuts, bamboo shoots, soy sauce, and duck sauce—you can save considerably when purchasing from Asian food stores in quantity.

Preparation Chart

Go through each recipe and decide what can be prepared in advance and frozen, what can be prepared a day or two ahead, and what requires last-minute preparation. If you see that too much has to be done at the last minute, change the menu or arrange for someone to help.

I need to rely on detailed lists of what to do and when to do it, because I find that what isn't written down sometimes is forgotten. For a particularly varied or complicated dinner, I make hour-by-hour time charts for the day of the dinner. For a major undertaking (such as a banquet), when there are several people helping, a detailed time chart is indispensable to me. I write each person's name across the top of the page, the times on the sides, and the tasks under each name, hour by hour.

Pots and Pans and Serving Pieces

Again, it is helpful to make a list of all pots, pans, casseroles, and utensils that will be needed for cooking and serving. Also plan for oven times and stove space. If you're using one or more electric skillets, have a knowledgeable person check the circuitry to prevent possible overloading. And make sure you can set up the skillets in an area where no one will trip over the cords. Be sure to use heavy duty extension cords.

A Sampling of Menus

Many people like to begin their experience with Chinese cooking by serving one appetizer, soup, main dish, or vegetable as part of an American dinner. For example, Chinese Beef Stew (page 185) goes wonderfully with noodles, a vegetable, and a tossed salad. Egg Drop Soup (page 160) will fit right in with a chicken dinner, and Stir-fried Vegetables (page 264) are good with chicken, steak, broiled chicken livers, and other meats. Fried rice makes use of leftovers, and you can serve it as the main dish, perhaps with peas and a salad. For special occasions Roast Duckling With Plum Sauce (page 231) is an elegant main course.

When you decide to progress to whole Chinese dinners, study the menus below. You will find complete menus for Chinese-style family dinners, a vegetarian menu, a teahouse meal, and two Chinese banquets. Following each menu is a discussion of how the dishes fit together to form the whole meal, and how the meal should be served.

If you are planning something more involved than a family meal, you may want to serve a beverage in addition to tea. Traditionally, warmed rice wine is served at Chinese banquets. It has become appropriate to serve white wine, beer, or even brandy during a Chinese meal. Although we think of brandy as an after-dinner drink, at present the Chinese do not drink intoxicating beverages following the meal. Tea is the last beverage to be served.

CHINESE HOME-STYLE DINNERS FOR SIX

I

Egg Drop Soup

Sweet-and-Sour Tofu "Meatballs"

Stir-fried Broccoli

Rice With Steamed Chicken
(one-half recipe)

Fresh Fruit

Tea

This is a nutritionally balanced meal. It is colorful, provides a range of textures, and uses a variety of cooking methods. The soup, *tofu*, broccoli, and rice dishes are set on the table at one time and eaten as integral parts of the whole meal, not as separate courses. The soup is served first, but it remains on the table through the meal to be taken as desired. Because this is a general menu with dishes common to Canton and other provinces, it would be appropriate to serve tea throughout the meal as the Cantonese do, or you may serve it following the meal as is customary in other parts of China.

No one dish is considered more important than the others. The broccoli is as essential as the *tofu* and rice dishes because it brings an important color contrast and crisp texture as well as a relatively strong taste compared to the soup and rice. The sweet-and-sour sauce of the *tofu* dish not only brings a lovely color to the meal but provides the most interesting taste. The *tofu* "meatballs" and the crisp vegetables in the sauce add a crunchy texture to offset the rice dish.

Because the rice is served as one of many dishes, it is not necessary to use the whole pound of chicken called for in the Rice With Steamed Chicken recipe. For American tastes, half a pound is more than adequate. In a real Chinese meal, two chicken legs chopped into one-inch pieces would very likely be used.

II

Chicken Broth

Home-style Steamed Crispy Duck

Salt and Pepper—Chinese Style

Steamed Rolls

Green Beans With Garlic

Stir-fried Carrots With Ginger

Fresh Fruit

Tea

In this home-style dinner a whole duck is placed in the center of the table and the diners "dig in" with chopsticks, breaking off small pieces of crisp skin and tender meat. In many Chinese meals, the diner takes a bit of food from the central dish and mixes it with the rice in his own rice bowl. In this one, the rolls take the place of rice, and the duck is eaten inside a piece of the roll, making a kind of sandwich.

The duck itself is a study in contrasts. The meat is exceptionally soft and tender, and the skin unusually crisp. The duck gets dipped into a dish of salt and spicy, aromatic Szechwan peppercorns before it is combined with the sweet roll.

Added to the meal are two colorful vegetables, both stir-fried to remain crisp but each cooked with a different seasoning. A clear soup, which remains on the table throughout the meal, is selected as the beverage. Because the duck and rolls are substantial, adding dumplings or noodles to the soup isn't necessary.

Tea is not served during the meal, but it takes its place at the end. If you want to vary the serving sequence and still fit into a Chinese pattern, serve tea before the meal begins, then the duck, rolls, and vegetables, and last, the soup. Tea should again be served with the fresh fruit.

III

Chicken and Corn Soup

Deep-fried Chicken Fu Yung

Peking Beef

Stir-fried Sweet Peppers

Steamed Carrots With Ginger

Plain Boiled Brown Rice

Tea

This lovely menu brings a delicate soup together with crunchy fried chicken shreds and a rich and flavorful beef. The peppers contribute color and a wonderful crispness. Steamed carrots balance out the meal, bringing a soft texture and gingery taste. Although nothing in this dinner is spicy, there is an excellent combination of seasonings, and the meal is full of good flavors, attractive colors, and a variety of textures.

Each diner takes morsels of food from the shared dish and eats them immediately or mixes the food first in his own rice bowl. For an authentic Chinese dinner, halving the quantities in the chicken and beef recipes would be more accurate. This is because Chinese families do not eat nearly as much meat as Americans. As with the other Chinese home dinners, the soup is made available throughout the meal. Tea is served following the meal.

IV

Beef-and-Vegetable Dumpling Soup

White-cut Chicken Breasts
(one-half recipe)

Szechwan Sauce

Sesame Sauce

Broccoli, Water Chestnuts, and Dried Hot Peppers

Cantonese Steamed Eggs

Plain Boiled Brown Rice

Fresh Fruit

Tea

A spicy, textured Szechwan sauce and a smooth, mild sesame sauce are used as dips for tender simmered chicken, which is served cold. Steamed eggs, soft and custardy in texture, contrast with every other dish in this meal. Broccoli with hot peppers is selected as the vegetable. Ordinarily you would not weigh down a meal with spicy foods, but since the Szechwan sauce is served as a condiment, and all the other foods are mildly seasoned, two spicy items are acceptable in this menu.

Beef-and-Vegetable Dumpling Soup rounds out the meal. The tasty little dumplings, which are loaded with vegetables, take the place of a second vegetable in this menu. Serve the dumplings in plenty of broth. Tea is not brought out until the fruit is served.

A Vegetarian Menu

Vegetarian Hot-and-Sour Soup

Tofu and Peanuts in Hoisin Sauce

Stir-fried Sweet Peppers

Steamed Vegetables

Plain Boiled Brown Rice

Eight-treasure Pudding

Tea

The strictly vegetarian Buddhists of China would enjoy this high protein meal—fit for a festival—which includes a grand variety of foods. Except for the rice, every dish selected for this menu uses at least two major ingredients. The rice, therefore, is not only a filler, but it serves as a buffer between all the tasty combinations.

A more simple vegetarian menu might include a clear vegetable broth, a large dish of stir-fried vegetables, *tofu* with a sweet-and-sour sauce, brown rice, fresh fruit, and finally tea. Some of the vegetarian recipes in this book—Vegetarian's Delight (page 262) and Vegetarian Brown Rice (page 291), for example—need only a clear broth and fresh fruit to make a complete meal.

A Teahouse Luncheon for Twelve

Spring Chicken Packages

Steamed Buns With Heavenly Beef Filling

Barbecued "Spareribs"

White-cut Chicken Breasts

Szechwan Sauce—Sesame Sauce—Duck Sauce

Chinese Mustard and other condiments

Pan-fried Scallion Cakes

Steamed Cantonese Dumplings

Chicken Livers With Water Chestnuts

Rabbi Belzer's Cold Hot Noodles

Tea

The tasty snacks, dumplings, buns, and other morsels known as *dim sum* are featured along with noodles and tea at teahouses in China. This menu includes a varied selection of *dim sum,* condiments, and a *lo mien* dish. It is appropriate to serve a variety of teas at this meal.

The menu opens with deep-fried crisp Spring Chicken Packages. Puffy steamed buns with a surprise beef filling are the next treat, followed by succulent "spareribs" (lamb breast). The lamb can be roasted in the oven for convenience or cooked over a carefully regulated charcoal fire. White-cut chicken is bland, balancing the richness of the "spareribs" and the steamed bun filling. The chicken is served cold, contrasting with the preceding hot *dim sum.* It is dipped into sauces of the diner's choosing, ranging from the sweet (duck sauce) to the hot and spicy (mustard, Szechwan Sauce).

Next come the scallion cakes, which are meatless but are rich in chicken fat. *Shao mai,* the small open-faced steamed dumplings, provide relief from the heavier scallion cakes. Now come the chicken livers, which bring a completely new taste to the meal. They are served hot because the final dish—Rabbi Belzer's Cold Hot Noodles—will be a cold one. The noodle dish is served because there are no other highly spiced dishes on the menu, unless the diner chooses to inundate the white-cut chicken with a very spicy sauce. A simple bowl of Sesame-Soy Lo Mien could be offered instead. If you have many helping hands, a noodle soup with meats and vegetables (see One-Dish Noodle Soup, page 164) is an excellent alternative.

This menu uses deep-fried, roasted, pan-fried, broiled, boiled, and steamed foods. It is a meal of widely varied textures and tastes, with the order carefully planned to make the most of the contrasts and to balance the hot and cold, the heavy and light, the bland and spicy.

Note: This kind of meal takes coordination, but all the dishes can be prepared in advance to some degree. Check each recipe to determine what can be done ahead.

A Chinese Banquet for Twelve

Rice Wine or Tea

Crispy Sweet Walnuts

Fruit Platter

Spiced Cold Brisket

White-cut Chicken Breasts served with Sesame Sauce

Stir-fried Steak, Snow Peas, and Chinese Mushrooms

Hot-and-Sour Soup

Chicken Livers With Water Chestnuts

Sweet Orange "Tea"

Boneless Pressed Duck
(double the recipe)

Sesame-Seed Red-Bean-Paste Dim Sum

Clear Chicken Broth

Pan-fried (or steamed) Whole Carp
With Sweet-and-Sour Sauce

Walnut "Tea"

Watermelon Basket

Tea

Wine is not typically served at Chinese meals, but banquets are an exception. The guests may sip wine or tea before the meal begins, and you can continue to serve rice wine during the meal. The walnuts are served before the guests proceed to the dinner table.

The three cold dishes—fresh fruit, spiced brisket, and white-cut chicken—are on the table when everyone sits down, and they are cleared before the first hot dish is brought out. The stir-fried steak makes a fine first course for a banquet: it is tasty, colorful, and interesting but not too strongly flavored. Hot-and-Sour Soup—because of its intriguing flavors and interesting ingredients—makes an appropriate next course. Chicken livers are served as a banquet dish in China because of the difficulty the average person has in accumulating them; and the Chicken Livers With Water Chestnuts—served on toothpick "spears"—are light and tasty.

Sweet Orange "Tea" is a wonderful refresher at this point. It is sipped slowly while everyone anticipates what is to come. Boneless Pressed Duck is selected for the next dish because it is made using cooking techniques that haven't yet been featured (steaming and deep-frying) and because a crisp skin and light sauce have yet to appear in any dishes served. Peking Duck would be a marvelous alternative. The much easier Chicken With Hoisin Glaze and Rice Stuffing is an acceptable substitute, especially since *hoisin* sauce has not flavored any of the other dishes.

A dessert-like *dim sum* follows as a change of pace, then a light chicken broth to quench the thirst and clear the palate. Fish, a sign of prosperity, is the last course to be served before dessert. The fish can be pan-fried or steamed, but it must be served whole. Walnut "Tea" and a Watermelon Basket, filled with expensive and exotic melons and fresh fruits, are good choices for dessert. Both are very refreshing, and neither is filling. The meal ends with tea.

You may have noticed that there is nothing very hot or spicy about this menu. The tasty but more subtle dishes of Peking are considered banquet fare, while the very peppery Szechwan cooking that many Americans have come to know and love is considered a sign of poverty by the Chinese. Szechwan dishes are therefore avoided at banquets.

How many people does this menu really serve? Keeping in mind that each recipe serves four to six people and that the portions will be small, twelve people will get more than halfway through the meal. At least three of those will make it to the end.

Chinese Banquet—Goldberg Style

Egg Rolls

Fried Wontons

Spring Chicken Packages

Steamed Buns With Heavenly Beef Filling

Northern Dumplings

Barbecued Chicken Wings

Very Tasty Cold Chicken

Deep-fried Noodles

Duck Sauce—Szechwan Sauce—Chinese Mustard

Chopped Scallions

Champagne Punch

Lo Mien and Meatball Soup

Mixed Fruit

Cashew Chicken With Hoisin Sauce

Stir-fried Vegetables

Special Fried Rice

Tea

Dessert and Fortune Cookies

This is the kind of menu I've used to feed as many as 120 people at synagogue fundraisers. Five to ten times the recipes are used, and I prepare in advance and freeze whatever possible. The menu reflects American tastes and expectations.

At our banquets we set up three electric skillets, and for about an hour the deep-fried appetizers are cooked. First egg rolls are fried in all three pans, then the *wontons,* then the chicken packages. Meanwhile, a kitchen crew is steaming the beef buns, boiling the dumplings, and baking the chicken wings. The cold chicken and fried noodles are set out from the start, along with the condiments. These appetizers are served with champagne punch, which everyone loves.

Now there is a break while we set up for the soup and main dishes. The soup and fruit are set out, and although champagne punch is made available throughout the meal, tea is now served as well. Our three electric skillets are drained and readied for the fried rice, vegetables, and chicken and nuts. This time a different item is cooked in each pan, so the meat, vegetable, and rice are served at once to about ten people, then the cooking begins again.

Finally, we serve dessert and fortune cookies. An identical set of fortunes is placed on each table, and other desserts are served from a central table.

Chinese Banquet—Goldberg Style exemplifies the adaptability of Chinese cooking. In that sense, it is authentically Chinese.

Part 2

Recipes

A Note on the Recipes

The dishes in this book, when prepared exactly as the recipes instruct, will be delicious and just the way *I* like them. If you adjust the seasonings or even change major ingredients, the dishes will be delicious and maybe more the way *you* like them. A friend aptly describes my recipes as "relaxed recipes"—they're meant to be adapted. The choice and exact quantities of ingredients are actually secondary to using the proper cooking techniques.

The recipes are grouped as follows: appetizers; condiments; congees and soups; beef and lamb; chicken, chicken livers, and duck; fish; vegetables and eggs; rice, noodles, and breads; and desserts. When looking for a particular dish, you should also check the Index under the appropriate heading.

Each recipe includes a notation indicating the province or city in which the preparation originated, whether it is a classic Chinese dish (Peking Duck), a kosher adaptation ("Shrimp" Toast), or a recipe modified to use ingredients that are available in the United States but are foreign to China (Stir-fried Beef and Broccoli). Dishes that are served in Chinese-American restaurants but that are not authentically Chinese—that is, not prepared in that manner in China—include the words "Chinese-American" in the notation. Finally, recipes that are my own creations based on my general experience with Chinese cooking include the word "influence" in the notation. For example, Deep-fried Stuffed Chicken Breasts has the notation "Peking influence," indicating that the recipe was developed in my kitchen but uses cooking methods and/or Chinese ingredients associated with Peking.

About the Chinese Characters and Transliterations

When my editor suggested that we include the authentic Chinese title of each recipe in the book, I called on the mother of one of my son's Chinese friends for help. Frankly, I was somewhat nervous before our first meeting. Would this Chinese woman, I wondered, be offended that an American with no Chinese background was attempting to write a Chinese cookbook? My fears were immediately allayed: Monica Yu was supportive, enthusiastic, encouraging. She immediately offered to read the entire manuscript and make corrections as needed. I was delighted when she called to inform me that she had learned something new about a particular Chinese ingredient, and I was even more thrilled to hear that she was trying some of my recipes and was planning to serve brisket (for the first time) to her daughter's college friends.

During the course of our meetings and phone conversations I got my first taste of the richness of the Chinese language. Monica labored many a late evening to find the most authentic Chinese name for each of the recipes. As I sat opposite Monica in her living room, waiting as she searched for the appropriate English words for a Chinese character, it occurred to me that we could write a book on the Chinese meanings of the recipe titles alone. When I asked Monica for the literal translation of eggs *fu yung,* expecting *fu yung* to mean pancake, she used her hands to fashion the words "wispy clouds" as though she were pulling the clouds out of the air and gently stretching them to make them light.

The English name of a given recipe often reflects the ingredients and cooking methods used in the preparation, and in many cases the English name of a recipe is a literal translation of the Chinese. However, many English recipe names have colorful and unusual Chinese counterparts. For example, Cellophane Noodles With Beef and Chicken is called *Ma Yi Shang Shu* in Chinese, which translates back to "Ants Climbing on a Tree." And the Chinese characters for broccoli, which is not native to China, mean "foreign green vegetable."

In this book the transliterations of the Chinese characters follow the Mandarin pronunciation. There are several systems used to transcribe Chinese sounds into English, none of which is altogether satisfactory. The *pin yin* system, in use on the Mainland, is employed here except in cases where common usage is otherwise.

One of the problems in learning to pronounce Chinese is that many Chinese sounds don't even occur in the English language. The truth of the matter is that one cannot learn to pronounce Chinese from a book. The best way to learn to correctly pronounce the names of the recipes is to learn to read the Chinese characters. Once you're proficient in Chinese cooking, who knows?

1

Appetizers

An appetizer, by definition, is something that stimulates the appetite. One might say, then, that every Chinese dish is an appetizer. However, what we think of as Chinese appetizers (egg rolls, spareribs, and the variety of steamed buns and dumplings we have come to know as *dim sum*) are not served in China as they are in the United States. Here, we are likely to find egg rolls or fried *wontons,* for example, served at cocktail parties or as the first course of a meal in a Chinese restaurant. The closest the Chinese come to a cocktail hour would be the time prior to a banquet, when guests are received. While waiting for everyone to arrive and dinner to begin, the guests might be served a little wine with nibbles of nuts and fresh or dried fruits. The first foods on the table would most likely be a selection of cold dishes and very attractively and unusually cut vegetables (plus the nuts and fruits if they have not already been served).

Dim sum, sometimes spelled *deem seem* or *dum sim,* translates literally to "dot heart" or "touch heart." These delightful morsels are sold from stands in the city streets of China, much the same as hot dogs and *knishes* are sold from pushcarts in large cities in the United States. Teahouses in China, and now also in the United States, serve *dim sum* as luncheon meals and daytime snacks. As part of a dinner, *dim sum* are served as appetizers in a very literal sense, but not at the beginning of the meal. They are brought out between courses as a change of pace in order to refresh the diner and indeed stimulate his waning appetite. Small thin-skinned spring rolls can be included in the general category of *dim sum,* but other egg rolls of China are more like omelets or *blintzes* and would therefore be more appropriately served as a luncheon dish or as one of the dinner dishes in a family meal.

Any one of the appetizers in this chapter can be incorporated into either an American or a Chinese dinner. Some make wonderful *hors d'oeuvres* for any occasion, others also work well in Chinese family meals, and some are particularly suitable for banquets. The recipe introductions will explain the place of some of the individual appetizers in Chinese meals.

Condiments are always expected to blend with or bring out flavors, not mask them. Many *dim sum* combine well with a variety of purchased and homemade sauces and dips. Therefore many of the appetizer recipes recommend that particular condiments be served with them. These should be considered suggestions, however, not requirements.

Uncooked Egg Roll Wrappers

春捲皮

Chun Juan Pi

Canton, Chinese-American

Makes twenty-four 7-inch triangles, enough for 1 recipe of egg roll filling

I have read many, many books on Chinese cooking, and I have talked with a number of Chinese about what egg rolls really are, but I have yet to find a definitive answer. Most sources agree that the Chinese-American restaurant-type egg roll, with which we're most familiar, is actually a spring roll, which in China is made with a much thinner wrapper than that used here. Chinese spring roll wrappers are made of a flour and water mixture, but commercially prepared egg roll wrappers as we know them are made with a flour, water, and egg dough; it is possible that egg rolls gained their American name as a reference to the egg in the wrapper.

The homemade wrappers in this recipe are prepared without egg, because they come out lighter when fried than do homemade wrappers made and tested with egg. The flour-and-water dough is reasonably easy to handle. It makes a light, crisp crust that is close in taste and texture to store-bought egg roll skins. These wrappers should be used as soon as they are rolled out. Therefore, the chilled filling must be ready before you start the wrappers.

2 cups unsifted all-purpose flour
½ teaspoon salt (optional)
¾ cup cold water

In a medium-size mixing bowl, combine the flour and the salt. Gradually add the water, stirring with a fork until the dough forms a ball. Transfer the dough to a clean, lightly floured work surface and knead for about 5 minutes—until the dough is very smooth. Divide the dough into 6 equal pieces.

Working consecutively, roll out each piece a little at a time into a rectangle whose final dimensions will be 7 × 14 inches. Keep the working surface lightly floured to prevent the dough from sticking. Roll out the first piece of dough to the largest rectangle you can easily manage (it may be very small at first), then roll out the second piece, then the third, and so on. When you come back to the first piece of dough after having rolled out all six, it will have relaxed and will be easier to roll. Continue the rolling until the desired size is reached. Occasionally pick up each piece of dough to make sure it is not sticking. Trim off uneven edges when the rectangles are about the correct size.

Cut each rectangle in half, yielding two 7-inch squares. For full-size egg rolls, cut each 7-inch square diagonally in half. For cocktail-size egg rolls, cut each square into quarters. Follow the directions in the recipe for Egg Rolls for filling and frying.

Cooked Egg Roll Wrappers

上海春捲皮

Shanghai Chun Juan Pi

Southern and eastern China

Makes twenty-four 7-inch rounds

One view of what egg rolls "really" are states that the egg roll of China is much like an omelet or a *blintz* rolled around a filling. It seems likely that this kind of egg roll is served in China at family meals, because the wrapping is not so difficult to prepare at home. In this recipe, the exposed parts of the wrapper become crisp when fried. Although the inside of the rolled-up wrapper does not become crisp, it is much tastier than other egg roll skins, so you will enjoy the taste of this wrapper as well as its texture.

2 cups unsifted all-purpose flour
½ teaspoon salt (optional)
3 eggs (graded large), beaten
2 cups cold water
A mildly flavored oil for coating the skillet

In a medium-size mixing bowl, mix together the flour and the salt. Stir in the beaten eggs. Gradually stir in the water, then beat the batter with a fork or a spoon until very smooth.

Heat a heavy 7-inch skillet over medium heat. Using a paper towel that has been dipped in a mildly flavored oil, coat the pan with a thin layer of oil.

Spoon 2 tablespoons of the batter into the pan. Now quickly tilt the pan so the batter covers the bottom of the pan thinly but completely. Cook the batter just until the pancake is set and the top surface has lost its wet look. Invert the pan, or use a pancake turner to remove the cooked wrapper from the pan. Repeat the process until all the batter is used up. Stack the pancakes, and cover until you are ready to fill them.

If the wrappers are not to be used within the hour, wrap them in foil as soon as they are cool. Refrigerate them overnight, or freeze them. Once frozen, the wrappers must be thoroughly defrosted or they cannot be separated.

To make the egg rolls, spread ¼ cup of filling in a straight line about an inch in from one edge of the wrapper. Roll the wrapper around the filling, forming a log (see Method Three for wrapping egg rolls, page 68). Secure the flap with one or two toothpicks if necessary. Place the filled egg rolls, flap side down, in a single layer on a plate lined with lightly oiled wax paper. Refrigerate the egg rolls until you are ready to fry them. The egg rolls can be filled as much as 2 hours in advance of frying.

Fry, drain, and serve the egg rolls according to the directions for Egg Rolls on page 69. Remove any toothpicks before frying. (If the skins open up during frying, leave the toothpicks in.) Filled egg rolls made with these cooked wrappers can be tray-frozen before frying. Do not defrost before frying.

Egg Rolls

春捲

Chun Juan

Southern and eastern China,
Chinese-American

Makes 24 egg rolls, 48 cocktail size

The egg rolls in this recipe resemble those served in most Chinese-American restaurants in this country. They call for the commercially prepared wrappers used by restaurants, and the filling is a stir-fried meat and vegetable mixture. The restaurant filling is likely to consist mainly of Chinese cabbage, celery, bean sprouts, and often a little chopped shrimp. The filling here relies more on meat (beef and chicken are used) and adds mushrooms, onions, and scallions to the vegetable mixture. You never come away feeling you've had a cabbage-and-bean-sprout sandwich.

The filling consists of three mixtures that are cooked separately and then combined when cold. This keeps the flavors and textures of each mixture distinctive. The vegetables remain crunchy, the beef is tasty but not overwhelming, and the chicken-egg mixture adds a softness and mild taste that complements the rest of the filling. The fried egg roll is golden brown and crisp on the outside, and fresh-tasting on the inside. Neither the crust nor the filling should ever be soggy.

If the beef, chicken, and vegetable mixtures are combined when hot and eaten immediately, they make a fine main dish to serve over hot rice or noodles.

Mixture I:

1 to 2 tablespoons peanut, corn, or other oil
¼ cup chopped onion
¼ cup thinly sliced scallion rounds (white and crisp green parts)
1 cup thinly sliced celery, cut into matchsticks about ⅛ × ½ inch
1 cup sliced celery cabbage or other Chinese cabbage, cut as above
1 cup coarsely chopped fresh mushrooms
1 cup fresh bean sprouts
½ teaspoon salt

In a 10-inch skillet or a wok, heat the oil until hot but not yet smoking. Stir-fry the onion and the scallion rounds to coat them with the oil, then add the celery and stir continuously for half a minute. Add the celery cabbage and continue stirring for about 30 seconds, then add the mushrooms and stir-fry for another 30 seconds. Mix in the bean sprouts, then mix in the salt. The vegetables should be crunchy. Remove the vegetables from the pan and refrigerate.

Mixture II:

½ pound beef, any kind, cut into very thin strips about ½ inch long
¼ teaspoon freshly ground black pepper
2 teaspoons soy sauce
1 tablespoon peanut, corn, or other oil
1 tablespoon cornstarch
1 tablespoon oil for stir-frying

Toss the beef strips with the pepper, soy sauce, 1 tablespoon of oil, and the cornstarch. Let the meat stand for 10 to 15 minutes. Coat a 7- or 8-inch skillet or a wok with about a tablespoon of oil. Heat the oil until very hot but not yet smoking, then stir-fry the meat for about 2 minutes, until it is cooked. Remove the beef from the pan and refrigerate.

Mixture III:

½ pound chicken meat, cut into ¼-inch cubes
½ teaspoon salt, or to taste
1 teaspoon cornstarch
2 tablespoons peanut, corn, or other oil
¼ cup chopped onion
¼ cup chopped scallions (white and crisp green parts)
2 eggs (graded large), beaten

Toss the chicken cubes with the salt and cornstarch. Using about 2 tablespoons of oil, coat a 7- or 8-inch skillet or a wok generously. Heat the oil, then add the chopped onion and scallions, stirring briefly to coat them with the oil. Add the chicken and stir immediately and constantly for about 2 minutes, until the chicken is cooked but not browned. Add the eggs and stir constantly, until they are set. Remove the mixture from the pan and refrigerate.

When the three filling mixtures are cold, combine them. The egg roll filling can be refrigerated overnight, but it should not be frozen. Drain off any liquid before filling the egg roll wrappers.

Wrapping and Frying the Egg Rolls:

1 pound egg roll wrappers (or 1 recipe homemade wrappers)
Oil for frying

Until you can work quickly, work with only a few egg roll skins at a time. Keep the remainder covered to prevent drying out. For square egg roll skins, use Method One or Method Two. For round skins, use Method Three.

Method One: Cut the wrappers in half diagonally. Using about ¼ cup of filling for each egg roll, follow the diagrams and directions below. For cocktail-size egg rolls, cut the wrappers into quarters, corner to corner, making 4 small triangles. Use about 2 tablespoons of filling for each.

Method Two: Cut the wrappers in half horizontally. Use ¼ cup of filling for each egg roll. If you are not adept at handling wrappers that have been cut in half, use the entire egg roll wrapper for each egg roll and increase the amount of filling. For cocktail-size egg rolls, cut the wrappers into 4 squares and use 2 tablespoons of filling for each.

Method Three: This method is used for round egg roll wrappers. Use ¼ cup of filling for each.

METHOD ONE

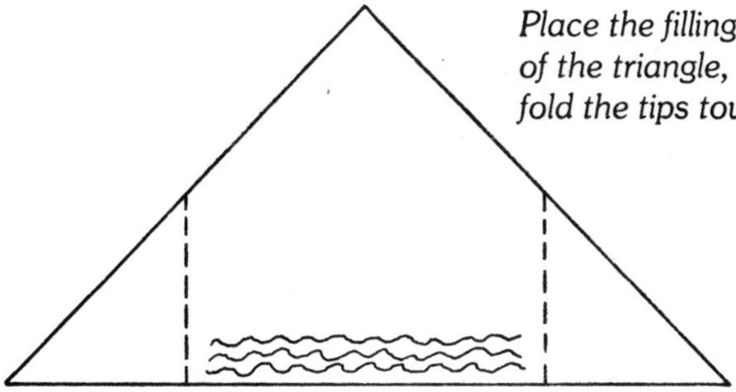

Place the filling along the bottom of the triangle, leaving room to fold the tips toward the middle.

Fold the tips toward the center, then seal by wetting the tips with a drop or two of water and pressing together.

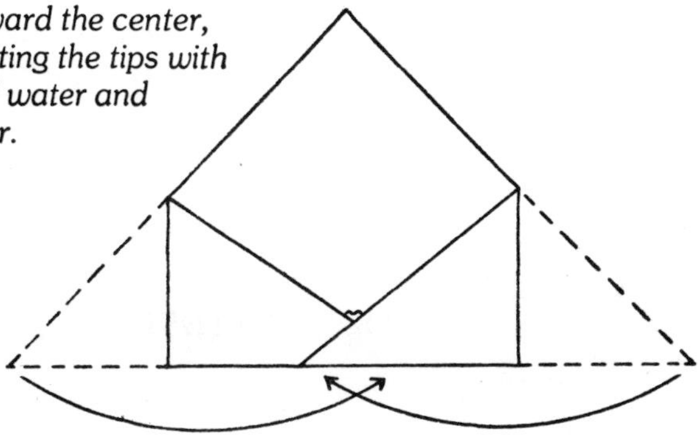

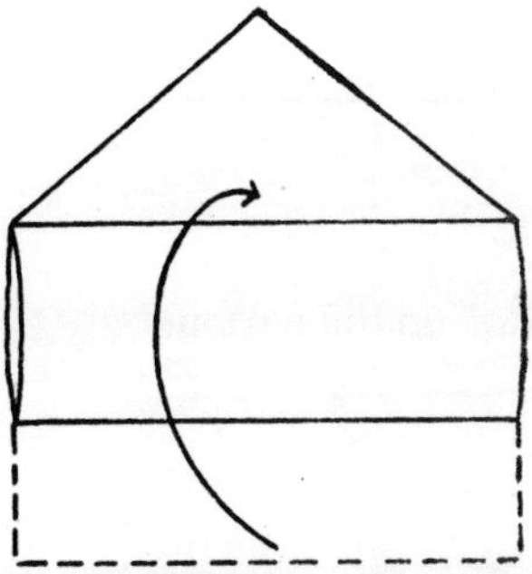

Keeping the filling toward the bottom, roll the wrapper up toward the tip.

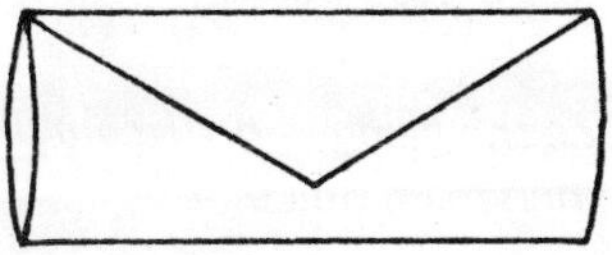

Seal the flap by wetting the tip with water and pressing closed.

METHOD TWO

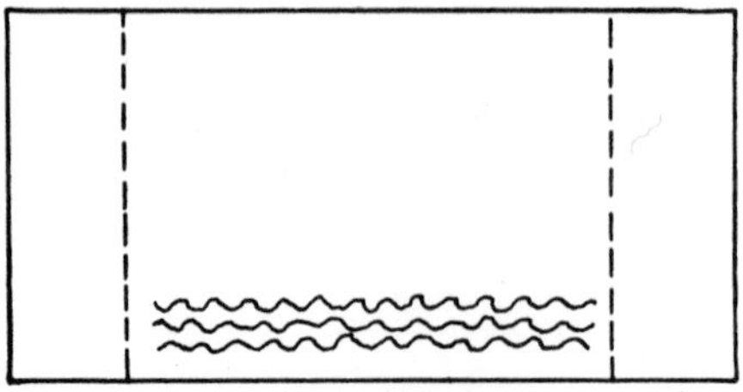

Place the filling along the bottom of the wrapper, leaving room to fold in the sides.

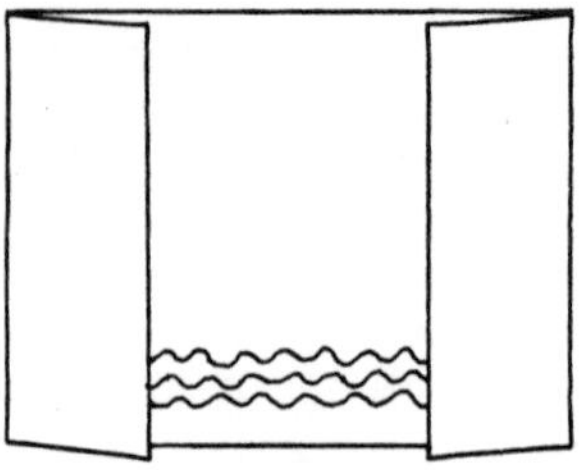

Fold in the sides to cover part of the filling.

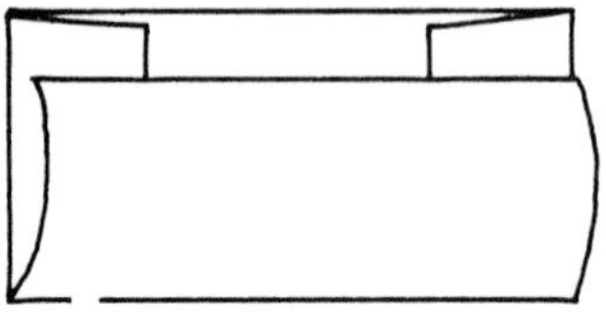

Roll up, pushing the filling in as you roll.

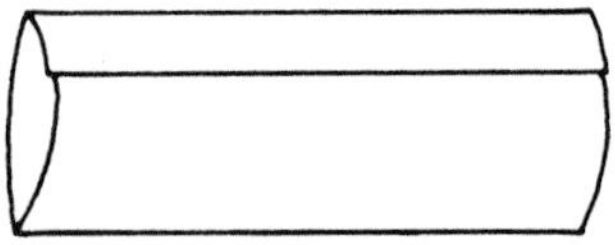

Seal the edge with water.

METHOD THREE

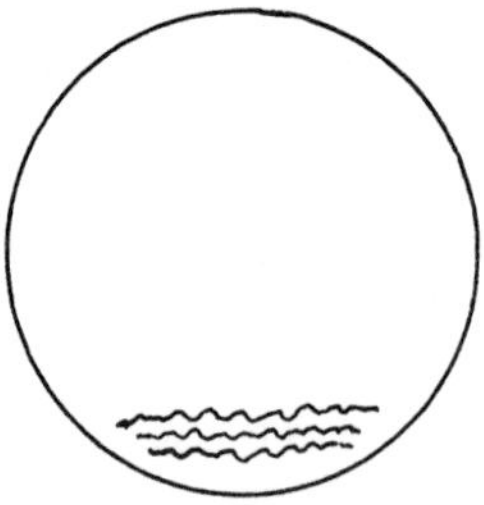

Place the filling in a straight line an inch from an edge.

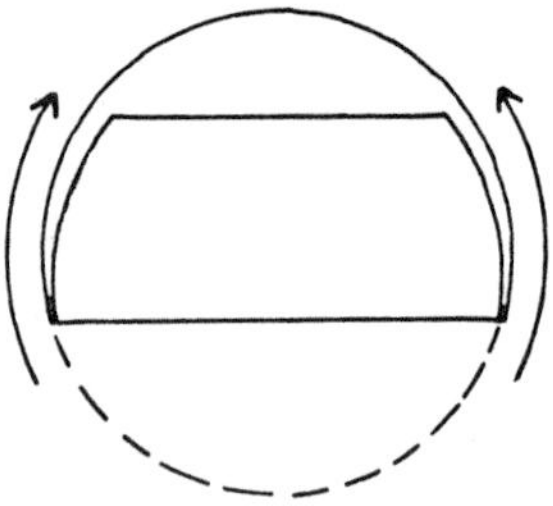

Roll up the wrapper.

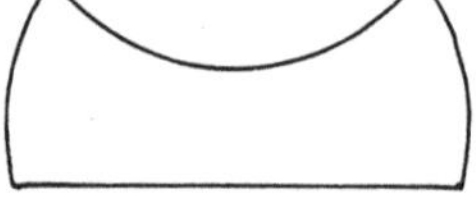

Secure the flap with toothpicks if necessary.

Once the egg rolls have been filled, they should be fried within 2 hours or the wrappers may become wet and soggy. Filled cocktail-size egg rolls can be tray-frozen before frying.

To fry the egg rolls, use a wok, electric skillet, deep fryer, or a pot with sides at least three inches high. Heat an inch or more of oil to 375 to 400 degrees F. A drop of water sprinkled (carefully) onto the oil will spatter instantly. Place the egg rolls into the oil flap side down. Do not crowd the pan or the temperature of the oil will be reduced and the egg roll wrappers will not brown properly. Fry the rolls until golden brown all over, turning once or as necessary. Drain very well on paper towels and serve immediately, with duck sauce and Chinese mustard as condiments. If preparing frozen cocktail-size egg rolls, do not defrost before frying.

Vegetarian Egg Rolls

炸素春捲

Zha Su Chun Juan

Southern and eastern China,
Chinese-American

Makes 24 egg rolls, 48 cocktail size

This recipe is prepared in two stages so that the stir-fried vegetables do not become overcooked when the eggs are added. The fresh, crisp taste is very important to the success of the filling.

The *tofu* is included mainly for protein, although if the *hoisin* sauce is used, the *tofu* will pick up that flavor and carry it through.

Vegetarians who do not eat eggs can prepare the filling without the eggs, and they can use the Uncooked Egg Roll Wrappers (page 62) as the skins. It would then be fitting to change the name of the recipe to Eggless Egg Rolls.

Mixture I:

2 tablespoons peanut, corn, or other oil
¼ cup chopped onion
¼ cup chopped scallions (white and crisp green parts)
1 cup thinly sliced celery, cut into matchsticks about ½ inch long
2 cups sliced celery cabbage or any Chinese cabbage, cut as above
1 cup sliced fresh mushrooms

→

2 cups fresh bean sprouts
½ teaspoon salt

Heat the 2 tablespoons of oil in a 10-inch skillet or a wok. Stir-fry the onion and scallions to coat them with the oil. Add the celery and stir constantly for about 45 seconds, then add the celery cabbage and continue to cook for another 30 seconds, stirring all the while. Now add the mushrooms and stir-fry for an additional half a minute, then mix in the bean sprouts and the salt. The vegetables should be only partially cooked. Remove the mixture from the pan and refrigerate until cold.

Mixture II:

2 tablespoons peanut, corn, or other oil
¼ cup chopped onion
¼ cup chopped scallions (white and crisp green parts)
½ pound firm tofu, cut into ¼-inch cubes
1 tablespoon soy sauce
1 tablespoon hoisin sauce (optional)
2 eggs (graded large), beaten

Heat the oil in an 8-inch skillet or a wok. Stir-fry the onion and scallions in the hot oil for one minute. Add the *tofu,* and stir gently to coat the *tofu* with oil and to mix it with the chopped vegetables. Mix in the soy sauce and, if desired, the *hoisin* sauce. Add the beaten eggs, scrambling them until set. Immediately remove the mixture from the pan and refrigerate it until cold.

When both mixtures are cold, combine them and drain off any liquid. The filling can be refrigerated overnight, but it should not be frozen. This recipe is enough to fill 1 pound of commercial egg roll wrappers or either recipe for homemade egg roll wrappers. Fill and fry the egg rolls according to the directions in the recipe for Egg Rolls on page 66. Cocktail-size egg rolls can be tray-frozen before they are fried, but they should not be defrosted before frying or they may lose their crunchy texture. Serve Vegetarian Egg Rolls with duck sauce, Chinese mustard, *hoisin* sauce, and sesame oil as condiments.

Spring Roll Wrappers

春捲皮

Chun Juan Pi

Shanghai

Makes twenty-four 5-inch squares

These can, of course, be used for any recipe calling for spring roll wrappers, or they may be used as egg roll wrappers (Method Two, page 68). The simple flour-and-water dough yields wrappers that are remarkably like the purchased Shanghai spring roll sheets. They fry beautifully, producing very crispy wrappings for the filling of your choice.

2 cups unsifted all-purpose flour
1½ cups cold water

In a small mixing bowl, mix together the flour and water. With a spoon, beat the mixture until completely smooth.

Heat a 5- to 7-inch cast-iron skillet or any size nonstick griddle over medium heat. Using a paper towel oiled with peanut or corn oil, coat lightly with oil. (It is not necessary to oil a nonstick griddle.) With a pastry brush, quickly paint a very thin layer of batter, 5 inches square, on the hot pan or griddle. When the dough begins to harden and the edges curl slightly, use a spatula or your fingers to turn the square over. Cook just until the wrapper dries out, only a few seconds longer. Do not brown the wrappers.

Stack the wrappers as soon as they are no longer hot—do not let them dry out. If the cooled wrappers are not to be used immediately, you may wrap them in foil for use within several hours, or freeze them for future use. Be sure to defrost the wrappers thoroughly before using. Peel them gently, one at a time, so they do not tear.

Use these wrappers as you would the purchased ones. However, because they are already small, they will not have to be cut for recipes such as Spring Chicken Packages or Hot Beef Packages. If the packages open up during frying, as sometimes happens, leave the toothpicks in until the wrappers set.

Spring Chicken Packages

春捲鷄

Chun Juan Ji

Canton and Shanghai influence

Makes 20 to 24 packages

The "spring" in the title refers to the fact that the chicken is wrapped in spring roll sheets or shells, which are sometimes sold as thin or very thin egg roll wrappers but actually resemble parchment more than egg roll skins. In experimenting with various wrappings for the marinated chicken, I discovered that the spring roll wrappers make an extraordinarily crisp enclosure for the succulent chicken.

The chicken is flavored by a soy sauce marinade, giving this tidbit an interesting taste as well as a unique texture. It can be served as an appetizer, American style, or as a *dim sum* in a Chinese meal. If served as the latter, it will appear as one of many morsels during a teahouse luncheon or between heavier courses at a banquet.

1 large whole chicken breast (1 pound), skinned and boned
3 scallions (white part only), cut into ¼-inch rounds (20 to 24 slices in all)
2 slices (⅛ inch thick) ginger root
1 tablespoon dry sherry
1 tablespoon soy sauce
½ teaspoon sugar
5 or 6 spring roll sheets (8½ inch square), each cut into 4 squares, or 1 recipe homemade Spring Roll Wrappers (page 70)
Toothpicks for wrapping
Oil for frying

Cut each half of the boned chicken breast into 10 or 12 chunks, each about 1 inch square. In a small mixing bowl combine the scallions, ginger root, sherry, soy sauce, and the sugar. Marinate the chicken in this mixture for 20 to 30 minutes. Stir the chicken occasionally to make sure all the pieces are bathed in the marinade.

To wrap the chicken, place a piece of chicken and a scallion slice on the center of each small square wrapper. Fold all 4 corners of the wrapper over the chicken, overlapping the corners to completely encase the chicken. Secure with a toothpick, which should go through all four corners, the chicken, and the other side of the wrapper. The chicken can be wrapped and refrigerated several hours before it is cooked.

To tray-freeze the chicken, do not secure the packages with toothpicks. Instead, place the chicken packets flap side down on the greased tray. Fry them while frozen, or allow them to thaw, flap side down, without touching each other.

To cook, heat at least ½ inch of oil in a wok, deep fryer, or a 10-inch skillet until the oil is hot but not yet smoking, 375 degrees F. Push the chicken packets off the toothpicks into the hot oil, making sure the folded side goes into the oil first. The hot oil will set the wrapper and keep the chicken enclosed. Fry each package until the wrapper is golden on one side, then turn and fry the other side until it is golden brown also. The cooking time is only a few minutes, so keep a careful watch. Using tongs or chopsticks, remove the chicken packages from the oil. As you lift out each package, shake it over the oil to get rid of any excess oil that may be trapped inside the wrapper. Drain the chicken packages well on paper towels. Serve hot with duck sauce and Chinese mustard.

Mock Spring Chicken Packages

紙包雞

Zhi Bao Ji

Canton

Makes 20 to 24 packages

In this recipe, the marinated chicken of the previous recipe is housed in wax paper instead of spring roll sheets. In China, rice paper would be used. The chicken is cooked and served in the paper, but the paper is of course discarded before the chicken is eaten. Actually, the taste of the chicken itself comes through better when it is cooked this way, but the delicious crunch of the wrapper is missing. Each diner is expected to open the chicken package to get to the goody inside, so plan on supplying plenty of paper napkins. There should also be receptacles available for discarding the wax paper.

Marinated chicken from Spring Chicken Packages (page 71)
20 to 24 squares (6 inches) of wax paper
A small amount of peanut, corn, or other oil
Oil for frying

Place a drop or two of oil just off center on each piece of wax paper. Put a piece of chicken and a piece of scallion on the oil. Make an envelope as pictured on page 74. The chicken packages can be made a day ahead and refrigerated, but they must be served immediately once cooked.

To cook, heat at least ½ inch of oil in a wok, deep fryer, or a 10-inch skillet until the oil is hot but not yet smoking, 375 degrees F. Carefully drop in the packages, flap side down, and fry for 1 minute on each side. The chicken will begin to brown inside the wax paper, but it must not be allowed to burn. Using tongs or chopsticks, remove the chicken packages from the oil. As you lift out each package, hold it with the flap side toward the oil, and shake the package to get rid of any excess oil that may be trapped inside the wax paper. Drain the chicken packages on paper towels. Serve immediately. The guests do the unwrapping with their fingers. The unwrapped chicken is picked up with chopsticks and dipped into duck sauce and Chinese mustard.

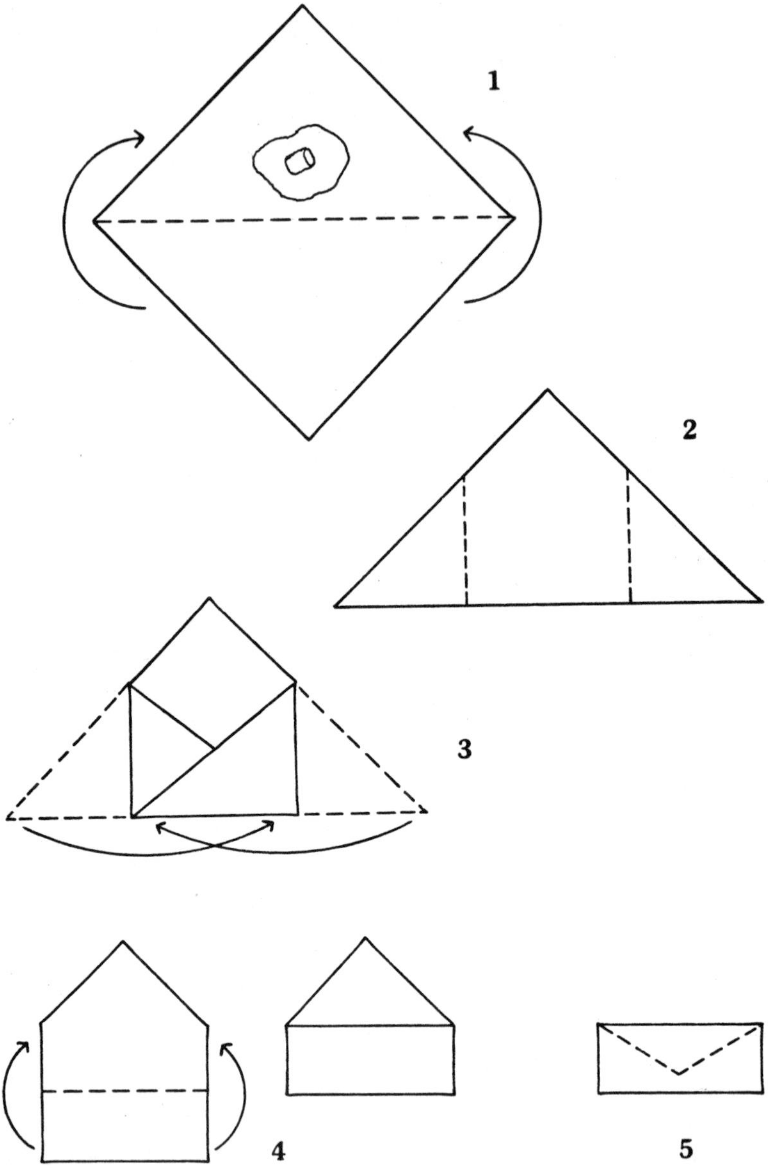

1.*Place the chicken and scallion on a square of wax paper; crease well at the fold line.* **2** *Fold the wax paper up over the chicken to make a triangle; crease the sides.* **3.** *Fold the sides toward the center so the tips go to the opposite edge.* **4.** *Push the chicken toward the bottom of the packet; crease and fold the envelope as pictured.* **5.** *Tuck the flap into the pocket.*

Hot Beef Packages
春捲牛肉
Chun Juan Niu Rou

Canton and Shanghai influence

Makes 24 packages

London broil marinates in a spicy soy sauce mixture before it is wrapped in spring roll sheets. The result is a crunchy delicacy with a bite supplied by five-spice powder and crushed red pepper.

This recipe is a variation on Spring Chicken Packages. The texture is different: the beef needs more chewing than the chicken. But the wonderful crunch of the wrapper remains a feature.

2 tablespoons dry sherry
2 tablespoons soy sauce
½ teaspoon five-spice powder
1 teaspoon crushed dried red pepper
48 very thin slices London broil, 1 inch square
6 spring roll sheets (8½ inch square), each cut into 4 squares, or 1 recipe homemade Spring Roll Wrappers (page 70)
Toothpicks for wrapping
Oil for frying

In a small mixing bowl, stir together the sherry, soy sauce, five-spice powder, and crushed red pepper. Add the beef and mix well to coat all the pieces with the marinade. Marinate the beef for an hour, stirring occasionally. To wrap and cook the beef packages, using 2 pieces of beef per package, follow the directions for Spring Chicken Packages, page 72.

Fried Wontons
炸餛飩
Zha Hun Tun

Canton

Makes about 32 wontons

When I cook fried *wontons* at informal Bar Mitzvah receptions for friends, I always have a hard time convincing some of the older guests that these are not fried *kreplach*. Of course they are very close to fried *kreplach*, but the scallions, water chestnuts, *hoisin* sauce, soy sauce, and sesame oil give them a distinct Chinese flavor—and they are folded differently from *kreplach*. If *hoisin* sauce and sesame oil are not available to you, try adding chopped bamboo shoots or a little minced ginger root to the ground beef mixture. Any cooked, cool filling can be used in fried *wontons*, but to keep the Chinese essence, you will want to add some ingredients associated with Chinese cooking.

In China, fried *wontons* would be considered one of many *dim sum*, and as such they are served in teahouses. As part of a dinner, fried *wontons* would appear between heavier courses as a light refreshment, but they would not be served as an *hors d'oeuvre*, the way they are likely to be served here.

Fried *wontons* freeze well after having been lightly fried, and they retain their crispness when refried. An outstanding item for a food festival or large party.

1 tablespoon peanut, corn or other oil
½ pound lean ground beef
1 to 2 tablespoons chopped scallions (white and crisp green parts)
2 or 3 diced water chestnuts
1 clove garlic, minced
1 teaspoon sugar
1 tablespoon soy sauce
1 tablespoon hoisin sauce
1 teaspoon cornstarch dissolved in 2 tablespoons cold water
½ teaspoon sesame oil
8 egg roll wrappers or 32 wonton wrappers
Oil for frying

In an 8-inch skillet, heat the 1 tablespoon of oil until moderately hot. (You will not need the oil if your pan has a nonstick surface.) Cook the ground beef in the hot oil, stirring constantly to keep the pieces broken up. Drain off all of the accumulated fat. Add the scallions, water chestnuts, garlic, sugar, soy sauce, and *hoisin* sauce, mixing well. Blend the cornstarch and water together to recombine them, then add this to the meat mixture, stirring constantly just until the cornstarch is blended in and the meat mixture is thickened and glazed. Stir in the sesame oil. Remove the filling to a bowl or container, and refrigerate until thoroughly cooled. The filling can be refrigerated overnight or frozen at this point, but defrost it completely before using.

Filling and Shaping the Wontons:

To make the *wontons,* cut square egg roll skins into quarters (4 squares each). *Wonton* wrappers are already the right size. Place about 1 teaspoonful of filling just off-center on each square, and moisten the edges of the square with a little water. Bring one corner of the wrapper over the filling to the opposite corner to make a triangle. Press the edges together firmly. Pull the two bottom corners around to meet behind the folded edge. Moisten your fingers and pinch the bottom of one point to the top of the other to seal the *wonton.* Until you can work quickly, work with only a few *wontons* at a time, keeping the remainder of the wrappers covered to prevent drying out. The uncooked *wontons* can be refrigerated overnight on a greased sheet of wax paper.

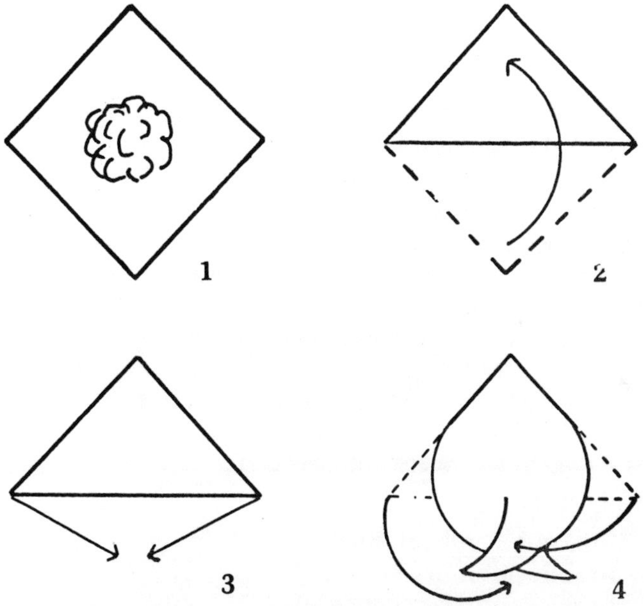

A 12-inch electric skillet is ideal for frying *wontons* because as many as 20 can be fried at once, but any deep fryer, wok, or pot with sides at least 3 inches high can be used. The *wontons* will cook well in as little as ½ inch of oil, or you may use more. Heat the oil to 375 to 400 degrees F. Carefully add the *wontons* one at a time so that they do not touch each other. Fry them until golden all over, turning as necessary. Drain well on paper towels. Serve the fried *wontons* with duck sauce, Chinese mustard, or any condiment of your choice.

Fried *wontons* freeze very well when partially cooked. Fry them lightly until they are set but still a pale color. Drain very well, cool completely, then freeze in freezer containers or bags. They do not first need to be tray-frozen. When ready to serve, defrost the *wontons* partially or fully, then refry them in hot oil until golden. If you prefer, heat the partially fried *wontons* in a 400-degree F. oven until they are golden and sizzling, which will take 10 to 15 minutes.

Steamed Cantonese Dumplings

燒賣

Shao Mai

Canton

Makes about 36 small dumplings

These open-faced steamed dumplings are made with ground pork in China, but the beef-and-vegetable filling used here works very well. Included in the list of ingredients below are a number of optional vegetables—any, all, or none of which may be added to the beef mixture. Bear in mind that the basic dumpling is smooth-textured and bland-tasting. Water chestnuts and celery cabbage do add textural contrast, but chopped onions and bamboo shoots would add a little more to bite into, the ginger root and garlic would add flavoring, and the spinach would add color as well as its own taste. The dumplings without any of the optional ingredients are very good, and any of the condiments in Chapter Two will complement these *dim sum*. Like other *dim sum*, in China these dumplings are served in teahouses and between courses at restaurant meals and banquets.

¾ pound lean beef, minced
1 tablespoon dry sherry
1 tablespoon soy sauce
2 or 3 scallions (white and crisp green parts), chopped
1 or 2 stalks celery cabbage or other Chinese cabbage, coarsely chopped then squeezed dry in paper towels
2 water chestnuts, finely chopped
Optional: ¼ cup chopped onion; ¼ cup chopped bamboo shoots; 1 teaspoon minced ginger root; 1 large clove garlic, minced; ¼ cup chopped spinach, squeezed dry in paper towels

1 teaspoon sugar
½ teaspoon salt
1 tablespoon cornstarch
7 to 9 egg roll wrappers or 36 wonton wrappers, cut into 2½- to 3-inch rounds with a cookie cutter or scissors

Mix together all of the ingredients for the filling. Hold a wrapper in the palm of your hand, and place about a tablespoon of filling in the middle of the wrapper. (Keep unused wrappers under a clean, dry kitchen towel so they don't dry out.) Make a pleated cup, pushing down the filling with one hand while pressing the wrapper securely around the filling with the other hand. Do not enclose the filling completely—it should be visible on top. Pinch or crimp the dough in small folds in four or five places. The filled uncooked dumplings can be covered and refrigerated overnight on a greased plate, or they can be tray-frozen. Do not defrost them before steaming or the wrappers might become wet.

Place the filled dumplings on a greased steamer tray, making sure that they do not touch each other. Steam the dumplings for 10 to 15 minutes, allowing a few minutes extra for frozen dumplings. Serve hot with a variety of condiments for dipping.

Northern Dumplings

水餃 餃子

Shui Jiao Jiaozi

Peking

Makes about 48 dumplings

The flour-and-water dough with which they are made and the soy sauce-and-vinegar dip with which they are served are distinguishing features of these crescent-shaped dumplings. Light to eat and mildly flavored, they are an excellent vehicle for many of the condiments that appear in Chapter Two.

It is very typically Chinese to contrast a mellow taste with a salty, hot and spicy, or piquant taste. Therefore it is appropriate to serve Northern Dumplings with either plain soy sauce and vinegar (with or without a little minced ginger root and/or garlic), the wonderfully flavorful Szechwan Sauce (page 130), a simple Hot Sesame-Soy Dip (page 127), or Fresh Ginger Sauce (page 132).

The simple wheat flour dough comes from northern China, where wheat is the predominant grain. The dough, which is easy to handle, is rolled thinly to provide a wrapping for the savory filling. The filled dumplings hold together nicely. Purchased egg roll or *wonton* wrappers can be substituted for the homemade dough for convenience. They will be thicker and have a little more taste than the more authentic flour-and-water dough.

Serve these dumplings boiled or fried as an appetizer, part of a luncheon, or as a light treat between heavy courses at a Chinese banquet.

The Filling:

⅓ pound fresh spinach or half a 10-ounce box of frozen chopped spinach, thawed
½ pound lean beef, minced
4 water chestnuts, chopped
2 tablespoons finely chopped bamboo shoots
1 small onion, minced, or ¼ cup chopped scallions (white and crisp green parts)
1 clove garlic, minced
½ teaspooon minced ginger root
2 tablespoons soy sauce
1 teaspoon sesame oil
1 teaspoon sugar

Swish the fresh spinach in cold water to remove all sand and dirt, changing the water until it remains clear. Chop the spinach finely. In paper towels, squeeze dry the fresh or thawed spinach. Combine the spinach and the minced beef with the remaining ingredients, mixing well to distribute everything evenly. Refrigerate the filling while preparing the dough, or freeze the filling for later use.

The Dough:

2 cups unsifted all-purpose flour
½ to ¾ cup cold water

Place the flour in a medium-size mixing bowl. Gradually add ½ cup of the water, working it in well with your fingers. Add a little more water, until the dough holds together. Knead for 3 to 5 minutes, sprinkling on a little flour if the dough begins to stick to the work surface or to your fingers. Knead until the dough is smooth, easy to handle, and not at all sticky.

If the dough is not to be used immediately, place it in a greased bowl and cover the bowl with plastic wrap. Plan to use the dough within a few hours. It is best to prepare the filling first and have it ready for the dough.

Divide the homemade dough into quarters, and work with one part at a time. Divide the first quarter into 12 pieces, then use a rolling pin to roll each piece out to a 3-inch circle. If the work surface is clean and the dough is not sticky, it may not be necessary to grease or flour the work surface. If the dough sticks, lightly grease or flour the work surface. For purchased egg roll or *wonton* wrappers, use a cookie cutter or scissors to cut the wrappers into 2½- to 3-inch rounds. Use leftover bits and pieces for fried noodles. Work with no more than a dozen wrappers at a time, keeping the remaining circles of dough covered with a dish towel to prevent drying out.

To wrap the dumplings, place a heaping teaspoon of filling slightly off-center on each circle. Moisten the edges of the purchased egg roll wrappers with water. (The homemade wrappers will seal well without water.) Fold the dough in half over the filling to form a semicircle, then press the edges together to seal well. Stand the dumpling on the folded edge and press it lightly to form a flattened bottom. Now you can make fancy pleats or crimps in the top, being careful not to break the wrappers. The dumplings can be tray-frozen at this point.

To boil the dumplings, bring 6 quarts of water to the boil in an 8-quart pot. Carefully drop in as many dumplings as you can without overcrowding. Cook the dumplings for 5 minutes, then taste one to make sure the dough is cooked through. Frozen dumplings should not be defrosted, but they will require an additional 3 to 5 minutes of cooking. With a slotted spoon transfer the cooked dumplings to a serving bowl. Boil the remaining dumplings. Serve the dumplings hot, making small bowls of dipping sauce available to each diner. Or, serve with any condiment of your choice.

An alternate method of cooking these dumplings is to fry them in ½ inch of hot (375 to 400 degrees F.) oil until they are golden brown on both sides. Drain well and serve with the dipping sauce or other condiments. Frozen dumplings can be fried without thawing.

The Dipping Sauce.

½ cup soy sauce
¼ cup vinegar, preferably an Oriental rice vinegar
Optional: Dash of sesame oil, ¼ teaspoon

→

crushed dried red pepper, up to 1
tablespoon minced garlic (to taste), up to 1
tablespoon minced ginger root (to taste)

Combine the soy sauce with the vinegar. Mix in any of the optional ingredients as desired. The dipping sauce can be prepared well in advance and does not need refrigeration.

Wheat Starch Dim Sum Wrappers

水晶皮

Shui Jing Pi

Canton

Makes about 48 small wrappers

Since eye appeal is an important consideration in Chinese cooking, this classic Cantonese dough is more than just a convenient wrapper. The combination of wheat starch and tapioca starch produces a dough that becomes translucent when steamed, so that the color of the filling shows through. The texture of the steamed dough differs from other wrappers in that it has a chewy, gelatinous consistency. The taste itself is bland. When fried, the dough makes a very crisp covering, but it must be eaten immediately or it softens. This dough is most often associated with a shrimp filling *(har gau* or *ha gow),* but there are numerous kosher alternatives that take advantage of both the appearance and the texture.

1 cup wheat starch
½ cup tapioca starch
1 cup water
1 teaspoon sesame oil or salad oil

In a small bowl, mix together the wheat starch and tapioca starch. Bring the water to a rolling boil, then add it all at once to the dry ingredients, stirring with a wooden spoon or chopsticks. Sprinkle the oil over the dough and work it in evenly. As soon as the dough is cool enough to handle, use your hands to shape it into a ball, then knead it for a few minutes, until very smooth.

If the dough is not to be used immediately, cover it with plastic wrap. Plan to use the dough within a few hours.

Divide the dough in half and roll each half into a 12-inch-long piece. Working with one 12-inch piece at a time, cut the piece into twenty-four ½-

inch slices. (I usually cut each 12-inch piece of dough in half, then cut each piece in half again, and once more in half. There are now 8 small pieces, each of which gets sliced into thirds.) Repeat with the other 12-inch piece of dough.

To Fill, Shape, and Cook:

Working on a clean, smooth surface, flatten each piece of dough with the palm of your hand to make a circle. With a rolling pin, roll out the dough to a thin circle of 2½ to 3 inches. If the dough sticks, rub a little oil into the work surface, but do not add flour of any kind to the dough. An alternative method of flattening the dough is to press each ball into a circle with the side of a lightly oiled Chinese cleaver.

Put a teaspoon of filling in the center of each wrapper, then fold the wrapper over the filling to form a half-moon. Press the edges together to seal, then use your fingers to make small pleats along the sealed edge.

Place the filled dumplings on a greased steamer tray. Steam the dumplings for 5 to 7 minutes, until translucent. Serve immediately, or cool thoroughly and tray-freeze. Resteam frozen dumplings without first defrosting for about 5 minutes, until the filling is hot.

Variation:

Fry the dumplings in a minimum of ½ inch of oil, turning once, until golden and crisp. Drain well on paper towels and serve immediately

Sub Gum Wheat Starch Dim Sum

四色餃

Si Se Jiao

Canton influence

Makes 48 dumplings

The first time I came home from the Chinese grocery with wheat starch and tapioca starch, I was eager to immediately try them for a *dim sum* dough. Because I hadn't planned a special filling, I literally threw together ingredients which happened to be in my refrigerator, explaining to my family that we were testing a new dough, and I didn't want any unpleasant comments about the filling. This prompted my fifteen-year-old to say that it was the first filling he ever really liked. I'm not sure if that was a compliment, but a spontaneously put-together filling can be as good as a very well-planned one.

The term *sub gum* is used for mixtures of vegetables and sometimes meat which are usually diced or cut small. Each little pocket of dough is a blend of textures and tastes. The dough itself is chewy, the celery undercooked and very crunchy, the mushrooms soft, the beef a little chewy but also tasty, and the scallions give the dumpling just the right amount of bite. Because of the contrasting tastes and textures these *dim sum* can be eaten plain, but they are even more appealing when first dipped in various condiments, including Chinese mustard, duck sauce, and any of the soy-sauce-based dips.

1 tablespoon peanut, corn, or other oil
½ cup diced celery (⅜-inch cubes)
½ cup chopped scallions (white and crisp green parts)
½ cup coarsely chopped fresh mushrooms
2 water chestnuts, chopped
½ cup diced beef (⅜-inch cubes)
A few drops of sesame oil
1 recipe Wheat Starch Dim Sum Wrappers (page 82)

In an 8-inch skillet or a wok, heat the tablespoon of oil until it is hot but not yet smoking. Stir-fry the celery for 15 seconds, then add the scallions and stir just to mix. Add the mushrooms, stirring constantly for another 15 seconds, then mix in the water chestnuts. Remove the vegetables from the skillet or wok to a medium-size mixing bowl.

Coat the same skillet or wok with a little more oil if necessary, then add the beef to the hot pan. Stir-fry the meat just until it is cooked. Mix the beef with the vegetables, then sprinkle with a few drops of sesame oil and combine everything well. Allow the beef and vegetables to cool while you prepare the dough. Follow the directions in the Wheat Starch Dim Sum Wrappers recipe for filling and cooking the *dim sum*. Serve the cooked *dim sum* immediately with a selection of condiments of your choice, such as Chinese mustard, sesame oil, duck sauce, soy sauce, or a soy sauce dip.

Steamed or Baked Buns

包子

Baozi

Peking

Makes 24 buns

These versatile filled buns are a teahouse attraction in China and the

United States. The steamed version produces a slightly sweet, very puffy white roll that surrounds a savory filling. The proportion of dough to filling is high, so it is nice to serve the steamed buns with a sauce—the Szechwan Sauce, for example—that will add interest to the dough.

In China the steamed buns would be served as any *dim sum*, either at teahouses or between courses at large meals. Although in the United States we would probably serve meat-filled buns as appetizers and those filled with a fruit and red-bean-paste filling as dessert, the Chinese would be unlikely to distinguish between the two. They would serve the Date and Red-Bean-Paste Buns (which appear in the dessert chapter of this book) at any point during a meal.

The baked version of the buns is an adaptation we in America can use because of the availability of ovens here. Baked buns come out very much like small, golden brown dinner rolls with a surprise filling inside. They can be served as an appetizer, soup accompaniment, or also as one of many *dim sum* at a luncheon or dinner. Once when I was working in a particularly warm kitchen, I let a very large tray of baked buns rise so much that they all merged together. Everyone thought I had created a new kind of *kugel* and dished out portions, which they loved. So if you want to make a Chinese *kugel*, let the filled dough rise until you can't distinguish one roll from another, then bake it until the crust is brown.

If you are used to proofing yeast for *challah*, you will be familiar with the method used for making the dough in this recipe.

1 teaspoon active dry yeast
2 tablespoons sugar
½ cup unsifted all-purpose flour
¼ cup warm water (110 to 115 degrees F.)
3 cups unsifted all-purpose flour
2 tablespoons sugar
¾ cup warm water
1 tablespoon peanut, corn, or other oil
1 recipe filling, chilled (see recipes below)

In a small bowl combine the yeast with the 2 tablespooons of sugar and ½ cup of flour. Stir with a fork to combine the dry ingredients, then stir in the ¼ cup warm water, mixing well. Let this mixture sit for about 5 minutes, until you see some activity—some bubbling, a little foaming. If nothing happens, there are three possibilities: the yeast was killed by water that was too hot; the water was so cool that the yeast isn't yet activated (place the bowl with the yeast mixture into a pan of warm water, which should start things going); or the yeast is outdated (check the expiration date on the package). If you think you started with water that was too hot or if the yeast is outdated, start over.

Now mix the 3 cups of flour and 2 tablespoons of sugar in a large mixing bowl. Stir in the ¾ cup warm water and the tablespoon of oil, then add the yeast mixture. Work the dough first with a spoon and then with your fingers until it holds together enough to handle. Knead the dough on a clean work surface until smooth, about 5 minutes. (To knead the dough, flatten the ball with the palm of your hand, fold the dough in half, press down to flatten it again, turn the dough 90 degrees and continue folding, pushing, and turning.) Continue kneading until the dough is ready. Poke your fingers into the dough—the indentation should not remain. If the dough is sticky, sprinkle a little flour on the work surface as necessary.

Place the kneaded dough in a large clean bowl. Cover the bowl tightly with plastic wrap, but first grease the underside of the plastic wrap in case the rising dough reaches the top and touches it. Let the dough rise until doubled in size. The time it will take the dough to rise depends partly on the temperature of the room. If it is a hot day and the temperature of the kitchen is about 85 degrees F., the dough should rise in 1½ to 2 hours if just left in the bowl on a kitchen counter. Keep it out of direct sunlight and away from drafts. If the kitchen temperature is about 72 degrees F., you can start the dough early and let it rise at room temperature for 3 to 4 hours. If the dough does not begin to rise after 2 hours, set the bowl over a pot or bowl of warm water to hasten the rising. The bottom of the bowl of dough should not touch the water. Or, set a pan of hot water on the bottom shelf of your oven, and place the bowl with the dough on a shelf above the water. If the dough has doubled before you are ready to use it, punch it down, re-cover the bowl, and let it rise again until it is time to fill the buns.

When the dough has risen sufficiently, it is ready to be filled. Punch down the dough and transfer it to a lightly floured work surface. Knead the dough for 30 seconds to work out any bubbles, then shape the dough with your hands into a long, thin roll. Using a sharp knife, divide the dough into 24 pieces. On a lightly floured surface, use a rolling pin to roll out each piece into a 3½-inch circle. There should be no thin spots in the circles.

Divide the chilled filling among the circles, using about a tablespoon per circle. Place the filling in the center, not too far out toward the edges or

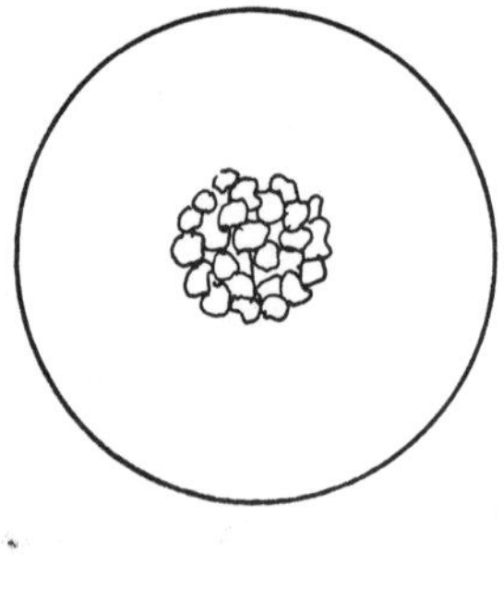

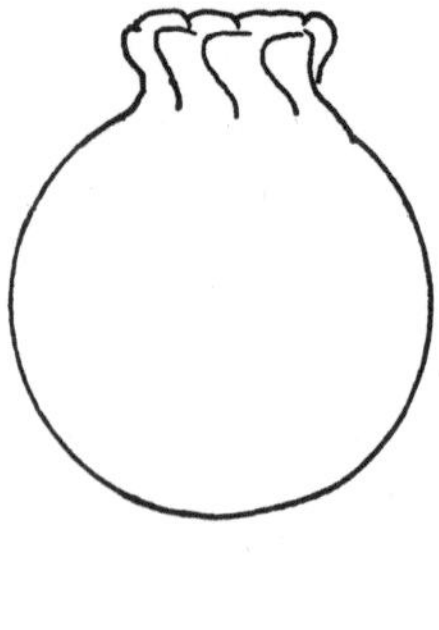

you may have difficulty sealing the buns. Now gather up the edges of the dough, pulling them together around the filling and twisting to seal the top. The top of the dough will have a puckered look.

To steam the buns, place the filled buns on a greased heatproof plate or greased steamer tray. Place them about an inch apart from each other as they expand considerably when steamed. You will probably need at least two 10-inch plates or trays to accommodate the 24 buns. Let the buns rise at room temperature for at least 20 minutes. For the puffiest of steamed buns, set the plates or trays in a steamer that has warm to hot water on the bottom, cover the steamer with a lid, and let the buns rise there. Steam the buns in a covered pot for 15 to 20 minutes or until puffy and cooked through. Serve them immediately, while still hot. The buns can be refrigerated and resteamed, and the cooked buns freeze well. They can be resteamed while still frozen, but will take less time if they are defrosted. Steam frozen buns just until they are heated through.

To bake the buns, arrange the filled buns in a greased baking dish. The buns should not touch each other. Let them rise at room temperature for 45 minutes to 1 hour. Brush the tops with beaten whole egg or egg yolk beaten with a little water. Approximately 15 minutes before the rising is complete, preheat the oven to 400 degrees F. Bake the rolls for 15 to 20 minutes, until golden brown. If you plan to freeze the buns, bake for 10 minutes only. Cool the partially baked rolls, then tray-freeze them. Bake thoroughly defrosted rolls in a 375 degree F. oven until they are heated through, which will take 10 to 15 minutes if you allow them first to come to room temperature. Frozen buns will take longer for the filling to heat through. If necessary, cover the tops with foil so they do not burn.

Heavenly Beef Filling
(for Steamed or Baked Buns)

肉餡兒包

Rou Xiar Bao

Peking

Makes enough filling for 24 buns

This is the best filling I know for steamed or baked buns, and the one that is most often requested. Since beef is uncommon in China, a pork filling is normally used for the buns, but this recipe uses steak which is marinated, broiled, then diced for use in a a rich delicious filling.

Heavenly Beef Filling has everything—the pieces of beef are small and tender and highly flavored with garlic and scallion, and the soy sauce mixture is sweetened with sugar, flavored with red bean paste and the smoky sesame oil, and then thickened. The beef starts out with an advantage because the marinade itself is exotic and tasty. As you will see, the strong and exotic flavors of the filling provide a wonderful contrast to the light, bland buns.

Step One:

½ to ¾ pound steak for broiling, ½ inch thick
2 slices (⅛ inch thick) ginger root
1 scallion (white and crisp green parts), sliced
1 clove garlic, coarsely chopped
2 teaspoons chili sauce (any store brand or name brand, not an Oriental chili sauce)
2 teaspoons hoisin sauce
1 tablespoon dry sherry
1 tablespoon soy sauce
1 tablespoon honey

In a bowl large enough to accommodate the beef, mix together all ingredients *except* the beef. Add the meat and marinate it in this mixture for 2 hours, turning once after an hour. Remove the steak from the marinade, then broil it on both sides until medium-rare. Now the steak is ready to use as the first ingredient in the filling below.

Step Two:

Broiled beef from above
2 tablespoons chopped scallions (white and crisp green parts)
2 large cloves garlic, finely chopped
3 tablespoons sugar
2 tablespoons soy sauce
1 tablespoon red bean paste
1 teaspoon sesame oil
3 teaspoons cornstarch
⅓ cup cold water
1 tablespoon peanut, corn, or other oil

Cut the steak into small cubes, less than ¼ inch. Combine the chopped scallions and garlic. Mix together the sugar, soy sauce, red bean paste, and sesame oil. In a small cup or bowl, blend the cornstarch and water. The cooking takes only a few minutes, so all the ingredients must be ready and at hand.

In an 8-inch skillet or a wok, heat the 1 tablespoon of oil. Add the beef and stir-fry briefly to heat the meat, then add the scallion-garlic mixture and stir continuously for 30 seconds. Add the soy sauce mixture, stirring rapidly. Stir the cornstarch and water together again until you have a smooth white liquid, then add the cornstarch to the beef mixture, stirring constantly. Cook until the cornstarch is blended and the sauce is thickened. Remove the beef from the heat, and transfer the mixture to a bowl or container. Refrigerate the filling until it is completely chilled. This filling can be frozen, but it must be thoroughly defrosted before it is used. The consistency of the sauce may change slightly, but this will not greatly affect the filled buns.

Prepare the dough as instructed in the preceding recipe, Steamed or Baked Buns. Fill and cook the buns as directed there. Serve the cooked buns with Szechwan Sauce (page 130), which has scallions, garlic, sugar, and soy sauce in common with this recipe but which contains other ingredients that make it hot and spicy. The fact that it repeats some of the taste of this filling but has intriguing differences adds double interest to the buns.

Very Flavorful Ground Beef Filling
(for Steamed or Baked Buns)

牛肉餡

Niu Rou Xian

Peking

Makes enough filling for 24 buns

This filling is easier and less expensive to prepare than the preceding Heavenly Beef Filling, but it is still well seasoned and flavorful. Biting into a bun filled with this ground beef mixture is akin to eating a hamburger on a roll—but this is a very, very special hamburger inside a most unusual roll. If you close your eyes and try to identify the ingredients you will probably come up with the garlic, fresh ginger root, the soy sauce, and the scallions; and if you are very familiar with Chinese food, you may even detect the *hoisin* sauce and the sesame oil. However, if like most people you prefer to just enjoy your food and not dissect it, you will find this a savory blend in which no one ingredient dominates.

1 tablespoon peanut, corn, or other oil
½ to ¾ pound very lean ground beef
3 tablespoons chopped scallions (white and crisp green parts)
3 cloves garlic, minced
½ teaspoon minced ginger root

→

1 tablespoon sugar
1 tablespoon soy sauce
1 tablespoon hoisin sauce
1 teaspoon cornstarch mixed with 1 tablespoon cold water
1 teaspoon to 1 tablespoon sesame oil

In a 7- or 8-inch skillet or a wok, heat the peanut, corn, or other oil. Add the ground beef and cook until no redness remains, stirring the beef constantly to keep the pieces broken up. Drain off all the fat that has accumulated. Add the scallions, garlic, and ginger root, and stir-fry for 1 minute to release the flavors. Stir in the sugar, soy sauce, and *hoisin* sauce. Again mix together the cornstarch and water, then add this to the meat mixture, stirring until the mixture is thickened and glazed. Turn off the heat, then add sesame oil to taste; mix in the sesame oil until it is well distributed. Refrigerate the ground beef to cool it completely before using as a filling for the buns. The mixture can be frozen, but it must be thoroughly defrosted before using.

Prepare the recipe for the dough in Steamed or Baked Buns (page 84). Fill and cook the buns as directed in that recipe. Serve with Chinese mustard, a Chinese mixed canned pickle, or any soy-sauce-based condiment.

Colorful Chicken-Vegetable Filling
(for Steamed or Baked Buns)

雞菜餡

Ji Cai Xian

Canton influence

Makes enough filling for 24 buns

Contrasting colors, textures, and flavors all contribute to the excellence of this filling. The chicken and mushrooms are soft, the red peppers are crisp and sweet, and the green peppers are crisp and slightly pungent. The soy sauce is added both for its saltiness and for its flavor. The baked buns are especially nice to serve with a clear chicken broth, and the steamed version is enhanced when duck sauce is used as a condiment.

1 tablespoon peanut, corn, or other oil
½ pound chicken meat, cut into ¼-inch cubes
1 small sweet red pepper, sliced into thin strips ½ inch long

1 small green pepper, sliced into strips ½ inch long
1 cup coarsely chopped fresh mushrooms
2 teaspoons soy sauce
½ teaspoon sugar (optional)

In an 8-inch skillet or a wok, heat the oil until it is hot but not yet smoking. Add the chicken pieces and stir-fry until they are cooked, which will take about 2 minutes. Add the red and green peppers and stir-fry for an additional 30 seconds, then add the mushrooms and stir-fry for 15 seconds longer. The vegetables will barely be cooked, but they will continue to cook as they cool. Mix in the soy sauce and sugar, then transfer the filling to a bowl or container. Refrigerate the mixture until it is cold. The filling can be refrigerated overnight in a covered container, but it should not be frozen.

Prepare the dough for Steamed or Baked Buns (page 84), and fill and cook the buns as directed in that recipe. Serve with duck sauce.

Note: The egg roll fillings that appear earlier in this chapter are not recommended for Steamed or Baked Buns, which rely on more heightened flavors and seasonings. In addition to the consideration of taste, although egg roll fillings stay crisp when egg rolls are fried, the fillings might soften inside buns that are steamed or baked.

"Shrimp" Toast

魚茸麵包

Yu Rong Mian Bao

Canton

Makes 24 pieces

This is a kosher version of shrimp toast, which is featured as an appetizer on most Chinese-American menus. Here, the mildly flavored fillets of flounder or sole are used because the main interest of this crispy, crunchy tidbit is its texture, and a strong-tasting fish would detract from that. Use very fresh fish, but use stale bread. Stale bread absorbs less oil than fresh bread and will come out more crispy. Serve the toast as part of a *dim sum* luncheon or as one of the lighter courses at a banquet.

½ pound flounder or sole fillets, finely chopped
½ teaspoon salt
½ teaspoon sugar

→

1 tablespoon cornstarch
4 water chestnuts, finely chopped
2 scallions (white and crisp green parts), chopped
1 egg (graded large), beaten
6 slices stale bread
Oil for frying

Sprinkle the chopped fish with the salt, sugar, and cornstarch. Mix in the chopped water chestnuts and scallions, then the beaten egg. If the mixture seems too wet to hold together, cover it well and refrigerate it for an hour or two.

Trim the crusts off the bread. Divide the mixture into 6 equal parts, and spread the mixture on the 6 slices of trimmed bread, covering the tops completely. With a sharp knife, cut each piece of bread into 4 triangles. If the fish is very fresh, the "Shrimp" Toast may now be refrigerated overnight. To do so, arrange the triangles on a plate or two in a single layer; cover them well with foil, crimping the edges around the plate so the fish odor doesn't permeate the refrigerator. When you are ready to proceed with the recipe, remove the foil slowly and carefully so it doesn't stick to the mixture.

To fry the toast, heat at least ½ inch of oil to 375 degrees F. in a large electric skillet, a wok, a deep fryer, or a pot at least 2 inches deep. A 10-inch skillet can be used, but be very careful of spattering and spilling oil. When the oil has reached the correct temperature, carefully drop in the bread, fish side down, adding one piece at a time to prevent the pieces from sticking to each other. When the fish is light brown, which will take only a minute or two, turn the bread over with tongs, chopsticks, or a large spoon. Fry until the toast side is a rich brown. Drain the "Shrimp" Toast on paper towels and serve immediately with duck sauce and Chinese mustard.

Prickly Fish Balls

炸魚丸

Zha Yu Wan

Fukien influence

Makes 16 to 20 fish balls

This appetizer sounds, looks, and tastes good: you hear the noodles crackle as they are dropped into the oil; you watch as they puff up and turn white almost instantly; the delicate taste of the codfish interior combines with the wonderfully crunchy fried cellophane or rice noodles to produce a winning combination.

This is an excellent appetizer to prepare at the table in an electric skillet. Serve it as you would any *dim sum*—either before the meal, as part of a *dim sum* Chinese luncheon, or between heavier courses at a Chinese banquet. In China, shrimp would be used in place of the fish. If cod is not available, substitute any mildly-flavored fresh fish.

½ pound cod fillets, finely chopped
1 egg (graded large), beaten
2 scallions (white and crisp green parts), chopped
3 water chestnuts, chopped
1 teaspoon sugar
¼ teaspoon salt
2 teaspoons cornstarch
2 ounces cellophane noodles or rice noodles, cut into 1-inch lengths
Oil for deep-frying

Combine the chopped fish with the beaten egg, chopped scallions and water chestnuts, the sugar, salt, and the cornstarch. Mix lightly until everything is well blended. Shape the mixture into 16 to 20 balls, each approximately an inch in diameter.

On a clean work surface, spread out the cut cellophane or rice noodles. Roll the fish balls in the noodles, pressing until the fish is lightly covered. If the fish is very fresh, the uncooked fish balls may now be refrigerated overnight. Arrange them on a flat plate in a single layer—don't crowd them—then wrap in foil and refrigerate.

When you are ready to cook the fish balls, pour at least 1 inch of oil into a large electric skillet, a wok, a deep fryer, or a pot at least 3 inches deep. (The oil must be a *minimum* of an inch deep or the noodles will not cook properly.) Heat the oil to 375 degrees F. Test the temperature by dropping in a few strands of uncooked noodles. They should puff up immediately. Add the fish balls one at a time to the hot oil, and avoid overcrowding. The fish balls should not touch each other or they may become tangled. Use chopsticks, tongs, or a big spoon to turn the fish after about 30 seconds to cook the other side. The noodles should puff up and turn white all over. The fish itself takes only about a minute to cook. Remove the fish balls with chopsticks, tongs, or a slotted spoon, and shake them as you lift them to get rid of excess oil. Drain well on paper towels. Serve with duck sauce, Chinese mustard, or any condiment. A mildly flavored condiment will preserve the delicacy of this appetizer, while a strong or hot sauce will provide a contrast.

Hot Prickly Fish Balls

辣子魚丸

La Zi Yu Wan

Hunan influence

Makes 16 to 20 fish balls

This is a spicy version of Prickly Fish Balls. A more strongly flavored fish is used to match the very hot chili paste with garlic. A mildly spiced condiment is recommended so there is no conflict with the already well-seasoned appetizer.

½ pound bluefish or red snapper fillets, finely chopped
1 egg (graded large), beaten
1 tablespoon finely chopped onion
½ teaspoon minced ginger root
1 to 3 teaspoons chili paste with garlic, to taste
2 teaspoons cornstarch
2 ounces cellophane noodles or rice noodles, cut into 1-inch lengths
Oil for deep-frying, at least 1 inch deep

Combine the chopped fish with the egg, onion, ginger root, chili paste with garlic, and cornstarch. Proceed as directed in the recipe for Prickly Fish Balls. Serve the Hot Prickly Fish Balls with soy sauce seasoned with a little ginger root, vinegar, or sesame oil.

Prickly Beef Balls

炸肉丸

Zha Rou Wan

General China influence

Makes 16 to 20 beef balls

Chinese food is supposed to delight the diner before he or she even tastes it. These morsels will do just that if cooked before the admiring eye of your guests. (If you don't have an electric skillet to bring to the table, invite your guests into the kitchen to watch the show.) The thin strands of cellophane or rice noodles in which the beef balls are rolled puff up in every different direction the instant they hit the hot oil.

One of my children claims that this appetizer tastes like salt-free potato chips with a hamburger inside. It is true that much of the interest of Prickly Beef Balls comes from its appearance, and it does remind one of a hamburger, but it is certainly a hamburger with a Chinese flavor. The texture is also extremely important in this tidbit, with each bite consisting of an unusually crunchy outside combined with a tender inside.

½ pound minced beef
3 tablespoons finely chopped scallions (white and crisp green parts)
3 or 4 water chestnuts, finely chopped
1 teaspoon sugar
½ teaspoon crushed dried red pepper
½ teaspoon salt
1 teaspoon dry sherry
1 teaspoon soy sauce
1½ teaspoons cornstarch
2 ounces cellophane noodles or rice noodles, cut into 1-inch lengths
Oil for deep-frying

Combine the beef, scallions, water chestnuts, sugar, crushed red pepper, salt, sherry, soy sauce, and cornstarch. Mix well. Shape the mixture into 16 to 20 balls, each approximately an inch in diameter. Roll each ball in the pieces of cellophane or rice noodles, covering well. If the noodles do not stick to the meatballs, dip the meatballs in beaten egg before rolling them in the dried noodles. The uncooked beef balls can be refrigerated overnight.

Cook the meatballs as directed in the recipe for Prickly Fish Balls (page 92). Serve immediately with duck sauce for a sweet complement to the beef and crisp noodles, or serve Szechwan Sauce (page 130) for more zip.

Baked Stuffed Mushrooms

鮮菇釀肉

Xian Gu Rang Rou

General China influence

Serves 6 to 10

These stuffed mushrooms are a Western appetizer with Chinese touches. The basic filling of rice, minced beef, spinach, and chopped mushroom stems is flavored with soy sauce, the universal Chinese seasoning. The scallions and water chestnuts add texture to the filling, and the scallions also add zest. From there you may wish to add bamboo shoots for flavor and a slightly chewy texture; ginger root, garlic, or *hoisin* sauce for additional and very distinctive flavoring; or minced Chinese hot turnip or radish for a jolt. These mushrooms make a fine addition to a *dim sum* luncheon, and they can be served as one dish in a family-style Chinese dinner.

1 pound medium-large fresh mushrooms, as uniform in size as possible
1 cup cooked rice (white or brown)
½ cup cooked spinach, finely chopped
½ cup minced beef
2 scallions (white and crisp green parts), finely chopped
3 water chestnuts, coarsely chopped
1 tablespoon soy sauce
½ teaspoon sugar
Optional additions: 1 tablespoon coarsely chopped bamboo shoots; 1 teaspoon minced ginger root; 1 or 2 cloves garlic, minced; 1 tablespoon hoisin sauce; 1 to 2 tablespoons minced Chinese hot turnip or radish
About 1 tablespoon peanut, corn, or other oil

Clean the mushrooms and remove the stems. Set aside the mushroom caps. Cut off and discard the ends of the stems if they are tough and discolored. Chop the stems then mix them with the rice, spinach, beef, scallions, water chestnuts, soy sauce, and sugar. At this point also add any of the optional ingredients. Combine the mixture well, then stuff the mushroom caps with this filling. Place the mushrooms in a greased or lightly oiled baking dish. They can be packed close together, but in a single layer only. Sprinkle a few drops of oil on each stuffed mushroom. The mushrooms can be covered and refrigerated overnight.

To bake the mushrooms, preheat the oven to 375 degrees F. Bake for 20 minutes or until the mushrooms are softened and the filling is sizzling. Serve immediately.

Steamed Chinese Mushrooms
魚釀香菇
Yu Rang Xiang Gu

Shanghai

Makes 25 mushrooms

In this adaptation of a classic Shanghai shrimp-stuffed mushroom, the exotic, smoky, chewy mushrooms are stuffed with a lightly seasoned bluefish filling. Hints of ginger root, sesame oil, and scallions come through to flavor the fish, and water chestnuts plus the crisp parts of the celery cabbage and scallions add an important contrast to the soft filling and the chewy mushrooms.

You must like Chinese mushrooms to appreciate this appetizer, because they are too expensive to use simply as a convenient holder for the filling. Serve as an appetizer preceding the meal or as a *dim sum* at a banquet.

25 medium-size dried Chinese mushrooms
Boiling water
½ pound bluefish fillets
1 tablespoon cornstarch
½ teaspoon salt
2 stalks celery cabbage or any Chinese cabbage
4 water chestnuts, chopped
½ teaspoon minced ginger root
2 scallions (white and crisp green parts), finely chopped
1 teaspoon sesame oil
1 egg (graded large), beaten

Put the Chinese mushrooms in a medium-size heatproof bowl and pour enough boiling water over them to cover completely. Soak the mushrooms for 20 minutes while you prepare the stuffing.

Finely chop the bluefish, then mix the fish with the cornstarch and salt. Coarsely chop the celery cabbage into ⅛-inch-square pieces; squeeze the cabbage dry in paper towels. Now mix the bluefish with the celery cabbage, water chestnuts, ginger root, scallions, and sesame oil. Blend in the egg. Set aside.

Drain the soaking mushrooms, then cut out and discard the stems, leaving the mushroom caps whole. Divide the bluefish filling evenly among the mushrooms, heaping the filling and packing it lightly. Place the mushrooms on a heatproof plate or a steamer tray. If there is leftover filling, shape it into balls and steam them with the mushrooms.

Place the plate or tray in a steamer or a pot for steaming, and steam the mushrooms for 15 minutes. Serve the mushrooms (and any fish balls) immediately with Szechwan Sauce (page 130) or any other soy-sauce-based condiment, Chinese mustard, or duck sauce.

Pearl Meatballs

珍珠丸

Zhen Zhu Wan

General China

Makes 24 meatballs

In this classic Chinese recipe, glutinous or "sticky" rice is used to coat meatballs made from ground beef mixed with a quintet of ingredients associated with Chinese cooking. As the meatballs are steamed, the rice softens and swells to resemble small shiny pearls. The cooked meatballs are moist and tender, and the rice is tender but chewy. Serve these sticky meatballs as an appetizer, as part of a *dim sum* luncheon, or as a main dish.

¾ cup glutinous rice
1 pound lean ground beef
3 scallions (white and crisp green parts), chopped
1 large clove garlic, minced
1 teaspoon minced ginger root
2 tablespoons sweetened red bean paste
2 teaspoons hoisin sauce

Soak the glutinous rice for 30 minutes in enough water to cover it by an inch. Drain the rice. While the rice is soaking, combine the ground beef with the remaining ingredients, mixing lightly with your fingers until everything is well distributed. Shape the mixture into 1¼-inch balls. Roll the meatballs in the drained rice, covering the meat all over. Place the meatballs on a greased steamer tray, leaving ¼ inch space for the rice to expand. Steam the meatballs for 1 hour. Check the steamer occasionally to make sure all the water hasn't evaporated. Serve the meatballs hot, either plain or with a dip.

Barbecued "Spareribs"

烤羊排

Kao Yang Pai

Chinese-American influence

Serves 6 to 10

When I asked one of the owners of an Asian grocery in my area if barbecued spareribs are served in China the way they are served in the United States, she laughed heartily. She then explained that the Chinese do eat spareribs, but the ribs are usually cut up into small pieces (with the bones) and cooked in a black bean sauce.

This recipe for "spareribs" is *not* authentically Chinese on two counts: (1) the ribs are barbecued and cooked the way you'd expect them in a Chinese-American restaurant and (2) the ribs are not spareribs at all—because spareribs, of course, are pork.

Here, breast of lamb is substituted not only because it is tender, juicy, and relatively inexpensive, but because it looks a little like spareribs. The lamb taste goes exceptionally well with the sauce used in this recipe. If you do not have the ingredients called for here, use the marinade from Barbecued Chicken Wings (the next recipe) or use a bottled sweet-and-pungent, sparerib, or duck sauce.

2 tablespoons hoisin sauce
2 tablespoons brown sugar
2 tablespoons soy sauce
2 tablespoons honey
2 tablespoons red bean paste
4 pounds breast of lamb, the leanest you can find

Mix together the *hoisin* sauce, brown sugar, soy sauce, honey, and the red bean paste. Cut away any excess fat from the lamb. Brush the lamb on both sides with the marinade. Put the lamb in a pan or bowl, and let the lamb marinate for a minimum of an hour, turning as necessary to make sure both sides are flavored with the sauce. The lamb may be placed in the refrigerator to marinate overnight.

About 1 hour and 30 minutes before you plan to serve the ribs, preheat the oven to 350 degrees F. Place the lamb on a rack so the fat can drain off. Bake the lamb for about an hour, until crispy on both sides. Turn the lamb as necessary to brown both sides. To serve, slice between the bones and arrange the ribs on a serving plate. Serve immediately with duck sauce and Chinese mustard.

Barbecued Chicken Wings

烤鷄翅

Kao Ji Chi

General China influence

Makes 36 to 40 pieces

These chicken wings work in well at a cocktail party, a Chinese family meal, or as one of the smaller tidbits at a Chinese banquet. Soy sauce and honey give the wings a *teriyaki*-like flavor, but the tomato base of the chili sauce and ketchup is also evident, and the scallions and garlic contribute a tang. Eight out of nine of the marinade ingredients are readily available, and the ninth (red bean paste, which adds a little color and a subtle taste) isn't vital. The marinade used here is good with all meats, including other chicken parts, lamb, and beef ribs.

18 to 20 chicken wings
2 scallions (white and crisp green parts), cut into 1-inch pieces
2 cloves garlic, finely chopped
2 tablespoons chili sauce (any store brand or name brand, not an Oriental chili sauce)
1 tablespoon ketchup
2 tablespoons soy sauce
1 tablespoon dry sherry
1 tablespoon red bean paste
½ teaspoon salt
1 tablespoon honey

With a cleaver or a sharp knife, cut the chicken wings at the joints. Save the tips for soup. You should now have 2 pieces from each chicken wing. Mix the remaining ingredients, and toss the chicken wings to coat them thoroughly. Refrigerate the chicken wings in the marinade for at least 2 hours, up to as long as overnight. Remove the wings from the refrigerator 1 hour before you plan to bake them.

Preheat the oven to 425 degrees F. Place the chicken wings in a clean baking pan and arrange them so they do not touch. Bake the wings for about 40 minutes, turning to brown them on both sides. When the chicken wings are crisp and lightly browned, transfer to a platter and serve immediately.

Pan-fried Barbecued Chicken Wings

乾燒鷄翅

Gan Shao Ji Chi

Southern and eastern China

Makes 16 pieces

After being marinated in a very typical Cantonese soy-sauce-and-wine mixture, these chicken wings are cooked in a little chicken broth and then stir-fried with *hoisin* sauce, scallions, and garlic. The result is an exceptionally tasty tidbit to stimulate the appetite. The wings are tender and succulent, with a reddish-brown glaze.

8 chicken wings
2 teaspoons cornstarch
1 tablespoon peanut, corn, or other oil
1 tablespoon soy sauce
1 tablespoon dry sherry
3 scallions (white and crisp green parts), sliced
1 large clove garlic, minced
1 teaspoon minced ginger root
2 tablespoons peanut, corn, or other oil
¼ cup chicken broth or water
2 tablespoons hoisin sauce

With a cleaver or sharp knife, cut the chicken wings into 3 sections each. Use the 2 meaty sections; save the tips for soup. You now have 16 pieces of chicken. Toss the wing pieces with the cornstarch, 1 tablespoon of oil, soy sauce, and sherry. Set the chicken wings aside while you prepare the remaining ingredients. Combine the sliced scallions, minced garlic, and minced ginger root, and set the mixture near the cooking pan. Keep the *hoisin* sauce within reach as well.

To cook the chicken wings, in a wok or a 10-inch skillet, heat 2 tablespoons of oil to 375 degrees F. Stir-fry the chicken wings for 5 minutes, until brown all over. Add the ¼ cup of chicken broth or water, then cover the pan or wok and cook the wings for 10 minutes over medium heat. Remove the cover and boil away any remaining liquid. (The chicken wings can be refrigerated at this point. If you refrigerate them, bring them to room temperature and stir-fry in a little oil to heat them through before proceeding.) Quickly add the scallions, garlic, and ginger root, stirring constantly for about 30 seconds. Blend in the *hoisin* sauce, coating the chicken wings well, which will give them a lovely glaze. Serve the chicken wings immediately.

Variation:

When pressed for time, try this simplified version of the above. Brown the chicken wings in the oil (or in 2 tablespoons of chicken fat), as above. Reduce the heat to low, and without adding any liquid cover the pan and cook the wings for 15 minutes. Remove the cover, and stir in the 2 tablespoons of *hoisin* sauce, coating the chicken wings well. Serve immediately.

Fried Chicken Wings With Hot Bean Sauce

辣豆瓣鷄翅

La Dou Ban Ji Chi

Hunan influence

Makes 16 pieces

Golden, crispy fried chicken wings stand well on their own, but they become exotic when dipped into this thick hot sauce. The chicken, arranged around the sauce to resemble a flower, is designed to appeal to the diner even before it is tasted, an important aspect of any well-prepared Chinese dish.

2 tablespoons hot bean sauce
2 tablespoons ketchup
2 tablespoons soy sauce
Pinch of sugar
Dash of sesame oil
8 chicken wings
Oil for frying
½ cup unsifted all-purpose flour
½ teaspoon salt

In a small bowl, mix together the hot bean sauce, ketchup, soy sauce, sugar, and sesame oil. This can be done several days in advance. Refrigerate the sauce if you don't intend to use it within a few hours. When you are ready to cook and serve the chicken, transfer the sauce to a small shallow bowl, and place it in the center of a serving plate large enough to hold the chicken wings when they are arranged petal-fashion around the bowl.

Use a sharp knife to cut each chicken wing into 3 pieces at the joints. Save the tips for soup. You should end up with 16 pieces of chicken to fry. Into a wok, 10-inch electric skillet, deep fryer, or pot at least 3 inches deep, pour a minimum of ½ inch of oil. Heat the oil to 375 degrees F.

Now combine the flour and salt in a heavy paper bag. Place 4 chicken pieces in the bag at a time, and toss them with the flour until the chicken is very well coated. Drop the wing pieces into the hot oil carefully—do not allow the chicken pieces to touch each other until the coating is set. Fry the wings until golden on one side, then turn them and fry until golden on the other side. Drain the chicken well on paper towels. Arrange the fried chicken wings petal-fashion around the sauce. Serve immediately.

Boneless Fried Chicken
生炸去骨鷄
Sheng Zha Qu Gu Ji

General China influence

Makes 40 to 48 pieces

Even fussbudgets like boneless fried chicken. What's not to like? Tender, juicy chunks of chicken are encased in a crisp, golden brown crust. This chicken makes a fine appetizer, or it can be served as the main meat dish at an American meat-vegetable-potato dinner or as one of several dishes at a Chinese-style family meal.

Chicken breasts or thighs or a combination of the two can be used. The breasts are easier to work with and can usually be cut a bit more evenly. The thighs are somewhat juicier than the breasts, but extra care must be taken to trim off all fat.

1 pound chicken meat (breasts, thighs, or a combination)
1 egg (graded large)
¼ cup water
½ cup unsifted all-purpose flour
½ teaspoon salt
½ teaspoon double-acting baking powder
½ teaspoon peanut, corn, or other oil
Oil for frying

Cut the chicken into 1-inch squares, taking care to trim off all the fat; set aside. To make the batter, in a medium-size mixing bowl beat the egg.

With a fork, beat in the water, then beat in the flour until the mixture is smooth. Stir in the salt, baking powder, and the ½ teaspoon of oil. Add a little water if the batter is too thick or heavy; add flour if the batter is thin and runny. The batter can be prepared a day ahead and refrigerated.

To fry the chicken, in a wok, deep fryer, or 10-inch skillet, heat at least ½ inch of oil to 375 degrees F. Mix the chicken pieces with the batter, coating the chicken completely on all sides. Carefully drop the coated chicken pieces one at a time into the oil, making sure they do not touch each other—if the pieces stick together, you will end up with a giant chicken pancake. Fry the chicken pieces until golden brown on one side, then turn them over and fry the other side. Drain well on paper towels and serve immediately while still hot and crisp.

To serve the chicken as an appetizer, spear the pieces with toothpicks and pass around with duck sauce or Fresh Ginger Sauce (page 132). The chicken has a delicate taste and should not be masked by a sauce that is too strong. As a main dish, this Boneless Fried Chicken is eaten plain, or it can be mixed with rice and/or stir-fried vegetables.

Chicken Livers With Water Chestnuts

荸薺雞肝

Bi Qi Ji Gan

Canton

Makes about 3 dozen small "spears," or 4 to 6 servings as a first course

In China, most cooking takes place over a stove. Ovens with top broiler elements are rarely seen. However, since broiling is a necessary step in kashering chicken livers (in order to remove the blood), the chicken liver recipes in this book call for broiling the livers rather than stir-frying them. This is but one example of how Chinese cooking can be successfully adapted to meet individual requirements or tastes. The broiled livers come out exceptionally well. They are cooked through and sufficiently firm that they don't fall apart when combined with other ingredients, but they remain soft enough to contrast well with crisp vegetables such as the water chestnuts used in this recipe.

The chicken livers are first marinated in a typically Cantonese marinade of soy sauce and sherry. The remaining ingredients add a little spiciness and a major contrast in textures. There are three ways of serving these chicken livers, which almost turn this into three different recipes. When the livers and water chestnuts are "speared" and served as *hors d'oeuvres* before dinner, the soy sauce flavor of the livers and their contrast in texture with the water chestnuts will be particularly noticeable. When served hot as a first course or as one of several main dishes, the livers carry the overtones of the other ingredients, offering the diner a familiar taste with a new background. When served chilled as an appetizer, the background flavors are more subtle.

1 pound chicken livers
¼ cup soy sauce
2 tablespoons dry sherry
1 tablespoon peanut, corn, or other oil
4 scallions (white and crisp green parts), chopped
1½ teaspoons minced ginger root
16 water chestnuts, fresh if possible, sliced along the broader side into halves or thirds

Remove the membranes and fat from the chicken livers. In a small bowl, mix the livers with the soy sauce and sherry; let marinate for an hour. Ready the remaining ingredients before broiling the livers. Remove the chicken livers from the marinade, and broil them on both sides until they are thoroughly cooked and no trace of redness remains. Cut the livers into 2 or 3 pieces each. In a 7- or 8-inch skillet or a wok, heat the oil. Add the scallions and ginger root and stir-fry for about 30 seconds. Mix in the water chestnuts and the cooked chicken liver pieces. The chicken livers can now be served hot, or they can be refrigerated and served cold.

To serve the chicken livers as an *hors d'oeuvre*, spear a piece of liver and a slice of water chestnut on a toothpick, and arrange these on a platter. For dipping, place a small cup of soy sauce mixed with a little minced ginger root in the center of the platter. As a hot first course in an American dinner, serve each person his own small plate of the chicken liver and water chestnut mixture. To serve hot in a Chinese meal, set out the chicken livers as one of several luncheon or dinner dishes. To serve this dish at a banquet, chill the livers and offer them as one of the cold dish appetizers at the beginning of the meal.

Chicken Livers, Onions, and Chicken Fat
洋葱鷄油炒鷄肝
Yang Cong Ji You Chao Ji Gan

Canton influence

Serves 4 to 6

You may well wonder what a recipe with this title is doing in a Chinese cookbook. However, the Chinese cook makes use of virtually every part of the chicken, and he or she would not waste the fat any more than an old-fashioned Jewish cook would. Butter is almost never available to the Chinese, so chicken fat becomes a nice change from the lard that is usually used in stir-frying. Water chestnuts and bamboo shoots are included in this dish to give it more of the expected Chinese touch, but they can be omitted.

Any dish containing this quantity of chicken livers would be considered a restaurant or banquet dish by the Chinese. (In China chickens are typically sold live—and therefore whole—and it would be almost impossible for the average family to buy enough chickens and store enough livers to amass a whole pound of livers.) Whether you prepare this as an appetizer for company or an inexpensive main dish for your family, it would be considered a luxury item in China.

¼ cup soy sauce
2 tablespoons dry sherry
1 tablespoon shredded ginger root
1 pound chicken livers
2 tablespoons rendered chicken fat
1 medium-size onion, chopped
¼ cup sliced water chestnuts
¼ cup sliced bamboo shoots

In a small mixing bowl, combine the soy sauce, sherry, and shredded ginger root. After removing the membranes and fat, add the chicken livers and marinate them for an hour. Remove the livers from the marinade, and broil them until no trace of redness remains. Cut each liver into 2 or 3 pieces.

In an 8-inch skillet or a wok, heat the chicken fat until it is very hot and beginning to smoke. Add the onions and immediately stir-fry until they are crisp-tender and just beginning to brown. Mix in the broiled chicken livers, stirring constantly just until they are heated through. Add the water chestnuts and bamboo shoots, and continue to stir-fry until everything is hot. Serve the chicken livers hot so the fat does not solidify.

Chicken Livers With Szechwan Peppercorns

花椒鷄肝

Hua Jiao Ji Gan

Szechwan

Serves 4 to 6

This is similar to Chicken Livers With Water Chestnuts, but the addition of Szechwan peppercorns changes the flavor enough for this to be considered a separate recipe. In fact, the unique fragrance of the peppercorns sets this dish apart even before it is tasted.

There are three forceful flavors here: the chicken livers themselves have a hefty flavor, the ginger root contributes a pungency that can't be missed, and the peppercorns are pleasantly spicy. Rather than conflicting with each other, the flavors actually seem to tone each other down—so instead of competition for attention, there is a balance and harmony.

A dish like this might be served to perk up the appetite between courses at a large Chinese banquet. It can also be served as an *hors d'oeuvre* with crackers, as an appetizer before a meal, or as a main dish.

1 pound chicken livers
¼ cup soy sauce
2 tablespoons dry sherry
2 tablespoons peanut, corn, or other oil
4 scallions (white and crisp green parts), chopped
8 water chestnuts, sliced
1½ teaspoons minced ginger root
1 teaspoon crushed Szechwan peppercorns

After removing the membranes and fat, marinate the chicken livers for 1 hour in the soy sauce and sherry. Drain off the liquid. Broil the livers until no trace of redness remains, turning the chicken livers as necessary. Cut each liver into 2 or 3 pieces.

In an 8-inch skillet or a wok, heat the 2 tablespoons of oil until it is hot but not yet smoking. Stir-fry the scallions, water chestnuts, ginger root, and peppercorns for about a minute to release the flavors. Add the chicken livers and continue stirring until the livers are hot and have had a chance to mingle with the other ingredients. Serve this hot as a main dish, or either hot or chilled as an appetizer.

White-cut Chicken Breasts

白切鷄

Bai Qie Ji

General China

Serves 10

White-cut chicken is the easiest and most common way of cooking chicken in China. The method is simply to cook the chicken in simmering water for a short time, then turn off the heat and allow the chicken to finish cooking from the heat that remains. The resulting chicken is very tender and juicy. And because it is bland-tasting, it combines well with any number of dips.

At a Chinese banquet, this dish would be served as one of the cold appetizers already on the table when the guests are seated. Attractive cutting and serving are an important part of the preparation. The recipe below uses very large chicken breasts from roasting chickens because they are easy to slice uniformly. Four one-pound chicken breasts can be substituted.

2 large whole roasting chicken breasts, at least 2 pounds each

In a 4- to 6-quart pot, bring 3 to 4 quarts of water to the boil. Place the chicken breasts in the water, making sure they are completely covered. When the water again comes to the boil, reduce the heat to a gentle boil. Partially cover the pot, and simmer the chicken breasts for 20 minutes. Turn off the heat, cover the pot completely, and leave the chicken in the pot for an additional 30 minutes.

Transfer the cooked chicken (without the liquid) to a bowl, cover the chicken with plastic wrap and refrigerate. When the chicken is cool enough to handle, pull off and discard the skin. Using your fingers—not a knife—pull the bones away from the meat, keeping each breast half in one piece. Return the chicken to the refrigerator.

When the chicken is completely cold, use a very sharp knife or a cleaver to slice the meat into thin pieces, approximately 1 inch × 1½ inches × ⅛ inch thick. Keep in mind as you slice the chicken that in Chinese cooking eye appeal is as important as taste. Take care to keep the slices all the same size, which should be small enough so they do not need further cutting to be eaten.

Overlap the slices attractively on a serving plate. Refrigerate the chicken, covered, until serving time. White-cut chicken goes well with virtually any dip. The diner takes a piece of meat with chopsticks and dips it into the condiment. It is nice to have several small bowls of condiments available to each guest.

Very Tasty Cold Chicken

醬鷄

Jiang Ji

Szechwan

Serves 6 to 10

The intriguing taste of this chicken will keep your guests guessing about its ingredients. In fact, most people will ask what kind of sauce is used for the beef, because when the chicken is prepared in advance the soy sauce turns the chicken dark, the flavors of all the ingredients penetrate the chicken, and it is no longer recognizable as chicken either in appearance or in taste. The sauce is salty, sweet, and subtly spicy (but not spicy hot) all at once, making such a well-balanced blend that no single ingredient stands out.

4 chicken thighs with legs, or 12 drumsticks
¼ cup soy sauce
2 tablespoons honey
1 clove garlic, very finely chopped
2 tablespoons peanut, corn, or other oil
2 scallions (white and crisp green parts), sliced into rounds and chopped
1½ teaspoons minced ginger root
½ teaspoon Szechwan peppercorns, crushed with the broad side of a cleaver or the back of a spoon
¼ teaspoon crushed dried red pepper

In a 6- to 8-quart pot, bring 4 quarts of water to the boil. Add the chicken, partially cover the pot, and boil gently for 15 to 20 minutes. Turn off the heat, but leave the pot on the burner. Cover the pot completely, and leave the chicken in the water for at least 20 minutes. This method of cooking keeps the chicken tender and juicy.

Meanwhile, prepare the sauce. In a medium-size bowl, combine the soy sauce, honey, and garlic. In a 1-quart pot, heat the remaining 5 ingredients over low heat for about 3 minutes, until sizzling but not browned. Add this slightly cooked mixture to the soy sauce mixture, blending the ingredients thoroughly. You now have a marvelously tasty sauce in which to bathe the chicken.

Remove the cooked chicken from the pot and let it drain in a colander. When the chicken is cool enough to handle, remove and discard the skin, then cut the meat into pieces about 1 inch square. If using drumsticks only, pull off the meat gently with your fingers—most of it will come off in bite-size pieces. Discard the bones. Mix the chicken meat with the sauce. The chicken can be served immediately or it may be refrigerated for up to 2 days. The longer it remains in the sauce, the stronger-tasting it will be. To serve the chicken after it has been refrigerated, remove from the refrigerator about an hour before serving, and stir the chicken 3 or 4 times during that hour. The gel which often forms from the liquid will dissolve as the chicken warms up.

Variation:

To substitute chicken breasts for the dark meat, use 2 whole chicken breasts (1 pound each). Cook the breasts as directed in the recipe, but instead of cutting the meat into bite-size pieces, remove and discard the skin, then shred the chicken into matchstick-size pieces about 1½ inches long. (White meat is drier than dark meat, and shredding the chicken gives it more surface area to be moistened by the sauce.) If desired, serve the shredded white meat over a bed of shredded lettuce as a main dish.

Spiced Cold Brisket

滷牛肉

Lu Niu Rou

Fukien

Serves 20 as part of a selection of appetizers

The licorice-like flavor of star anise (so named because the whole spice is shaped like a star) combines with the cinnamon and cloves in this recipe to make a blend that is detectable in many Chinese stews. The barbecued ducks and ribs that can be seen hanging in the windows of Chinese groceries and the more informal restaurants are also often seasoned with star anise or five-spice powder, which contains star anise, cinnamon, and cloves as three of its major ingredients. For a more subtle and less spicy taste, see Red-cooked Whole Brisket (page 183).

Cold spiced meat is attractively cut into evenly sliced, bite-size pieces and placed on the table as one of several first-course cold dishes at Chinese banquets. Spiced Cold Brisket fits in very well at the American cocktail party, where numerous appetizers are often passed around. It can be prepared completely in advance, and it is the right size to be speared with a toothpick.

Although most recipes for similar dishes use shin beef, brisket works marvelously well. We are used to cooking brisket slowly to tenderize it and bring out its flavor, and when it is cooked in soy sauce and spices it absorbs just enough to heighten its own good taste. Red-cooked (cooked in soy sauce) dishes are typical of the eastern province of Fukien, but they are known throughout China as well.

2 cups Red-cooked Starter Sauce (see Ingredients, page 21), or 1 cup soy sauce and 1 cup water
1 cup additional water
2 whole star anise
1 piece (3 inches) stick cinnamon
¼ teaspoon whole cloves
1 large piece fresh brisket of beef, flat cut (about 4 pounds)

Combine the Red-cooked Starter Sauce, water, and the spices in a 6- to 8-quart pot with a tight-fitting lid. Bring the liquid to the boil, then add the brisket. Bring the liquid to the boil again, then reduce the heat so the meat simmers in the gravy. Cover the pot and cook the brisket for about 2½ hours, until very tender. Turn the meat every half-hour so all the sides are bathed in the gravy. When the brisket is tender, remove the pot from the heat and take out the star anise, stick cinnamon, and cloves. Allow the meat to cool in the liquid, then refrigerate the meat right in the gravy. The brisket and gravy can be frozen at this point, or you may refrigerate the brisket for up to two days before slicing.

When it is thoroughly chilled, remove the brisket from the sauce, allowing any sauce that has jelled around the meat to cling to it. Slice the brisket with the grain into 1½-inch strips. Then cut each strip across the grain thinly on the diagonal, making dozens of slices in all. Dip each slice into the cold gravy. If the gravy has jelled too much, warm it slightly so it can be used to flavor each piece of meat. Layer the meat slices attractively on a platter. This beef is usually served plain, or with small chilled cubes of the jellied sauce. If you would like to serve it with a condiment, Chinese mustard, plum sauce, or a canned Chinese pickle would all go well.

Romaine Stuffed With Beef and Water Chestnuts

生菜包

Sheng Cai Bao

Peking influence

Makes 12 to 16 stuffed leaves

Fresh romaine leaves are more than a convenient receptacle for this appetizer, which I developed when I needed a new cold dish for a Chinese banquet. It is especially nice to serve as part of a buffet. The lettuce adds color and crispness to a tasty ground beef mixture flavored with fresh ginger root, garlic, scallions, soy sauce, *hoisin* sauce, and sesame oil. The water chestnuts are included mainly for their crisp texture, but if you can get fresh water chestnuts, the mixture will be even better. No one taste predominates, but the combination is exotic. Because this appetizer is served cold, it would be appropriate to serve at a banquet as one of several first-course dishes that would be placed on the table at once.

1 tablespoon peanut, corn, or other oil
1 pound lean ground beef
½ teaspoon minced ginger root
1 clove garlic, minced
¼ cup chopped scallions (white and crisp green parts)
¼ cup coarsely chopped water chestnuts
2 tablespoons soy sauce
2 tablespoons hoisin sauce
1 teaspoon sesame oil
12 to 16 medium-size romaine leaves

Coat an 8-inch skillet with a tablespoon of oil. When the oil is moderately hot, add the ground beef, stirring constantly to brown the beef quickly and to keep the pieces broken up. Spoon off all of the accumulated fat. Add the ginger root, garlic, scallions, and water chestnuts, mixing these ingredients in very well. Now add the soy and *hoisin* sauces, stirring until these are blended in very well also. Turn off the heat, then stir in the sesame oil. Refrigerate the mixture until it is completely chilled. The filling can be made a day in advance, or it can be frozen as long as it is thoroughly defrosted before using.

Within 3 hours of serving time, wash each romaine leaf thoroughly and pat the leaves dry with a clean towel or with paper towels. Use scissors to trim off the bottom of each leaf as well as any wilted or dark areas. Place the romaine leaves attractively on a large platter or on two plates. Divide the filling among the leaves, using the romaine as a kind of cup to partially but not completely enclose the filling. This is served as "finger food," so the romaine leaves must be small enough to pick up easily.

Crispy Sweet Walnuts

酥炸核桃

Su Zha He Tao

General China

Makes 1 cup

These sweet, crisp treats make a wonderful afterschool nosh. It has never been possible for me to find out how long they can be stored, because they disappear before I have a chance to hide them. They are included with the other appetizers because they are used as a before-the-meal nibble at Chinese banquets. They might also be served during the day as a sweet with tea in China, and they can be used as a dessert or to garnish other desserts such as Peking Dust.

2 cups water
1 cup walnut halves (pecans may be substituted)
¼ cup sugar
Oil for frying

In a 2-quart pot, bring the water to the boil. Add the walnut halves, remove the pot from the water, and let the walnuts sit in the hot water for 2 minutes. Drain the walnuts in a colander or strainer, return them to the pot, and immediately mix in the sugar. Stir the walnuts and sugar until the nuts are well-coated and the sugar is dissolved. Spread the walnuts out on a sheet of wax paper and allow them to cool.

In a 1-quart pot, heat 1 inch of oil until it is hot but not yet smoking, 375 degrees F. Add ¼ cup of the walnuts at a time. Fry each batch for 2 minutes, stirring occasionally to keep the walnuts from sticking together. Watch them carefully as they cook, and make sure they don't burn. If they are browning too rapidly, lower the temperature of the oil. When the walnuts are nicely browned, remove them with a slotted spoon, and spread them out on a clean piece of wax paper or a lightly oiled plate. Continue frying until all the walnuts are glazed. While the walnuts are cooling, gently move them around to make sure they don't stick to the wax paper. When they are completely cool, transfer the walnuts to a container. Cover tightly and store.

Crisp Spiced Sugar Pecans

香烤核桃

Xiang Kao He Tao

General China influence

Makes 1 pound

These crisply baked, lightly spiced pecans will always be "Break-the-Fast Pecans" to me. When the past-president of our local sisterhood and her family joined us for break-fast following Yom Kippur services one year, she brought these wonderful treats along with pickled herring and a noodle *kugel*. These pecans are as much at home at a Chinese banquet as they are at a traditional Jewish meal. They can be served interchangeably with Crispy Sweet Walnuts.

1 egg white (from an egg graded large)
1 tablespoon cold water or orange juice
1 pound pecan halves
½ cup firmly packed light or dark brown sugar
½ teaspoon ground cinnamon, or more to taste
¼ teaspoon ground nutmeg, or more to taste

Preheat the oven to 250 degrees F. Grease a jelly roll pan or a large cookie sheet, preferably with sides; set aside. Using a fork, in a medium-size mixing bowl beat the egg white with the water or orange juice until the egg white is frothy. Add the pecans and, using a large spoon, mix the pecans with the beaten egg white; coat the nuts well. Combine the sugar and spices in a cup or a small bowl, then sprinkle the mixture over the pecans. Gently mix the sugar and spices with the pecans.

Spread the pecans on the greased pan or cookie sheet and bake for 1 hour. Every 15 minutes, stir the nuts around with a large spoon. Transfer the baked pecans to a flat plate or pan, and allow them to cool before storing in a tightly covered container.

2

Condiments

Garnishes, pickles, dips, dressings, marinades, seasonings, and cooking sauces—these condiments are used by the Chinese to blend with, complement, or bring out the flavors of other foods, never to mask them. Chinese do not use sweet-and-pungent sauces to cover up the flavor of a fish that is no longer fresh; they do use sweet-and-pungent sauces to balance the delicate taste of freshly caught fish. Nor do the Chinese sprinkle soy sauce over everything the way we use salt, ketchup, and pancake syrup—the chef does the seasoning during the cooking and additional seasonings aren't usually necessary if the dish has been properly prepared.

There are exceptions, of course. Many Chinese appetizers are enhanced when dipped into a flavorful sauce. Soy sauce, the near-ubiquitous seasoning, is at the base of numerous dips and dressings, each of which has the distinctive flavor of the additional ingredients. Other dipping sauces—for example, Chinese mustard and duck sauces—have spices or fruit as their primary ingredients.

As in other cuisines, garnishes are used in China to make foods look more attractive by adding a contrasting color or unique shape. Sometimes they also add a fresh taste (scallions) or an interesting texture (fried noodles). This chapter begins with some simple garnishes used by the Chinese in home cooking, and continues with a broad range of condiments.

Scallion Garnish

葱花

Cong Hua

General China

Scallions, also known as green onions, figure prominently in Chinese cooking, especially as a garnish. Just a touch of raw chopped scallion adds color, texture, and a little zing to soups, vegetables, rice, noodles, and meat dishes. You don't need to add scallions to already colorful and highly seasoned foods or to dishes that have a delicate balance of flavors; nor would you sprinkle scallions over every dish at a given meal. However, when you're looking for a color contrast, a bit of bite, or a light crunch, think scallions.

1 bunch scallions, more or less

Cut off the root ends and the soft parts of the green tops. Peel off any tough outer layers, but don't peel away more than two layers or there won't be any scallion left. Wash the scallions, being careful to remove any sand. Pat dry. Slice the scallions lengthwise down the middle, then chop them thinly, crosswise. Or, just slice the scallions into thin rounds. Be sure to include the crisp parts of the green tops. Leftover chopped scallions will keep in a covered jar, refrigerated, for a few days. They keep best if there isn't much air space left at the top of the jar. After a while, the scallions soften and cannot be used.

Vegetable "Flowers"

刻菜花

Ke Cai Hua

General China

Vegetable carving is an art, and I am not an artist. But I can share with you a simple technique for transforming scallions, broccoli stems, and celery tops into attractive "flowers." The vegetables are cut into two-inch pieces, then the ends are slit into an X or a crosshatch pattern. The ends open up when the vegetables are placed in ice water. The flowers can be used to garnish platters, as paintbrushes for dips (see Peking Duck), or in stir-fried dishes.

Scallions
Broccoli stems
Celery tops, where the leaves break off from the stalks

For the scallions, trim off the root ends, peel off any tough outer layers, then wash. Starting at the root end, cut the scallions into 1½- to 2-inch pieces. You can cut each scallion up to the part where it begins to split. Set aside.

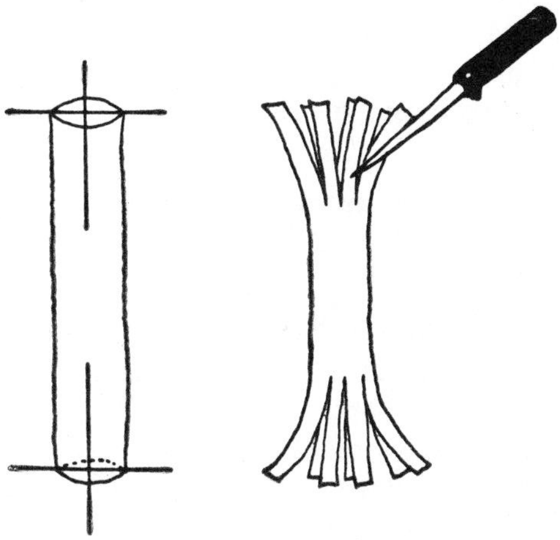

For the broccoli, peel the stems. Cut the stems into 2-inch pieces that are ⅜ to ½ inch in diameter. Trim thicker pieces into rounds of uniform size.

The celery comes out best when you use the thin ends to which the leaves are attached—they are automatically the right diameter. Trim off the leaves, and cut the stems into 2-inch pieces. If you like, use the thick stalks, paring them into ⅜-inch rounds. Using a small sharp knife, such as a good paring knife, slit an X into both ends of the vegetables, cutting at least ½ inch deep. Cut extra slits in the broccoli and celery and they will "flower" better. Be careful not to slice off pieces, and don't slice too much of the way through or the vegetables will split in half.

Place the vegetables in a small bowl or container of cold water. If you're in a hurry, put a piece of ice in the water. If you have time, leave the vegetables in the refrigerator, in the container of water. The ends will open up within an hour. The vegetables will become very crisp when left in the water for several hours. Leave them in the water as long as overnight, then drain the vegetables and refrigerate them in a plastic bag, a container, or on a plate. If so treated, they will keep for a day or two longer.

Egg Garnish
蛋絲
Dan Si

General China

Makes one 8-inch pancake, many strips

Strips of egg made from a plain egg pancake are often used in Chinese cooking to dress up soups, rice, noodles, vegetables, and meat-vegetable combinations. They are used mainly to add color and sometimes to add textural interest.

1 tablespoon peanut, corn, or other oil
2 eggs (graded large)

In an 8-inch skillet, heat the oil until it is moderately hot but not yet smoking. Beat the eggs in a small mixing bowl. Pour the beaten eggs into the hot oil. Swish them around to cover the bottom of the pan. Using a spoon, gently push cooked egg toward the middle, and allow uncooked egg to flow around the edges, making a flat pancake. Remove the pan from the heat before the eggs brown. Using a pancake turner, remove the eggs from the pan in one piece. When it is cool enough to handle, cut the pancake into thin strips.

Deep-fried Noodles
脆炸麵條
Cui Zha Mian Tiao

Chinese-American

Makes about 6 cups

The fried noodles found on the tables in Chinese restaurants are easy and inexpensive to duplicate. They are sold already prepared as "*chow mein* noodles" in many grocery stores, but they taste better when made at home. The name "*chow mein* noodles" is itself incorrect on two counts. The word *chow* is a corruption of the Chinese *chao,* which means "stir-fried," and these noodles as we know them are deep-fried. Secondly, *mein* is an alternate spelling of *mien,* which means "noodles," so the literal translation of "*chow mein* noodles" is "stir-fried noodles noodles."

Notwithstanding that the title of the dish is technically inaccurate and that the noodles themselves are a Western invention rather than an authentic Chinese condiment, this is a crisp and wonderful garnish or snack. Serve the noodles with soups, sprinkle them on vegetable dishes, mix them with rice, add them as a garnish to any stir-fried dish, dip them into duck sauce and mustard, munch them plain, or serve them in place of nuts on a hot fudge sundae.

1 pound egg roll or wonton wrappers
Oil or shortening for deep-frying

Slice the egg roll or wonton wrappers into pieces about 2 inches × ⅛ inch—or make them wider if you like. Into a deep fryer, electric skillet, wok, or any pot at least 3 inches deep, pour at least 1 inch of oil. Heat the oil until it reaches 375 to 400 degrees F., hot enough to fry the noodles quickly without burning them. Carefully scatter some of the noodles into the oil; cook them in several batches so the noodles don't touch each other. Fry the noodles until golden brown, turning as necessary to fry both sides. Drain the fried noodles very well on paper towels, then store them in a heavy plastic bag at room temperature, or freeze them in plastic bags when completely cool. The noodles will keep for several weeks at room temperature and for months in the freezer.

Deep-fried Cellophane or Rice Noodles

炸粉絲

Zha Fen Si

Fukien

Makes about 6 cups

Fried cellophane noodles (made from mung beans) are light and airy, and while they have little flavor of their own, they'll pick up some of the taste of the oil in which they are fried. Fried rice noodles, which have a mild ricelike flavor, are a little thicker than cellophane noodles. Both noodles are fun to cook—they curl, puff up, and turn white immediately on contact with hot oil. Their color makes them show up especially well on beef, lamb, and colorful vegetable dishes. Serve them as a nibble or on top of stir-fried dishes for a uniquely crisp but light texture.

8 ounces cellophane or rice noodles
Oil for deep-frying

Break the noodles with the fingers, or cut them with scissors, into 1- to 2-

inch pieces. Do *not* soak the noodles first. Into a deep fryer, electric skillet, wok, or any pot at least 3 inches deep, pour at least 1½ inches of oil. Heat the oil to at least 375 degrees F.—it should be hot but not yet smoking when the noodles are added. Test one noodle to make sure the oil is hot enough. The noodle should puff up immediately and turn from clear to white.

When the oil has reached the correct temperature, scatter a handful of noodles around the oil, being careful not to overcrowd. Remove the noodles as soon as they puff up. If they do not puff up immediately, they never will. Remove them, heat the oil again, and try with another batch. Drain the fried noodles well on paper towels. Store the cooled noodles in heavy plastic bags at room temperature for a week, or freeze them.

Peanut-Scallion-Hoisin Relish

三色醬

San Se Jiang

Peking influence

Makes about 1½ cups

There are only three ingredients in this relish (and they are all in the title), but each brings a different color, texture, and flavor. The peanuts are crunchy, flavorful, salty, and a good source of protein. The scallions bring a fresh, bracing taste and two colors at once, green and white. The *hoisin* sauce adds color, body, and its distinctive sweet-spicy taste. Each ingredient is readily identifiable in each bite, but the parts harmonize well and the contrasts enhance each other. This relish can be served on lettuce as an unusual appetizer or as a condiment.

1 cup chopped salted peanuts
8 scallions (white and crisp green parts), cut into rounds
¼ cup hoisin sauce

Mix the ingredients together in a small bowl. Serve immediately, or refrigerate the relish in a covered container. The scallions will become soft after a day or two, so it is best to prepare this in small quantities and serve it fresh each time. Set the relish out as a condiment, or serve it in individual portions on a bed of lettuce.

Monica's Chinese Pickles

泡菜

Pao Cai

Peking

Makes 2 cups

Monica Yu, who is originally from Peking, is one of the people I had the pleasure of meeting as I was gathering background information for this cookbook. As we sat and sipped green tea in her Connecticut living room, she looked through my manuscript and discovered that I had no recipes for Chinese pickles. Monica told me she had just started a batch in a large mason jar, and offered to give me her recipe. It immediately became apparent that getting a recipe from a Chinese housewife is no different from getting a recipe from a Jewish grandmother. "I throw in a little of this . . . I taste and see how salty it is . . . "—these were Monica's measurements. Here is her recipe as she gave it to me:

> Fill a jar with water. Throw in some salt—I don't know how much—I taste it after a week and add salt, or if it's too salty I divide it in half, add water, and make two jars of pickles. Throw in a few dried Chinese red peppers, some Chinese peppercorns, ginger root, and a few drops of a good brandy. Cut cabbage into nice triangular pieces. Here, I'll get a jar I just started to show you what I mean. You can also use broccoli, and Chinese radish cut into pieces like French fries. Leave the jar in the refrigerator for a month, and then it's ready. I guess you could leave it out at room temperature for a week or two.

The pickles are served as an accompaniment to meats, congees, and other dishes. They are both salty and spicy. Here is a more precise version of the recipe:

2 cups water
2 tablespoons salt
3 dried hot chili peppers
¼ teaspoon Szechwan peppercorns
1 slice (⅛ inch thick) ginger root
¼ teaspoon cognac
2 cups raw vegetables, such as broccoli stems, peeled and cut into even-size pieces; cauliflower florets; carrots, peeled and cut on the diagonal into 1-inch pieces; Chinese radish, cut into long, thin pieces; green cabbage (not a Chinese cabbage), cut into

→

small triangular pieces; cucumbers, unpeeled, cut on the diagonal into ½-inch slices

In a 1-quart glass jar, mix together the water and salt, stirring to dissolve the salt. Add the dried peppers, peppercorns, ginger root, and cognac. Shake the jar gently to mix the ingredients. Now add the sliced vegetables. Cover the jar and refrigerate. Stir the mixture once a week. Taste the liquid and correct the seasoning as needed. Some of the vegetables, such as the Chinese radish and the cucumbers, will be ready within a few days. Keep tasting—when the vegetables are permeated by the lovely spicy flavors of the pickling liquid, they are ready. Store in the refrigerator.

Chinese Mustard

芥末

Jie Mo

General China

Makes ¾ cup

I remember seeing a road sign along a 50-mph road in Upstate New York which said: STOP SIGN AHEAD. Somewhere in close proximity to the actual stop sign was another sign, which read: YOU WERE WARNED. When this Chinese mustard sauce is freshly prepared, it is HOT. *You are warned!* You will do well to warn guests also, and have cold water available for those who don't believe you.

Chinese mustard differs from the deli mustard used with corned beef or pastrami on rye in that (1) it is more of a sauce than a spread, (2) it is bright yellow, and (3) it is sharper. The mustard and turmeric flavors come through unadulterated by other spices.

When Chinese mustard is recommended as a condiment, use this recipe or a purchased Chinese mustard sauce. For the dry mustard powder, Colman's brand consistently works well, and it is available in the two-ounce cans required for this recipe. We've experimented with the dry mustard powders sold in Chinese groceries, but they are too bitter.

My husband developed this recipe many years ago using a postage meter scale. I have translated most of the weights into standard measurements.

2 ounces dry mustard powder (weight is on the can)
½ teaspoon ground turmeric, slightly heaped

2 tablespoons sugar
¼ teaspoon, scant, freshly ground black pepper
¼ teaspoon salt
1 ounce (by weight) cornstarch (about 3 level tablespoons)
2 teaspoons distilled white vinegar
3 to 4 ounces (6 to 8 tablespoons) cold water

In a small mixing bowl, combine the dry ingredients. Use a spoon to stir in the vinegar and 2 tablespoons of the water. Blend the mixture well, which may take some time. (My husband is very patient.) The mixture must be completely free of lumps. Add water a tablespoon at a time to make a smooth sauce that is about the consistency of heavy cream. Refrigerate the mustard sauce in a tightly covered container. If it appears to be drying out, blend in a little water from time to time. Stir just before serving. The mustard will form a crust when exposed to the air. If you want to have your condiment bowls arranged early, cover the dish of mustard with plastic wrap until serving time.

Fresh Fruit Duck Sauce

桃杏李酱

Tao Xing Li Jiang

Canton

Makes 1½ cups

Fresh fruits are cooked with a hint of sweet and sour ingredients to make a sauce which serves the same purpose as commercially prepared duck sauce but has a considerably more fruity taste. Serve it as an accompaniment to many *dim sum.* When the fruit is put through a food mill, the sauce takes on the consistency of applesauce and is used as a dip. When left in chunks, like a chutney, it can be eaten on its own as a relish or used to accompany other foods.

1 pound mixture of fresh peaches, apricots, and prune plums
1 cup water
1 tablespoon sugar
1 tablespoon light corn syrup

→

1 tablespoon distilled white vinegar
1 tablespoon cornstarch dissolved in 2 tablespoons cold water

Cut the fruit into chunks; discard the pits. In a 2-quart pot, combine the fruit with the cup of water. Bring to the boil, reduce the heat to the simmer, cover the pot, and cook the fruit until it is soft, about 15 minutes. Stir the mixture as necessary to keep it from sticking. If desired, put the fruit through a food mill before proceeding with the recipe; return the fruit to the pot. Stir in the sugar, light corn syrup, and vinegar. Bring the mixture to the boil again, stirring to keep it from sticking. Boil the fruit for 1 minute, then taste a bit. Add a little additional sugar or corn syrup to sweeten the sauce, or vinegar to increase the sour taste. Stir together the cornstarch and 2 tablespoons cold water until the mixture is smooth. Blend the mixture into the boiling fruit, and cook and stir until the mixture is thickened, which should take less than half a minute. Transfer the sauce to a bowl or a container. Let cool then place in a covered container and refrigerate. This duck sauce will keep for several days in the refrigerator. The mixture can be frozen, although the fruit will break down a bit and the cornstarch-thickened sauce will lose some of its smoothness when thawed.

Apricot Duck Sauce

杏醬

Xing Jiang

Canton influence

Makes 2 cups

Canned apricots packed in water or fruit juice are the basis of this condiment. The remaining ingredients are almost the same as those in Fresh Fruit Duck Sauce, but the minced garlic added here produces a flavor that is closer to many commercially prepared duck sauces. Small, soft chunks of fruit are a feature of this sauce (the fruit is cut into pieces with a spoon as it cooks), which is used as a dip or spooned over other foods. When Apricot Duck Sauce and Fresh Fruit Duck Sauce are combined, a richly flavored fruit sauce with a garlicky sweet-sour tang results.

1 can (1 pound) pitted apricots packed in unsweetened juice or water
1 clove garlic, finely chopped

1 tablespoon sugar
1 tablespoon light corn syrup
1 tablespoon distilled white vinegar
1 tablespoon cornstarch dissolved in 2 tablespoons cold water

In a 2-quart pot, place the apricots with their juice (or water). Add the garlic, sugar, corn syrup, and vinegar. Over medium heat, bring the liquid to the boil, stirring frequently. With the edge of the spoon, cut the apricots into small pieces as the mixture cooks. Cook the apricots for about 3 minutes after it has come to the boil. Stir together the cornstarch and water until the cornstarch is completely dissolved, then add the cornstarch mixture to the boiling apricots. Stir rapidly for about 15 seconds, until the mixture is thickened and has a glazed look. Transfer the sauce to a bowl or a container. Let cool, then cover and refrigerate. The duck sauce will keep for several days in a covered container in the refrigerator. The sauce can be frozen, but as with other cornstarch-thickened products it will lose some of its smoothness when thawed.

Plum Duck Sauce
蘇梅醬
Su Mei Jiang

Canton influence

Makes 2 cups

This homemade plum sauce, seasoned with lemon juice and ginger root, is another marvelous sauce that will enhance many appetizers. Actually a very simplified version of the sauce used in Roast Duck With Plum Sauce, it is especially nice with "Spareribs," "Shrimp" Toast, and fish and chicken appetizers.

1 can (1 pound) purple plums in heavy syrup
Juice of ½ lemon
½ teaspoon minced ginger root

In a 1- or 2-quart pot, place the plums with their syrup. Remove all pits. Stir in the lemon juice and ginger root. Bring the mixture to the boil. Using the edge of a spoon, cut the plums into smaller pieces as they cook. Cook the plums for about 5 minutes to boil down the liquid a bit, stirring as necessary to prevent sticking. Transfer the cooked plums to a bowl or container. Let cool, then cover and refrigerate. The plum sauce will keep for several days in the refrigerator, or it can be frozen.

Salt and Pepper—Chinese Style

椒鹽

Jiao Yan

Szechwan

Makes about ¼ cup

The Chinese do not use salt and pepper the way we do, but salt and pepper do find a place in Chinese cooking when aromatic Szechwan peppercorns are crushed and toasted with salt. Kosher salt is used in this recipe to match the coarseness of the crushed peppercorns. The salt-and-pepper mixture is characteristically served as a dip (it is not sprinkled on) with home-style duck and steamed rolls, but it also makes a tasty seasoning for some of the plainer appetizers such as white-cut chicken.

2 teaspoons Szechwan peppercorns
4 tablespoons kosher salt

Crush the peppercorns with a broad knife or the side of a cleaver. Heat a 5- to 7-inch cast-iron skillet over medium heat. Add the salt and peppercorns, and cook the mixture for 5 minutes, shaking the pan often. The salt and pepper should brown lightly, but do not allow the mixture to burn. Transfer the mixture to a bowl, and when cool, store it in a small jar that can be tightly capped. If there is not much room for air in the jar and the lid or stopper is airtight, the mixture will keep its flavor for months.

"Hot" Oil

辣油

La You

Szechwan

Makes ¼ cup

"Hot" oil is prepared by combining heated oil with some form of hot peppers. The oil is then cooled and strained. It can be purchased or prepared at home for use as a seasoning in cooking, as a condiment to sprinkle on food at the table, or as an ingredient in other condiments. The recipe here is for one-quarter cup because that is the amount used in Szechwan Sauce, which appears later in this chapter (page 130).

The flavor of the oil is determined by the oil used. Peanut oil is suggested for a mild flavor and pleasant taste, while sesame oil can be used for a strong, smoky flavor. The hotness depends largely on the pepper selected. We once used a hot cayenne powder purchased in the Southwest. The choking and eye irritation began as soon as the hot pepper hit the oil, and we were unable to use that batch of hot oil because we couldn't get near enough to taste it.

This recipe calls for crushed dried red pepper, which is readily available in all supermarkets. You may adjust the amount of pepper to suit personal taste, and the recipe can be increased to yield any quantity desired. The "hot" oil will keep well unrefrigerated, although in time it will lose some of its kick.

¼ cup peanut oil or sesame oil
1½ teaspoons crushed dried red pepper (more or less, to taste)

In a 1-quart pot, heat the oil just until it starts to smoke. Remove the pot from the heat, wait 5 to 10 seconds, then stir in the crushed red pepper. The pepper can be irritating to the eyes and throat, so take a breath before adding it, and don't have your face too near the pot. Allow the oil to cool to room temperature, then strain out the crushed red pepper. We use a small tea strainer that we keep for this purpose only. If you use a strainer that will be used for tea also, it must be washed thoroughly to get rid of the oils from the hot pepper. Store the "hot" oil on a pantry shelf in a tightly covered jar, or transfer to a bottle with a shaker top so it can be used conveniently as a condiment.

"Hot" Sesame-Soy Dip

辣味麻醬汁

La Wei Ma Jiang Zhi

Peking

Makes about ⅓ cup

Soy sauce and sesame oil are used as condiments for many appetizers, and here they are mixed together for convenience. A little liquid pepper sauce is included for zip. This flavorful combination can be used as a dip, or it may be sprinkled on the food. In China the food is usually seasoned during cooking, but Americans like to season to taste at the table, and this can be considered a general seasoning. The sesame oil and moderate use of hot peppers make this a northern-style condiment.

¼ cup soy sauce
2 tablespoons sesame oil
2 to 4 drops liquid pepper sauce (such as Tabasco), or to taste

In a small bowl, mix the soy sauce and sesame oil. Blend in the liquid pepper sauce one drop at a time until you reach a comfortable "hot." Serve this sauce in small condiment bowls, or transfer it to a shaker-top bottle. The sauce keeps well unrefrigerated.

Basic Soy-Sauce-and-Vinegar Dip

鹹酸汁

Xian Suan Zhi

Peking

Makes ¾ cup

A plain soy-sauce-and-vinegar dip is associated with the northern dumplings known as *jiaozi,* but this basic condiment can be served with almost all *dim sum.* Although the soy sauce is salty and flavorful, and the vinegar is perky, neither interferes with the taste of the appetizer. Use a light or thin soy sauce, not a black soy, which is made with molasses and can be overpowering. The vinegar can be a rice vinegar, for authenticity, or a red wine vinegar, which may not be quite as sharp.

The plain dip or one of its variations is especially nice to serve with the more doughy appetizers, giving the diner something to savor until the filling is reached. When a soy-vinegar dip is served with *jiaozi,* each person gets a small condiment bowl. The dumpling is picked up with chopsticks (not always an easy task), dipped, and then eaten. Soy sauce and vinegar could also be served in separate shaker-top bottles or cruets, the way vinegar and oil are often served in Italian restaurants.

½ cup soy sauce
¼ cup rice vinegar or red wine vinegar

Combine the ingredients in a small mixing bowl, a measuring cup, or a jar. Store unrefrigerated in a covered jar. Serve the dip in small condiment bowls.

Soy-Sauce-and-Vinegar Dip With Fresh Ginger
生薑鹹酸汁
Sheng Jiang Xian Suan Zhi

Peking

Makes about ¾ cup

It isn't enough to enjoy the pungent fragrance of fresh ginger root to appreciate this dip. You must also like the *taste* of the aromatic root. The pieces of grated ginger root are sharp on the tongue, and the liquid has the unmistakable fresh ginger taste. The dip is served with dumplings and other *dim sum*. Or mix it with plain boiled rice or noodles, or use it to perk up a plain congee.

½ cup soy sauce
¼ cup rice vinegar or red wine vinegar
1 tablespoon grated ginger root

Combine the ingredients in a small mixing bowl. To serve, transfer to an attractive bowl or individual condiment bowls. If you serve this in several smaller bowls, make sure to distribute the ginger root evenly. This dip will keep unrefrigerated for several days in a covered jar.

Soy-Sauce-and-Vinegar Dip With Garlic
蒜泥鹹酸汁
Suan Ni Xian Suan Zhi

Peking

Makes about ¾ cup

Here, the garlic permeates the soy sauce and vinegar, and anything the sauce touches picks up the garlic taste. Crushed red pepper may be added to make the sauce spicy hot as well. Serve this variation of the basic soy-vinegar dip with Northern Dumplings (page 79) and other dumplings.

½ cup soy sauce
¼ cup rice vinegar or red wine vinegar
1 tablespoon minced garlic
¼ to ½ teaspoon crushed dried red pepper (optional)

Combine the ingredients in a small bowl. Stir just before serving. Serve in an attractive bowl or in individual condiment bowls. This dip will keep unrefrigerated for several days in a covered jar, but the garlic flavor is nicest when the dip is freshly prepared.

Szechwan Sauce
四川辣汁
Si Chuan La Zhi

Szechwan

Makes about 1 cup

This hot and spicy sauce packs a wallop: five of the seven ingredients contribute a tang ranging from piquant to fiery hot. The soy sauce and the touch of sugar do tone down the mixture a bit, and the scallions and minced Chinese turnip or radish add a crispness and softness, thereby increasing the interest of this sauce.

We began using Szechwan Sauce to go with the puffy Steamed Buns. However, we soon found that we liked it with other dumplings as well, and we now use it also to flavor mild soups and some rice and noodle dishes. Szechwan Sauce is devoured in quantity at the annual Chinese banquet held at our synagogue. One year I made a note that ten times the basic recipe was not enough. I doubled that the next year, which was just about right for the 120 people who came to our "Teahouse of the Cheshvan Moon."

¼ cup "hot" oil, purchased or homemade (see recipe, page 126)
¼ cup soy sauce
4 teaspoons red wine vinegar
1 teaspoon sugar
4 or 5 large cloves garlic, finely chopped
3 to 4 tablespoons minced Chinese hot turnip or radish with chili
4 scallions (white and crisp green parts), chopped

Combine all the ingredients in a small mixing bowl. If you do not serve the Szechwan Sauce right away, stir it again just before serving. This sauce is at its best within a day of preparation, because the scallions soften quickly. To prepare it a few days ahead, mix together everything but the scallions; add them at the last minute. Leftovers can be stored in the refrigerator.

Very Tasty Soy Sauce
美味醬汁
Mei Wei Jiang Zhi

Szechwan

Makes about ½ cup

This subtly spicy sauce is used for Very Tasty Cold Chicken, but it also makes a very good condiment when served separately. It is more mellow than Szechwan Sauce, much like a beautifully enriched soy sauce blend of sweet, salty, and spicy, textured with dots of scallion, ginger root, Szechwan peppercorns, and garlic.

¼ cup soy sauce
2 tablespoons honey
1 clove garlic, finely chopped
2 tablespoons peanut, corn, or other oil
2 scallions (white and crisp green parts), chopped
1½ teaspoons minced ginger root
½ teaspoon Szechwan peppercorns, crushed with the side of a cleaver
¼ teaspoon crushed dried red pepper

In a small mixing bowl, stir together the soy sauce, honey, and garlic; set aside. In a 1-quart pot, combine the remaining ingredients. Cook this mixture over low heat for 3 minutes, until sizzling hot. The ingredients should not brown. Stir the hot mixture into the soy sauce mixture, blending very well Serve the sauce immediately, or cool and transfer to a covered jar. You may store it at room temperature for a day or two, but after that time place it in the refrigerator, where it will keep for about a week. Bring the sauce up to room temperature before serving.

Fresh Ginger Sauce
生薑五味汁
Sheng Jiang Wu Wei Zhi

Szechwan influence

Makes about ½ cup

A gingery version of Very Tasty Soy Sauce. The ginger flavor dominates, but it is tempered by the honey, resulting in a sweet yet tangy taste.

¼ cup soy sauce
2 tablespoons honey
1 clove garlic, minced
1 tablespoon peanut, corn, or other oil
1 slice (1 inch diameter, 1 inch thick) ginger root, minced
¼ teaspoon crushed dried red pepper

In a small mixing bowl, combine the soy sauce, honey, and garlic; set aside. Put the oil, minced ginger root, and crushed red pepper in a 1-quart pot. Heat over medium-low heat until the mixture is sizzling but not browned, which will take about 3 minutes. Blend the hot ingredients into the soy sauce mixture, stirring well. Serve warm or at room temperature. Store the sauce in a covered container. It will keep for several days at room temperature and for two weeks in the refrigerator.

Hot Bean Sauce
香辣豆醬
Xiang La Dou Jiang

Hunan influence

Makes ½ cup

This is a rich and flavorful hot dip that begins with the very spicy canned hot bean sauce. Bits of bean and scallion contribute to the robust character of the sauce. Top a dish of plain noodles with a tablespoon of this mixture, or use it as a condiment for white-cut chicken, dumplings, *tofu*, or fish.

2 tablespoons hot bean sauce
2 tablespoons ketchup
2 tablespoons soy sauce
Dash of sesame oil
4 scallions (white and crisp green parts), chopped

In a small bowl, combine the ingredients. This mixture should be refrigerated after a day or two, but bring it back to room temperature before serving. It will keep for about a week in a tightly covered jar in the refrigerator.

Sesame Sauce

芝麻醬

Zhi Ma Jiang

General China influence

Makes ½ cup

Sesame-based sauces are used in Chinese cooking as dips and to dress salads. This smooth, tasty dip starts with sesame paste, which is made from ground sesame seeds and tastes like unsweetened *halvah*. Sesame paste, sold as *tahini* or *tahina* in Middle Eastern groceries and in health food stores, is also available in Asian groceries. It can be made at home by pulverizing sesame seeds in a blender with a little water.

This Sesame Sauce, a mixture of sesame paste and sesame oil, has the consistency of Chinese Mustard (page 122). It tastes much like a thickened sesame oil and can be served as is or perked up with the addition of a little liquid hot pepper. The sauce makes a wonderful dip for barbecued meats and Chinese hot pots. Drizzle it over salads and *tofu* cubes for a unique dressing.

½ cup sesame paste
2 tablespoons sesame oil
A few drops of hot pepper sauce, such as Tabasco (to taste)

In a small bowl, mix together the sesame paste and oil. Stir in the liquid hot pepper. Taste a dab, and add more hot pepper as desired. Store at room temperature for up to 3 weeks.

Sesame-Peanut Butter Sauce

花生香醬

Hua Sheng Xiang Jiang

General China influence

Makes ⅓ cup

One of the rabbis at the synagogue we once belonged to used to say that when a prospective member came up to him after a service and said, "That was interesting, Rabbi," he knew he'd never see that person again. So it was that I was wary when I began experimenting with the following sauce and found myself saying, "Now, that's interesting." When I added soy sauce to a peanut butter-sesame oil-lemon juice combination, I expected the mixture to thin out, but it became thicker and more like a spread. My husband's first reaction was, "That's great if you like salt bagels." I switched from a light and very salty soy sauce to a dark, less salty soy, and the mixture wasn't quite as salty, although it still thickened.

The sauce below has the consistency of a spread, and it is indeed interesting—with four strong tastes coming through all at once. Use it as a dip for raw vegetables, barbecued meats, and plain cooked meats.

¼ cup peanut butter, preferably all-natural with no additives
1 tablespoon fresh lemon juice
2 teaspoons sesame oil
1 to 3 teaspoons soy sauce
Water

In a medium-size bowl, blend together the first 3 ingredients. Add soy sauce to taste. Thin the mixture as necessary with water. Store in the refrigerator; it will keep for months but will thicken. Thin again by blending in water to the consistency desired.

Salad Dressings

涼拌調味品

Liang Ban Tiao Wei Pin

The three dressings which follow are intended to add zest to raw or blanched vegetables. They are all variations on the same theme: sesame oil, soy sauce, and vinegar (the basics) plus sweet, hot, or spicy ingredients (the accessories). The Sesame Sauce and Sesame-Peanut Butter Sauce that precede these recipes also make excellent salad dressings. Use all the dressings sparingly—they are meant to enliven, not to inundate, the salad.

Dressing I

Peking

Makes about ½ cup

Ginger root adds pungency and scallions bring texture to this sweetened dressing.

1 teaspoon minced ginger root
2 scallions (white and crisp green parts), chopped
3 tablespoons soy sauce
2 tablespoons sesame oil
2 tablespoons rice vinegar or red wine vinegar
1 tablespoon sugar

In a small bowl, combine all the ingredients. Store the dressing at room temperature in a tightly covered jar. It will keep for a few days, but the scallions will soften after a while.

Dressing II

Peking

Makes ½ cup

Equal amounts of vinegar, oil, soy sauce, and sugar make this an easy recipe to remember. Vinegar and oil with seasonings will remind you of a classic French dressing, but when the oil is sesame oil and one of the seasonings is a heavy dose of soy sauce, you know you're reading a Chinese recipe. The dressing gets a hot and spicy touch from crushed red pepper and garlic.

2 tablespoons rice vinegar or red wine vinegar
2 tablespoons sesame oil
2 tablespoons soy sauce
2 tablespoons sugar
¼ teaspoon crushed dried red pepper
1 clove garlic, finely chopped

In a small bowl, combine all the ingredients. Store the dressing at room temperature in a tightly covered jar. It will keep for several weeks.

Dressing III

Peking

Makes ½ cup

This dressing uses the basics of soy sauce, sesame oil, and vinegar, but it is much thicker than the previous two recipes, with much the consistency of Sesame Sauce (page 133). Its color (tan) is that of the sesame paste, not the soy sauce.

2 tablespoons sesame paste
2 teaspoons sesame oil
¼ cup soy sauce
2 tablespoons rice vinegar or wine vinegar
1 clove garlic, finely chopped
Water

In a small bowl, stir the sesame paste with the sesame oil until smooth. Blend in the remaining ingredients. Store the dressing for a few days in a covered jar at room temperature. It should be refrigerated for longer storage, although it will thicken. Thin with water as necessary.

Fresh Ginger Root, Garlic, and Scallions
清香三調味
Qing Xiang San Tiao Wei

Peking

Yield flexible

This splendid combination of seasonings, which is intended to be used with other recipes, can make the most mundane dish special. The moment these three ingredients come into contact with hot cooking oil, a unique aromatic spicy pungency is released, awakening the appetite before the food is even cooked. After the flavors are released, meats and vegetables are added to the pan and stir-fried with the seasonings.

The combination of ginger, garlic, and scallions reflects the deliciousness of good Peking cooking, which seasons, enhances, and enriches but does not mask the basic food. These seasonings work well in stir-fried dishes, which are so quickly cooked that their flavor isn't dissipated. They are especially good with stir-fried vegetables, fried rice, *lo mien,* and broiled chicken livers.

The amounts of fresh ginger root, garlic, and scallions you use can be varied to suit personal taste, but fresh ingredients are a must. Powdered or freeze-dried substitutes will not do. If you have Szechwan peppercorns on hand, use them for increased fragrance and their pleasant spiciness.

2 tablespoons peanut, corn, or other oil
1 piece (1 inch thick) ginger root, minced
4 large cloves garlic, minced
4 scallions (white and crisp green parts), chopped
1 teaspoon crushed Szechwan peppercorns (optional)

Heat the oil to 375 degrees F. Stir-fry the ginger root, garlic, scallions, and peppercorns for 30 to 60 seconds. Now add your first vegetable or meat, stir-frying as directed in the recipe you are preparing. Proceed as directed in the recipe.

Soy Sauce and Rice Wine (Sherry) Marinades

醃泡調味汁

Yan Pao Tiao Wei Zhi

Canton

Soy sauce and rice wine, in combination, are the basis of the meat marinades used in Chinese cooking, particularly those used to prepare the meats for the stir-fried dishes of southern China. Dry sherry substitutes for rice wine in the United States with fine results. Cornstarch, sugar, and ginger root are frequent additions, and scallions and garlic are used also.

Thin slices of uncooked meat, poultry, or fish, are combined with small quantities of soy sauce and wine, but not for too long. The seasonings should contribute to the tastiness of the dish, not play a commanding role. The meat usually stands in the marinade for a period of only ten to twenty minutes before being cooked, just long enough for the marinade to cling to the meat. The moment the meat is removed from the marinade, it goes right into the pan and the stir-frying begins. The quality of the marinade is important, for it may be the primary flavoring of the dish. Here is a typical marinade for half a pound of thinly sliced beef.

1 tablespoon cornstarch
2 tablespoons soy sauce
1 tablespoon rice wine or dry sherry

⟶

1 teaspoon sugar
2 slices (1/8 inch thick) ginger root
2 scallions (white and crisp green parts), cut into 1-inch pieces

In a medium-size bowl, toss the meat with the cornstarch, then mix in the remaining ingredients. Let the mixture stand for 20 minutes. Remove the ginger root and scallions before the cooking begins.

Egg White Coatings

蛋白糊

Dan Bai Hu

General China

Egg white and cornstarch mixtures, sometimes seasoned with soy sauce or salt, are often used to coat chicken and fish before they are stir-fried or deep-fried. The coating keeps the pieces of food separated and gives them a light crust. Heavier batters are used for more substantial crusts. The simple, light mixture here is for half a pound of uncooked chicken (boneless) or fish, cut into shreds or cubes. Deep-fried chicken pieces (bone in) come out with a lovely crisp coating when they are dipped into this batter before they are fried.

1 egg white (from an egg graded large)
2 tablespoons cornstarch
1 teaspoon soy sauce

In a medium-size bowl, combine the egg white and cornstarch with a fork until the cornstarch is blended in very smoothly. It is not necessary to beat the egg white. Stir in the soy sauce. Mix the chicken or fish with the egg white mixture, stirring gently but thoroughly to coat all the pieces.

Red Bean Paste (Sweetened)

豆沙

Dou Sha

General China

Makes 2 cups

I thought perhaps red bean paste was something you had to grow up with to enjoy, but I found out that at least some Chinese children don't like it any more than mine do. The paste is not served plain as a condiment or a garnish, but it finds its way into diverse stews and fillings, where it adds color, body, and a subtle flavor. Its bean flavor and thick, pasty texture are most apparent in desserts, where its presence is considered a treat (by adults).

Red bean paste can be purchased in cans, but if you can get hold of the beans, it is a simple matter to make it yourself. The beans are a dark red, the color of kidney beans, which can in fact be substituted in a pinch. A minimum amount of water is used in the processing, which makes for a very thick purée.

Sweetened red bean paste was used in testing the recipes in this book, and it should be used in making pastries and desserts. If you want to avoid sugar, don't sweeten red bean paste that is to be used in stews and meat fillings.

1 cup Chinese red beans
2 cups water, plus additional water as necessary
½ cup sugar

Wash the beans. Place them in a 2-quart pot with 2 cups of water. Bring the water to a boil, reduce the heat so the water boils gently, cover the pot, and simmer the beans for 1½ to 2 hours, until very tender. Add a little water from time to time if the beans begin to dry out. They should always be covered with water.

With a slotted spoon, transfer the beans to the container of a food processor or a food mill. Purée the beans until very smooth, adding water only if needed to process them. Blend in the sugar. Red bean paste must be refrigerated. It can be frozen, but unlike the more salty bean sauces, it freezes solidly. You might want to freeze the paste in ice cube trays so you have to defrost only a little at a time, as many recipes call for solely a tablespoon or two.

Red-cooked (Starter) Sauces

滷汁

Lu Zhi

Fukien

Makes 3 cups

Although Fukien is most famous for it, red-cooking is a classic cooking method used all over China. It involves cooking meat slowly in soy sauce, which flavors the meat and turns it a reddish color. The addition of just a few select spices or a sweet and pungent mixture transforms the sauce into a savory gravy. Any leftover gravy is saved and used to start the next red-cooked dish. Throughout this book I refer to this leftover gravy from a red-cooked dish as Red-cooked Starter Sauce.

Of the two sets of ingredients below, the first produces a spicier sauce, with an anise flavor that is perceptible but not too strong. The second recipe calls for ginger root, lemon juice, and sugar, and comes out tasting remarkably like a subdued version of the first. Both start with three cups of liquid, combining a cup of soy sauce and two cups of water. Two cups of any leftover starter sauce can be combined with one cup of water for an even richer beginning. *Tamari* and mushroom soy sauce are recommended for red-cooking, because they are less salty than many other soys.

Red-cooked Sauce I

1 cup soy sauce
2 cups water
2 whole star anise
1 stick cinnamon
¼ teaspoon whole cloves

Red-cooked Sauce II

1 cup soy sauce
2 cups water
Juice of 1 large lemon
2 teaspoons grated or minced ginger root
2 tablespoons firmly packed light or dark brown sugar

Combine the ingredients for the sauce in a pot that will be big enough to hold the meat you will be cooking. Bring the ingredients to the boil, then add the meat, poultry, or fish. Reduce the heat to a gentle boil, cover the pot, and simmer the meat until very tender, turning it occasionally if it isn't completely covered by the sauce. Refrigerate or freeze leftover sauce, and use 2 cups of it to replace the soy sauce and 1 cup of the water in the recipes for Red-cooked Sauce

Sweet-and-Pungent Sauces

甜酸汁

Tian Suan Zhi

Sweet-and-pungent (or sweet-and-sour) sauces are used in Chinese cooking in combination with meat, poultry, fish, fried *wontons*, dumplings, *tofu*, and other vegetables. They are usually prepared separately and poured, hot, over the cooked foods. There are numerous recipes in this book for sweet-and-pungent sauces. The most delicate and loveliest of all relies on pineapple and sweet pickle juices for the sweet-and-sour effect. The others use sugar and vinegar as their foundation. Modifications include the addition of lemon juice, chicken broth, and Chinese vegetables. Four recipes are presented here to illustrate some of the variations.

Sweet-and-Pungent Sauce I

Canton

Makes 1½ cups

This mellow sauce uses pineapple and sweet pickle juices to create a perfect sweet-and-pungent combination. Garlic is used to lightly flavor the oil; it is removed before the other ingredients are added. This sauce can be used without reservation in all recipes calling for a sweet-and-pungent or sweet-and-sour sauce. Even if you never eat the pickles, it's worth keeping the sweet pickle juice on hand.

1 tablespoon peanut oil
2 large cloves garlic, each cut in half
1 cup unsweetened pineapple juice
½ cup pickle juice from a jar of sweet pickles
2 tablespoons soy sauce
1 tablespoon cornstarch dissolved in ¼ cup cold water

In a 1-quart pot, over moderate heat, heat the oil. Add the garlic and let it sizzle in the oil for a few seconds, then stir the garlic around for a minute. Remove the garlic. Add the pineapple and pickle juices and the soy sauce. Bring the mixture to the boil. Stir the cornstarch and water together until smooth, then blend the cornstarch paste into the sauce. Turn off the heat, or turn it down to low, as soon as the mixture thickens and is smooth. Cornstarch-thickened products do not freeze well, but the sauce can be refrigerated and reheated over low heat.

Sweet-and-Pungent Sauce II

Honan

Makes 1¼ cups

This sweet-and-pungent sauce has sugar and vinegar as its base. The quantities of these ingredients can be adjusted to suit personal taste. If you substitute some lemon juice for part of the vinegar, the taste will be a bit more sour but less sharp.

Ketchup is added to the sauce for extra richness. Although this tomato product is not authentically Chinese, it has a place here because it enhances the sauce without dominating.

5 tablespoons sugar
¼ cup rice vinegar or red wine vinegar
2 tablespoons ketchup
1 tablespoon soy sauce
½ cup water
1 tablespoon cornstarch dissolved in ¼ cup cold water

In a 1-quart pot, combine the sugar, vinegar, ketchup, soy sauce, and ½ cup of water. Bring the mixture to the boil over medium heat, stirring often. Let the mixture boil for a minute, then stir in the cornstarch-and-water paste to thicken the liquid. Keep the sauce warm over low heat until ready to use.

Sweet-and-Pungent Sauce III

Southern and eastern China

Makes about 1½ cups

Here, Chinese vegetables give the basic sweet-and-pungent sauce added interest. The respectively chewy, crisp, and crunchy textures of the mushrooms, snow peas, and water chestnuts make this especially nice served over soft foods such as *tofu* and poached fish.

4 medium-size dried Chinese mushrooms
Boiling water
6 snow peas, tips and strings removed, sliced on the diagonal into ¼-inch pieces
6 water chestnuts, sliced
½ cup sugar
6 tablespoons rice vinegar or wine vinegar
2 tablespoons soy sauce
2 tablespoons tomato sauce
1 tablespoon cornstarch dissolved in ¼ cup cold water

Place the Chinese mushrooms in a bowl and add enough boiling water to cover—the water must cover the mushrooms completely. Soak them until softened, about 15 minutes. Drain the mushrooms and slice them thinly, discarding the stems. Combine the mushrooms, snow peas, and water chestnuts and set aside.

In a 1-quart pot, mix together the sugar, vinegar, soy sauce, and tomato sauce. Bring the mixture to the boil over moderate heat; boil for 1 minute. Now add the vegetables and continue to cook a minute or two longer. Stir the cornstarch and water until smooth, then add this mixture to the sauce, stirring until the sauce is smooth and thickened. Turn the heat to low and keep the sauce warm until ready to serve.

Sweet-and-Pungent Sauce IV

Fukien influence

Makes 1½ cups

Chicken broth and lemon juice are featured in this sauce, which is especially nice with chicken.

1 cup seasoned chicken broth
2 tablespoons rice vinegar or distilled white vinegar
2 tablespoons fresh lemon juice
¼ cup sugar
1 tablespoon cornstarch dissolved in 2 tablespoons cold chicken broth

In a 1-quart pot, combine the chicken broth, vinegar, lemon juice, and sugar. Bring the mixture to the boil; boil for about a minute. Mix together the cornstarch and 2 tablespoons of cold chicken broth, then stir them into the sauce, cooking until the sauce is thickened. Turn the heat to very low and keep warm until ready to serve.

3

Congees and Soups

"Chicken Broth and Congee" could be the title of a book about Chinese soups. Chicken broth is used as the base for many soups, and it is also used extensively in sauces in Cantonese cooking. The home cook all over China makes chicken broth from all the edible parts of the chicken that aren't used for other dishes. However, when you see chicken broth called for in a recipe, use whatever you would for *kreplach* or *knaidlach* soup. Of course, a rich homemade chicken stock is best, but there are satisfactory alternatives available in this country.

Fish skins and bones are used for broth in Chinese home cooking much the same as chicken skins and bones. However, because fish broths are generally stronger-tasting than chicken- or vegetable-based broths and hence can take over in a recipe, I tend not to use them in Chinese cooking. For a simple homemade vegetarian broth to use in recipes containing fish, cook three stalks of Chinese cabbage, two scallions, a carrot or two, a clove of garlic, a thin slice of ginger root, and salt to taste in a quart of water until the vegetables are tender. Simmer about half an hour. For extra richness, allow the vegetables to remain in the liquid for an additional half hour before straining the broth.

Congee—a home-style thick rice soup known universally in China—is served for breakfast or throughout the day as a snack. It is inexpensive, uses readily available ingredients, and is easy to prepare. There are basic recipes for congee, with probably as many variations as there are households in China.

At family meals in many parts of China, soup is set out with all the other dishes and is sipped during the meal or at the end of the meal in place of a beverage. The soup can be as basic as boiled greens served in their broth. Chinese banquets usually feature several soups, which appear between other courses. A heavy soup might be served after several stir-fried dishes, to be followed by the major attraction of the banquet (if there is one) and one or two other dishes. Then a clear, light soup refreshes the palate and quenches the thirst before the next series of dishes is served. There are also dessert soups, such as the Walnut "Tea" which appears in Chapter Nine.

Glutinous Rice Congee

糯米粥

Nuo Mi Zhou

General China

Serves 4

Congee, known as *jook* in Cantonese, is a thick cereal-like soup, a porridge, made by cooking a small amount of rice in a large quantity of water. The cooking time can be as brief as forty minutes or as long as six hours, depending on the recipe and the rice used. The two hours recommended in this recipe produces a congee with the consistency of a thick barley soup.

In China, glutinous rice is used to prepare congee, and rice from the new season is preferred because it is most sticky. The glutinous rice becomes puffy and very tender, and the broth itself is thick and has a glazed appearance. If the rice sticks to the bottom a bit between stirrings, the congee takes on a reddish hue.

Plain congee is very bland-tasting. Because of its soothing qualities, it is often fed to babies, the aged, and the infirm. As a breakfast food, it is served with something salty or spicy, but when combined with a little soy sauce and bits of meats or fish and vegetables, the soup makes a satisfying and tasty lunch or snack. Congee is usually cooked plain, then during the last few minutes uncooked ingredients are sprinkled into the thick soup and cooked. Congee is eaten with a porcelain spoon, although pieces of food are sometimes picked up with chopsticks.

Although you will probably find plain congee uninteresting, bear in mind that seasoned and spiced it becomes a pleasant change from more elaborate dishes. Start with the basic recipe, then follow some of the serving suggestions. Soon you will create dozens of variations of your own.

½ cup glutinous rice
6 cups cold water

In a 4-quart pot, combine the rice and the water. Bring the water to the boil, stirring occasionally. Reduce the heat until the water is gently boiling, then cover the pot and continue to simmer the rice for 2 hours. Stir at least every 20 minutes to keep the rice from sticking to the bottom of the pot. As the rice thickens, there is a tendency for the liquid to boil up and over, so watch the pot carefully and reduce the heat as necessary. Serve the congee plain or any of the ways suggested below. Leftover congee will keep for several days in the refrigerator. Reheat over low heat, stirring the rice occasionally to prevent sticking.

SERVING SUGGESTIONS

For Meat Meals:

1. *Variation on Basic Congee:* Substitute chicken broth for the water in preparing the congee. This will produce a more flavorful congee no matter what seasonings and additional ingredients are used.
2. *Chinese Lunch, Light Dinner, or Snack:* Prepare the congee with chicken bones, rice, and water. Remove the bones before serving. Season the congee, and add other ingredients as desired (see suggestions 3 through 7).
3. *Chinese Lunch or Light Dinner I:* During the last 15 minutes of cooking, drop in small uncooked meatballs made of minced or ground beef mixed with water chestnuts, scallions, soy sauce, and any other ingredients of choice.
4. *Chinese Lunch or Light Dinner II:* Cut the meat of a whole chicken breast into ⅛-inch cubes. Combine with a little soy sauce and sherry, and add the chicken to the congee during the last 5 minutes of cooking. Serve with additional soy sauce and chopped scallions.
5. *Chinese Lunch or Light Dinner III:* Add 2 whole chicken legs to the congee during the last half-hour of cooking. When the meat is cooked through, chop the legs—bone and all—into 1-inch pieces and mix them back into the congee. Season with soy sauce and ginger root.
6. *Lunch or Dinner—American Style I:* Five minutes before serving, mix in 1 cup of diced cooked lamb, 1 can of mushrooms (with their liquid if the congee is very thick), and 1 package of frozen peas, thawed. Cook until the peas are hot.
7. *Lunch or Dinner—American Style II:* Ten minutes before the cooking time is over, add 2 cups diced uncooked beef that has been tossed with soy sauce and sherry. (Two cups would be a lot for a Chinese meal, and the Chinese family would eat pork, not beef.) Serve the congee with additional soy sauce and chopped scallions.

For a Dairy Meal:

8. *Chinese Breakfast—American Style:* Serve with milk, brown or white sugar, and cut-up fresh or canned fruit

For Pareve Meals:

9. *Chinese Breakfast I:* Season with soy sauce, then poach eggs in the congee just before serving.
10. *Chinese Breakfast II:* Season with soy sauce, then serve with salted hard-cooked eggs and/or spicy Chinese pickles.
11. *Chinese Breakfast, Snack, or Lunch:* Just before serving the congee, stir in beaten eggs. Serve with a spicy vegetable or a relish.
12. *Chinese Snack:* During the last 5 minutes of cooking, mix in 2 tablespoons of shredded ginger root; add soy sauce to taste. Top off individual servings with chopped scallions.
13. *Chinese Snack or Dessert—American Style:* Mix the cooked rice with ½ cup sugar, 1 teaspoon ground cinnamon, ¼ teaspoon ground nutmeg, 2 tablespoons *pareve* margarine, and 1 teaspoon vanilla extract. Remove the pot from the heat. Stir in 1 well-beaten egg. Transfer the rice to a heatproof casserole and broil it until very lightly browned. Watch the rice constantly so it does not burn. Cool the dish to room temperature, then refrigerate and serve this rice pudding cold.
14. *Chinese Lunch or Light Dinner IV:* Season with soy sauce and grated ginger root. Top individual bowls of the congee with stir-fried vegetables.
15. *Chinese Lunch or Light Dinner V:* Combine 1 cup of shredded uncooked fresh fish with 1 teaspoon grated ginger root and 1 tablespoon soy sauce. Add to the congee 5 minutes before the cooking time is over. Serve with additional soy sauce and chopped scallions.
16. *Chinese Lunch or Light Dinner VI:* Five minutes before serving, add ½ cup sliced dried Chinese mushrooms which have been soaked in boiling water and the stems discarded. Just before serving, add soy sauce to taste, stir in 4 beaten eggs, and season with 1 tablespoon of sesame oil. Garnish the individual servings of congee with chopped scallions.
17. *Chinese or American-style Lunch or Snack:* During the last 5 minutes of cooking, add 1 cup of sliced fresh mushrooms and ¼ pound of well-washed fresh spinach leaves, shredded. Season the congee with soy sauce, and garnish it with chopped scallions.

18. Use your imagination. Good luck!

White Rice Congee

稀飯

Xi Fan

General China influence

Serves 4

Glutinous rice and brown rice are the everyday rices of China. White rice, which is so readily available in the United States, is a sign of prosperity in China, and as such it would not ordinarily be served at a home-cooked meal. (For further discussion on the various types of rice used in China, see Chapter Eight—Rice, Noodles, and Breads.)

After two hours of cooking, white rice breaks down much more than glutinous rice and the resulting congee is not as chewy as that made with the glutinous rice. Whereas the white rice falls apart completely when bitten into, the glutinous rice retains a little substance. Short-grain rice produces a congee a little more sticky than the long-grain rice.

The broth of this White Rice Congee is white, so the soup looks like a creamy rice pudding made with milk. It is very bland in taste and texture, and benefits from the addition of sauces, meats or fish, and vegetables.

½ cup white rice, long-grain or short-grain
6 cups cold water

In a 4-quart pot, combine the rice and the water. Cook and serve as directed in the preceding recipe for Glutinous Rice Congee.

Brown Rice Congee

黄稀飯

Huang Xi Fan

General China

Serves 4

Brown rice made into congee takes additional cooking to evaporate enough water to thicken the broth. The congee has bits of bran here and there, adding coarseness to the otherwise soft rice. Because the rice has the bran covering, congee made from brown rice is more nutritious than white rice congee. Brown rice congee, which is light tan in color, is somewhere between the nearly disintegrated white rice and the slightly chewy glutinous rice congee in texture.

½ cup brown rice
6 cups cold water

In a 4-quart pot, combine the rice and the water. Bring the water to the boil, then reduce the heat so the water boils gently. Cover the pot and continue to simmer the rice for 2 hours, stirring every half-hour or as necessary to keep the rice from sticking to the bottom of the pot. The rice will be tender at this point, but the broth will be thin. To thicken the broth, remove the lid and regulate the heat so the water continues to boil. Cook the rice an additional 15 to 30 minutes, stirring occasionally, until the congee thickens to the consistency desired. See the recipe for Glutinous Rice Congee for serving suggestions.

Chicken Broth

雞湯

Ji Tang

General China influence

Makes about 4 quarts

If you ask 100 Jewish cooks how to make chicken soup, you'll get at least 150 recipes, and probably a lot of arguments about the virtues of one over another. The recipe here is for a chicken broth made from uncooked chicken necks, backs, gizzards, bones, and skin, which I accumulate and freeze when I cut up whole chickens and bone the breasts. In the tradition of my Grandma Jennie, who never wasted a thing, after the broth is strained, I pick the meat off the cooked bones and use that for croquettes, fried rice, or chicken-mushroom *kreplach*.

Chicken broth made from parts that might otherwise be discarded is perhaps not as rich as soup made from a stewing hen, but it is much more economical and has a fine flavor. The recipe here follows the example of all Chinese cooking, because the method is more important than the exact ingredients or quantities used.

Uncooked chicken bones, wing tips, necks, backs, gizzards, skin, etc., enough to fill an 8-quart pot up to 4 inches from the top
Water

→

A selection of washed fresh vegetables, such as 2 or 3 whole carrots, unpeeled; 2 or 3 stalks celery; 2 stalks bok choy or other Chinese cabbage; 2 whole onions, peeled
Seasonings: 2 to 4 cloves garlic; a good handful of fresh chives; fresh parsley; salt to taste

Select a heavy 8-quart pot that will hold the chicken bones with at least 4 inches to spare on top. Add enough water to cover the chicken bones by ½ inch. Scatter around the vegetables and the seasonings except for the salt. Bring the water to the boil, then reduce the heat to the simmer. Cover the pot partially and cook for about 2 hours, until the meat and skin are tender and the thinner bones are beginning to soften. After the first hour of cooking, add salt to taste. Stir the contents occasionally and keep an eye on the pot to make sure it doesn't boil over.

When the broth is done, remove all the bones and vegetables with a slotted spoon. Skim off the fat and save it in a heatproof jar (refrigerate or freeze the chicken fat when cool), or discard it in a metal container. (Don't pour fat down the drain.) To strain the broth, line a strainer or colander with a single layer of sturdy white paper towels. Place the strainer in a clean 4- to 6-quart pot, and ladle the soup into the strainer. The soup will pass through the towel while the fat stays on top. Change the paper towels as necessary. Put the strained chicken broth into plastic freezer containers, leaving 1 inch of headspace. (Liquid expands as it freezes, and glass is never recommended for freezing—it may crack.) When the broth is cool, refrigerate it or freeze for later use. Chicken broth can also be frozen in ice cube trays then transferred to a freezer bag for use when a small quantity of chicken broth is needed for a sauce.

Wonton Wrappers I

餛飩皮 (一)

Hun Tun Pi (Yi)

Canton

Makes 32 wrappers

Wonton soup is a familiar item not only in Chinese restaurants but also in the frozen food departments of many supermarkets. There are ready-made kosher *wontons* available that may say "Wonton (Kreplach) Soup" on the labels. As sold in the United States, the difference between kosher *wontons* and *kreplach* is largely a matter of the seasonings used and the shape of the filled pockets of noodle dough.

Wonton wrappers can be store-bought or prepared at home. The light and tender egg dough of this recipe is similar in texture to commercially prepared wrappers, but because it has more egg, it also has more taste. The recipe for Wonton Wrappers II, which follows, substitutes a second egg for part of the liquid, making a more substantial dough.

Wonton fillings should be prepared before the wrappers are made. Two recipes for fillings (pages 152 and 154) follow Wonton Wrappers I and II. Or, prepare any filling of your choice—approximately one cup of filling is used for 32 wrappers.

2 cups unsifted all-purpose flour
½ teaspoon salt (optional)
1 egg (graded large), beaten
½ cup cold water, approximately

In a medium-size to large mixing bowl, combine the flour and salt. With a fork, stir in the egg, then gradually add the water, stirring rapidly until the dough forms a ball. Knead gently for a minute or two, until the dough is smooth. Cover the dough with the mixing bowl or with plastic wrap and let it rest for 10 minutes.

Divide the dough in half. Keep one half covered, and on a floured surface roll out the other half to a 12-inch square. Cut the dough into sixteen 3-inch squares. Divide half of the filling (page 152 or 154) among the squares, placing a rounded teaspoonful of filling just off-center on each square. Following the diagrams on page 77, fold the dough over the filling to form a triangle. Press together the edges of the dough to firmly enclose the filling—if you stopped at this point you would have *kreplach*. Bring the tips of the long edge of the triangle back behind the folded edge, pinch together the tips of the dough—now you have *wontons*. Repeat the procedure with the other half of dough. The *wontons* can be tray-frozen at this stage.

To cook the wontons, in a 5- to 6-quart pot bring 3 or 4 quarts of chicken broth to the boil. Drop in the *wontons* and cook them for 4 to 7 minutes, until the dough is tender. Taste one after the minimum time. Keep the broth boiling, but not too violently or the dough will toughen.

Wonton Wrappers II

餛飩皮（二）

Hun Tun Pi (Er)

Canton

Makes 32 wrappers

This rich egg dough can also be used for *lo mien* or other noodles. It is heavier and more substantial than commercially prepared *wonton* wrappers, and it has more of a taste of its own. The rolled-out dough is thicker than that of the purchased wrappers and it requires a few more minutes of cooking—and a little more chewing.

2 cups unsifted all-purpose flour
½ teaspoon salt (optional)
2 eggs (graded large)
¼ cup cold water or chicken broth, approximately

In a large bowl, mix together the flour and the salt. With your fingers, work in the eggs. Now work in the water or chicken broth, 1 tablespoonful at a time, to make a soft but not sticky dough. Form the dough into a ball and turn it out onto a clean, floured surface. Invert the mixing bowl over the dough and let the dough rest, covered, for 10 minutes.

Continue as directed in the preceding recipe, Wonton Wrappers I. Follow the cooking directions, increasing the cooking time to 7 to 10 minutes.

Wonton Soup

餛飩湯

Hun Tun Tang

Canton

Makes 32 wontons, serves 6

In China, *wontons* are almost invariably filled with pork. *Wonton* soup may appear on the table with other dishes, or it may be a complete luncheon meal in which as many as a dozen *wontons* are served in a small amount of broth. Garnishes of cooked greens, chopped scallions, and ham are used in China.

In the United States, *wonton* soup is most often served as a course preceding the main dish(es), although it can be presented as a complete lunch also. Chinese-American restaurants tend to garnish *wonton* soup with *bok choy* and strips of barbecued meat. Other garnishes can be used to further enhance the soup.

Cook the *wontons* directly in the chicken broth to increase the flavor of both the broth and the *wontons*. Some of the broth will be absorbed by the wrappers, and some will evaporate during the cooking, so start with a larger quantity of chicken broth than you hope to end up with.

½ pound minced beef
2 tablespoons chicken broth or water
1 teaspoon peanut, corn, or other oil
1 tablespoon soy sauce
1 tablespoon dry sherry
2 tablespoons chopped scallions (white and tender green parts)
1 tablespoon cornstarch
½ teaspoon salt
½ teaspoon sugar
1 recipe Wonton Wrappers I (page 150) or Wonton Wrappers II (page 152), or 32 wonton wrappers, or 8 sheets egg roll wrappers
3 quarts seasoned chicken broth
Garnishes: chopped scallions (white and tender green parts); diagonally-cut strips of Chinese cabbage; bite-size pieces of fresh spinach, washed thoroughly; diced cooked chicken or beef; thinly sliced fresh mushrooms; sliced water chestnuts; dried Chinese mushrooms, soaked in hot water then sliced; fried noodles

Mix together the minced beef, 2 tablespoons of chicken broth or water, the oil, soy sauce, sherry, 2 tablespoons of chopped scallions, cornstarch, salt, and sugar. Use a fork or your fingers to distribute all the ingredients evenly.

Prepare a homemade dough, use *wonton* wrappers (which are cut to the right size), or cut each egg roll wrapper into 4 squares. Work with only 6 to 8 of the wrappers at a time, keeping the remainder covered with a clean kitchen towel so they do not dry out.

To wrap *wontons* made with a homemade dough, follow the directions for Wonton Wrappers I, page 150. To wrap *wontons* using commercially prepared wrappers, follow the same directions but seal the wrappers by moistening the edges lightly with an egg that has been beaten with a little water. *Wontons* can be tray-frozen before they are cooked. Do not thaw before cooking.

To cook the *wontons*, in a 5- or 6-quart pot bring the chicken broth to the boil. Gently drop in the *wontons*, bring the soup back to the boil, then lower the heat so the *wontons* cook gently—a rolling boil is likely to make them fall apart. For Wonton Wrappers I and commercially prepared wrappers, cook the *wontons* for 4 to 7 minutes, until the dough is tender and the filling is done. For Wonton Wrappers II, cook for 7 to 10 minutes. The soup with the *wontons* can now be refrigerated overnight and reheated over a low burner. Although cooked *wontons* can be frozen directly in the soup, they have a tendency to fall apart when reheated. They will taste as delicious but will no longer be so attractive.

Before serving the soup, have the garnishes at room temperature. In China, the vegetables would not be served raw to avoid potential hygienic problems, but in the United States the vegetables can be left in their crisp, uncooked state. If serving the soup in a tureen at the table, garnish the serving bowl with scallions, Chinese cabbage, and/or spinach for color. Place whatever garnishes you're offering (except for the fried noodles, which become soggy quickly in the soup) in each individual bowl in advance—this will ensure an even distribution of the garnishes. Serve the soup hot. Some people like to add soy sauce, Chinese mustard, or a spicy sauce, such as Szechwan Sauce, to their soup. The Chinese prefer not to mask the delicate flavor of the broth, so when you invite your Chinese friends over, you may not need to use these condiments (unless their tastes have become Westernized).

Red-cooked Brisket Wontons

醬肉餛飩

Jiang Rou Hun Tun

Fukien and Canton

Makes 32 wontons

These Red-cooked Brisket Wontons will add so much flavor to the soup that you can literally water it down if you need to stretch a meal for unexpected company. The recipe uses the savory top piece from Red-cooked Whole Brisket, combined with scallions and water chestnuts to increase the Chinese influence. Incidentally, the recipe calls for more filling than you will need for 32 *wontons*, because you won't be able to resist tasting the filling, and one little taste probably won't do, so I've given you leeway.

1 cup minced top piece of brisket from Red-cooked Whole Brisket (page 183)
4 scallions (white and crisp green parts), chopped
4 water chestnuts, chopped
1 egg (graded large), beaten
1 recipe homemade wonton wrappers, or 8 sheets egg roll wrappers, or 32 wonton wrappers
3 quarts seasoned chicken broth
Garnishes: chopped scallions (white and crisp green parts), diagonally-cut strips of Chinese cabbage, bite-size pieces of fresh spinach (washed thoroughly), thinly sliced fresh mushrooms

Mix together the minced brisket, chopped scallions and water chestnuts, and the beaten egg. Refrigerate the filling until ready to use. Prepare the homemade wrappers, or cut the egg roll skins into 4 squares each, or use commercially prepared *wonton* wrappers. Wrap and cook the *wontons* as directed in Wonton Wrappers I, page 150, or Wonton Soup, page 152. Garnish the serving bowl lavishly, and be sure each person gets some greens and mushrooms in each serving.

Beef-and-Vegetable Dumpling Soup

菜肉餛飩

Cai Rou Hun Tun

Canton and Peking

Makes about 48 dumplings

Offer your guests a change from the popular *wonton* soup. This variation uses a dumpling that's easier to shape than a *wonton*, with a very nice meat-vegetable filling. Either a homemade flour-and-water dough or commercially prepared egg roll skins can be used for the wrappers. The filling gets flavor from the typically Cantonese soy sauce and wine seasonings, and texture from the celery cabbage and scallions. The scallions also provide a zing, but they do not overpower.

This is a good recipe with which to experiment. There are many ingredients—minced ginger root, garlic, sweet red or green peppers, and bamboo shoots are some—that will contribute flavor if added in small quantities (a tablespoon or less).

The garnishes will also add interest. They are very important for color (scallions, *bok choy* leaves, Chinese mushrooms), texture (soft *tofu*, crunchy water chestnuts, chewy Chinese mushrooms), and taste.

6 stalks celery cabbage or other Chinese cabbage
½ pound beef, minced
½ cup chopped scallions (white and crisp green parts)
1 tablespoon soy sauce
1 tablespoon sherry
1 teaspoon sugar
1 pound egg wrappers, approximately, or 1 recipe dough in Northern Dumplings (page 79)
4 quarts chicken broth
Garnishes: chopped scallions (white and crisp green parts), ¼-inch cubes of cooked chicken, quartered or sliced fresh mushrooms, slices of presoaked dried Chinese mushrooms, slices of water chestnuts, shredded celery cabbage or bok choy, ¼-inch cubes of fresh bean curd (tofu)

Chop the cabbage finely, and squeeze it dry in paper towels or a clean kitchen towel. Mix together the cabbage, beef, scallions, soy sauce, sherry, and sugar.

Using a cookie cutter or scissors, cut 2½- to 3-inch rounds from the egg roll skins. Use the leftover bits and pieces for fried noodles. If you are using homemade wrappers, divide the homemade dough into quarters, and work with one part at a time. Divide the quarter into 12 pieces, then use a rolling pin to roll each piece out to a 3-inch circle. If the work surface is clean and the dough is not sticky, it may not be necessary to grease or flour the work surface. If the dough sticks, lightly grease or flour the work surface.

To fill, work with no more than a dozen wrappers at a time, keeping the remaining dough or wrappers covered to prevent drying out. Place a heaping teaspoonful of filling in the center of each circle. Moisten the edges with water. Fold the dough in half to make a semicircle, and press to seal the edges well. Now you can make fancy pleats or crimps in the top if you wish, being careful not to break the wrapper. Proceed to fill all wrappers. The dumplings can be tray-frozen at this point.

To cook the dumplings, in a 5- or 6-quart pot bring the chicken broth to the boil. Gently drop in the dumplings, and cook them for about 5 minutes, stirring occasionally. Taste to see if they're cooked through.

To serve the soup at the table from a tureen, garnish the soup attractively, and take care to ladle some of the garnishes into each bowl. Or, arrange the garnishes in the individual soup bowls before the bowls are set out, and at the table ladle the soup over the garnishes. If your dining table isn't too big, you can place the soup tureen in the center of the table, surrounded by the soup bowls. This is most attractive when using Chinese porcelain bowls and spoons.

Hot-and-Sour Soup

酸辣湯

Suan La Tang

Szechwan

Serves 4 to 6

This used to be considered a very unusual, exotic soup, but in recent years it has been popularized by restaurants featuring Szechwan cooking. The first time we served Hot-and-Sour Soup at a Chinese banquet the reception to it was lukewarm, and I couldn't help but notice that the expensive tree ears and Chinese mushrooms remained at the bottom of most bowls. Some years later, at our synagogue's annual banquet, we filled two five-quart crockpots with Hot-and-Sour Soup and could barely keep up with the demand.

Well-prepared Hot-and-Sour Soup will not be so peppery that it burns the throat, but it should provide an intriguing balance between the pungent vinegar and spicy peppers and the bland *tofu.* The tree ears, Chinese mushrooms, and tiger lily buds bring more of a chewy consistency than flavor, but they do add a "woodsy" taste important to the soup. Sesame oil is an essential flavor as well, but it should add a subtle dimension, not dominate.

¼ pound chicken or beef, cut into small cubes or shreds (optional)
1 teaspoon peanut, corn, or other oil
1 tablespoon dried tree ears
2 to 4 medium-size dried Chinese mushrooms
6 to 8 dried tiger lily buds (golden needles)

→

Boiling water
1 quart seasoned chicken broth
¼ cup thinly sliced bamboo shoots
¼ to ½ pound tofu, cut into ¼-inch cubes
1 teaspoon soy sauce
½ teaspoon sugar
2 to 3 tablespoons red wine vinegar
¼ teaspoon freshly ground black pepper
¼ teaspoon crushed dried red pepper
Salt to taste
2 tablespoons cornstarch dissolved in 3 tablespoons cold water
1 egg (graded large), beaten
1 to 3 teaspoons sesame oil, to taste

Mix the chicken or beef with the 1 teaspoon of oil so the meat will not stick together when it is cooked. Place the tree ears, dried Chinese mushrooms, and the tiger lily buds in a small heatproof mixing bowl. Pour in enough boiling water to cover; let these ingredients soak for 10 to 20 minutes, until softened. If all the water is absorbed, add more boiling water to cover. Drain off the water when the dried ingredients have softened. Cut up the larger pieces of tree ears, slice the mushrooms thinly, discarding the stems, and cut the golden needles in half or into thirds. Have all the remaining ingredients at hand before the cooking begins.

In a 2-quart pot, bring the chicken broth to the boil. Add the chicken or beef, tree ears, dried mushrooms, tiger lily buds, bamboo shoots, and *tofu*. Reduce the heat to a gentle boil and cook the soup for 4 to 5 minutes, until the meat is done. Stir the soup as necessary to keep the pieces of meat from sticking together. Now add the soy sauce, sugar, red wine vinegar, black pepper, and the crushed red pepper. Cook a minute longer, then taste the soup; add salt if necessary, then correct the other seasonings. The soup can be refrigerated or frozen before the cornstarch and egg are added.

To complete the cooking, bring the soup to the boil. Stir together the cornstarch and water until smooth, then blend the cornstarch paste into the soup. Turn off the heat as soon as the soup thickens. Add the beaten egg, stirring constantly. The egg will curdle to form long strands. Blend in the sesame oil and serve the soup, passing around additional sesame oil for those who like it. Leftovers can be refrigerated and reheated.

Vegetarian Hot-and-Sour Soup

素酸辣湯

Su Suan La Tang

Szechwan

Serves 4 to 6

This soup has the same pungent-peppery combination as the regular Hot-and-Sour Soup. Extra *tofu* is used both because it is the foundation of many vegetarian diets in this country and because it is an extremely important source of protein in China, especially in areas where both meat and fish are unavailable. A strict vegetarian will omit the egg, which will not alter the soup's flavor but will affect its appearance and texture.

1 tablespoon dried tree ears
4 medium-size dried Chinese mushrooms
8 dried tiger lily buds (golden needles)
Boiling water
1 quart seasoned vegetarian broth
¼ cup thinly sliced bamboo shoots
1 pound fresh firm tofu, or 4 cakes fresh tofu, cut into ½-inch cubes
1 tablespoon soy sauce
3 tablespoons wine vinegar
¼ teaspoon freshly ground black pepper
¼ teaspoon crushed dried red pepper
1 teaspoon sugar (optional)
2 tablespoons cornstarch dissolved in 3 tablespoons cold water
1 egg (graded large), beaten (optional)
1 to 3 teaspoons sesame oil, to taste

Place the tree ears, dried Chinese mushrooms, and the tiger lily buds in a small heatproof mixing bowl. Pour in enough boiling water to cover these ingredients and let them soak for 10 to 20 minutes, until softened. If all the water is absorbed, add more boiling water to cover. Drain off the water when the dried ingredients have softened. Cut up the larger pieces of tree ears, slice the mushrooms thinly, discarding the stems, and cut the golden needles in half or into thirds. Have all the remaining ingredients at hand before the cooking begins.

Bring the vegetable broth to the boil in a 2-quart pot. Add all the ingredients except the dissolved cornstarch, beaten egg, and sesame oil. Stir gently to mix, then simmer for a few minutes to blend the flavors.

Taste for seasoning, and adjust as necessary. The soup can be frozen at this point.

To complete the cooking, bring the soup to the boil, then stir in the dissolved cornstarch. Turn off the heat as soon as the soup thickens, then add the beaten egg, stirring constantly to distribute the strands of egg. Blend in the sesame oil. Pass around additional sesame oil when serving the soup.

Egg Drop Soup
蛋花湯
Dan Hua Tang

General China

Serves 4

This is a nice, light soup to serve with any Chinese meal, and it makes a wonderful extender if you're trying to stretch a dinner for unexpected company. The Chinese like to preserve the delicacy of light soups, and both the tomato sauce (which is not native to China) and the soy sauce are added in small enough quantities to increase the richness without taking over. The eggs cook instantly when they are stirred into the soup, forming irregular yellow strands throughout. The scallion garnish adds color, a crunchy texture, and a bit of pizazz.

1 quart chicken broth
1 tablespoon tomato sauce (optional)
1 tablespoon soy sauce
2 eggs, beaten
4 scallions (white and tender green parts), chopped

In a 2-quart pot, combine the chicken broth, tomato sauce, and soy sauce. Bring the soup to the boil, turn off the heat, then stir in the beaten eggs. Stir rapidly for about 30 seconds to distribute the eggs. Transfer the soup to a tureen or a serving bowl, sprinkle the scallions over the top, and serve at once.

Chicken and Corn Soup (Chicken Velvet Soup)
鷄茸玉米湯
Ji Rong Yu Mi Tang

Canton

Serves 6

It took me eighteen years to try this soup. First, it didn't seem Chinese enough. Second, I didn't see how the chicken could cook in such a limited amount of time. But when one evening I decided to try the soup, I was delighted to find that everyone loved it. The use of canned corn is of course a shortcut, as fresh ears of corn would be scraped in a more authentic recipe. Two cups of freshly scraped corn kernels can be substituted for the canned corn.

An important feature of this recipe is the egg whites, which are beaten until they form soft mounds and are added with the chicken just before the soup is served. The egg whites cook slightly but remain on top of the soup to look like puffy clouds. In the Chinese version, bits of ham are sprinkled on top, but the soup is very attractive and tasty without garnishes.

½ chicken breast
1 quart seasoned chicken broth
1 can (1 pound) corn kernels, drained
1 tablespoon cornstarch dissolved in ¼ cup cold water
3 egg whites (from eggs graded large)

Remove all the meat from half of an uncooked chicken breast; mince the meat with a sharp knife or cleaver or in a food processor. Set aside.

In a 3- or 4-quart pot (a 2-quart pot is too small), heat the chicken broth to boiling. Add the corn and again bring the soup to the boil. Stir together the cornstarch and water until very smooth, then blend the mixture into the boiling soup. When the soup is thickened, reduce the heat to low.

In a small mixing bowl with a whisk, or in the small bowl of an electric mixer, beat the egg whites until foamy. Continue to beat until the whites form soft mounds when the beaters are lifted. Gently mix the chicken into the egg whites, then stir this chicken and egg white mixture into the soup. Raise the heat to moderate, and stir the egg white mixture *very gently* so the chicken makes some contact with the hot broth but the egg whites don't dissolve into the soup. As soon as the soup comes back to the boil, transfer to a bowl and serve.

Cellophane Noodle Soup With Chicken and Mushrooms

鮮菇雞丁粉絲湯

Xiang Gu Ji Ding Fen Si Tang

General China

Serves 6 to 8

This is not chicken noodle soup the way grandma used to make it—unless grandma was Chinese. Cellophane noodles, or bean thread, become transparent when soaked in hot water, and they may seem to disappear into the soup. The elusive noodles are a bit slippery as well, but when you do catch them on the spoon, they are a nice surprise. The noodles pick up the flavor of the broth and are soft in texture, contrasting with the more substantial mushrooms and the chicken.

This is a light soup, well suited to the role of beverage. It is appropriate to serve as a first course, as one of several dishes in a Chinese family meal, or as a refreshing change between courses at a Chinese banquet.

8 ounces cellophane noodles
2 quarts chicken broth
2 tablespoons soy sauce
1 tablespoon tomato sauce
2 tablespoons peanut, corn, or other oil
¼ pound chicken, cut into ¼-inch cubes
½ pound fresh mushrooms, sliced
Chopped scallions (white and crisp green parts) for garnish

Soak the cellophane noodles in hot water for 10 mintues or until softened. Drain the noodles and, with kitchen scissors, cut them into 2-inch pieces. Place the noodles in a 3- or 4-quart pot with the chicken broth, soy sauce, and tomato sauce. Bring the soup to the boil, stirring occasionally, then reduce the heat and keep the soup warm while you cook the chicken and mushrooms.

In a wok or an 8-inch skillet, heat the oil until it is hot but not yet smoking. Stir-fry the chicken for about 3 minutes, until it is no longer pink. Add the mushrooms and continue to stir-fry for 30 to 60 seconds, until the mushrooms are barely tender. Mix the cooked chicken and mushrooms into the soup. Serve the soup, passing around the chopped scallions as a separate garnish. Leftovers can be refrigerated and reheated. The mushrooms darken when the soup is frozen.

Lo Mien and Meatball Soup

肉丸捞麵

Rou Wan Lao Mian

Canton

Serves 6

Tiny meatballs are the attraction of this noodle soup. The *lo mien* is cooked directly in the broth, which thickens the broth slightly and also flavors the noodles a little. Tomato sauce enhances the broth. Scallions are used as a garnish for color, texture, and the bit of sharpness they bring to any dish.

1 pound very lean ground beef
¼ cup soy sauce
2 tablespoons dry sherry
2 water chestnuts, chopped
2 scallions (white and crisp green parts), chopped
1 egg (graded large), beaten
2 quarts seasoned chicken broth
¼ cup tomato sauce
1 pound lo mien
Soy sauce to taste
Chopped scallions (white and crisp green parts) for garnish

In a medium-size bowl, combine the ground beef, soy sauce, sherry, water chestnuts, scallions, and egg, mixing lightly with your hands. Shape the meat into very small balls, 40 to 50 in all. Set aside.

In a 4-quart pot, bring the chicken broth and tomato sauce to the boil. Add the *lo mien* and cook for 1 minute, stirring constantly. Now add the meatballs and cook them gently for 3 to 4 minutes, until done. Taste the soup and add soy sauce to taste. Serve the soup from a tureen. Garnish it with chopped scallions just before serving.

One-Dish Noodle Soup

一品鍋

Yi Pin Guo

Canton

Serves 6

Years ago, there was an unpretentious-looking coffeehouse in New York's Chinatown that was frequented almost exclusively by Chinese. As we looked in the window, we noticed bowl upon bowl of a noodle soup topped with roast and barbecued meats and bright green vegetables. At the time we had never seen a soup of this kind. As Chinese teahouses have become more and more popular in this country, this noodle soup has gained more of the recognition it deserves. It can be served as a main dish luncheon soup or as a featured dish for dinner.

The basic idea is this: a bowl of noodles is topped with slices of meat and vegetables, then a rich chicken broth is poured over all. The meat in a Chinese restaurant would most likely be barbecued roast pork, or small pieces of roast duck cut and served with the bone. This adaptation uses marinated broiled steak and roast duck. It is the kind of recipe for which one could benefit from a large kitchen and numerous cooks, at least two of whom can handle Chinese cleavers impressively. Slices of roast lamb or chicken can be substituted for the more elaborately prepared steak and duck.

2 slices (⅛-inch thick) ginger root
1 scallion, sliced
1 clove garlic, coarsely chopped
1 tablespoon ketchup
1 tablespoon hoisin sauce
1 tablespoon dry sherry
1 tablespoon soy sauce
½ pound London broil
Half of a 5-pound duck
1 tablespoon soy sauce
1 tablespoon dry sherry
½ teaspoon five-spice powder
½ pound bok choy or ¼ pound fresh spinach leaves
1 pound lo mien
1 tablespoon sesame oil
2 quarts well-seasoned chicken broth

Preheat the oven to 350 degrees F. In a bowl just large enough to accommodate the steak, combine the first 7 ingredients. Marinate the steak in this mixture for about 2 hours, turning it occasionally.

Meanwhile rub the duck all over with a mixture of 1 tablespoon soy sauce and 1 tablespoon dry sherry, then rub the five-spice powder into the duck skin. Prick the duck skin all over with a fork, then place the duck, skin side up, on a rack in a roasting pan. Roast the duck in the preheated oven for about 2 hours, until the meat is tender and the skin is a lovely rich brown color. Prick the skin with a fork from time to time to allow the fat to run off.

While the duck is roasting, wash the *bok choy* or spinach leaves thoroughly. Slice or chop the *bok choy* evenly into pieces that can be handled easily with a soup spoon or chopsticks. Tear the spinach leaves into bite-size pieces.

About 15 minutes before the duck is done, in a 5- or 6-quart pot, begin to bring 3 or 4 quarts of water to the boil. The *lo mien* will be cooked in this water. At the same time, bring the chicken broth to the boil in another pot big enough to hold the 2 quarts of broth. When the soup has come to the boil, reduce the heat to low and keep the soup hot.

After you put up the water for the *lo mien* and the soup is heating, remove the steak from the marinade. Broil the steak a few inches from the heat until it is done, turning once during the cooking. Meanwhile, cook the *lo mien* as soon as the water in the 5- or 6-quart pot has come to the boil. Drop in the noodles, and cook them for about 4 minutes, stirring occasionally to keep them from sticking. Drain the *lo mien,* return it to the pot, and mix it with 1 tablespoon of sesame oil. Keep the noodles warm on top of the turned-off burner. Slice the steak thinly on the diagonal and transfer the slices to a heated plate. Cover the steak loosely with foil to keep it warm. The duck should be cooked by now. Use a sharp cleaver to chop the duck, bone and all, into pieces that can be handled with the fingers, chopsticks, or a spoon. (Or carve the duck American style, making sure to get at least six nice pieces to serve, one per bowl.)

To serve this noodle soup, divide the noodles among 6 soup bowls. Arrange slices of steak, pieces of duck, and the *bok choy* or spinach on top of the noodles. Now pour the hot chicken broth over all, which will cook the vegetables slightly. Serve the soup immediately.

Simplified One-Dish Noodle Soup

一品鍋(易做)

Yi Pin Guo (Yi Zuo)

Canton

Serves 6

This recipe differs from the preceding more authentic soup in two major ways. Although it remains a bowl of noodles seasoned by meats, vegetables, and chicken broth, it is prepared as a *lo mien* dish. The meats and vegetables are already combined with the noodles before the broth is poured over the mixture. Most of the preparation is completed in advance, and the final cooking takes but a few minutes and does not require the coordination of the previous recipe.

This hefty soup calls for considerably more meat and vegetables than the One-Dish Noodle Soup, a concession to American tastes. I generally serve it as the main course following four or five appetizers.

1 pound lo mien
1 tablespoon sesame oil
1 pound boneless chicken, cut into ½-inch cubes
1 tablespoon peanut, corn, or other oil
1 tablespoon soy sauce
1 tablespoon dry sherry
¼ pound beef, very thinly sliced
1 large clove garlic, minced
2 quarts chicken broth
2 tablespoons peanut, corn, or other oil
3 or 4 stalks celery cabbage, sliced thinly on the diagonal
1 pound fresh mushrooms, thinly sliced
4 to 6 water chestnuts, sliced
2 tablespoons peanut, corn, or other oil
4 scallions (white and crisp green parts), sliced

In a 4- or 5-quart pot, bring at least 3 quarts of water to the boil. Drop in the noodles and cook them until they are just tender, about 2 or 3 minutes. (For convenience, the *lo mien* may be cut into 2-inch pieces before cooking.) Drain the noodles well, then toss them with the sesame oil. The cooked *lo mien* can now be refrigerated or frozen, but it should be brought to room temperature before being used in this recipe.

Mix the chicken cubes with a tablespoon each of oil, soy sauce, and sherry. Cut the thinly sliced beef into thin strips, and mix the beef with the garlic. Place the chicken and beef in separate bowls or containers, and refrigerate them until you are ready to begin the cooking.

Heat the chicken broth in any pot that will accommodate it. The soup should be kept hot but not boiling. Meanwhile, in a wok or a 12-inch skillet, heat 2 tablespoons of oil. Stir-fry the celery cabbage in the hot oil for 30 seconds; add the mushrooms and continue to stir-fry for half a minute longer, until the mushrooms are coated with oil and slightly cooked. Mix in the water chestnuts. Remove the vegetables to a clean bowl.

Now heat 2 or more tablespoons of oil in the same wok or skillet; add the chicken to the hot oil, and stir-fry until all the pieces turn white. Add the beef strips, and continue to stir-fry until the beef is cooked. The total cooking time for the chicken and beef should be only 3 or 4 mintues, if that much. Mix the cooked vegetables into the meat, then add the cooked *lo mien*. You will probably need to use chopsticks, two spoons, or tongs to distribute the ingredients evenly. Continue to cook and stir just until everything is hot and mixed together.

To serve, spoon some of the *lo mien* mixture into each soup bowl. Add hot broth to cover, and sprinkle scallions over each portion. Pass around soy sauce and sesame oil as condiments.

Chinese Hot Pot (Fire Pot)

火鍋

Huo Guo

Peking

Number of servings flexible

Nearly twenty years ago, a friend told us about a wonderful meal she'd enjoyed at the home of her Chinese neighbor. It was a do-it-yourself dinner in which slices of all kinds of meat, fish, vegetables, and noodles were cooked in hot broth. The cooking implement was an unusual metal piece which consisted of a hot charcoal-filled cylinder set into a large attractive bowl. The broth in the bowl was kept hot by the charcoal. Each guest had a small wire basket in which to cook the array of uncooked foods. Our friend went on to describe her delight in finding that the broth became a rich and tasty soup, which the guests then ate.

The idea of soup following the meal was new to us at the time, but we tried it and found it very satisfying. We have since deglamorized the meal somewhat for use as a family dinner. (This is actually quite appropriate because the hot pot—which describes both the name of this classic dish and the utensil in which it is cooked—is served as a family meal all over China.) We use an electric skillet, which works very well, and we use fondue forks for spearing and cooking the food. Chopsticks are a most appropriate alternative to fondue forks. Substitutions for an authentic Chinese fire pot include a fondue pot or chafing dish, as long as there is enough heat to keep the broth hot enough to cook the foods.

The selection of ingredients for this dish and the amount they will serve will vary according to the number of people being served, of course, and the place the hot pot has in the meal. If it is the major attraction of the meal, you will need a good variety of ingredients in ample quantity. If you are serving this as an appetizer-soup combination to be followed by other dishes, you will not need as much. Variations on the meat and vegetable hot pot presented below include (1) a fish and vegetable hot pot, which substitutes fish fillets for the meats and a vegetarian broth for the chicken broth and (2) a vegetarian hot pot, which uses vegetables only in a vegetarian broth.

To serve the hot pot, arrange the uncooked foods on a platter as artistically as you can. Make sure to slice the raw meats very thinly so they will cook quickly.

2 quarts seasoned chicken broth, with additional broth or water available
Beef, sliced thinly into bite-size pieces
Chicken, sliced as above
Lamb, sliced as above
Chicken livers, broiled and cut into bite-size pieces
Fresh mushrooms, sliced or quartered
Dried Chinese mushrooms, soaked in hot water and sliced (discard stems)
Bamboo shoots, sliced
Celery cabbage or any Chinese cabbage, cut into bite-size pieces
Fresh spinach, thoroughly washed, torn into bite-size pieces
Scallions (white and crisp green parts), cut into 1-inch pieces
Cucumber slices
Fresh tofu, cut into ½-inch cubes
Fresh snow peas, tips and strings removed (sliced if large)

Lo mien, cut into 2-inch pieces
Cellophane noodles, soaked in warm water and cut into 2-inch pieces
Dips: soy sauce, duck sauce, Chinese Mustard (page 122), Szechwan Sauce (page 130), Sesame-Peanut Butter Sauce (page 134), any soy-sauce-based condiment, sesame seeds

The soup can be heated directly in an electric skillet or a Chinese hot pot. Or heat the soup in any pot on the stove and transfer the hot broth to a fondue pot, chafing dish, or whatever cooking implement will be used. Since some of the liquid evaporates during cooking, it will probably be necessary to add hot broth or water to the cooking pan from time to time, so keep extra broth simmering on the stove.

Everything should be in reach of all the people eating. Use either a Lazy Susan or numerous platters, or provide individual plates of uncooked food for each guest. Each diner gets a selection of condiments for dipping. The procedure is simple: each person selects a piece of food, cooks it in the broth, dips the cooked food, and eats it. If the table is large, it may be necessary to use more than one cooking implement. (I use two electric skillets plugged into different circuits.)

If you like, you can have precooked *lo mien* or rice ready to add to the soup after all the ingredients have been cooked and eaten and it's time to serve the broth.

4

Beef and Lamb

Most of the recipes in this chapter have been adapted to American tastes for American usage. There is considerably more meat in each recipe than you would find on a Chinese table, and the recipes are designed to serve four to six as the main dish. If you want to use a more authentically Chinese approach, cut an entire recipe in half or thirds and serve two or three times as many dishes, or reduce the amount of meat by at least half and serve an extra vegetable combination or two.

Beef has almost no place in the average Chinese diet. Cows require much space, so when cattle are raised by the Chinese at all, they are used for food only after their plowing days are over. Thus, veal is virtually unknown.

Pork is the meat of China. Pigs are small, they eat almost anything, and they are easier to butcher than cows. Both beef and veal substitute well (for pork) in all kinds of Chinese cooking. London broil is particularly suited to stir-fried dishes because it can be sliced very thin and holds up well when cooked. For the thinnest possible slices, always freeze beef partially before slicing it, and use a sharp knife or cleaver. Brisket is superb in red-cooked dishes, and cubed chuck makes wonderful Chinese stews.

Lamb is known mostly in northern China, among the nomadic Mongolians. The most famous Chinese lamb dish is the Mongolian barbecue, which is increasingly seen in cookbooks and on menus in this country. Lamb adapts especially well to all kinds of Chinese cooking, including stir-fried dishes, rice combinations, and stews.

Stir-fried Steak, Mushrooms, and Celery Cabbage
鲜菇白菜炒牛肉
Xian Gu Bai Cai Chao Niu Rou

Canton

Serves 4 to 6

This is a basic stir-fried beef-and-vegetable dish. Because of the quantities involved, the cooking is done in two stages. First the vegetables are briefly stir-fried until partially cooked. Then, they are transferred to a bowl, where they continue to cook from their own heat. It is very important to undercook the vegetables so they remain crisp. Next the beef is stir-fried in at least two batches, the meat and vegetables are combined, and then the mixture is thickened with cornstarch. If this were more typically Chinese, it would have at most one-half pound of meat. The meat would be stir-fried first and pushed aside in the wok (or left in the skillet) while the celery cabbage and then the mushrooms were quickly cooked.

Fresh mushrooms are chosen for this recipe because of their soft texture and delicate taste. The dish stands alone as just Steak and Mushrooms, especially if a scallion garnish is added for color. Celery cabbage contributes color, a fresh taste, and a contrasting crisp texture. The water chestnuts are added primarily for texture.

The mixture in which the steak marinates is the only seasoning in this dish. You may be tempted to douse the cooked steak and vegetables with extra soy sauce, but then you will lose the contrasting subtleties of the crisp, garden-fresh-tasting celery cabbage, the barely tender mushrooms, and the very flavorful beef.

1½ pounds London broil, partially frozen then sliced very thinly on a 45-degree angle
3 tablespoons dry sherry
3 tablespoons soy sauce
1 teaspoon sugar
1 tablespoon peanut, corn, or other oil
2 large cloves garlic, minced
2 teaspoons minced ginger root
2 tablespoons peanut, corn, or other oil
1 pound celery cabbage or other Chinese cabbage, sliced on the diagonal into ½-inch pieces
¾ pound fresh mushrooms, sliced

→

2 tablespoons peanut, corn, or other oil
8 to 10 water chestnuts, sliced
1 tablespoon cornstarch dissolved in ¼ cup cold water or broth

Cut the sliced steak into 1-inch pieces. In a medium-size mixing bowl, combine the sherry, soy sauce, sugar, tablespoon of oil, the garlic, and the ginger root. Add the steak slices and mix gently but thoroughly; marinate the steak for a minimum of an hour. The uncooked marinated steak can be refrigerated overnight.

Coat a large wok or a 12-inch skillet with 2 tablespoons of oil. Heat the oil until it is hot but not yet smoking, between 375 and 400 degrees F. Swish the oil around the wok or pan so the oil coats the sides. Add the celery cabbage and stir it immediately and continuously for no longer than 1 minute. Now add the mushrooms and continue to stir-fry for about 30 seconds. The vegetables will be underdone and may seem to be hardly cooked. Remove them to a clean bowl at this point.

Add 1 more tablespoon of oil to the wok or skillet; heat it to a temperature of about 375 degrees F. The beef will stick if the temperature is too high, but it will not cook quickly enough if it is too low. A drop of water sprinkled onto the oil should spatter instantly. Add half the steak to the oil, and stir the beef continuously until it is cooked. If you are using a wok, toss the beef around so it comes in contact with the sides of the wok as well as the bottom—it will cook more quickly. Remove the cooked beef to a clean bowl.

Add the remaining tablespoon of oil to the wok or pan, and repeat the procedure to stir-fry the rest of the beef. Now combine all the steak, vegetables, and the water chestnuts in the cooking pan. Toss the ingredients quickly to mix them well without cooking them further. Again stir together the cornstarch and water until the mixture is smooth. Add the cornstarch paste to the steak and vegetables. Cook, stirring constantly, only until the paste is mixed in and the liquid is thickened and glazed. Serve this dish immediately, with rice or noodles.

Stir-fried Steak, Snow Peas, and Chinese Mushrooms

雪豆香菇炒牛肉

Xue Dou Xiang Gu Chao Niu Rou

Canton

Serves 4 to 6

A splendid taste and texture combination makes this stir-fried steak suitable for a very special meal. Fresh snow peas remain crisp and bright green, and the chewy, somewhat smoky Chinese mushrooms add a touch of the exotic. So although this is essentially a variation on the basic steak-and-vegetables of the preceding recipe, the snow peas and Chinese mushrooms make it more festive. Serve it as the main dish in an American dinner, or feature it in a multicourse Chinese dinner.

1½ pounds London broil, partially frozen then sliced very thinly on a 45-degree angle
3 tablespoons dry sherry
3 tablespoons soy sauce
1 tablespoon peanut, corn, or other oil
1 teaspoon sugar
2 large cloves garlic, minced
1 teaspoon minced ginger root
8 dried Chinese mushrooms
Boiling water
¼ to ½ pound fresh snow peas
3 tablespoons peanut, corn, or other oil, approximately
8 water chestnuts, sliced
1 tablespoon cornstarch dissolved in ¼ cup cold water or broth

Cut the sliced steak into 1-inch pieces. In a medium-size mixing bowl, combine the sherry, soy sauce, 1 tablespoon of oil, the sugar, garlic, and the ginger root. Add the steak slices and mix them gently but thoroughly; marinate the steak for a minimum of an hour. The uncooked marinated steak can be refrigerated overnight.

Place the Chinese mushrooms in a small heatproof bowl and pour in enough boiling water to cover the mushrooms completely. Let the mushrooms soak until they are soft, about 15 minutes. Slice the mushrooms into thin strips, discarding the stems. Break off the tips of the snow peas and pull down along the seams to remove any strings. The beef, mushrooms, and snow peas can be made ready for cooking up to a day ahead, but final cooking should not begin until you are ready to serve. Dissolve the cornstarch in the water or broth before cooking begins.

Heat a large wok or 10- to 12-inch skillet with 1 tablespoon of oil until the oil is hot but not yet smoking, between 375 and 400 degrees F. Swish the oil around to coat the pan completely. Add the snow peas, stirring immediately so they do not stick or burn. Stir-fry the snow peas for 1 minute, until they are well coated with oil and just barely cooked. Mix in the Chinese mushrooms, then remove the vegetables to a clean bowl.

Add another tablespoon of oil to the wok or pan, and heat it to about 375 degrees F., until a drop of water spatters instantly. Add half the steak to the oil, and stir-fry for a minute or two until the beef is just cooked. Transfer the steak to a clean bowl. Again, coat the wok or pan with a little oil, and cook the remaining steak. Combine all the steak, the snow peas, the Chinese mushrooms, and the water chestnuts in the wok or pan. Quickly toss the ingredients together to distribute them evenly. Again stir together the cornstarch and water until the mixture is smooth; add this cornstarch paste to the steak and vegetables and blend it in, stirring constantly. Cook only until the mixture comes to the boil and becomes thickened and glazed, which is a matter of seconds. Remove from the heat and serve immediately.

If you wish to prepare this as a more authentically Chinese dish, use only ½ pound of beef and ¼ pound of snow peas. First stir-fry the beef in enough oil to coat the wok or pan. Cook the beef until it is nearly done, then add the snow peas and continue to stir-fry over high heat until the peas are barely tender. Mix in the Chinese mushrooms and water chestnuts, then the cornstarch thickener. Serve this in small portions as one of several "main" dishes.

Stir-fried Beef and Green Beans

四季豆炒牛肉

Si Ji Dou Chao Niu Rou

Canton influence

Serves 4 to 6

To me, Sunday mornings in New York City always meant bagels and lox, and in my family Sunday afternoons meant window-shopping. My father, a retail clothier, liked to see how all the windows were dressed. He and my mother enjoyed pointing to things they'd like to have, but there was no danger of impulse-buying because all the stores were closed. I was never particularly interested in clothing or jewelry, but I enjoyed peering into the delis, bakeries, and restaurant windows to observe what was going on in the food world. Eventually I became so good at imagining what various goodies tasted like, I felt as though I'd actually eaten them.

This Stir-fried Beef and Green Beans recipe comes from a dish I saw and savored mentally but never actually tasted. I developed the recipe after observing the owner of a Chinese restaurant and his family about to divide up a wonderful-looking dish heaped high with a juicy-looking mixture of beef and green beans. In China, many dishes are available only in restaurants because they are too expensive or time-consuming to prepare at home. The reverse seemed to be true of this dish: it was not prepared as a standard restaurant dish, but was obviously specially made for the owner and his family.

Fresh green beans, cut attractively on the diagonal, are stir-fried with ginger root and garlic until they are crisp-tender. The pungent aroma is tantalizing. The beef is then cooked quickly and seasoned, and the beef and beans are then combined, glazed, and finally topped off with the distinctively flavored sesame oil, which also contributes color and adds to the effect of the glaze.

This dish is delicious in every way. It appeals directly to the sense of smell. It is colorful and lustrous. The beans bring a crisp contrasting texture. And the balance of tastes so important in Chinese cooking is achieved by a blend of seasonings released at just the right time.

I have always characterized this dish as relatively mildly flavored, but the addition of a few sprinkles of crushed dried red pepper while the beans are stir-frying would turn it into a tasty Peppery Beef and Green Beans without destroying the essential balance of the other ingredients.

1 tablespoon peanut, corn, or other oil to mix with the beef
1½ pounds London broil, partially frozen then sliced very thinly on a 45-degree angle, then cut into 1-to 1½-inch pieces
2 tablespoons peanut, corn, or other oil
1 pound fresh green beans, cut on the diagonal into 1-inch pieces (discard tips)
1 tablespoon finely minced garlic (4 large cloves)
½ teaspoon minced ginger root
½ teaspoon crushed dried red pepper (optional)
2 tablespoons peanut, corn, or other oil for cooking the beef
¼ cup soy sauce

→

2 tablespoons dry sherry
1 tablespoon sugar
2 teaspoons cornstarch dissolved in 2 tablespoons cold water
1 teaspoon or more sesame oil for flavoring, to taste

Sprinkle the 1 tablespoon of oil over the beef and mix lightly. Set aside.

In a large wok or a 12-inch skillet, heat the 2 tablespoons of oil until it is hot but not yet smoking, 375 to 400 degrees F. Stir in the green beans, and toss them around immediately to coat them with the oil. Sprinkle on the garlic and ginger root, and continue to stir quickly and constantly. Stir-fry for 4 to 5 minutes, until the beans are partially cooked but are still bright green and crisp. If you are using the crushed hot pepper, sprinkle it in toward the end of the cooking. If the garlic begins to burn or the beans stick to the pan, reduce the heat or add a little more oil. Remove the partially cooked beans to a clean bowl.

In the same wok or skillet, heat another tablespoon of oil to 375 degrees F. Add half the steak and stir-fry until it is just done. Transfer the cooked steak to a clean bowl, then add more oil to the pan and stir-fry the remaining steak. The meat is cooked in at least two batches so that it cooks quickly and doesn't have a chance to simmer in its own juices. Put all the cooked steak back in the pan; mix in the soy sauce, sherry, and sugar. Add the green beans, and toss the ingredients quickly to mix them well without cooking them further. Again stir together the cornstarch and water until smooth, then blend the mixture into the beef and green beans. Turn off the heat as soon as the cornstarch paste is evenly distributed and the mixture is thickened and glazed. Blend in the sesame oil, then heap the beef and green beans beautifully in a bowl. Serve immediately with rice.

Stir-fried Beef and Broccoli

番芥蘭炒牛肉

Fan Jie Lan Chao Niu Rou

Canton

Serves 4 to 6

In the United States, broccoli sees considerable use in Chinese cooking because (1) it is readily available, (2) it holds up very well in stir-frying, (3) it retains an attractive green color when cooked properly, and (4) it adds contrast to many dishes with its crisp texture and tart flavor. In addition, broccoli looks pretty without even trying. Individual pieces of the flower-like heads make attractive raw garnishes, and the stems can be cut to resemble florets also.

The broccoli in this recipe combines with thinly sliced stir-fried beef for an excellent budget-stretching meal. Chopped onion adds a touch of sweetness when it is stir-fried with the broccoli, and the shredded ginger root brings its familiar pungency. If this were served at a banquet, the host would pick out the choice slices of beef and the most attractive florets for his most important guest. At a Chinese family dinner, each person picks his own food out from the central dish and may mix it with rice before it is eaten. Although my children all eat broccoli, I fear that if I gave them the option of selecting their own tidbits, the steak would disappear instantly and we'd be left with Stir-fried Beef-flavored Broccoli. Therefore, as a family dinner, I add a simple gravy and spoon out servings over rice.

1½ pounds beef (a steak or roast), partially frozen then cut into very thin slices approximately 1 × 2 inches
2 large cloves garlic, minced
2 tablespoons soy sauce
1 tablespoon dry sherry
1 tablespoon peanut, corn, or other oil
1 medium-size bunch broccoli (1 pound)
2 tablespoons peanut, corn, or other oil
1 to 2 teaspoons shredded ginger root, to taste
1 large onion, chopped (about 1 cup)
1 teaspoon sugar (optional)
2 tablespoons peanut, corn, or other oil
Optional: 1 cup seasoned beef or chicken broth; 1 tablespoon cornstarch dissolved in 2 tablespoons cold water or broth

Mix the beef slices with the garlic, soy sauce, sherry, and 1 tablespoon of oil. Marinate the beef in this mixture for a minimum of 1 hour. The marinating beef can be refrigerated overnight.

Cut off the broccoli florets. Cut the large florets in half or quarters so that all the pieces are about the same size. Peel the stems with a vegetable peeler or a sharp knife. Slice the stems into long, thin pieces about 1½ × ¼ × ¼ inches. Discard the bottom inch or two of the stems. Keep the stems and florets in separate piles, as they will be cooked separately.

When you are ready to cook, in a large wok or a 12-inch skillet, heat 2 tablespoons of oil until it is hot but not yet smoking, 375 to 400 degrees F. Add the shredded ginger root and stir it around to coat it with the oil, then add the chopped onion and stir-fry for half a minute. Add the broccoli stems and stir-fry for an additional 5 minutes, then add the florets and continue to stir-fry for 1 more minute. Sprinkle the sugar on the vegetables, mix well, and transfer the contents of the wok or pan to a clean bowl.

Coat the wok or skillet with a tablespoon of oil and heat it to 375 degrees F. Add half the beef, and stir-fry just until the beef is no longer pink. Remove the cooked beef to a clean bowl, add a little more oil to the pan, and cook the remaining beef. Now mix together all the beef and vegetables. Serve immediately, or first make a sauce by adding a cup of beef or chicken broth to the cooked beef and broccoli. Bring the broth to the boil, stirring gently. Again blend the cornstarch with the water, then stir the cornstarch paste into the cooking broth. Mix well, turn off the heat, and serve immediately over cooked rice.

Stir-fried Beef and Broccoli in Sweet Bean Sauce

醬爆芥蘭炒牛肉

Jiang Bao Jie Lan Chao Niu Rou

Peking

Serves 4 to 6

This beef-and-broccoli dish relies on only three ingredients (plus oil for stir-frying) for all of its interest. The beef picks up a rich, salty taste from the thick reddish-brown bean sauce. The broccoli is crisp and green, with a fresh and slightly pungent taste. Although soy sauce and a little sugar can be used in preparing this kind of stir-fried dish, the sweet bean sauce adds bod, and a color that is hard to duplicate.

1 medium-size bunch broccoli (1 pound)
3 tablespoons peanut, corn, or other oil
1½ pounds London broil, partially frozen then sliced on a 45-degree angle, then cut into 1-inch pieces
3 tablespoons sweet bean sauce

Cut off the broccoli florets, then cut the large florets in half or into quarters so all the pieces are about the same size. With a vegetable peeler or a paring knife, peel the stems, discarding the bottom inch or two of the stems. Slice the stems into long, thin pieces about $1\frac{1}{2} \times \frac{1}{4} \times \frac{1}{4}$ inches. Cook the broccoli in a pot of boiling water for 5 minutes. Drain the broccoli in a colander, and set it aside until you are ready to cook the beef. If the broccoli will not be used within a few minutes, run it under cold water so it will not continue to cook from its own heat.

In a large wok or a 12-inch skillet, heat a tablespoon of oil until it is hot but not yet smoking, between 375 and 400 degrees F. Add the broccoli and toss it around for a minute to coat it with oil and cook it a bit. Remove the broccoli to a clean bowl. Add another tablespoon of oil to the wok or skillet, heat it to 375 degrees F., and stir-fry half the beef until it is just done. Remove the beef to a clean bowl, heat another tablespoon of oil, and stir-fry the remaining beef. Return all of the cooked beef to the pan, then blend in the sweet bean sauce. Now add the cooked broccoli, toss the beef and broccoli together just until mixed, and serve immediately.

Steak and Shredded Scallions

葱炒牛肉

Cong Chao Niu Rou

Szechwan

Serves 4

Crushed red pepper and loads of scallions signal this spicy dish as one which would be from Szechwan Province. A whole pound of beef and no vegetables to stretch the meat mean that the dish is out of the grasp of most Chinese households, but it is easy to prepare at home. Stir-fried steak is lightly seasoned with minced ginger root, soy sauce, sherry, and just enough crushed red pepper to notice. The sauce that forms when the dish is cooked is mildly spicy, but the dish gets its real bite from the scallions, which are added at the very end so they remain crisp and sharp-tasting. Serve this dish with plenty of plain rice, which will absorb some of the sharpness of the scallions while allowing their special tang to come through.

1 pound London broil, partially frozen then sliced very thinly on a 45-degree angle
8 scallions (white and crisp green parts)
2 tablespoons peanut, corn, or other oil
½ teaspoon minced ginger root
¼ teaspoon crushed dried red pepper
¼ cup soy sauce
2 tablespoons dry sherry
1 tablespoon cornstarch dissolved in ¼ cup cold water or broth

Cut the steak slices into pieces approximately 1 × ½ inch. Cut the roots and the tough green ends off the scallions. Slice the scallions, including the tender parts of the green ends, lengthwise into quarters, then crosswise into 1-inch pieces. Have all the ingredients measured and at hand for final cooking.

In a wok or a 10- to 12-inch skillet, heat a tablespoon of oil until it is hot but not yet smoking, 375 degrees F. Stir-fry half the beef until barely pink, then transfer it to a clean bowl. Heat another tablespoon of oil in the wok or skillet, and stir-fry the remaining beef until it is almost done. Return the other half of the cooked beef to the wok or skillet. Raise the heat so the beef sizzles instead of simmers, and sprinkle on the ginger root and crushed red pepper. Continue to stir-fry over high heat until the meat loses all its redness. Now mix in the soy sauce and sherry, and bring the liquid to the boil. Again blend the cornstarch with the water and stir this thin paste into the beef. Continue cooking only until the liquid thickens, stirring constantly. Turn off the heat, then mix in the shredded scallions, and serve immediately.

Peking Beef

京爆牛肉

Jing Bao Niu Rou

Peking

Serves 4

Garlic and scallions in a light brown sauce are distinguishing features of this stir-fried beef preparation. Although Peking cooking sometimes is strong-tasting, it never has the fire of Szechwan dishes. The flavor of the garlic here cannot be missed, but the blend of ingredients is much more subtle than one finds in the hot Szechwan combinations. The thick sweet bean sauce will add body, a reddish hue, and saltiness. Soy sauce, although thinner, is an acceptable substitute because it adds color and is salty as well.

This amount of steak can be cooked in one batch if you are willing to triple the amount of oil. The extra oil will keep the temperature high even when a lot of meat is added.

1 pound London broil, partially frozen then sliced very thinly on a 45-degree angle
2 tablespoons peanut, corn, or other oil
4 large cloves garlic, finely chopped

3 tablespoons sweet bean sauce or 4 tablespoons soy sauce
1 tablespoon red wine vinegar
4 scallions (white and crisp green parts), cut into ¼-inch rounds
2 teaspoons sesame oil (optional)

Cut the thinly sliced steak into strips approximately 1½ × ½ inches. In a wok or a 10- to 12-inch skillet, heat a tablespoon of oil until it just begins to smoke. Add half the garlic and stir immediately and quickly to coat the garlic with oil, which will take only a few seconds. Add half the steak slices. Stir-fry the steak until the redness disappears, then transfer it to a clean bowl. Repeat the cooking procedure with the other half of the oil, garlic, and steak.

In the wok or skillet, mix together all of the cooked beef, then stir in the sweet bean sauce or soy sauce and the vinegar. Allow the mixture to come to the boil while stirring. Toss in the scallions. Turn off the heat, then blend in the sesame oil. Serve immediately.

Pepper Steak With Tomatoes

番茄青椒炒牛肉

Fan Qie Qing Jiao Chao Niu Rou

Canton, Chinese-American

Serves 6

Striking colors; a wonderful blend of aromas; crisp, soft, and chewy textures; distinctive tastes that maintain their individuality while contributing to a delicious whole—everything central to good Chinese cooking is in this beautifully glazed stir-fried dish. The ingredients—beef, peppers, onions, tomatoes—are standard American menu items, but the method of cutting up and cooking them is unmistakably Chinese. The finished dish looks a little like a stew, but it has the contrasting textures typical of stir-fried combinations.

1½ pounds London broil, partially frozen then sliced thinly on a 45-degree angle
3 cloves garlic, minced
3 tablespoons peanut, corn, or other oil
1 large onion, sliced thinly
2 medium-large green peppers, cut into strips

→

2 tablespoons dry sherry
¼ cup soy sauce
½ cup beef bouillon
1 tablespoon cornstarch dissolved in 3 tablespoons cold water
1 pound fresh ripe tomatoes, cut into wedges

Cut the steak slices into uniform pieces about 1 inch long. Mix the steak with the minced garlic.

In a large wok or a 12-inch skillet, heat 1 tablespoon of the oil until it is hot but not yet smoking, 375 to 400 degrees F. Add the onion and peppers, and stir-fry for 2 minutes until they are very hot but still crisp. Remove the vegetables to a clean bowl. Add another tablespoon of oil to the cooking pan, again bring the temperature to 375 degrees F., and stir-fry half the steak until most of the redness disappears. Transfer the steak to a clean bowl, add the remaining tablespoon of oil to the pan, and stir-fry the rest of the meat until done.

Now, in the wok or skillet, combine all the beef, onions, and peppers; then stir in the sherry, soy sauce, and beef bouillon. Bring the contents of the pan to the boil. Again blend the cornstarch with the water until they are well combined, then stir the cornstarch paste into the liquid in the pan. Cook just until the mixture boils and thickens, stirring gently to blend in the cornstarch evenly. Add the tomato wedges, and mix them in until distributed evenly and heated through. The tomatoes should not actually cook or they will soften too much, but they should be warmed up. Serve this dish at once, with rice.

Beef and Vegetables With Cellophane Noodles

粉絲鮮炒牛肉

Fen Si Xian Chao Niu Rou

General China influence

Serves 4 to 6

This recipe combines two Chinese ingredients with everyday American foods to produce a remarkable one-dish meal. The soft cellophane noodles give body to the dish and pick up the flavors of the steak and the *hoisin* sauce. The onions contribute a sweet crispness, and both the steak and the mushrooms are plentiful enough to be noticed in every bite.

Green peas add color, sweetness, and texture, and the *hoisin* sauce lends its distinctive sweet-salty pungency to the preparation, which would otherwise be too bland.

8 ounces cellophane noodles
1 pound London broil, partially frozen then sliced very thinly on a 45-degree angle
3 tablespoons peanut, corn, or other oil
½ cup coarsely chopped onions
½ pound fresh mushrooms, sliced
1 box (10 ounces) frozen green peas, thawed
¼ cup hoisin sauce

Soak the cellophane noodles in hot water for 10 mintues or until they are soft enough to cut. Drain the noodles, then cut them with kitchen scissors into pieces 2 inches long. Cut the steak slices into uniform strips about 1½ × ½ inches.

In a large wok or a 12-inch skillet, heat 1 tablespoon of the oil until it just begins to smoke. Stir-fry the onions until they just begin to brown, then add the remaining 2 tablespoons of oil. When the oil is hot but not yet smoking, about 375 degrees F., add the beef strips all at once and stir-fry until the redness disappears. Next add the mushrooms, and stir continuously half a minute longer. Mix in the peas, then add the cellophane noodles. Toss the contents of the pan to distribute the ingredients evenly. Add a cup of water, and continue to stir the mixture over moderate heat until everything is hot. Blend in the *hoisin* sauce. Taste the noodles. If they are not soft enough to eat, cover the pan and cook over moderately low heat for 5 minutes. This dish can be served immediately after it is cooked, or it can be kept warm over low heat until serving time. Reheat leftovers by steaming.

Red-cooked Whole Brisket

滷牛肉

Lu Niu Rou

Eastern China

Serves 6 to 8

The first time I tried cooking brisket this way I made a big noodle-applesauce *kugel* and heated up leftover spaghetti and meatballs in case my family didn't like the brisket. I ended up with leftover *kugel* and untouched spaghetti and meatballs.

The brisket comes out very tender, with a wonderful hint of spiciness from the ginger root and lemon juice. The lean straight cut is used as a main dish, while the top portion is saved for Red-cooked Brisket Wontons (page 154). The soy sauce makes the gravy very salty, and when the brisket is served hot with the gravy, a spicy or tart Chinese pickle or relish should be served with it for contrast. When served cold, the flavor of the sauce permeates the meat but it doesn't taste overly salty.

To serve the brisket Chinese style, cut the the meat into pieces of uniform size that can be handled with chopsticks. Or, cook the meat for four or five hours, until it just about falls apart when pierced with a fork. Then place it at the center of the table, and instruct everyone to break off pieces of the meat with chopsticks.

2 cups Red-cooked Starter Sauce (page 21) or 1 cup soy sauce and 1 cup water
1 cup additional water
Juice of 1 large lemon
2 teaspoons grated or minced ginger root
2 tablespoons firmly packed light or dark brown sugar
1 whole fresh brisket, well trimmed

In an 8- to 12-quart heavy pot with a good lid, combine all the ingredients except the brisket. Bring the liquid to the boil. Add the brisket (cut the brisket into two pieces if necessary). Bring the liquid to the boil again, and adjust the heat so the meat simmers. Cover the pot. Cook the brisket for 2½ to 3 hours, turning it every half hour, until it is very tender. A large fork should pierce the meat easily.

Cut off the top portion of the brisket, place it in a bowl or container with enough of the cooking sauce to cover; refrigerate it for use in Red-cooked Brisket Wontons. After a day of marinating in the sauce, the piece can be removed and frozen for later use or used immediately for the *wontons*.

Serve the brisket hot or cold. If serving it cold, allow the brisket to chill in the gravy. A spicy relish, chutney, or pickle is an appropriate accompaniment. Save any leftover gravy for your next Red-cooked Starter Sauce.

Chinese Beef Stew

紅燒牛肉

Hong Shao Niu Rou

Eastern China

Serves 4

Chinese restaurant cookery may lead us to think of *dim sum* and stir-fried dishes as the major attractions of Chinese cooking, so it is up to the cookbook authors to introduce Westerners to the slow-cooked dishes of China. Although this kind of stew would be at home in Peking, it is more readily associated with the cooking of China's eastern coast.

The joy of this aromatic beef stew is that it tastes just as good as it smells. The beef becomes very tender, and the blend of the ginger root, soy sauce, sugar, and lemon juice, along with a touch of hot pepper, gives it a delicately spiced taste with a hint of sweet-sour. The rich, flavorful gravy thickens as the beef cooks.

2 pounds well-trimmed stewing beef, cut into ½-inch cubes
2 teaspoons cornstarch
2 tablespoons peanut, corn, or other oil
2 medium-size onions, cut in half crosswise, then quartered
2 slices (⅛ inch thick) ginger root
3 tablespoons soy sauce
2 teaspoons sugar
2 teaspoons lemon juice
½ cup water
A pinch of ground hot chili pepper, more if you like it hot

Toss the beef cubes with the cornstarch. In a 2-quart pot, heat the oil over medium heat. Add the onions, ginger root, and the beef. Stir the ingredients to separate the onions into individual pieces and to coat the meat with oil. When the beef is slightly browned, add the soy sauce, sugar, lemon juice, water, and hot pepper, mixing well. Bring the mixture to the boil, then reduce the heat. Cover the pot and simmer the beef over low heat until the meat is very tender, 1½ to 2 hours. Boil away some of the liquid if the gravy is very thin. Remove the ginger root before serving. Serve the stew over hot rice or *lo mien,* or Westernize it with potatoes. This recipe can be prepared in advance and refrigerated or frozen.

Red-cooked Beef Stew With Vegetables

胡蘿蔔燒肉

Hu Luo Bo Shao Rou

General China influence

Serves 4 to 6

This is not a classic Chinese dish—I developed it in my own kitchen—but it is based on the classic method of red-cooking. The *hoisin* sauce, fresh ginger root, and soy sauce give the stew a distinctive Chinese flavor, and the *hoisin* sauce also enriches the reddish color that comes from slow-cooking the meat in soy sauce. Carrots and green beans are selected because they are readily available and colorful, but virtually any vegetables you like in stew can be substituted.

2 pounds well-trimmed stewing beef, cut into ½-inch cubes
2 teaspoons cornstarch
1 teaspoon minced ginger root
¼ cup soy sauce
2 tablespoons hoisin sauce
¼ pound fresh green beans, sliced on the diagonal into ½-inch pieces
4 medium-size carrots, peeled and sliced on the diagonal into ½-inch pieces
2 cups water
½ cup sliced water chestnuts
2 tablespoons cornstarch dissolved in ¼ cup cold water

Toss the beef cubes with the 2 teaspoons of cornstarch. In a 2-quart pot, combine the beef, ginger root, soy sauce, and *hoisin* sauce. Cover the pot and cook for 1 hour over low heat, stirring from time to time. Add a little water if necessary to keep the beef from sticking.

Now add the sliced green beans, carrots, and the 2 cups of water to the beef. Bring the mixture to the boil, then reduce the heat to a gentle boil. Cover the pot and cook until the meat and vegetables are tender, about 30 minutes longer. The stew can be frozen at this point. To finish cooking bring the stew to the boil again and stir in the water chestnuts. Again mix together the cornstarch and water, then blend this smooth paste into the stew. Cook and stir just until the cornstarch is blended in and the gravy is thickened. Turn off the heat, or keep the stew warm over very low heat until serving time.

Star Anise Beef Stew With Hot Bean Sauce and Broccoli

五香豆瓣牛肉

Wu Xiang Dou Ban Niu Rou

Szechwan influence

Serves 4 to 6

The strong flavors of hot bean sauce, star anise, and broccoli blend well in this stew, and the gravy is lovely over rice. The hot bean sauce mellows during the slow cooking, and the licorice flavor of the star anise gently permeates the stew. Broccoli adds a slightly tart tinge. Turnips, parsnips, carrots, green beans, or any other "stew" vegetables can be substituted for the broccoli.

2 pounds well-trimmed stewing beef, cut into ½-inch cubes
2 teaspoons cornstarch
¼ cup hot bean sauce
2 whole star anise
1 cup broccoli florets
1½ cups water
2 tablespoons cornstarch dissolved in ¼ cup cold water

Toss the beef cubes with the 2 teaspoons of cornstarch, then place the beef in a 2-quart pot. Stir in the hot bean sauce and the star anise. Cover the pot and cook *gently* over moderately low heat, stirring occasionally. A rich gravy should be accumulating within 30 minutes. If no gravy forms, you are probably cooking the beef too rapidly, so try reducing the heat. Add a little water if necessary to keep the beef from sticking. Cook for about 1½ hours, until the beef is tender. The stew can be refrigerated or frozen at this point.

Now add the broccoli florets and the 1½ cups of water. Bring the liquid to the boil, and continue to cook the stew until the broccoli is tender, 10 to 15 minutes, stirring occasionally. Just before serving, again mix together the 2 tablespoons of cornstarch and the ¼ cup of cold water, then add this paste to the boiling liquid. As you blend in the cornstarch paste, cook it only until the gravy thickens and takes on a glazed look. Try to remove the star anise before the dish is served.

Sweet-and-Pungent Meatballs

咕咾肉

Gu Lao Rou

Canton

Serves 4 to 6

Tasty meatballs made of beef or veal (pork would be used in China) are seasoned with garlic, ginger, soy sauce, and sherry to give them an obvious Chinese flavor. These meatballs are delicious even before they are combined with the sauce.

The sweet-and-pungent sauce is prepared with the juices of canned pineapple and sweet pickles, which makes a more delicate blend than a sugar and vinegar sweet-sour sauce. Red and green peppers are used for color and crisp texture; and the canned pineapple chunks not only add color and a contrasting soft texture but also contribute to the sweet-sour effect.

2 pounds lean ground beef or veal
2 tablespoons soy sauce
1 tablespoon dry sherry
6 water chestnuts, finely chopped
2 medium-size cloves garlic, minced
½ teaspoon minced ginger root
1 egg (graded large), beaten
3 tablespoons peanut, corn, or other oil
1 medium-size clove garlic, minced
1 medium-size onion, cut into chunks, none larger than 1 inch square
1 large green pepper, cut into ¾- to 1-inch squares
1 large red pepper, cut into ¾- to 1-inch squares
1 can (20 ounces) pineapple chunks in unsweetened juice, drained (reserve the juice)
½ cup juice from the canned pineapple
¼ cup juice from any sweet pickles
1 tablespoon soy sauce
2 teaspoons cornstarch dissolved in 2 tablespoons cold water

For the meatballs, mix together the ground beef or veal, 2 tablespoons of soy sauce, the sherry, water chestnuts, 2 cloves of minced garlic, minced ginger root, and the egg. Shape into 1-inch meatballs. In a 12-inch skillet, heat 2 tablespoons of the oil until moderately hot. Brown the meatballs in the oil, shaking the pan lightly so they brown evenly and don't stick. Reduce the heat to low, cover the pan, and cook the meatballs for about 5 minutes.

Meanwhile, prepare the sauce. In a 10-inch skillet, heat 1 tablespoon of oil until the oil just begins to smoke. Add the garlic and onion, and stir-fry for 1 minute over high heat. Add the peppers and continue to stir-fry for an additional 2 minutes. Reduce the heat to medium, then mix in the pineapple. Blend in the pineapple and pickle juices and the soy sauce. Remix the cornstarch and water until smooth, then stir the cornstarch thickener into the liquid. Turn off the heat as soon as the mixture is thickened and glazed. Transfer the cooked meatballs to the sauce, using a slotted spoon. Stir in the meatballs gently to coat them with the sauce.

This dish can be prepared in advance and refrigerated. The peppers may soften a bit, but the sauce permeates the meatballs more, so it's a trade-off. Reheat over low heat until everything is nice and hot.

Meat Sauce and Chinese Noodles

肉末拌麵

Rou Mo Ban Mian

General China

Serves 4

This sauce is rich and surprisingly tasty for its simplicity. The secret ingredient is the chopped onions, which bring a sweet crispness to the ground beef. Unlike many slowly simmered Italian sauces, this Chinese meat sauce is stir-fried over high heat and is ready in minutes. The noodles and sauce are mixed together by the cook for convenience and even distribution. In China, however, a sauce such as this would more likely be placed in a separate bowl, and the diner would top a portion of noodles with a small amount of meat.

1 pound lo mien
1 tablespoon sesame oil
2 tablespoons peanut, corn, or other oil
2 large cloves garlic, finely chopped
3 medium-size onions, chopped
1½ pounds lean ground beef
¼ cup soy sauce

→

6 to 8 water chestnuts, coarsely chopped
Chopped scallions (white and crisp green parts) for garnish

Fill a 4- or 5-quart pot about three-fourths full with water. Bring the water to the boil. Cook the *lo mien* in the boiling water, stirring often, until the noodles are tender. Taste after 2 or 3 minutes to see if the noodles are cooked enough, then keep tasting frequently until they are done. Drain the noodles in a colander, rinse them with cold water to keep them from sticking together, then return the *lo mien* to the pot. Mix the *lo mien* with the tablespoon of sesame oil, and set the pot over low heat to keep the noodles warm while the sauce is prepared.

To cook the sauce, in a wok or a 10- to 12-inch skillet heat the 2 tablespoons of peanut, corn, or other oil until the oil just begins to smoke. Add the garlic and onions, and stir-fry until the onions soften and some are beginning to crisp. Add the ground beef, stirring constantly until the beef is cooked. Break up any large pieces of ground beef that may come together. Blend in the soy sauce and water chestnuts.

Toss the noodles with the sauce. Transfer the mixture to a large platter, and garnish with chopped scallions.

Variation:

Add ½ pound sliced fresh mushrooms after the onions are crisp, stir-frying for half a minute before adding the beef. Then, after the beef is cooked, mix in 1 package frozen green peas (thawed), stirring gently until the peas are hot. Proceed with the soy sauce and water chestnuts. Serve this meat-vegetable sauce over *lo mien*.

Hot Meat Sauce and Chinese Noodles

辣味麵

La Wei Mian

Peking

Serves 4

This highly spiced meat sauce uses ingredients (hot turnip and hot chili paste) associated with Szechwan cooking, but the dish is adapted from a Peking recipe. Bowls of meat sauce and cold vegetables are set out, and the diner takes small amounts of everything to mix in his own bowl of noodles. Cucumbers are used to cool down the very hot sauce, and both the cucumbers and the bean sprouts bring a contrasting crisp texture to the soft noodles and sauce.

1 pound lo mien
1 tablespoon sesame oil
2 tablespoons peanut, corn or other oil
3 large cloves garlic, minced
6 scallions (white and crisp green parts), sliced thinly into rounds
2 pounds lean ground beef
¼ cup soy sauce
3 tablespoons Chinese hot turnip, or radish with chili, or a hot Chinese pickled vegetable
1 teaspoon to 2 tablespoons chili paste with garlic, depending on the hotness desired
2 cups peeled chopped cucumbers
2 cups fresh bean sprouts

To cook the *lo mien,* fill a 4- or 5-quart pot about three-fourths with water; bring the water to the boil. Drop in the noodles, and cook, stirring often, until the noodles are tender. Taste after 2 or 3 minutes, and continue to cook until the noodles are done, tasting often. Drain the noodles in a colander, rinse them with cold water to keep them from sticking together, then return the *lo mien* to the pot. Mix the noodles with the tablespoon of sesame oil, and set the pot over low heat to keep the noodles warm while the sauce is prepared.

For the sauce, in a wok or a 10- or 12-inch skillet heat the 2 tablespoons of peanut, corn, or other oil until the oil just begins to smoke. Stir in the garlic and scallions; stir continuously and rapidly for about half a minute. Add the ground beef, and stir-fry until all the beef is brown. Break up any clumps of meat while you are stirring. Blend in the soy sauce, hot turnip (or radish or pickled vegetable), and the chili paste, mixing well.

Put the meat sauce, cucumbers, and bean sprouts in separate bowls. Each person gets a bowl of noodles, adds the toppings, and mixes them together.

Hunan Meat Sauce
湖南肉末
Hunan Rou Mo

Hunan influence

Serves 4

Creating recipes for Chinese meat sauce is a good way of learning about regional variations in Chinese cooking. This robust meat sauce will make your eyes water if you're not careful. The more chili paste you use, the more this becomes a Hunan dish, and Hunan (culinarily speaking) is synonymous with hot. The scallions add a fresh-tasting sharpness. Serve the sauce over *lo mien*, rice, or even hamburger rolls.

1 tablespoon peanut, corn, or other oil
1 bunch scallions (white and crisp green parts), sliced into rounds
6 water chestnuts, coarsely chopped
1 pound lean ground beef
¼ cup soy sauce
1 to 3 teaspoons chili paste with garlic, to taste
½ cup beef broth

In a wok or 8- to 10-inch skillet, heat the oil to 375 degrees F. Stir in the scallions and water chestnuts, coating them with oil. Add the ground beef, and stir constantly until the beef is completely browned. Raise the heat if necessary so the beef cooks quickly. Drain off any fat that accumulates. Reduce the heat, mix in the soy sauce, then add the chili paste. Start with a little and work your way up. You can always add more to make the beef spicier, but it is very difficult to dilute the effect of the hot chili paste once it has been added. Stir in the beef broth, and continue cooking until the broth is heated through. Keep warm over low heat until serving.

Beef Chop Suey
李公雜碎
Li Gong Za Sui

Chinese-American

Serves 3 or 4

It is generally agreed that *chop suey* originated in the United States, not in China, but just how it was "invented" is open to discussion. According to one version, a Chinese diplomat traveling in Europe in the 1800s became ill from the food (or, at best, grew tired of it) and in desperation his aide concocted a bland-tasting stir-fried dish from ingredients at hand. Others say that out-of-work Chinese laborers who had been brought to America to work on the transcontinental railroads opened food stalls featuring quick-cooked cut-up vegetables and meats. The mixtures were inexpensive, palatable, and resembled Chinese cooking enough to attract Chinese workers, but they were different enough from American cooking for *chop suey* to catch on as an interesting "foreign" dish.

Humble in origin, and more an American dish than an authentic Chinese food, *chop suey* ("mixed assorted," "fragments," or more loosely, "odds and ends") continues to occupy a place on many Chinese restaurant menus all over the United States. In keeping with the thread common to all stories about the origins of *chop suey,* the dish as presented here uses vegetables that most people have on hand—celery, carrots, and onions. Mushrooms, bean sprouts, and tomato wedges are common ingredients in *chop suey,* so they are included in the recipe as "additional possibilities."

Although we see *chop suey* on restaurant menus, it is really a home-style dish that makes use of whatever happens to be in the refrigerator. Leftover beef from a roast is used in this recipe, but thinly sliced broiled steak or uncooked beef that is thinly sliced and then stir-fried can be mixed with the cooked vegetables.

3 tablespoons peanut, corn, or other oil
1 cup thinly sliced celery, cut on the diagonal
1 cup thinly sliced carrots, cut on the diagonal
½ pound small onions (1½- inch diameter), sliced into rounds
Additional possibilities: 1 cup thinly sliced mushrooms; 1 cup fresh bean sprouts; 2 medium-size ripe tomatoes, each cut into 6 to 8 wedges

→

1 to 2 cups very thinly sliced leftover roast beef, cut into pieces about 1 inch square
2 tablespoons soy sauce
1 teaspoon sugar
Salt to taste

In a wok or a 12-inch skillet, heat the oil until it just begins to smoke. Stir-fry the celery for 2 minutes, then add the carrots and continue to stir-fry 3 minutes longer. Toss in the onions, and stir continuously for another 2 minutes. If you are using mushrooms, add them now, stir-frying for half a minute. Mix in the cooked beef slices, stirring until the beef is hot. Next toss in the optional bean sprouts, then the optional tomato wedges; cook, stirring all the while, until the sprouts and tomatoes are warmed through. Finally, sprinkle on the soy sauce and sugar, add salt if you like, and mix the contents of the pan once more. Serve the *chop suey* at once with hot rice.

Stir-fried Lamb and Vegetables

青椒炒羊肉

Qing Jiao Chao Yang Rou

Canton influence

Serves 4

This looks and tastes like a Cantonese preparation, but it was developed in a Connecticut kitchen. The individual tastes of the lamb, peppers, mushrooms, and tomatoes come through beautifully in this colorful dish. A simple beef broth, thickened and glazed with cornstarch, is added at the very end so there is no chance for the crisp peppers and partially cooked mushrooms to lose their textures. The broth picks up some of the flavor of the lamb, and it increases the eye appeal of the dish as it glazes all the ingredients. The optional sesame oil lends an exotic quality, but it is not an essential ingredient in an already tasty combination.

4 shoulder lamb chops
2 large cloves garlic, minced
1 teaspoon minced ginger root
2 tablespoons peanut, corn, or other oil
2 large green peppers, cut into strips
¾ pound fresh mushrooms, sliced
1 tablespoon peanut, corn, or other oil
4 fresh plum tomatoes, quartered

⅔ cup beef broth, undiluted if canned
2 tablespoons cornstarch dissolved in 6 tablespoons cold water
2 teaspoons sesame oil (optional)

Slice the meat from the lamb chops into thin strips, discarding the bones, gristle, and fat. Mix the lamb with the minced garlic and ginger root.

In a wok or a 12-inch skillet, heat the 2 tablespoons of oil to 375 degrees F. Add the green pepper strips and stir-fry for 1½ minutes, then add the mushrooms. Continue to stir-fry half a minute longer. Remove the vegetables to a clean bowl.

Add about a tablespoon more oil to the wok or skillet, enough to coat it. Stir-fry the lamb strips over moderately high heat just until they are cooked. Stir in the peppers and mushrooms, then the uncooked tomato quarters. Add the beef broth, and bring it to the boil. Again stir together the cornstarch and cold water until blended well, then mix the cornstarch paste into the broth, stirring constantly until the broth is thickened and glazed. Remove the pan from the heat, blend in the sesame oil, and serve the lamb and vegetables immediately.

Ground Lamb and Peas

雪豆羊末

Xue Dou Yang Mo

General China influence

Serves 4

My daughter would like to omit peas from all recipes, but they contribute a sweet taste and bright color to this dish. Garlic, ginger root, and soy sauce bring out the best in lamb in any form, including the ground lamb used here. This dish takes only a few minutes to cook, and unlike many recipes for Chinese cooking it requires almost no cutting up of ingredients.

2 tablespoons peanut, corn, or other oil
3 large cloves garlic, finely chopped
1 teaspoon minced ginger root
1½ pounds lean ground lamb
¼ cup soy sauce
1 package (10 ounces) frozen green peas, thawed

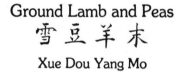

In a wok or a 10- to 12-inch skillet, heat the oil to 375 degrees F. The oil will be hot but not yet smoking. Add the garlic and ginger root, and stir them in the oil continuously for 30 seconds. Add the ground lamb, stirring constantly until the lamb is cooked. Drain off any accumulated fat. Mix in the soy sauce, then add the peas. Continue to cook, stirring constantly, until the peas are heated through. Keep the pan warm over low heat until you are ready to serve. Leave the pan uncovered so the peas do not overcook. Serve the lamb and peas over rice or *lo mien.*

Ground Lamb and Chinese Noodles

羊肉末拌麵

Yang Rou Mo Ban Mian

Peking

Serves 4

This piquant meat sauce features lamb and scallions seasoned with garlic, ginger root, and soy sauce. The scallions add color and bring a contrasting consistency to the ground lamb. The meat is served over *lo mien* tossed with sesame oil, another flavor that goes very well with lamb.

1 pound lo mien
1 tablespoon sesame oil
2 tablespoons peanut, corn, or other oil
3 medium-size cloves garlic, finely chopped
1½ teaspoons minced ginger root
8 scallions (white and crisp green parts), chopped
1½ pounds lean ground lamb
¼ cup soy sauce

In a 4- to 6-quart pot, bring 3 to 4 quarts of water to the boil. Add the *lo mien* to the boiling water and cook until it is just tender, stirring often. Taste for tenderness after 2 or 3 minutes, and keep tasting frequently until it is done. Drain the cooked noodles, rinse them with cool water, and return them to the pot. Mix the *lo mien* with the sesame oil, and set the pot over the lowest possible heat to keep the noodles warm.

For the sauce, in a wok or a 10- to 12-inch skillet heat the 2 tablespoons of oil until hot but not yet smoking, about 375 degrees F. Add the garlic, ginger root, and scallions and stir continuously for a minute to coat them with oil and release their flavors. Add the ground lamb, stir-frying until the lamb is cooked. Spoon off any accumulated fat from the lamb, then mix in the soy sauce. To serve American style, put the noodles on a platter or in a very large bowl, and pour the sauce over the *lo mien*. Mix the *lo mien* and sauce before serving. To serve Chinese style, each person gets a bowl of noodles and spoons a small amount of sauce over the noodles, along with vegetable accompaniments such as chopped cucumbers and fresh bean sprouts.

Sweet-and-Pungent Baked Lamb Breast

咕咾羊排

Gu Lao Yang Pai

Canton influence

Serves 4 to 6

This is a kosher alternative to sweet-and-sour pork, which is very popular in Chinese-American restaurants. The lamb is served as pork would be in China, with the bone in. The lamb must be eaten with the fingers, which means that you get to taste every drop of that delicious sauce (if you lick your fingers). The lamb itself is crisp and very flavorful, and the green peppers, pineapple chunks, and tomatoes make this dish exceptionally pretty to look at.

4 pounds breast of lamb, the leanest you can get
8 ounces bottled sweet-and-pungent sauce or sparerib sauce
1 tablespoon peanut, corn, or other oil
1 large clove garlic, cut in half
2 medium-large green peppers, cut into 1-inch squares
1 can (20 ounces) pineapple chunks in unsweetened juice, drained (reserve the juice)
2 fresh red tomatoes, cut into 8 wedges each

Preheat the oven to 350 degrees F. Slice the lamb into individual ribs. Cut off as much fat as you can. Roast the lamb on a rack for about 45 minutes, until it begins to brown and some of the fat drips out. Transfer the lamb to a clean roasting pan. Place the lamb directly in the pan, not on a rack.

Brush all sides of the ribs with sweet-and-pungent sauce. Bake for another half-hour or until the lamb is crisp and well glazed, brushing every 10 minutes with sweet-and-pungent sauce.

In a 7- or 8-inch skillet, heat the oil until it is hot but not yet smoking, 375 degrees F. Stir the garlic in the oil for a minute or two to flavor the oil, then remove the garlic. Add the peppers and stir-fry for 1 minute. Remove the pan from the heat.

When the lamb is crisp, add the stir-fried peppers, the pineapple chunks, and the tomatoes to the roasting pan. Pour in half the juice from the canned pineapple and part of the remaining sweet-and-pungent sauce. Blend the liquids gently. Taste the resulting sauce, and add more pineapple juice or sweet-and-pungent sauce according to taste. Bake only until everything is heated through, stirring occasionally. Serve this with rice so you don't lose any of the sauce.

Sweet-and-Sour Lamb Stew

甜酸羊肉

Tian Suan Yang Rou

General China influence

Serves 4 to 6

Here, onions, ginger root, and garlic are ground to a smooth paste. (A blender or food processor takes the place of a mortar and pestle). The paste is fried lightly to evaporate the water, then the lamb is browned in the spicy mixture. The browned lamb simmers in soy sauce; sugar is added for sweetness and a little lemon juice adds pungency to the ginger root flavor. A bit of hot pepper contributes a zesty touch. If you like very spicy foods, increase the amount of chili pepper and turn this into a hot-and-sour lamb. Slow-cooked dishes usually have a wonderful aroma as they cook, and this one is no exception.

2 pounds lamb, cut into ½-inch cubes
2 teaspoons cornstarch
2 medium-size onions
1 slice (1 inch thick) ginger root
3 large cloves garlic
2 or 3 tablespoons water
2 tablespoons peanut, corn, or other oil

3 tablespoons soy sauce
2 teaspoons sugar
2 teaspoons lemon juice
½ cup water
A pinch of ground hot chili pepper, or to taste

Mix the lamb with the cornstarch and set it aside. Chop the onions, ginger root, and garlic. Place them in a blender or food processor; add 2 or 3 tablespoons of water, just enough to puree the ingredients. Blend the mixture until a smooth puree or paste is formed.

In a 2-quart pot, heat the oil until it just begins to smoke. Add the pureed onion mixture and stir immediately and constantly so the onions do not burn. Cook and stir until the water evaporates. Do not let the onions brown. Add the lamb; stir it until it browns lightly. Add the remaining ingredients. Mix well. Bring the liquid to the boil, then reduce the heat, cover the pot, and simmer the lamb over low heat until tender, 1 to 1½ hours. If the sauce is thin, uncover the pot and boil away some of the liquid before serving the stew. This lamb can be prepared in advance and refrigerated or frozen. Serve it with rice, which will soak up the flavor of an exceptional gravy.

Lamb Kebobs
火燒羊肉串

Huo Shao Yang Rou Chuan

General China influence

Serves 4

In China, two pounds of meat would be stretched to cover numerous meals, so a dish like this would be found only at a banquet. Lamb adapts well to all kinds of Chinese cooking, and this thick sweet-and-spicy marinade is absolutely wonderful with lamb. The rich red-brown color and beautiful glaze sharpen the appetite, and the sizzling lamb cubes taste every bit as good as they look. Serve these barbecued *kebobs* over plain rice or rice mixed with a little sesame oil, soy sauce, and chopped scallions.

2 tablespoons hoisin sauce
2 tablespoons firmly packed light or dark brown sugar
1 tablespoon red bean paste

→

2 tablespoons soy sauce
2 tablespoons honey
2 large cloves garlic, finely chopped
2 pounds lean lamb, cut into 1½-inch cubes

In a medium-size mixing bowl, blend together the *hoisin* sauce, brown sugar, red bean paste, soy sauce, honey, and garlic. Add the lamb cubes and mix them with the sauce, coating the lamb very well on all sides. Marinate the lamb for a minimum of 4 hours, or as long as overnight. Refrigerate the lamb after 2 hours. From time to time, stir the lamb around.

Spear the marinated lamb onto skewers, allowing as much of the marinade as possible to cling to the lamb. The lamb cubes should not touch each other. Broil the lamb under a broiler or grill it over a charcoal fire, turning to cook the lamb evenly. Do not allow the lamb to catch fire: it should be sizzling and crisp but not burned. Serve the lamb with rice, and pass around sesame oil if you like. The lamb has a good flavor of its own, but it can be served with a sesame-based condiment for people who like to dip.

Mongolian Barbecue
蒙古烤肉
Meng Gu Kao Rou

Mongolia

Serves 4

Lamb has long been basic to the diet of the nomadic sheepraising peoples of Mongolia. In this esteemed Mongolian lamb dish, served in Chinese-American restaurants, strips of lamb are cooked over a charcoal fire (a large outdoor grill or hibachi is ideal for the cooking), dipped into any one of a number of spicy sauces, and eaten with pieces of steamed or baked breads. This is a do-it-yourself meal in which the diners skewer and cook their own pieces of meat.

1 recipe Steamed Rolls or Bread (page 307)
1 pound boneless lamb
Szechwan Sauce (page 130)
Sesame Sauce and/or Sesame-Peanut Butter Sauce (page 133 and 134)
"Hot" oil, purchased or homemade, and/or "Hot" Sesame-Soy Dip (page 127)

Prepare the rolls, timing them so they are hot when you are ready to cook the lamb. The rolls can be steamed or baked.

Freeze the lamb partially to make the slicing easier. Slice the meat into uniform-size pieces about 1 inch wide × 2½ inches long × ⅛ inch thick. Do not make the slices paper-thin or they will be too difficult to handle when they are cooked. Arrange the lamb attractively on plates.

To cook in the style of the nomads, everyone gathers around the fire, spears a piece of meat with some kind of long skewer, cooks the meat, dips it into a spicy sauce, and stuffs it into a roll before it is eaten. For convenience, you may want to broil the meat all at once and bring it to the table already cooked.

If this is to be served as a complete meal rather than as one course, have mushroom caps, squares of red and green peppers, and tomato wedges available for grilling after the meat is cooked and enjoyed.

5

Chicken, Chicken Livers, and Duck

Chicken is the most common poultry in China. Chickens are raised at home or purchased live. Once killed, a chicken must be eaten within a few days because there is little refrigeration outside of the cities. One chicken is cut up and used for several meals. The breasts might be used for white-cut chicken or a stir-fried dish (perhaps along with the livers), the legs and thighs for a steamed chicken-and-rice dish, and the wings in a congee. The back bones and giblets are used for chicken broth, just as we use them. Chicken thighs are usually cooked and served with the bones in; special chopping cleavers are used to chop the chicken into small pieces—bone and all—that can be handled easily with chopsticks or the fingers. In keeping with American tastes, most of the recipes in this chapter use boneless chicken breasts or thighs—and they call for at least two or three times more meat than you would expect to find on a Chinese table.

Ducks are more likely to be cooked whole than chickens are, possibly because they have less meat per pound. Even when ducks are cooked whole, however, they are served for more than one meal, and the carcass is used to make soup. Ducks can appear on the family dinner table (see the recipe for Home-style Duck) or, as the more aristocratic Peking duck, at a banquet. It is not at all unusual to see duck recipes that combine at least two methods of cooking, such as steaming and deep-frying or simmering and deep-frying.

In the United States, chicken livers are inexpensive and readily available. In China, however, a recipe using more than one or two chicken livers would almost certainly be for a restaurant or banquet dish, because the Chinese housewife simply doesn't have a way of storing chicken livers for eventual use in cooking (home freezers being almost nonexistent).

The chicken liver recipes in this book use authentic Chinese cooking methods and ingredients, but they are not classic Chinese dishes—they were developed in my kitchen. The requirement that chicken livers be broiled to be made kosher turns out to be an advantage in Chinese recipes. Broiled livers which are then stir-fried briefly come out tender and tasty without becoming too soft.

Stir-fried Chicken With Soy Sauce

炒鷄丁

Chao Ji Ding

Canton

Serves 4

In this classic Cantonese dish, chicken cubes are stir-fried, then simmered briefly in a little soy sauce, sherry, and sugar. The result is a juicy, richly flavored chicken with an attractive reddish color. This dish is exceptionally easy to prepare, and it fits remarkably well into an American-style meat-vegetable-potato (or rice) dinner or almost any kind of Chinese dinner.

3 tablespoons peanut, corn, or other oil
1½ pounds boneless chicken breasts or thighs, cut into 1-inch cubes
3 tablespoons soy sauce
3 tablespoons dry sherry
2 teaspoons sugar

In a wok or a 10-inch skillet, heat half the oil until it is hot but not yet smoking, about 375 degrees F. Add half the chicken, and stir the chicken cubes constantly until no pink color remains. Remove the chicken to a clean bowl. Heat the remaining oil, and stir-fry the rest of the chicken. Mix all of the chicken together in the pan, scraping in any liquid that has accumulated in the bowl. Reduce the heat to low, then stir in the soy sauce and sherry, and sprinkle the sugar over the chicken. Mix everything well. Cover the pan and cook over low heat for 10 to 15 minutes. Keep warm over very low heat until serving time.

Stir-fried Chicken, Peppers, and Mushrooms

青椒鮮菇炒雞丁

Qing Jiao Xian Gu Chao Ji Ding

Canton

Serves 4 to 6

This recipe is related to the popular Chinese-American restaurant dish known as *moo goo gai pan*. (*Moo goo* is mushrooms, *gai* is the Cantonese word for chicken, and *pan* means sliced.) It is an example of a Cantonese stir-fried preparation which relies only on the contrasts of the major ingredients to make a tasty and interesting dish. The seasoning is minimal, and—unlike the restaurant dish—there is no sauce.

1½ pounds boneless chicken breasts
3 tablespoons dry sherry
1 tablespoon cornstarch
6 tablespoons peanut, corn, or other oil
1 large sweet red pepper, cut into thin strips
1 large green pepper, cut into thin strips
2 cups sliced fresh mushrooms
1 teaspoon salt (optional)
½ teaspoon sugar (optional)

Partially freeze the chicken breasts until firm but not solidly frozen. Using a sharp cleaver or knife, make thin, horizontal slices approximately 1 × 1 × ⅛ inches. Toss the chicken slices with the sherry and cornstarch. In a large wok or a 12-inch skillet, heat 2 tablespoons of the oil until it is hot but not yet smoking, 375 degrees F. Add half the chicken slices, and stir-fry until all the chicken turns white on the outside. Remove the chicken to a bowl, heat 2 tablespoons more oil, and stir-fry the other half of the chicken. Return the first batch of cooked chicken to the cooking pan. Add the remaining 2 tablespoons of oil to the pan, raise the heat so the ingredients sizzle, then add the red and green pepper strips and stir-fry for 1 minute. Now throw in the mushrooms and continue cooking for 30 seconds longer, stirring constantly. Turn off the heat. Sprinkle the salt and sugar over the chicken and vegetables; mix them in and serve immediately

Variation:

For a preparation more similar to the Chinese-American restaurant *moo goo gai pan*, omit the peppers. After the chicken and mushrooms are cooked, stir in ½ cup of seasoned chicken broth. Bring to the boil, then thicken with a cornstarch paste made of 1 tablespoon cornstarch dissolved in ¼ cup cold chicken broth.

Chicken, Mushrooms, and Bean Sprouts

豆芽炒雞丁

Dou Ya Chao Ji Ding

Canton

Serves 4

This is another *moo goo gai pan*—chicken and mushrooms—with bean sprouts added. Fresh bean sprouts are essential to this combination, so if you cannot get them, omit the sprouts and call the dish by its Cantonese name, that is, *moo goo gai pan*.

Chicken, Mushrooms, and Bean Sprouts can be served over rice and topped with crisp fried noodles (as the American *chow mein* is). Because it does not have the color usually important to Chinese dishes, it should be served with one or two brightly colored vegetables or with a colorful meat-and-vegetable dish. People who do not like spicy foods will appreciate this mixture.

1 pound boneless chicken breasts
2 teaspoons cornstarch
½ teaspoon salt (optional)
½ teaspoon sugar
1 pound medium-size fresh mushrooms
¼ cup peanut, corn, or other oil
½ cup cold chicken broth mixed with 1 teaspoon cornstarch
4 cups fresh bean sprouts

Partially freeze the chicken breasts until firm but not solidly frozen. Using a sharp cleaver or knife, make thin, horizontal slices approximately 1 × 1 × ⅛ inches. Mix the chicken slices with the 2 teaspoons of cornstarch and the salt and sugar. Cut the mushroom caps into quarters, and slice the stems into ½-inch pieces.

In a large wok or a 12-inch skillet, heat the oil until it is hot but not yet smoking, 375 degrees F. Stir-fry the chicken slices until no trace of pink remains. Add the mushrooms and stir-fry 1 minute longer, partially cooking the mushrooms. Mix together the cold chicken broth and the cornstarch until the cornstarch is dissolved, then stir the liquid into the chicken and mushrooms. Cook until the broth boils and thickens, stirring constantly. Now toss in the bean sprouts, mixing them in thoroughly. Serve as soon as the sprouts are heated through. Make soy sauce available at the table.

Stir-fried Chicken, Mushrooms, and Snow Peas

醬爆鷄丁

Jiang Bao Ji Ding

Canton

Serves 4 to 6

Chicken, mushrooms, and snow peas ought to associate with each other often, because they go together wonderfully well. Moist, tender chicken seems to have a natural affinity for fresh mushrooms, and the crisp, bright green snow peas help whet the appetite on appearance alone. The sweet bean sauce adds a glaze and lends an attractive red hue to the chicken and mushrooms. It is used as the only seasoning, adding saltiness and a pleasant, mild bean flavor. A sprinkling of soy sauce and sesame oil might be substituted for the bean sauce.

¼ cup peanut, corn, or other oil
1 pound boneless chicken breasts or thighs, cut into 1-inch cubes
½ pound fresh mushrooms, sliced
¼ pound fresh snow peas, uniformly small if possible, tips and strings removed
2 tablespoons sweet bean sauce

In a wok or a 12-inch skillet, heat the oil until moderately hot—a drop of water should spatter instantly. Stir-fry the chicken until it is no longer pink. Raise the heat to about 400 degrees F., then add the mushrooms and continue to stir constantly for 30 seconds longer. Now add the snow peas, and stir-fry another half-minute. Turn off the heat, blend in the sweet bean sauce, and serve at once.

Stir-fried Chicken and Mushrooms With Lemon and Parsley

鮮味鷄丁

Xian Wei Ji Ding

Canton influence

Serves 4

Chinese cooking techniques applied to common American ingredients produce this refreshing chicken and mushrooms. Lemon juice perks up the lightly sauced stir-fried mixture, and parsley adds color and garden-fresh flavor. The texture of the dish is tender all the way, and suitable for those who have just had their braces tightened by the orthodontist.

¼ cup peanut, corn, or other oil
1 pound boneless chicken breasts or thighs, cut into 1-inch cubes
1 pound small whole fresh mushrooms
Juice of 1 lemon
1 teaspoon sugar
½ cup seasoned chicken broth
¼ cup chopped fresh parsley

In a wok or a 12-inch skillet, heat the oil until it is hot but not yet smoking, 375 degrees F. Stir-fry the chicken until it is no longer pink. Add the mushrooms and stir-fry for about 1 minute, until they are coated with oil and just beginning to darken. Raise the heat if necessary to keep the pan sizzling hot. Stir in the lemon juice, then sprinkle the sugar over the chicken and mushrooms. Now blend in the chicken broth, and turn off the heat as soon as the broth comes to the boil. Sprinkle the parsley over everything, give the contents of the pan a quick toss, and serve this dish over rice or *lo mien.*

Stir-fried Chicken With Broccoli

番芥蘭炒鷄丁

Fan Jie Lan Chao Ji Ding

Canton

Serves 4

The first time I paired chicken and broccoli in a stir-fried preparation I expected the broccoli to be overpowering. It was a pleasant surprise, then, to discover that this colorful combination offers a tasty balance.

1 medium-size bunch broccoli (1 pound)
2 tablespoons peanut, corn, or other oil
1 pound boneless chicken breasts or thighs, cut into ½-inch cubes
2 tablespoons soy sauce
1 teaspoon sugar

Cut off the broccoli florets. Quarter or halve the large florets so that all the pieces are about the same size. Reserve the stems for another use. In a 4-quart pot, bring 3 quarts of water to the boil. Cook the broccoli florets in the boiling water for 5 minutes, then drain them in a colander and rinse with cold water until cool. Set aside until ready to use. The broccoli can be parboiled in advance and refrigerated overnight.

In a wok or a 12-inch skillet, heat the oil until it is moderately hot, 350 to 375 degrees F. Add the chicken cubes to the oil and stir-fry until all the chicken pieces turn white, which will take about 2 minutes. Sprinkle on the soy sauce and sugar, continue to stir-fry the chicken for 30 seconds, then toss in the partially cooked broccoli florets. Stir-fry for an additional minute or two, until the chicken is cooked and the broccoli is crisp-tender. Serve immediately with hot rice. Pass around soy sauce and sesame oil.

Cashew Chicken With Hoisin Sauce

腰果鷄丁

Yao Guo Ji Ding

Peking

Serves 4

Cashew nuts bring their sweet, rich taste to this pleasantly spicy chicken dish, and the Chinese mushrooms and *hoisin* sauce add a touch of the exotic. You may stretch the dish by adding half a pound of *tofu* cubes, which will also contribute a very soft and contrasting texture. This chicken is fit for a banquet, and it makes a nice treat for a family meal.

1 pound boneless chicken breasts or thighs, cut into ½-inch cubes
2 tablespoons dry sherry
2 teaspoons cornstarch
4 dried Chinese mushrooms
Boiling water
¼ cup peanut, corn, or other oil
6 water chestnuts, sliced
¼ cup thinly sliced bamboo shoots
½ cup roasted cashew nuts (salted or unsalted, to taste)
¼ cup hoisin sauce

In a medium-size bowl, toss the chicken cubes with the dry sherry and the cornstarch. Place the Chinese mushrooms in a small bowl and pour boiling water over them to cover. Allow the mushrooms to soak until soft, about 15 minutes. Slice the mushrooms into strips, discarding the stems.

In a wok or a 10- to 12-inch skillet, heat the oil until it is hot but not yet smoking, 375 degrees F. Add the chicken and stir-fry until it is cooked through. Now mix in the mushrooms, water chestnuts, bamboo shoots, and the cashews. Stir quickly until the ingredients are distributed well and heated through. Blend in the *hoisin* sauce, turn off the heat, and serve.

This is one stir-fried dish that can be prepared ahead and reheated, as long as the nuts have not been added. Refrigerate the cooked chicken, vegetables, and *hoisin* sauce, and steam to reheat. Just before serving, mix in the cashew nuts.

Sub Gum Chicken Almond

五色鷄丁

Wu Se Ji Ding

Chinese-American

Serves 4 to 6

Thanksgiving and Passover are both big "food" holidays, and it may have surprised my Grandma Lillie to know that of all the wonderful foods we enjoyed on those occasions, her toasted salted almonds stand out in my mind. It would surprise Grandma even more to learn that her toasted almonds found their way into a Chinese kosher cookbook.

Nuts are frequently used in Chinese cooking for their crunch, for their taste, and because they add protein to the meal. The crisp salted almonds in this mixture (*sub gum* means mixture) of chicken and vegetables contrast well with the tender cubes of chicken and lovely mushrooms. Sweet red peppers and green peas contribute color and sweetness, canned pineapple tidbits and juice add a subtle tartness, and chicken broth is used to moisten the mixture and tie everything together.

2 tablespoons peanut oil
1 cup whole blanched almonds
½ teaspoon salt
¼ cup peanut, corn, or other oil
1 sweet red pepper, cut into ¼-inch squares
1 pound chicken breasts or thighs, cut into ½-inch cubes
½ pound fresh small whole mushrooms
1 cup fresh or frozen peas, thawed if frozen
½ cup canned pineapple tidbits in unsweetened juice (reserve the juice)
¼ cup juice from the canned pineapple
½ cup seasoned chicken broth
1 teaspoon soy sauce
2 teaspoons cornstarch dissolved in 2 tablespoons water (optional)

First toast the almonds. To do so, in an 8-inch skillet heat the 2 tablespoons of oil until moderately hot. Add the almonds, and stir-fry immediately to coat the nuts with oil and brown them. Remove the nuts as soon as they are golden brown and crisp—be very careful not to burn them. In a small bowl mix the almonds with the salt, then drain them very well on paper towels. They should be crisp and dry, not the slightest bit oily. The almonds can be prepared several days ahead. Store them at room temperature in a covered container.

In a wok or a 12-inch skillet, heat the ¼ cup of oil. When the oil just begins to smoke, stir in the red pepper, then immediately add the chicken cubes. Stir-fry the chicken until all the pieces turn white. Add the mushrooms, and continue to stir-fry for about 1 minute, until they barely begin to soften. Mix in the peas and pineapple, then the pineapple juice, chicken broth, and soy sauce. Bring the mixture to the boil. Thicken with the cornstarch paste if desired. Transfer the cooked chicken and vegetables to a platter, or heap the mixture in a large bowl. Garnish the chicken and vegetables attractively with the toasted almonds. Serve with rice.

Chicken in Rich Brown Sauce

紅燒鷄

Hong Shao Ji

Fukien and Szechwan influences

Serves 4

This red-cooked chicken features a superb gravy that is uncommonly rich and reasonably spicy. In creating this recipe, I combined a cooking method popular on the eastern coast of China with a bit of the spiciness associated with Szechwan dishes. Although boneless cubes of chicken can be used, the more authentic method of cooking cut-up pieces of unboned chicken makes a more flavorful gravy. The Chinese chop the cooked chicken pieces into two-inch pieces. The larger pieces here are easier for us to eat, but the chicken can be served either way.

1 frying chicken (3 to 3½ pounds)
½ cup unsifted all-purpose flour
Oil for shallow-frying
1 large onion, coarsely chopped
2 thin slices (1/16 inch) ginger root, cut into thin slivers
2 small cloves garlic, minced
½ teaspoon crushed dried red pepper
¼ cup soy sauce
2 tablespoons dry sherry
1 cup water

Cut the chicken into pieces: disjoint the wings, cut the thighs into 2 pieces each, cut the breasts into 3 pieces each. Roll the chicken pieces in the flour to coat them well all over. Or put the flour in a bag, and shake one or two pieces of chicken in the bag at a time to coat with flour.

Into a 12-inch skillet, pour ⅛ inch of oil. Heat the oil until moderately hot, between 350 and 375 degrees F. Add the chicken pieces, skin side down, and cook them until nicely browned. Turn to brown the other side. Adjust the heat so the chicken browns without burning. Sprinkle on the remaining ingredients (except for the water) to distribute them evenly. Add the water and bring the liquid to the boil. Cover the pan, reduce the heat so the chicken cooks gently, and cook for 30 to 40 minutes, until the chicken is tender and the sauce is a rich brown color. Keep the chicken warm over low heat until you are ready to serve.

This chicken can be refrigerated and reheated. It can also be frozen but may lose some of its spiciness. Correct the seasoning by adding a little crushed red pepper while the chicken heats up.

Red-cooked Chicken Thighs

紅燜雞腿

Hong Men Ji Tui

Eastern China

Serves 6

This very tender, richly flavored, and notably salty chicken is easy to prepare and can be served several ways. It is lightly seasoned with ginger root and garlic, which add flavor to the chicken and the gravy. When served hot with its own gravy, it is most salty and therefore goes especially well with a spicy Chinese pickle.

The Chinese most frequently allow this chicken to cool in the gravy, then they chop it into two-inch pieces, bone and all, and serve it cold. Another method of cutting and serving the chicken cold is presented in the body of the recipe.

8 whole chicken thighs
1 slice (½ inch thick) ginger root
1 large clove garlic, cut in half
1 cup soy sauce
1 cup water
1 tablespoon sugar
4 scallions (white and crisp green parts), chopped

Rub the chicken thighs with the ginger root and garlic. Place the chicken in a 12-inch skillet or in any skillet large enough to accommodate it. If necessary, cut the thighs into pieces at the joints. Chop the piece of ginger root finely and scatter it on and around the chicken. Add the soy sauce and water to the pan, then sprinkle the sugar into the liquid. Bring the liquid to the boil, cover the pan, and regulate the heat so the chicken cooks gently. Cook the chicken for 30 minutes, then turn off the heat and let the chicken cool in the pan for 20 minutes. To serve hot, transfer the chicken to a platter, spoon some of the sauce over the chicken, and garnish with chopped scallions. Serve the hot chicken with Steamed Rolls or Bread (page 307) and spicy Chinese pickles.

To serve the chicken cold, allow it to cool completely in the gravy. Pull off the skin, then use your fingers to gently pull the meat off the bones in the largest pieces possible. Now cut the chicken into uniform-size pieces. Arrange it attractively on a platter, and serve the cold chicken with several condiments or dips such as sesame oil, Sesame Sauce (page 133), any soy-sauce-based dip, or Peanut-Scallion-Hoisin Relish (page 120).

Refrigerate or freeze extra gravy and use it the next time you cook chicken this way.

Smoked Chicken

燻鷄

Xun Ji

Peking

Serves 6

This classic method of cooking chicken comes from Peking. A whole chicken is flavored with aromatic seasonings, steamed, then smoked over carmelized brown sugar and tea leaves. (In China, for the smoking process sawdust is used in place of the brown sugar.) The chicken picks up a smoky flavor, and if served chilled, it also has the definite taste of tea.

In the Chinese method of cutting and serving, the chicken is chopped into small pieces which can easily be managed by the fingers, but it is reshaped on the serving platter to resemble a split-open chicken. I have simplified the recipe a bit by using chicken thighs only, but they are chopped with a cleaver into one-inch pieces and reshaped to look like whole thighs.

1 teaspoon Szechwan peppercorns
1 tablespoon salt
1 slice (½ inch thick) ginger root
6 whole chicken thighs with legs
½ cup firmly packed dark brown sugar
½ cup tea leaves (optional)
2 teaspoons sesame oil, approximately

Crush the Szechwan peppercorns and combine them with the salt in a 5-inch skillet. Roast them over moderate heat for about 5 minutes, shaking the pan occasionally, until the salt turns light brown and the aroma of the peppercorns is very much evident. Allow the roasted salt and pepper to cool. Rub the chicken thighs all over with the ginger root, then rub in the roasted salt and pepper. Leave the chicken in the refrigerator overnight, or let stand in a cool room (not over 65 degrees F.) for 5 to 6 hours.

Place the chicken thighs on a large steamer tray, and steam them for 25 minutes. Be sure you have enough water in the pot to last that long. Turn off the heat but leave the chicken in the steamer for an additional 15 minutes.

Cover the bottom of a large heavy pot with aluminum foil. (The foil is absolutely necessary unless you want a big mess to clean up later.) Sprinkle the brown sugar and tea leaves over the foil. Place the chicken thighs, skin side down, on a wire rack or a steamer tray with very large holes; set the rack over the foil. Cover the pan tightly, and set the pan over moderately high heat. The temperature must be high enough to caramelize the sugar and create smoke, but not so high that you burn out the bottom of the pot. Allow the chicken to smoke for about 15 minutes, then turn off the heat and let the chicken remain in the pot for at least 15 minutes longer.

Rub the chicken thighs all over with a thin coating of sesame oil. Chop the chicken thighs with a sharp cleaver into even-size pieces, then arrange the chicken on a platter, reassembling the pieces in the shape of the thighs. Serve the chicken warm or chilled.

Sub Gum Chicken Salad

涼拌鷄丁

Liang Ban Ji Ding

Canton influence

Serves 4 to 6

Chicken salad takes on a Chinese look in this unusual creation. Water chestnuts and pecans are used not only for their crisp texture and the taste of the pecans but for their salad decoration. Bamboo shoots contribute to the Chinese effect, and raw peas add color. Instead of our typical mayonnaise moistener, *hoisin* sauce binds the ingredients together, adding color, spiciness, and its very distinctive taste. Start with leftover cubes of chicken or turkey, or for the most moist and tender chicken salad use the method below for white-cut chicken (see also page 108).

1 frying chicken (3½ pounds) or 3 cups cooked cubed chicken or turkey (½-inch cubes)
2 tablespoons peanut, corn, or other oil
1½ cups pecan halves
1 cup shelled fresh raw peas
¼ cup thinly sliced bamboo shoots
¼ cup coarsely chopped water chestnuts
4 to 6 tablespoons hoisin sauce
Lettuce leaves
10 whole water chestnuts, preferably fresh

In a 5- or 6-quart pot, bring 4 quarts of water to the boil. Add the whole chicken, which should be completely covered with water. When the water comes back to the boil, regulate the heat so the water boils gently. Partially cover the pot with a lid, and simmer the chicken for 20 minutes. Turn off the heat, cover the pot completely, and allow the chicken to remain in the water, over the turned-off burner, for 30 minutes or until the chicken is tender. Remove the chicken from the water, and cool it in the refrigerator. When the chicken is cool enough to handle, pull off the skin, and gently pull the chicken off the bones in the largest sections possible. Now cut the chicken into ½-inch cubes.

While the chicken is cooking, fry the pecans. In an 8-inch skillet, heat the 2 tablespoons of oil until hot but not yet smoking, about 375 degrees F. Stir-fry the pecans for 3 or 4 minutes, until crisp and golden. Drain the pecans on paper towels. Chop ½ cup of the pecans coarsely, reserving the remaining cup for garnish.

In a large mixing bowl, toss together the chicken cubes, chopped pecans, the uncooked peas, sliced bamboo shoots, and the ¼ cup of chopped water chestnuts. Blend in 4 tablespoons of *hoisin* sauce. Taste the mixture, and add more *hoisin* sauce if the salad is too dry or if you want to increase the spicy flavor.

Arrange lettuce leaves on an 8-inch plate or in a shallow 8-inch bowl. Heap the chicken salad on the plate, and pat it with your hands to make a smooth domelike shape. Cut the 10 whole water chestnuts in half. Arrange the pecan halves and the water chestnuts attractively around the salad mound, pressing them in lightly. Refrigerate the salad until serving time. A wonderful dish on a hot summer day.

Sweet-and-Pungent Chicken

咕咾鷄

Gu Lao Ji

Canton

Serves 4

Sweet-and-pungent sauces, which are common in Chinese cooking, are usually prepared separately and poured over cooked poultry, meat, fish, or dumplings. In this kosher adaptation of a Cantonese dish, the chicken and sauce are cooked in the same pan, increasing the flavor of both. The sweet and sour tastes are firmly established in every mouthful, but the pineapple and pickle juices bring a delicacy not found in sauces that depend on vinegar and sugar to achieve the sweet-and-pungent effect.

Texture is an important aspect of this dish, which contains soft tomatoes, slightly more firm pineapple, tender chicken, and crisp green peppers. The pungent aroma of the dish is attractive and the colors are appealing, both of which are important considerations in Chinese cooking.

1 pound boneless chicken breasts or thighs, cut into ¾-inch cubes
1 teaspoon cornstarch
3 tablespoons peanut, corn, or other oil
2 large cloves garlic, each cut in half
2 medium-large green peppers, cut into ¾-inch squares
1 can (20 ounces) pineapple chunks in unsweetened juice (reserve the juice)
½ cup juice from the canned pineapple
¼ cup juice from a jar of sweet pickles
2 tablespoons soy sauce
2 teaspoons cornstarch dissolved in 2 tablespoons cold water
2 medium-size tomatoes, each cut into 6 wedges

Mix the chicken cubes with the 1 teaspoon of cornstarch and 1 tablespoon of the oil. In a wok or a 12-inch skillet, heat the remaining 2 tablespoons of oil until it is hot but not yet smoking, 375 degrees F. Add the garlic and stir it in the oil for about 2 minutes, then remove the garlic from the oil and discard. This will flavor the oil with garlic but will preserve the delicacy of the sauce.

Add the chicken cubes to the oil, and stir-fry until the chicken is cooked. Adjust the temperature so the chicken cooks as quickly as possible without sticking or burning. Add the green peppers and continue to stir-fry for 1 minute longer. The peppers will cook enough to release their pungent flavor, but will remain crisp. Now stir in the pineapple chunks, then blend in the pineapple and pickle juices and the soy sauce.

Remix the 2 teaspoons cornstarch and the 2 tablespoons of water until smooth, then add the cornstarch mixture to the sauce. Cook, stirring constantly, until the sauce boils and thickens. Add the tomato wedges, mixing them in gently just until they are heated through. If you will not be serving this dish immediately, keep it warm over very low heat—and don't add the tomatoes until just prior to serving.

Deep-fried Chicken Fu Yung

芙蓉雞片

Fu Rong Ji Pian

General China

Serves 4

We are accustomed to seeing the words *fu yung* attached to "eggs," and we've come to know eggs *fu yung* as pancake-like omelets. *Fu yung* translates loosely to "wispy clouds," and *fu yung* dishes in China are those that use egg whites beaten to the wispy cloud stage. This recipe uses beaten egg whites as the only coating for deep-fried chicken pieces. The result is a golden crust which surrounds the chicken as a most delicate enclosure. It is crisp at first, then softens upon standing.

As a variation, roll the chicken in cornstarch before coating it with the egg white. This will produce more of a fusion between the chicken and the crust, making the chicken pieces more crunchy but less smooth in appearance, and less delicate in texture and taste.

2 egg whites (from eggs graded large)
1 pound boneless chicken breasts or thighs, shredded or cut into ¾-inch cubes
Oil for frying

In a small clean, dry mixing bowl, beat the egg whites with an electric mixer or a whisk until they begin to mound (just before the soft peak stage). Meanwhile, in a 10- to 12-inch skillet heat the oil to 375 degrees F. A few pieces at a time, add the chicken to the egg whites, coating them well. Drop the coated chicken into the hot oil, and fry the chicken pieces until golden brown, turning once to cook them on both sides. Don't overcrowd the pan—the chicken pieces should not touch each other. Drain the chicken well on paper towels, then serve immediately.

Stir-fried Chicken Fu Yung

芙蓉鷄絲

Fu Rong Ji Si

General China

Serves 4

Here, chicken shreds are mixed with beaten egg whites and then stir-fried. This is a common method of cooking chicken all over China. The chicken comes out soft and tender, with just a light coating of egg. Ginger root and scallions add a wonderful flavor.

1 pound boneless chicken breasts or thighs, cut into 1½ × ¼-inch shreds
1 tablespoon cornstarch
2 tablespoons peanut, corn, or other oil
2 egg whites (from eggs graded large)
1 teaspoon minced ginger root
4 scallions (white and crisp green parts), chopped

Toss the chicken shreds with the cornstarch, using your fingers to distribute the cornstarch evenly. In a wok or a 12-inch skillet, start heating the oil to 375 degrees F. Meanwhile, in a small clean, dry mixing bowl beat the egg whites with an electric mixer or a whisk until they begin to mound (just before the soft peak stage). Mix the chicken lightly with the beaten egg whites.

When the oil has reached 375 degrees F., stir-fry the ginger root and scallions for about a minute, then add the chicken and stir-fry until the chicken is done. The egg whites have the effect of insulating the chicken from the heat, so the chicken will take a little longer to cook than uncoated stir-fried chicken. Serve the chicken immediately. Complement the soft texture of the dish by serving it with crisp stir-fried snow peas and water chestnuts.

Boneless Fried Chicken on Chinese Vegetables

軟炸鷄球

Ruan Zha Ji Qiu

Canton

Serves 4

This is a festive dish, full of wonderful textures and a fine medley of Chinese vegetables. Golden crusted chicken cubes top a colorful platter of stir-fried vegetables. Crisp snow peas, Chinese cabbage, and water chestnuts are balanced with chewy Chinese mushrooms and tender chicken pieces. Uncooked scallions are sprinkled over the vegetables to add the only sharp taste in an otherwise bland combination.

8 medium-large dried Chinese mushrooms
Boiling water
1 egg (graded large)
2 tablespoons unsifted all-purpose flour
½ teaspoon salt (optional)
1 pound boneless chicken breasts, cut into 1-inch squares
Oil for frying the chicken
2 tablespoons peanut, corn, or other oil
5 stalks celery cabbage or other Chinese cabbage, cut on the diagonal into ½-inch slices
¼ pound fresh small snow peas, tips and strings removed
6 water chestnuts, sliced
¼ cup thinly sliced bamboo shoots
½ cup seasoned chicken broth
1 tablespoon soy sauce
2 teaspoons cornstarch dissolved in 2 tablespoons cold water
4 scallions (white and crisp green parts), sliced into ¼-inch rounds

In a small heatproof bowl, pour boiling water over the dried mushrooms, covering the mushrooms completely. Allow them to soak for about 15 minutes, until soft. Cut the mushrooms into quarters, discarding the stems.

In a small mixing bowl, beat the egg. Stir in the flour and the salt, and beat with a fork until the mixture is very smooth. Add the chicken pieces to the egg batter, and mix them around to coat well.

In a 10- to 12-inch skillet, heat a minimum of ½ inch of oil to a temperature of 375 degrees F. Drop in the chicken pieces individually so they do not touch each other, adding as many pieces as will fit comfortably. Do not overcrowd the pan. Fry the chicken on both sides until the pieces are golden all over. Remove the chicken from the pan, and drain it well on paper towels. Repeat until all the chicken is cooked.

As soon as the chicken is done, cook the vegetables. In a clean 10- or 12-inch skillet or a wok, heat the 2 tablespoons of peanut, corn, or other oil. When the oil reaches 375 degrees F., stir-fry the celery cabbage for 1 minute. Add the snow peas, stir-fry a minute longer, then mix in the water chestnuts, bamboo shoots, and the soaked Chinese mushroom quarters. Stir in the chicken broth and soy sauce, and when the mixture comes to the boil, remix the cornstarch and water then blend in this paste. Cook until the broth is thickened and the cornstarch is blended in thoroughly. Place the vegetables on a platter, then garnish with the scallions. Arrange the fried chicken chunks on top of the vegetables, and serve immediately.

Deep-fried Stuffed Chicken Breasts

火鷄卷

Zha Ji Juan

Peking influence

Serves 4

These golden brown chicken rolls have a thin crust of egg and flour—and a unique stuffing consisting of Chinese vegetables and pecans spiced with *hoisin* sauce. The filling is served also as a relish to accompany the chicken.

Unlike many Chinese dishes, this preparation is not designed as a meat stretcher. A luxurious whole chicken breast (two rolls) makes one serving.

8 dried Chinese mushrooms
Boiling water
8 water chestnuts
½ cup thinly sliced bamboo shoots
½ cup coarsely chopped pecans
3 tablespoons hoisin sauce

4 whole boneless chicken breasts (8 halves)
1 egg (graded large), beaten well
⅔ cup unsifted all-purpose flour, mixed with
½ teaspoon salt (optional)
Oil for deep-frying

Place the Chinese mushrooms in a small heatproof bowl. Add enough boiling water to cover, and soak the mushrooms until soft, about 15 minutes. Drain the mushrooms, then cut out and discard the stems. Chop the mushrooms, water chestnuts, and bamboo shoots coarsely. Combine them with the chopped pecans and *hoisin* sauce. Divide the filling in half, and set one half aside to serve with the chicken as a relish.

Pound the chicken thinly between two sheets of wax paper. Divide the remaining half of the filling among the chicken breasts. Spread the filling down the center of each chicken breast, then roll up the chicken tightly, lengthwise, making a long, thin roll. Secure the rolls with toothpicks if necessary. Dip each roll into the beaten egg, coating completely, then roll the chicken in the flour. The chicken breasts can be fried immediately or refrigerated for up to 4 hours.

To cook the chicken, you may use a deep fryer or a 4- to 6-quart pot. If using a deep fryer, add oil to the manufacturer's recommended level; if using a pot, add 2 to 3 inches of oil. Heat the oil to 375 degrees F. Carefully place the chicken rolls in the oil, seam side first. Cook half the rolls at a time, frying them until golden all over. Turn the chicken as necessary. Drain the chicken rolls very well on paper towels, and serve them hot, with a small bowl of the extra filling as a relish.

Roast Chicken With Hoisin Glaze and Rice Stuffing

四寶烤鷄

Si Bao Kao Ji

Peking influence

Serves 6

For some families, Friday night is not Friday night without roast chicken. This kind of roast chicken, beautifully glazed with *hoisin* sauce, is stuffed with a mushroom-and-rice combination that contains water chestnuts, scallions, and *hoisin* and soy sauces. The *hoisin* sauce, which can have a very strong effect on a dish, is used more as a background in this recipe, subtly tying together the chicken, stuffing, and gravy. Glutinous rice is used for stuffings in China. Both glutinous and brown rice will make a more chewy stuffing than white rice.

¼ cup peanut, corn, or other oil
¼ cup sliced scallions (white and crisp green parts)
2 cups sliced fresh mushrooms
½ cup coarsely chopped water chestnuts
6 cups cold cooked rice (glutinous, brown, or white), fluffed up with a fork
2 tablespoons hoisin sauce for the stuffing
3 tablespoons soy sauce
1 roasting chicken (6 pounds)
2 tablespoons hoisin sauce, approximately, for brushing the chicken
1 cup seasoned chicken broth
1 tablespoon hoisin sauce for the gravy
2 teaspoons cornstarch dissolved in 2 tablespoons cold water

In a large wok or a 12-inch skillet, heat the oil until moderately hot, 350 to 375 degrees F. Stir in the scallions to coat them with the oil, then add the mushrooms and stir-fry for 1 minute. Mix in the water chestnuts, then add the rice, stirring quickly so the rice does not stick. Toss the rice to coat the grains with oil, then blend in 2 tablespoons *hoisin* sauce and the 3 tablespoons of soy sauce. The stuffing can be prepared a day in advance and refrigerated. Allow 15 mintues extra cooking time if the stuffing is cold.

Preheat the oven to 350 degrees F. Stuff the chicken with the rice mixture, packing it lightly. Put the extra stuffing in a greased ovenproof casserole; cover the casserole with a lid or foil. Roast the chicken uncovered for 1 hour, then add to the oven the casserole with the extra rice. At this point, brush the chicken all over with a thin coating of *hoisin* sauce. Roast the chicken 15 minutes longer, then again brush it with *hoisin* sauce. Continue to cook the chicken, and now baste the chicken every 15 minutes with the juices that have accumulated in the pan. Roast the chicken for a total of 2 to 2½ hours, using whatever guides for doneness you usually use (a meat thermometer placed in the center of the stuffing will register 185 degrees F., the leg will move easily, and so on).

Transfer the chicken to a carving platter. Remove the stuffing and keep it warm in a casserole in a very slow oven or on top of the stove. To prepare the gravy, heat the drippings in the roasting pan, or transfer the drippings to a 1-quart pot, scraping the bottom of the roasting pan well. Add 1 cup of chicken broth to the drippings and bring to the boil, stirring constantly. Stir in the tablespoon of *hoisin* sauce, blending it in well. Again stir together the cornstarch and water until very smooth, then add the cornstarch paste to the gravy. Cook and stir until the mixture thickens and is smooth, then turn down the heat and keep the gravy warm over very low heat, stirring it occasionally.

Stir-fried Chicken Livers and Bean Sprouts

豆芽炒鷄肝

Dou Ya Chao Ji Gan

Canton

Serves 4

This mildly flavored dish depends on an unusual combination of textures for its interest—the chicken livers are very soft while the fresh bean sprouts remain crunchy. Sweet bean sauce adds saltiness and flavor. If it isn't available, substitute half a cup of a well-seasoned chicken broth mixed, if you like, with a tablespoon of soy sauce.

½ pound chicken livers
1 tablespoon peanut, corn, or other oil
2 tablespoons sweet bean sauce
3 to 4 cups fresh bean sprouts

Remove the membranes and fat from the chicken livers, then broil the livers until no trace of redness remains. Slice them into uniform pieces. In a wok or a 12-inch skillet, heat the oil until it is about 350 degrees F. Add the broiled chicken livers and stir until they are hot. Blend in the sweet bean sauce. Toss in the bean sprouts, cooking and tossing them around just until the sprouts are heated through. Serve immediately.

Stir-fried Hot Hot Chicken Livers

辣子鷄肝

La Zi Ji Gan

Hunan

Serves 4

The first "hot" refers to temperature, the second to spiciness. The softness of the chicken livers plays well against the very spicy tastes of the minced hot turnip and the chili paste with garlic. A little goes a long way, and this makes a nice topping for a dish of noodles.

1 pound chicken livers
2 tablespoons peanut, corn, or other oil
1 teaspoon minced ginger root
2 tablespoons minced hot turnip
1 teaspoon chili paste with garlic, or to taste
2 scallions (white and crisp green parts), chopped

Remove the membranes and fat from the chicken livers, then broil the livers until no trace of redness remains. Cut the livers into 3 pieces each. In a wok or a 10- to 12-inch skillet, heat the oil to 350 degrees F.—it does not need to be any hotter because the ingredients only need heating through. Stir the chicken livers in the oil until they are hot, then mix in the ginger root, hot turnip, and the chili paste. Continue to heat, stirring constantly, until everything is hot. Keep the livers warm over low heat until you are ready to serve. Transfer to a serving plate or bowl, and sprinkle the livers with the chopped scallions.

Chicken Livers, Onions, and Peas

雪豆鷄肝

Xue Dou Ji Gan

General China influence

Serves 4

These lightly spiced, lightly sauced chicken livers are tasty, colorful, economical, and very easy to prepare. Serve this with rice to take advantage of the beautifully seasoned gravy.

1 tablespoon peanut, corn, or other oil
1 large onion, coarsely chopped
½ teaspoon minced ginger root
1 large clove garlic, minced
¼ to ½ teaspoon crushed dried red pepper
¼ cup soy sauce
1 tablespoon lemon juice
1 cup water
1 pound chicken livers
1 package (10 ounces) frozen peas, thawed

In a wok or a 10-inch skillet, heat the oil until it is moderately hot, 350 to 375 degrees F. Add the onion, ginger root, and garlic, and stir-fry for 2 minutes. Mix in the crushed red pepper, soy sauce, and lemon juice, then stir in the water. Bring the liquid to the boil, then cover the pan and reduce the heat to a gentle boil.

While the sauce cooks, remove the membranes and fat from the chicken livers, then broil the livers until no trace of redness remains. Cut each liver into 3 or 4 pieces of uniform size. Add the cooked livers to the pan, and mix them around. Continue to simmer the ingredients for about 5 minutes longer, so the flavors in the sauce can permeate the livers. Mix in the peas. Cook until the peas are heated through, then turn down the heat to very low until you are ready to serve.

Stir-fried Chicken Livers, Onions, Snow Peas, Mushrooms, and Water Chestnuts

醬爆鷄肝

Jiang Bao Ji Gan

Canton

Serves 4 to 6

The title gives a partial listing of the ingredients, but it doesn't describe what makes the combination work so well. The chicken livers are soft but have the strongest flavor of all the ingredients. The onions and mushrooms are softened but somewhat chewy, and the snow peas, water chestnuts, and fresh bean sprouts bring a fresh crisp touch. *Hoisin* sauce is used to add flavor, which it does quietly so the emphasis remains on the meat and vegetables.

1 pound chicken livers
2 tablespoons peanut, corn, or other oil
1 large onion, sliced
1 cup fresh snow peas, tips and strings removed
2 cups sliced fresh mushrooms
¼ cup sliced water chestnuts, fresh if possible
¼ cup hoisin sauce
2 cups fresh bean sprouts

Remove the membranes and fat from the chicken livers, then broil the livers until no trace of redness remains. Cut each liver into 3 uniform pieces. In a large wok or a 12-inch skillet, heat the oil until it just begins to smoke. Add the onions and stir-fry until they are lightly browned. Add the snow peas and continue to stir-fry a minute longer. Lower the heat if the snow peas begin to brown. Now add the mushrooms and stir-fry half a minute to 1 minute longer, partially cooking the mushrooms. Mix in the water chestnuts, then the broiled chicken livers. Continue to cook, stirring constantly, until the livers are heated through. Now mix in the *hoisin* sauce. Finally, toss in the bean sprouts, cooking just until everything is hot and well blended. Serve at once.

Chicken Livers With Stir-fried Vegetables

白菜炒鷄肝

Bai Cai Chao Ji Gan

Canton

Serves 4 to 6

This is typical of Chinese stir-fried dishes in that a small amount of meat is combined with lots of vegetables. If this were a Jewish dish, the vegetables would probably be cooked until they were very soft and a delicious blend. Since this is a Chinese stir-fried preparation, it is important to cook the vegetables briefly so they retain their individuality.

½ pound chicken livers
¼ cup cold chicken broth or water
2 tablespoons soy sauce
1 tablespoon cornstarch
2 tablespoons peanut, corn, or other oil
1 large Spanish onion, sliced
6 scallions (white and crisp green parts), sliced
1 pound celery cabbage or other Chinese cabbage, sliced on the diagonal into ½-inch pieces
½ pound fresh mushrooms, sliced
½ pound fresh bean sprouts

Remove the membranes and fat from the chicken livers, then broil the livers until no trace of redness remains. Cut each liver into 3 uniform pieces. In a small bowl or a cup, blend together the cold chicken broth, soy sauce, and cornstarch until the cornstarch is dissolved and the liquid is smooth. Set aside.

In a large wok or a 12-inch skillet, heat the oil until it just begins to smoke. Add the onion and scallions and stir-fry for 2 minutes, then toss in the celery cabbage and continue to stir-fry for another minute.

Now add the mushrooms and continue to stir-fry for half a minute to a minute longer, until the mushrooms just begin to darken and wilt. Stir in the chicken livers, cooking only until they are hot. Toss in the bean sprouts, mixing lightly.

Remix the chicken broth, soy sauce, and cornstarch until smooth, then stir this mixture into the chicken livers and vegetables, mixing well. Cook only until the liquid is thickened and glazed, which should be less than a minute. Turn off the heat and serve over rice or noodles.

Chicken Livers, Peppers, and Mushrooms

白炒雞肝

Bai Chao Ji Gan

Canton

Serves 4

Many people shy away from Chinese cooking because so many of the recipes call for soy sauce, which has a high sodium content. This recipe relies on the distinctive taste and softness of chicken livers, the permeating flavors of ginger root and garlic, the sweet crispness of red peppers, the slightly tart taste of crisp green peppers, and the earthy flavor of softened mushrooms. You'll be too busy enjoying this variety to miss the soy sauce.

1 pound chicken livers
2 tablespoons peanut, corn, or other oil
2 teaspoons minced ginger root
2 cloves garlic, minced
1 large sweet red pepper, sliced into thin strips
1 large green pepper, sliced into thin strips
½ pound fresh mushrooms, sliced

Remove the membranes and fat from the chicken livers, then broil the livers until no trace of redness remains. Slice the cooked livers into strips. Set aside.

In a wok or a 10-inch skillet, heat the oil to 375 degrees F. Add the ginger root and garlic, and stir them around the oil constantly to release their flavors and season the oil. Add the red and green pepper strips and stir-fry for 30 seconds, coating the peppers with oil. Now toss in the mushrooms and continue to stir-fry a minute longer. If the pan becomes too dry, add a little more oil. Drizzle the oil down the side of the wok or skillet instead of pouring it directly over the vegetables—it will become hot more quickly this way. Mix in the cooked chicken livers, tossing the ingredients around until the livers are hot and mixed in. Serve immediately with rice or *lo mien* seasoned with sesame oil.

Chicken Livers and Summer Squash

南瓜炒鷄肝

Nan Gua Chao Ji Gan

General China influence

Serves 4

This dish is an interesting study in contrasts: the heftiness of the chicken livers against the sweet, mild taste of the summer squash; the dark brown meat vs. the bright yellow skin of the vegetable; the softness of the livers contrasting with the crisp, barely cooked squash. Crushed red pepper adds zip as the only seasoning.

1 pound chicken livers
2 tablespoons peanut, corn, or other oil
1 pound yellow (or green) summer squash, cut lengthwise into quarters then sliced into ½-inch pieces
½ teaspoon crushed dried red pepper

Remove the membranes and fat from the chicken livers, then broil the livers until no trace of redness remains. Cut each liver into 3 pieces of uniform size. Set aside.

In a wok or a 10-inch skillet, heat the oil to 375 degrees F. Add the summer squash and stir-fry for about 2 minutes, until just barely cooked. Mix in the chicken livers and continue to cook and stir until the livers are heated through. Now sprinkle on the crushed red pepper, and stir 1 minute longer to distribute evenly.

Peking Duck
北京烤鴨
Beijing Kao Ya

Peking

Serves 4 to 8

Duckling roasted to crisp perfection is cut into pieces and eaten in an extraordinary sandwich. The "bread"—a thin steamed wrapper made of flour and water—is chewy but has little taste. Scallion "paintbrushes" contrast sharply with the meaty duck, crisp skin, and the bland pancake-like wrapper. The scallions are used to brush on the tangy *hoisin* sauce, adding just the right touch of flavor.

The ducks in China are literally force-fed to become very fat, and the dish known as Peking duck is served in China with meat, skin, and a lavish slice of fat. The duck prepared in this recipe is served without fat.

Peking duck takes twenty-four hours to prepare, but most of that is waiting time. The duck hangs overnight in a cool, airy place until there is no dripping and the skin is completely dry. Then it marinates in sherry (rice wine in China) and hangs again until it is dry. The hanging time can be shortened by setting a fan to blow air on the duck for several hours. Drying the duck is an important step because it contributes to the crisping of the skin. In some recipes, the duck is pumped with air prior to cooking to separate the skin from the meat. In this recipe that step is omitted, with very satisfactory results.

Peking duck is served most easily as an appetizer. (Because it is time-consuming to cut the duck attractively, it is difficult to fit in the cutting between courses.) As an appetizer, allow two or three pieces per person. Peking duck is also served most appropriately as the featured attraction at a banquet. As part of a multicourse banquet, one duck can serve as many as ten. In an American-style meal, it will serve four as the main course.

1 duckling (5 pounds)
2 cups dry sherry
12 to 15 scallions
1 recipe Mu Shu Pancakes (page 309)
6 tablespoons hoisin sauce mixed with 1 tablespoon sugar

If the duck is frozen, defrost it thoroughly before beginning. Wash the duck inside and out and pat it dry. Hang the duck overnight in a cool place; place a pan underneath it to catch the drippings. Where can you hang the duck? An unheated room that is protected from animals is excellent in cool weather. The duck might be suspended from a plant hook in the ceiling or from some kind of laundry line arrangement. In warmer weather, or if no cool area is ever available, you can hang the duck from the back of a chair and blow a fan on it for several hours. Use a strong metal wire (pieces of coat hanger will work) and securely pierce the duck so it won't fall during the hanging. If there is no alternative, set the duck, unwrapped, on a rack with a pan underneath to catch the drippings. Refrigerate the duck, turning it occasionally.

The next morning, marinate the duck in the sherry for 2 hours, turning it from time to time. Rehang the duck for 5 or 6 hours, or dry it out with a fan.

When you are about ready to cook the duck, preheat the oven to 350 degrees F. Remove all the visible fat from the duck before cooking, and prick the skin all over with a large kitchen fork. Place the duck on the rack of a roasting pan and roast it in the 350-degree F. oven for 1 hour, turning it two or three times. Turn the duck carefully so no skin sticks to the rack. Prick the skin from time to time so the fat can drip out. After the hour, reduce the heat to 325 degrees F. and cook the duck for another 30 minutes, then increase the heat to 400 degrees F. for a final browning of the duck. Continue to prick the skin and turn the duck from time to time for even browning. Be very careful when pulling out the pan to turn the duck, as a lot of fat accumulates and it is possible to start a fire if any fat spatters or spills. Remove the duck when it is crispy brown all over. The total cooking time is 2 to 2½ hours.

While the duck is roasting, make the scallion paintbrushes. Cut the root ends off the scallions, and cut off the green tops where they begin to separate. Using one or two 1½- to 2-inch pieces from each scallion, use a small sharp knife to cross-slit both ends about half an inch. Soak the scallions in ice water for an hour or longer. The slit ends will open up like a flower. (See illustrations on page 117.) Once they have opened, the scallion brushes can be transferred from the ice water to a covered container and refrigerated overnight.

If the *mu shu* pancakes haven't been made in advance, prepare them while the duck is roasting. Allow at least 1½ hours for the wrappers. If they were made in advance, steam them until hot a few minutes before you're ready to serve.

Before the duck is sliced, arrange the scallion brushes attractively on two plates, and put the *hoisin* sauce mixture into two small bowls. The steamed pancakes will be arranged in an overlapping circle on two plates just before the duck is served.

Cutting up the duck is tricky. You are aiming for 20 to 24 reasonably even-sized pieces of duck and skin. Cut off the wings and legs and set aside. Leaving the remainder of the duck intact, first cut the skin into pieces roughly 1 inch square, scoring the meat as you cut the skin. Scrape all the fat off the skin with a sharp knife, then scrape any fat off the duck meat. Now, use a boning knife to cut the meat into uniform pieces the size of the skin. If there are enough meat and skin from the body of the duck to make up the 20 to 24 pieces, serve the legs whole. If not, cut the meat and skin from the legs for the remainder. Serve the wings whole, or save them for a private treat.

If you are not ready to serve immediately, put the meat on a warming tray, and put the skin on a cookie sheet or baking sheet. Just before serving, place the skin pieces several inches from a preheated broiler. Watching *constantly,* broil the skin so that it crispens without burning. The meat and skin are usually served on separate plates, but if your cutting technique is not yet skillful, cover each piece of meat with one of skin.

Set out on the table the duck and skin, pancakes, scallion brushes, and the *hoisin* sauce. Each person opens up a pancake and paints on some *hoisin* sauce with the scallion. A piece of duck, skin, and the scallion are then rolled up in the pancake and enjoyed.

Roast Duckling With Plum Sauce

梅醬烤鴨

Mei Jiang Kao Ya

General China influence

Serves 4 generously

A rich, sweet, mildly pungent sauce uses canned plums as the basis for an exquisite blend. The sauce is used to glaze and flavor the roast ducklings, and there is plenty of sauce left to serve as an unusual gravy for rice. This plum sauce is also a wonderful glaze for roast leg or breast of lamb.

2 ducklings (5 pounds each)
1 large can (30 ounces) purple plums in heavy syrup
2 tablespoons peanut, corn, or other oil
1 medium-size onion, chopped
1 can (6 ounces) frozen lemonade, thawed but undiluted
⅓ cup chili sauce (any store brand or name brand, not an Oriental chili sauce)
¼ cup soy sauce

→

1 teaspoon minced ginger root
1 large clove garlic, minced

Preheat the oven to 350 degrees F. Remove the solid pieces of fat from the ducks. Cut the ducks into quarters, and prick the skin all over. Place the duck quarters, skin side up, on racks in roasting pans (you will probably need two pans). Roast in a preheated oven for 1½ hours. Prick the skin every half-hour with a large fork. If using two roasting pans, reverse the pans on the shelves after 45 minutes to insure even cooking.

Meanwhile, prepare the sauce. Go through the purple plums carefully to remove all pits. In a blender or a food processor, puree the plums with their syrup. In a 2-quart pot, heat the oil until it is hot but not yet smoking. Stir-fry the onion until it is soft but not brown. Add the pureed plums and the remaining ingredients. Simmer the sauce over medium heat for about 15 minutes, then return it to the blender and puree the entire sauce. Return the puree to the pot, and keep it warm over low heat. The sauce can be prepared in advance and refrigerated overnight, or frozen for later use.

After the duck quarters have roasted for 1½ hours, carefully remove the pans from the oven, remove the racks from the pans, and pour off the fat. An empty coffee can is a good receptacle for the fat. Place the duck quarters directly in the roasting pan (the racks are no longer used). Try to fit them into one large pan if possible. Baste the duck quarters liberally with the purple plum sauce. Return them to the oven for 10 minutes, and baste again every 10 minutes until the duck is crisp and beautifully glazed. Allow about 40 minutes after the first 1½ hours of roasting.

Serve the duck quarters with rice, and pass around the extra sauce. Serve plain vegetables with this roast duck, such as steamed carrots and stir-fried green beans with almonds sprinkled on top. You do not want any strongly flavored accompaniments to compete with the plum sauce.

Home-style Steamed Crispy Duck

香酥鴨

Xiang Su Ya

Szechwan

Serves 4 to 6

This dish combines two cooking methods—steaming and deep-frying—to produce an exceptionally tender and crispy duck. It is considered a home-style dish because the duck is placed in the center of the table and everyone pulls off pieces with chopsticks. The pieces of duck are dipped into the Szechwan peppercorns and salt and then stuffed into the slightly sweet steamed dinner rolls to be eaten as a sandwich. The contrasting textures of the crisp skin, tender meat, and soft rolls are important. The roasted salt and pepper add flavor and pep.

The duck and the rolls both take many hours to prepare, but most of the time is either in the rising (the rolls) or in the unsupervised steaming and cooling (the duck). The rolls can be made well in advance and frozen, and the duck can be steamed ahead and refrigerated overnight, leaving last-minute cooking (resteaming the rolls and deep-frying the duck) that will take only a matter of minutes.

1 duckling (5 pounds)
1 slice (½ inch thick) ginger root
1 recipe Steamed Rolls or Bread (page 307)
1 recipe Salt and Pepper—Chinese Style (page 126)
Oil for deep-frying

Rub the duck inside and out with the fresh ginger root. Steam the duck on a rack or steamer tray over boiling water for 2 hours. (If you don't have a rack or steamer tray, you may place the duck on a plate, in which case it will be necessary to drain off the accumulated juices before cooling the duck.) An 8-quart pot should hold the duck. Make sure the water doesn't completely boil away or you will have uncooked duck and a burned pot. Remove from the pot the rack, steamer tray, or plate with the cooked duck on it—don't attempt to take off the duck until it is completely cool, or it will fall apart. The duck can be refrigerated after it is cool enough to handle, or fried as soon as it is cooled.

If the rolls have not been prepared in advance, start them as soon as you put up the duck to steam. The salt and pepper can be roasted at this time also. Have the rolls steamed and hot before you start the deep-frying. Leave them in the steamer to stay warm until serving time.

The cooled whole duck is easiest to fry in a wok, which is exactly the right shape for easy handling. An 8-quart pot will also do, although it's a little difficult to turn the duck in a pot. In the wok or pot, heat at least 3 inches of oil to 375 degrees F. (a drop of water will spatter instantly). Carefully lower the duck into the oil, using two large kitchen spoons. Extra special care must be taken to avoid spilling and spattering with this quantity of oil. When the duck is brown on one side, turn it and brown the other side as well. If you have an enormous pot and plenty of oil, it may be possible to deep-fry the whole duck without any turning. Drain the duck carefully on paper towels, then transfer it to a serving platter. Serve the duck with the roasted salt and pepper and the steamed dinner rolls—and chopsticks for everyone.

Boneless Pressed Duck

去骨酥鴨

Qu Gu Su Ya

Canton, Chinese-American

Serves 4

This is a restaurant or banquet dish requiring time, patience, and skill. The creation of Cantonese chefs working in Chinese-American restaurants, the dish is known as *wor shew opp* on restaurant menus. To prepare it, a whole duck is either steamed or simmered until tender. When cool enough to handle, the entire duck is boned then pressed with the hands into pieces of uniform size and thickness. The tender duck is coated with a light batter and deep-fried until golden and crisp. It is served in small pieces on a bed of shredded lettuce, topped with a smooth thickened brown sauce and chopped almonds. The result is a fine dish of contrasting textures and delicate flavors.

¼ cup coarsely chopped almonds
1 tablespoon peanut, corn, or other oil
1 duckling (5 pounds)
1 slice (½ inch thick) ginger root
1 tablespoon soy sauce
¼ cup unsifted cornstarch
3 tablespoons cold water
1 egg white (from an egg graded large)
Oil for deep-frying
1 cup seasoned chicken broth
1 tablespoon soy sauce
1½ tablespoons cornstarch dissolved in 2 tablespoons cold water
2 cups shredded lettuce

First, toast the almonds. To do so, in a 7- or 8-inch skillet heat the oil to 375 degrees F. Stir-fry the almonds until lightly browned, then drain them on paper towels. Reserve the almonds for later use as garnish.

Rub the skin of the duck all over with the ginger root, then rub in the soy sauce. Steam the duck on a rack over boiling water for 1 hour. (An 8-quart pot should accommodate the duck.) Remove the duck and allow it to cool thoroughly.

Now, bone the duck. Cut through the breastbone as neatly as you can, then lay the duck out flat, with the skin on the work surface and the inside (the cavity) facing you. Use a boning knife to cut out the rib cage, disjointing the wing and leg bones when you get to them. Work the boning knife between the bones and the meat until all the meat is free from the bones, except for the wing and leg meat. Now turn the duck over so the skin faces you. Remove the wings and set aside for another use—they are not served with the finished dish. Use your fingers or a boning knife to carefully scrape the meat off the leg bone toward the thigh, leaving the meat and skin as whole as possible.

Place the duck between two sheets of wax paper. With the palms of the hands, press the duck firmly into a square measuring 6 to 8 inches, of even thickness. Cut the square into 4 equal pieces. (If you haven't been able to bone the duck in one piece and it is already in 2 or 4 pieces, press each section out separately.) The duck can be refrigerated at this point.

In a shallow bowl, stir together the ¼ cup cornstarch and the 3 tablespoons cold water. This will be used as a batter and should be very smooth. Use a clean fork and a clean shallow bowl to beat the egg white until foamy. Meanwhile, in a deep fryer, a wok, or a 4-quart pot heat 2 inches of oil until hot but not yet smoking, about 375 degrees F.—a drop of water will spatter instantly.

Dip the pieces of duck first into the egg white and then into the cornstarch batter, coating them well all over. Gently lower the coated duck into the hot oil, frying on both sides until the duck is a lovely golden color. Drain well on paper towels.

While the duck is frying, in a 1-quart pot bring the chicken broth and a tablespoon of soy sauce to the boil. Stir in the 1½ tablespoons of dissolved cornstarch, mixing until the cornstarch paste is blended in and the sauce is thickened. Turn off the heat.

Place the shredded lettuce on a small platter or a plate. Cut the duck into even-size pieces about 1 × 2 inches. Arrange the pieces of duck attractively over the lettuce, drizzle the sauce over the duck, sprinkle with the toasted almonds, and serve at once.

6

Fish

Fish has a special place in both Jewish and Chinese cooking. Many traditional Jewish meals, including the weekly Sabbath dinner, feature some kind of fish dish as a first course. In China, where fish is said to be a symbol of prosperity, a whole fish is the last course served at a banquet, ending the meal on a prosperous note.

Although fish generally is considered *pareve* ("neutral") and can be eaten at either dairy or meat meals, some Orthodox groups do not mix fish and meat in the same dish. Therefore, where Chinese fish recipes originally called for chicken broth, the simple substitution of a vegetable broth makes the dish fit into the strict laws of *kashrut*—and it keeps the dish *pareve*.

Freshly caught fish is a staple in the coastal regions of China, and it is a major protein source in many diets. Westerners who visit China cannot help but be impressed by the numbers and kinds of fish dishes served every day. Steaming, pan-frying, and deep-frying are common ways of cooking fish. Bits of fish are used to flavor rice and vegetable dishes.

Numerous authentic Chinese dishes call for kosher fish (those with fins and scales), so no kosher adaptation is necessary. However, shellfish—which is never permitted in the kosher kitchen—is eaten extensively in the coastal areas of China. In Chinese-American restaurants, shrimp, lobster, and scallops are said to be the shellfish most frequently ordered. To make a dish calling for any of these items kosher I have substituted fish with fins and scales for the shellfish.

For example, in the first recipe in this chapter, Fillets of Fish Cantonese, fresh sole or flounder fillets substitute for the shrimp. The ground pork that is sometimes called for in authentic Chinese recipes for this dish is replaced by chopped mushrooms without compromising on the basic taste of the sauce.

Dried shrimp and other dried seafood are used in inland areas of China where there is no access to fresh fish, and dried seafood is likely to appear in small quantities in congees, vegetable dishes, and steamed or baked egg custards. Because the dried seafood is already a substitute for fresh seafood, in making the kosher modification it is an easy matter to just use a kosher fresh fish or any other tasty ingredient. In Baked Peking Custard, for example (Chapter Seven, page 275), ground beef or veal is a fine alternative to the dried shrimp used by the Chinese.

Fillets of Fish Cantonese

豆豉魚

Dou Shi Yu

Canton

Serves 4

If Marjorie (Morgenstern) Morningstar had tasted this, she never would have given in to the temptation to eat that first shrimp. This is a kosher answer to Shrimp in Lobster Sauce. "Lobster Sauce" refers to the sauce used to prepare Lobster Cantonese—the sauce itself contains no lobster. In China, ground pork is used in the sauce. Although ground beef is usually an acceptable alternative to pork, because of the prohibition against eating meat and fish together mushrooms are substituted here.

The sauce is tasty and nicely flavored, but no ingredient is overpowering, so it provides a nice background for the delicate fish. The amount of broth used makes this a sauce that flows, but it is dotted with bits of fermented black beans, the mushrooms, and sliced scallions. The eggs give the sauce a whitish appearance, similar to that of a cream sauce.

2 tablespoons peanut, corn, or other oil
2 teaspoons finely chopped fermented black beans
2 large cloves garlic, finely chopped
1 cup coarsely chopped fresh mushrooms
1½ tablespoons soy sauce
½ teaspoon sugar
2 scallions (white and crisp green parts), sliced into thin rounds
1½ cups seasoned vegetable broth
3 tablespoons cornstarch dissolved in ¼ cup

→

cold vegetable broth or water
3 eggs (graded large), beaten lightly so the whites and yolks aren't thoroughly combined
1½ pounds fresh sole or flounder fillets
Lemon juice (optional)

First prepare the sauce. In an 8-inch skillet, heat the oil to 350 degrees F. Add the fermented black beans and the garlic; stir them in the oil until coated well. Add the chopped mushrooms and stir-fry for 30 seconds. Mix in the soy sauce and the sugar, then the scallions. Stir in the 1½ cups of vegetable broth and bring it to the boil. Again stir together the cornstarch and the ¼ cup of broth or water until the mixture is smooth, then blend the cornstarch paste into the sauce. Cook until the sauce thickens and becomes smooth and glazed, stirring constantly. Turn off the heat, then add the beaten eggs, stirring constantly. The eggs may curdle somewhat as they are blended in—this will give the sauce an interesting consistency, but don't overcook the eggs or they will toughen. Turn the heat to the lowest possible point to keep the sauce warm—be very careful that the sauce doesn't boil.

For the fish, fill a 10-inch skillet halfway with water. Add a little lemon juice if you like. Bring the water to the boil, then carefully add the fish in one layer. The water should cover the fish. Immediately adjust the heat so the liquid simmers. Poach the fish, uncovered, until it turns white and flakes, which should take only a few minutes. Transfer the fish to a platter and cover it with the sauce. Or cut the fish into bite-size or serving-size pieces and mix it gently with the sauce. Serve the fish immediately over rice.

Fillets of Flounder With Sweet Pepper Sauce

甜酸魚

Tian Suan Yu

Canton influence

Serves 4

A mellow red and green pepper sauce pairs with delicately flavored flounder or sole fillets in this colorful dish, which I developed as one of several versions of sweet-and-sour fish. The sauce itself is a simple sweet-and-pungent combination of pineapple and sweet pickle juices, reinforced by the sweetness of red peppers and the slight pungency of green peppers. The peppers are briefly stir-fried to release their flavors, so they remain crisp in sharp contrast to the soft poached fish.

1 tablespoon peanut, corn, or other oil
2 cloves garlic, cut in half
1 large green pepper, sliced into thin strips
1 large sweet red pepper, sliced into thin strips
½ cup unsweetened pineapple juice
¼ cup juice from a jar of sweet pickles
2 teaspoons cornstarch dissolved in 3 tablespoons cold water
1½ pounds fresh flounder or sole fillets, cut into serving-size pieces
Juice of ½ lemon

In a wok or an 8-inch skillet, heat the oil to 350 degrees F. Add the garlic and stir it in the oil for a minute to season the oil, then remove the garlic and discard. Increase the heat to 375 degrees F. and stir-fry the pepper strips for 2 minutes. Stir in the pineapple and pickle juices, and bring the mixture to the boil. Again mix together the cornstarch and water until smooth, then blend the cornstarch paste into the liquid. Cook just until the sauce boils again and thickens, stirring constantly. Turn off the heat, but leave the pan on the turned-off burner.

Now, poach the fish. To do so, fill a 10-inch skillet halfway with water. Add the lemon juice, bring the liquid to the boil, then carefully add the fish in one layer. The liquid should cover the fish. Immediately adjust the heat so the liquid simmers. Cook the fish, uncovered, just until it turns white and flakes, which should take only a few minutes. Carefully transfer the fillets to a serving platter. Stir the sauce one more time, then pour the sauce over the fish and serve at once.

Sweet-and-Sour Cod Fillets

瓦塊魚

Wa Kuai Yu

Honan

Serves 4

In China, fish is either freshly caught for immediate use in the coastal regions or dried for later use in the interior parts of the country. Unlike

China, in the United States we have access to many kinds of frozen fish throughout the country. Although it is difficult to match the delicacy and flavor of fresh-caught fish, there are ways to bring out the best in frozen fish, and this is one of them.

Here, the fish is sliced and cooked before it is completely defrosted, which lessens the chances of a fishy taste or smell. The fish is coated with batter then deep-fried to produce a crisp golden crust. The crust softens somewhat when the fish is mixed with the sauce, giving it a very interesting texture. Because frozen fish has a less delicate taste than fresh fish, the sauce used here is stronger than the sweet-and-pungent sauces made with pineapple juice and vinegar.

5 tablespoons sugar
¼ cup rice vinegar or red wine vinegar
2 tablespoons ketchup
1 tablespoon soy sauce
2 eggs (graded large)
5 tablespoons unsifted all-purpose flour
3 tablespoons unsifted cornstarch
Water, up to 4 tablespoons
Oil for frying
1 pound frozen cod fillets
1 tablespoon cornstarch dissolved in ½ cup cold water

In a 1-quart pot, combine the sugar, vinegar, ketchup, and soy sauce. Bring the mixture to the boil, reduce the heat, cover the pot, and keep the sauce warm over very low heat. The cornstarch thickener will be added after the fish is cooked.

In a small mixing bowl, beat the eggs well. Stir in the flour and then the cornstarch, blending the mixture with a fork until completely smooth. Add water, 1 tablespoon at a time, if the batter is too thick. The batter should be about the consistency of pancake batter. In a 12-inch skillet, start heating oil for deep-frying—the oil should be at least ½ inch deep. Heat the oil to 375 degrees F. Meanwhile, use a sharp cleaver or a large sharp knife to slice the partially frozen fish into uniform pieces approximately 2 × 3 inches × ¼ inch thick. Uniform size is more important than the actual dimensions.

Drop the fish slices into the batter and coat each slice all over. Fry the fish in the hot oil until it is golden brown on one side, then turn it over and fry the other side. Drain the cooked fish well on paper towels.

Now bring the sauce back to the boil. Again stir together the 1 tablespoon of cornstarch with the ½ cup cold water until the mixture is smooth, then blend this mixture into the sauce. Continue to cook and stir until the sauce boils and thickens. Place the fish on a platter or in a bowl, pour the sauce over the fish, and serve immediately.

Pan-fried Whole Carp With Sweet-and-Sour Sauce

糖醋鯉魚

Tang Cu Li Yu

Honan

Serves 4 to 6

Until I began investigating the authenticity of the Chinese recipes I've used for years, I did not realize that carp is one of the principal fishes of China. I have always associated carp with Jewish cooking—it is one of the fishes used in *gefilte* fish—and with Jewish literature.

Because in the United States it is sometimes difficult to find whole carp small enough to fit into the home skillet or wok, Chinese cookbooks tend to call for sea bass and bluefish in recipes requiring whole fish. The recipe here is based on the classic sweet-and-sour carp of Honan, and although sea bass and bluefish are acceptable substitutes, ask your fish dealer to order a small carp for you so you can try the authentic Chinese recipe.

Whatever you buy, the fish must be able to fit into your largest pan, because serving the fish whole, with head and tail intact, is very important in Chinese cooking. The Chinese consider a fish without head or tail incomplete, not pleasing to look at. There are also culinary reasons for cooking and serving the fish whole: the whole fish retains the juices better than a fish with the head and tail removed, and the tender meat inside the fish's head is highly prized by the Chinese. The fish should even be placed on the serving platter so it looks as though it is still alive and swimming—eyes intact, back slightly arched as though the fish is jumping, perhaps mouth slightly open—an indication that freshly caught fish was used.

Whole fish is commonly served as the last course in a Chinese banquet. Chopsticks are used to pull the meat off the fish, and the host serves the most important guest himself.

1 whole carp (2 to 3 pounds, or a size that will fit into your skillet or wok)
1 slice (1/8 inch thick) ginger root
1 clove garlic
1 tablespoon peanut, corn, or other oil

→

2 tablespoons cornstarch, approximately
5 tablespoons sugar
1 tablespoon lemon juice
3 tablespoons rice vinegar or red wine vinegar
2 tablespoons ketchup
1 tablespoon soy sauce
1 tablespoon cornstarch dissolved in ½ cup cold water
⅓ cup oil, approximately, for frying

First prepare the fish for cooking. Wash the fish inside and out, then pat it dry with paper towels. Rub the fish inside and out with the ginger root and garlic. Now rub the fish on the outside with the tablespoon of oil, which will help keep the fish from sticking when it is fried. Pat the 2 tablespoons of cornstarch all over the outside of the fish. Set the fish aside while you prepare the sauce.

For the sauce, in a 1-quart pot combine the sugar, lemon juice, vinegar, ketchup, and soy sauce. Bring the mixture to the boil, then reduce the heat and simmer the sauce, uncovered, for 2 to 3 minutes. Again stir together the tablespoon of cornstarch and ½ cup of cold water until the mixture is smooth. Blend the cornstarch-water mixture into the sauce, stirring until it boils and thickens. Keep the sauce warm over very low heat.

To cook the fish, in a wok or a 12-inch skillet heat the oil to 350 degrees F. If the oil is too hot, the fish will stick. If you use a wok, swish the oil around the sides so the fish will not stick to the sides. Carefully place the fish in the pan or wok, and cook the fish for 3 minutes, all the while spooning oil over the top surface of the fish. Cover the pan or wok and cook the fish for 5 to 10 minutes, depending upon its size. Uncover and with two large spoons carefully turn the fish over. Brown the other side for about 2 minutes. Very carefully transfer the fish to a large platter. Pour the sauce over the fish and serve immediately.

Sweet-and-Sour Fish Fillets
(Squirrel Fish)
松鼠魚
Song Shu Yu

Shanghai

Serves 4 to 6

In this recipe, fish fillets are deeply scored, coated with a batter, and deep-fried until wonderfully crisp. The fish curls up as it cooks, remotely resembling a squirrel's tail, hence the popular use of the name Squirrel Fish on restaurant menus. Although the whole fish is used in China, it is difficult for the home cook to deep-fry a whole fish and achieve the crispy crust, which is important to the taste and appearance, so fillets are substituted here. The sweet-and-sour sauce spooned over the fish contains vegetables which contribute to the appearance and taste of the preparation.

4 medium-size dried Chinese mushrooms
Boiling water
1 cup seasoned vegetable broth
¼ cup rice vinegar or red wine vinegar
¼ cup sugar
¼ cup ketchup
10 fresh snow peas, tips and strings removed, cut on the diagonal into ¼-inch pieces (substitute ½ cup frozen peas and carrots, thawed)
6 water chestnuts, sliced
1 tablespoon cornstarch dissolved in 2 tablespoons cold vegetable broth or water
Oil for deep-frying
2 pounds fish fillets with the skins on (sea bass, bluefish, carp, pike, red snapper)
2 eggs (graded large)
½ cup water
1 cup unsifted all-purpose flour
½ teaspoon salt
1 teaspoon peanut, corn, or other oil

In a small heatproof bowl, pour boiling water over the dried mushrooms and soak them for 15 to 20 minutes, until soft. Slice the mushrooms thinly, discarding the stems.

In a 1-quart pot, bring the cup of vegetable broth, the vinegar, sugar, and ketchup to the boil, stirring occasionally. Mix in the mushrooms, snow peas, and water chestnuts. Cook for 1 minute over moderately low heat. Again stir together the tablespoon of cornstarch and 2 tablespoons of cold broth or water to recombine them, then blend the cornstarch paste into the sauce. Cook until the liquid boils, thickens, and is smooth. Reduce the heat to very low to keep the sauce warm without cooking it further.

In a large electric skillet, a deep fryer, or a pot at least 4 inches deep, heat at least 2 inches of oil to 375 degrees F. Meanwhile, cut the fish fillets into even-size pieces approximately 2 × 3 inches. Score the meat of the fish deeply in a tic-tac-toe pattern, but be careful not to cut through the skin.

In a small mixing bowl, beat the eggs well. Blend in the ½ cup of water, then stir in the flour and salt, beating until the mixture is smooth. Blend in the teaspoon of oil. Drop the fish pieces into the batter, coating the fish completely. Work the batter into the areas where the fish has been scored. With a fork, remove the pieces of fish one at a time, letting the excess batter drip back into the bowl. Carefully drop the fish into the oil, meaty side down. Cook only a few pieces at a time. Fry the fish until golden and crisp, then turn the pieces to brown the skin side. Drain the fillets very well on paper towels. Arrange the fried fish on a platter, pour the sauce over the fish, and serve at once.

Steamed Rainbow Trout

蒸全魚

Zheng Chuan Yu

General China

Allow 1 per person

My mother once sent me a birthday card that said, "Treat yourself like company." This trout is something I prepare as a lunch treat just for myself when my husband's at work and the children are at school.

This recipe is a good example of how to adapt available ingredients to Chinese cooking methods. Steaming is a very common method of cooking a whole fish in China, and trout comes out moist and tender. Carp, sea bass, bluefish, and many other kinds of whole fish can be used, as long as they'll fit into your steaming pot. Most fish fillets also take to steaming, because they cook quickly and don't dry out.

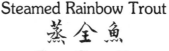

Ginger root and soy sauce are the seasonings used in this recipe. Although the trout comes out sweet, tender, and juicy and is enjoyable just as is, it is also good served with a spicy dip such as the one presented here. Other ingredients used often in preparing steamed fish in China are garlic, fermented black beans, and scallions.

1 tablespoon soy sauce
1 teaspoon sesame oil
1 slice (½ inch thick) ginger root
1 teaspoon chopped fresh hot pepper (jalapeno or milder) or ¼ to ½ teaspoon crushed dried red pepper
1 small whole rainbow trout (about ½ pound), cleaned and ready to cook
1 slice (⅛ inch thick) ginger root
Soy sauce, about 2 teaspoons

In a small bowl, combine the first 4 ingredients for use as a dip. The amount is meant for one serving and should be increased according to the number of people being served.

Rub the trout inside and out with the second slice of ginger root, then sprinkle about 2 teaspoons of soy sauce on the fish, on both the inside and the skin. Rub the soy sauce into the fish. Place the trout on a steamer rack or tray. Steam 10 to 15 minutes for one trout, a few minutes longer if you're doing several at a time or if you're using a larger fish. Serve one whole trout per person, with one side dish of the dip per person.

Although the Chinese do not typically remove the bones before serving whole fish, the bone in cooked trout is reasonably easy to remove, and many Americans prefer to have the fish served without the bones. First dislodge the bone from the tail end, using a sharp knife if necessary. Carefully lift the bone up and out, dislodging it again as you come to the head of the fish. The spine and most if not all of the smaller bones will come out as one piece.

Steamed Fresh Pollock Fillets With Hoisin-Soy Sauce

海鮮醬蒸魚

Hai Xian Jiang Zheng Yu

General China influence

Serves 4

This sweet, mild-tasting fish is enhanced but not overpowered by the light coating of *hoisin* and soy sauces. It is one of the easiest recipes in this book, and one of the tastiest. I developed it as an alternative to recipes requiring chopping or measuring numerous ingredients.

1½ pounds fresh pollock fillets
1½ teaspoons hoisin sauce
1½ teaspoons soy sauce

Cut the fresh pollock into serving-size pieces. Place the fish on a heatproof plate that will fit into the steaming pot. The plate should also be suitable for use as a serving platter because the fish will be difficult to remove after it is cooked. A plate without holes can be used, as the juices will collect on the plate and can be used as a light sauce.

Mix together the *hoisin* and soy sauces. Brush the top of the pollock fillets lightly with the mixture. Steam the fish for 10 to 15 minutes, depending on its thickness. Serve at once.

Steamed Flavorful Fish Fillets on Rice and Chinese Cabbage

豆豉蒸魚

Dou Shi Zheng Yu

Canton influence

Serves 4

This unusual one-dish meal pairs seasoned fish fillets with rice and Chinese cabbage, all of which are steamed on the same plate. The result is a subtle blending of flavors as the rice picks up flavor from the cabbage, the fish, and all the seasonings. Although we most often see vegetables stir-fried to a crisp-tender stage in Chinese cooking, steamed vegetables are also used, especially when something else is being steamed.

1½ pounds fish fillets, any kind
4 cups slightly undercooked brown rice
3 cups shredded Chinese cabbage, any kind
2 cloves garlic, minced
3 scallions (white and crisp green parts), chopped
2 teaspoons fermented black beans, chopped
1 teaspoon minced ginger root

Cut the fish fillets into serving-size pieces. Place the rice on a heatproof plate that will fit into a steamer. The plate will also be used as the serving dish. Spread the rice evenly over the plate, and place the shredded Chinese cabbage over the rice.

Mix together the minced garlic, chopped scallions and fermented black beans, and the minced ginger root. Arrange the fish over the shredded cabbage. Sprinkle the fish with the mixture of seasonings. Steam the fish, cabbage, and rice for 10 to 15 minutes, depending on the thickness of the fish. The fish will flake easily and change color when it is cooked. Serve individual portions of fish surrounded by rice and cabbage.

Steamed Stuffed Fish

釀全魚

Rang Chuan Yu

General China influence

Serves 4 to 6

It would not surprise me to discover someday that the Jews of China who were found to be living in the province of Honan in the seventeenth century were the originators of our old-fashioned *gefilte* fish. We know that the Chinese like to serve fish whole, and it isn't too farfetched to imagine a Chinese version of chopped seasoned fish that is stuffed back into the skin and then cooked and served as though it were a whole fish. Here is such a recipe, which uses a whitefish-pike-carp combination with ingredients associated with Chinese cooking. The fish is steamed, a common method of cooking fish in China.

1 whole whitefish (2 to 3 pounds)
1 whole carp (3 to 4 pounds) or 2 pounds carp fillets
1 whole pike (1½ to 2 pounds) or 1 pound pike fillets
¼ cup unsifted cornstarch
1 tablespoon chopped ginger root
6 scallions (white and crisp green parts), chopped
¼ cup chopped water chestnuts
2 eggs (graded large), slightly beaten
2 tablespoons soy sauce

Have the fish filleted when you buy it (unless you're a do-it-yourselfer), but be sure to ask the person doing the filleting to keep the fish skin intact, including the head and tail. You'll be stuffing either the whitefish or the carp skin, whichever looks nicer and will fit in your steaming pot. In both Jewish and Chinese cooking the more authentic approach is to leave in the fish spine and stuff the fish mixture around the bones, because the bones add some flavor when the fish is cooked. However, if you prefer, have all the bones removed.

With a cleaver, chop the fish fillets coarsely. Continue to chop while you work in the cornstarch, ginger root, scallions, and water chestnuts. With your hands, mix in the eggs and the soy sauce. When the mixture is combined well, stuff the fish casing.

Place the stuffed fish on a lightly oiled steamer tray. Steam the fish for about 20 minutes, until done. Bring the fish to the table whole, and use a very sharp knife to cut off slices which include the skin, or spoon out servings. This fish can be served hot or cold.

Red-cooked Red Snapper Fillets

紅燒魚

Hong Shao Yu

Coastal China

Serves 4 to 6

Here, fish fillets are first pan-fried then red-cooked in a flavorful soy sauce mixture. This combination of cooking methods is popular in regions of China where fresh fish is caught. You'll want to serve plenty of rice with the rich gravy. The fish has a soft crust and is tender inside, and the sauce is very slightly pungent. Bluefish fillets and cod steaks also work well in this recipe. A whole fish can be used (as it would be in China), but because the sauce makes the bones difficult to see, it is best to bone the fish for this recipe.

1½ pounds red snapper fillets
All-purpose flour for coating the fish, about ¾ cup
Oil for frying
1 small onion, chopped
1 teaspoon minced ginger root
1 clove garlic, minced
¼ cup soy sauce

2 tablespoons dry sherry
1 cup water
4 scallions (white and crisp green parts), chopped

Wash the fish fillets and pat them dry. Cut the fish into serving-size pieces. Roll each piece in flour to coat it well; or put the flour in a paper bag and, one or two pieces at a time, shake the fish in the flour. In a 10- or 12-inch skillet, heat ⅛ inch of oil until it is moderately hot, between 350 and 375 degrees F. Cook the fish fillets for 3 to 4 minutes on one side, until golden brown, then turn them carefully and brown the other side. Leaving the fish in the pan, spoon off all but 1 tablespoon of oil. Scatter the onion, ginger root, and garlic over and around the fish, sprinkle the fish with the soy sauce and sherry, and pour in the water. Mix the ingredients *gently.* Be sure to handle the fish with care, or it may fall apart. Bring the liquid to the boil, then reduce the heat to a simmer, cover the pan, and cook the fish and gravy over low heat for 15 minutes. Transfer the fish fillets to a serving platter, pour the sauce over the fish, and sprinkle the fish with the chopped scallions.

Spicy Red Snapper Fillets

辣豆瓣魚

La Dou Ban Yu

Hunan influence

Serves 4 to 6

The hot bean sauce makes this recipe representative of the Hunan school of cooking. The spicy dip served with this hot and tasty broiled fish carries through the theme.

2 tablespoons hot bean sauce
2 tablespoons soy sauce
4 scallions (white and crisp green parts), chopped
2 tablespoons hot bean sauce
1 tablespoon peanut, corn, or other oil
Quarter of a large lemon
2 pounds red snapper fillets

In a small bowl, combine the first 3 ingredients. This spicy condiment will be served with the fish. Set aside.

In a small bowl, mix together the remaining 2 tablespoons of hot bean sauce with the oil. Squeeze the lemon quarter over the mixture, then blend in the lemon juice. Cut the fish into serving-size pieces, then place the fillets on a greased baking sheet. (If you cover the baking sheet with foil, then grease the foil, clean-up will be easier.) Preheat the broiler so it is hot when you put in the fish. Brush the hot bean sauce-oil-lemon juice mixture over the fish fillets. Broil the fish 5 inches from the heat for about 5 minutes, until the topping is bubbly and the fish flakes easily. Serve immediately with the dip.

Baked Stuffed Whiting
烤魚
Kao Yu

General China influence

Serves 4 to 6

Ovens are about as rare in China as they are common in the United States, so you would not expect this recipe for baked fish to be authentically Chinese, and you would be right. In China, a whole fish stuffed with an interesting rice mixture would be steamed or perhaps roasted over an open fire, so this baked fish dish is definitely an American adaptation. The fish and the stuffing flavor each other reciprocally, and bits of scallion, mushroom, and water chestnut add interest to the soft rice. Whiting is selected for this recipe because the spine is particularly easy to remove before the fish is cooked, but a whole bluefish, whitefish, or bass can also be used. The final taste, of course, depends on the fish used.

2 whole whitings, each about 1 pound, or one whole 2- to 3-pound bluefish, whitefish, bass, or any fish suitable for baking
1 slice (½ inch thick) ginger root
¼ cup peanut, corn, or other oil
3 scallions (white and crisp green parts), thinly sliced
½ cup sliced fresh mushrooms
4 water chestnuts, coarsely chopped
2 cups cold cooked rice—white, brown, or glutinous
2 teaspoons hoisin sauce
2 teaspoons soy sauce
Oil for brushing the fish

Preheat the oven to 400 degrees F.

Wash each fish inside and out then pat dry. Using a sharp boning knife and your fingers, work out the entire spine of each fish. Be sure to remove all of the small bones. Rub the ginger root over the fish, inside and out.

In a wok or a 10- to 12-inch skillet, heat the oil to 350 degrees F. Stir in the scallions and mushrooms, then add the water chestnuts. Now stir in the rice, coating the grains well with the oil. Mix in the *hoisin* and soy sauces, then remove the pan from the heat.

Brush the fish inside and out with a little oil. Lightly oil or grease a baking pan or dish large enough to hold the fish, preferably one on which the fish can be served as well. Stuff the fish with the rice mixture. If the stuffing is popping out too much, which may happen if you're using the 1-pound whitings, turn each fish from its side to its belly so the fish rests on the stuffing. Keep any extra stuffing warm over low heat, and serve it as a side dish.

Bake the stuffed fish at 400 degrees F. for 20 to 30 minutes, until it flakes easily when poked with a fork. To serve, cut the fish crosswise into thick slices. Use a broad spatula to transfer the stuffing and fish together as one piece.

7

Vegetables and Eggs

In the United States, vegetable dishes are often served as accompaniments to the main dish, which usually consists of meat or fish. In China, where meals are not built around a main dish, vegetables play an especially significant role. At Chinese family meals, dishes usually consist mainly of vegetables, with bits of meat added for color, flavor, and protein. Sometimes vegetables are used to add color and flavor to rice or noodles.

Milk products are nearly nonexistent in China, and meat is not often available to most people, so vegetable products are nutritionally important. *Tofu,* made from pressed soybeans, is the only source of protein for many Chinese, and fortunately for the vegetarian world, this soybean curd combines well with other ingredients—poultry, many vegetables, and virtually all sauces and spices. A diet consisting mainly of rice or noodles, *tofu,* and greens can still offer impressive variety. The Buddhists of China, who are strict vegetarians, rely heavily on bean curd and wheat gluten, which they use inventively to simulate meat dishes.

Bok choy and other Chinese cabbages and greens are used extensively in China, as are root vegetables such as Chinese turnip and radish. Vegetables of the sea—seaweeds—are used in soups and steamed dishes. Seaweeds are also dried for use in the interior portions of China, and dried seaweed products are available in Asian groceries in the United States.

Although many of the recipes in the vegetable portion of this chapter are exclusively vegetarian and therefore *pareve,* some of the vegetables are cooked with chicken broth, making them meat dishes. Substituting a vegetable broth will make these preparations suitable for meat, dairy, or vegetarian meals. The one *bok choy* recipe that calls for a cream sauce must be served as part of a dairy meal only. Throughout the book, especially in Chapter Eight—Rice, Noodles, and Breads—you will find other strictly vegetarian recipes that will fit very well into the vegetarian diet and can be used for all meals in the kosher home.

Because many Chinese vegetable recipes stress the importance of stir-frying the vegetables briefly so they remain crisp, we tend to overlook the fact that in China vegetables are also steamed and slow-cooked in stews. This chapter covers a range of cooking methods for fresh produce. Most of the vegetable dishes are intended to fit into our American meat-vegetable-potato meals as well as Chinese-style meals. The *tofu* recipes can be served as main dishes in American dinners or as one of the dishes set out for a Chinese family dinner. Combining a soup, a *tofu* preparation, and two or three vegetable dishes, one of which is prepared with a small amount of meat or fish, along with rice, comes close to duplicating an everyday Chinese meal.

In Chinese cooking, eggs are most often used as additions to other dishes. They may be poached in congee for breakfast or stirred into congee the way they are stirred into egg drop soup. Uncooked eggs are mixed with rice or noodles, creating an unusual texture while adding protein. Eggs are also used as a garnish to add color to foods that might otherwise be colorless, such as plain rice, *lo mien,* steamed cabbage, or congee. Steamed eggs with soy sauce and bits of meat or dried fish are also popular in China.

The recipes in this chapter reflect the various ways of treating eggs. Eggs *fu yung,* which is a Western concoction, is presented along with other more authentic Chinese recipes. Because many of the egg preparations in this chapter are suitable only for meat meals, alternatives to make them *pareve* are suggested in the recipes.

Vegetable Dishes

Sweet-and-Sour Tofu "Meatballs"

素獅子頭

Su Shizi Tou

Canton influence

Serves 4

Chinese Buddhists, who favor vegetable creations that resemble meat dishes, would particularly enjoy this dish. The *tofu* "meatballs" do not taste like meat, but they offer a low-cost high-protein alternative to beef. To prepare them, *tofu* is mixed with water chestnuts and scallions, and eggs and cornstarch are used as binders. Deep-frying creates a crisp, golden crust that adds eye and taste appeal. The meatballs are presented in a sweet-and-pungent vegetable sauce that brings a rich flavor and additional texture to this dish.

3 medium-size dried Chinese mushrooms
Boiling water
1 cup fresh snow peas, tips and strings removed
1 tablespoon peanut, corn, or other oil
6 tablespoons red wine vinegar
½ cup sugar
2 tablespoons soy sauce
2 tablespoons tomato sauce
1 pound tofu
4 water chestnuts, chopped
2 scallions (white and crisp green parts), chopped
2 eggs (graded large), lightly beaten
1 tablespoon soy sauce
2 tablespoons cornstarch
Oil for deep-frying

First prepare the sauce. In a small heatproof bowl, pour boiling water over the mushrooms; let the mushrooms soak for about 15 minutes, until soft. Slice the mushrooms very thinly, discarding the stems. Shred the snow peas on the diagonal into small pieces.

In an 8-inch skillet, heat the 1 tablespoon of oil over moderate heat. Stir-fry the mushrooms and shredded snow peas for 2 minutes. Add the vinegar, sugar, soy sauce, and tomato sauce. Bring the sauce to the boil, simmer it for a few minutes, then reduce the heat to very low and keep the sauce warm.

For the meatballs, mash the *tofu* with a fork and combine it with the water chestnuts, scallions, eggs, 1 tablespoon soy sauce, and the cornstarch. Shape the mixture firmly into 1-inch balls. In a deep fryer, a large electric skillet, or a pot at least 4 inches deep, heat a minimum of 1½ inches of oil to 375 degrees F. Carefully drop the *tofu* balls into the oil, avoiding over-crowding. Fry the balls until golden all over, then drain them on paper towels and mix them gently with the sauce. Serve the *tofu* balls and sauce over rice.

Sweet-and-Sour Batter-fried Tofu

甜酸豆腐

Tian Suan Dou Fu

Canton influence

Serves 4

Soft cubes of *tofu* are encrusted with a puffy, golden casing and served with a zesty sweet-and-pungent sauce. This is a *tofu* dish for people who don't like *tofu*—not because the *tofu* in it is so tasty but because it is so well-disguised. I developed this recipe as a vegetarian alternative to sweet-and-pungent chicken or fish preparations.

3 tablespoons red wine vinegar
¼ cup sugar
1 tablespoon soy sauce
1 tablespoon tomato sauce
¼ cup water
1 tablespoon cornstarch dissolved in ¼ cup cold water
1 pound tofu
Oil for deep-frying
1 egg (graded large), beaten
½ cup water
½ cup unsifted all-purpose flour
1 teaspoon double-acting baking powder
½ teaspoon salt
1 teaspoon peanut, corn, or other oil

For the sauce, in a 1-quart pot combine the vinegar, sugar, soy sauce, tomato sauce, and ¼ cup water. Bring the ingredients to the boil over moderate heat, stirring occasionally. Again stir together the cornstarch and ¼ cup cold water until completely smooth, then stir this mixture into the sauce. Cook and stir only until the sauce is thickened and smooth, then reduce the heat and keep the sauce warm.

Cut the *tofu* into ½-inch cubes. In a 2-quart pot, heat 2 inches of oil to 375 degrees F. The oil should be hot but not yet smoking. While the oil is heating, make the batter for the *tofu*. In a small to medium-size mixing bowl, combine the egg, ½ cup water, the flour, baking powder, salt, and 1 teaspoon of oil. Stir rapidly with a fork to blend the ingredients until they are very smooth. Mix the *tofu* cubes gently but thoroughly with the batter to coat the *tofu* completely. Drop the cubes into the hot oil one piece at a time, cooking as many as you can at once without overcrowding. Fry the *tofu* cubes until they are a nice golden brown all over. The *tofu* doesn't have to be turned—the cubes will turn by themselves and puff and brown evenly. Drain the cooked *tofu* well on paper towels. When all the *tofu* is cooked, place it in a serving bowl and pour the sauce over it. Serve immediately.

Deep-fried Tofu With Hot Bean Sauce

家常豆腐

Jia Chang Dou Fu

Hunan influence

Serves 4

Tofu cubes puff out all over when fried in hot oil, adding a special lightness to this soft soybean product. Here, hot bean sauce is used to offer a complete contrast to the very bland *tofu*. Those who are accustomed to fiery hot foods may want to just mix the *tofu* and hot bean sauce, but for those with average taste buds, diluting with vegetable or chicken broth is recommended.

1 pound tofu
Oil for deep-frying
2 tablespoons hot bean sauce (or more, to taste)
1 cup seasoned vegetable or chicken broth
2 teaspoons cornstarch dissolved in 2 tablespoons cold water

Cut the *tofu* into ½-inch cubes. In a 2-quart pot, heat 1 inch of oil to 375 degrees F. Carefully drop in the *tofu* pieces, giving them room to expand as they cook. Deep-fry the cubes until they are puffy and golden brown all over, then drain the *tofu* on paper towels. Continue cooking until all the *tofu* cubes are fried.

In an 8-inch skillet, toss the fried *tofu* cubes with the hot bean sauce. Stir in the broth and bring the mixture to the boil over moderate heat. Again stir together the cornstarch and water until smooth, then blend the cornstarch paste into the boiling liquid, stirring gently. Turn off the heat as soon as the broth is smooth and thickened. Serve the *tofu* over hot rice.

Deep-fried Tofu With Scallions

葱燒豆腐

Cong Shao Dou Fu

Peking influence

Serves 4

By changing one ingredient in the previous recipe, Deep-fried Tofu With Hot Bean Sauce, the dish is converted from spicy hot to sharp. The uncooked scallions add wonderful color and zip to the delicate *tofu* cubes.

1 pound tofu
Oil for deep-frying
1 cup seasoned vegetable or chicken broth
2 teaspoons cornstarch dissolved in 2 tablespoons cold water
8 scallions (white and crisp green parts), chopped

Cut the *tofu* into ½-inch cubes. In a 2-quart pot, heat 1 inch of oil to 375 degrees F. Carefully drop in the *tofu* pieces, giving them room to expand as they cook. Deep-fry the cubes until they are puffy and golden brown all over, then drain them on paper towels. Repeat until all the *tofu* cubes are fried.

In a 2-quart pot, bring the vegetable or chicken broth to the boil. Again stir together the cornstarch and water until smooth, then blend the cornstarch mixture into the broth. Continue to cook, stirring constantly, just until the broth is thickened and the cornstarch is blended in smoothly. Remove the pot from the heat, gently stir in the fried *tofu,* and transfer the *tofu* and sauce to a serving platter. Sprinkle the *tofu* lavishly with the scallions. Serve immediately over rice.

Tofu in Black Bean Sauce

鮮菇豆腐

Xian Gu Dou Fu

Canton

Serves 4

This could be called Tofu in Mushroom Sauce, but the fermented black beans add a special saltiness and deserve their name in the title. Garlic and scallions season the sauce beautifully, and additional scallions are sprinkled on top for color. The soft *tofu,* the slightly more resilient mushrooms, and the crisp scallions add to the enjoyment of the tasty sauce, which is actually a variation on the sauce for Fillets of Fish Cantonese (page 237).

1 tablespoon peanut, corn, or other oil
1 tablespoon fermented black beans, minced
2 cloves garlic, minced
4 scallions (white and crisp green parts), chopped (save half for garnish)
1 cup sliced fresh mushrooms
1 cup unsalted vegetable or chicken broth
1 pound tofu, cut into ½-inch cubes
2 teaspoons cornstarch dissolved in 2 tablespoons cold water
2 eggs (graded large), slightly beaten

In an 8-inch skillet, heat 1 tablespoon of oil until moderately hot, 350 to 375 degrees F. Stir in the fermented black beans, garlic, and half the scallions. Coat these ingredients well with the oil, then add the mushrooms and stir-fry for 1 minute. Now add the vegetable or chicken broth and bring it to the boil, then gently stir in the *tofu* cubes. Again stir together the cornstarch and water until smooth, then stir the cornstarch paste into the liquid in the pan. Blend in the cornstarch gently but thoroughly until the sauce is thickened and smooth. Finally, turn off the heat and immediately stir in the beaten eggs. The eggs may curdle slightly. Transfer the *tofu* to a serving platter, and sprinkle the *tofu* and sauce with scallions. Serve over brown or white rice.

Tofu and Peanuts in Hoisin Sauce

醬豆腐

Jiang Dou Fu

General China influence

Serves 4 to 6

I think of this as a vegetarian variation on Cashew Chicken With Hoisin Sauce, (page 208), but the two recipes have only one ingredient in common, and that is the *hoisin* sauce. *Tofu* takes the place of the chicken, peanuts are substituted for the cashews (although cashews could certainly be used), dried Chinese mushrooooms become fresh small whole mushrooms, and frozen green peas don't replace anything but are added for color, texture, and taste. The result is a *tofu* dish that is very easy to prepare and full of exceptional contrasts.

2 tablespoons peanut, corn, or other oil
½ pound fresh small whole mushrooms, cleaned but not sliced
1 package (10 ounces) frozen green peas, thawed
1 pound tofu, cut into ½-inch cubes
¼ cup hoisin sauce
1 cup dry roasted peanuts, salted or unsalted

In a wok or a 10- or 12-inch skillet, heat the oil until moderately hot, about 350 degrees F. Stir-fry the mushrooms for 2 minutes, until they are well coated with the oil and just beginning to soften. Add the peas and continue to stir the contents of the wok or pan until the peas are hot. Now toss in the *tofu,* gently stirring until it is mixed in and hot. Blend in the *hoisin* sauce. Turn off the heat, mix in the peanuts, and serve at once before the peanuts become soggy.

Tofu With Mushrooms and Sweet Red Peppers in Sweet Bean Sauce

豆腐三吃

Dou Fu San Chi

Peking influence

Serves 4 to 6

It is very easy for me to keep coming up with new recipes for *tofu* dishes. Everytime I say we're having *tofu* for dinner, the children want to know how I'm preparing it. If I say I'm testing a recipe with mushrooms and sweet red peppers, my eldest son wants to know why there won't be peanuts in it. So, I tell him I'll divide it in half and make some with peanuts. My second son doesn't like nuts in foods, but he'll eat *tofu* with peanuts and *hoisin* sauce, and now we have a different dish. My third son doesn't like cooked red peppers, so I assure him that I'll make some with peas instead of peppers. My daughter, of course, doesn't like peas, but she doesn't like *tofu* either. My husband likes virtually all foods except *borscht,* so he's interested in everything, especially this dish of *tofu,* mushrooms, and sweet red peppers. Now I have to buy more *tofu*. Do I always bend to the pleasures of my family? Only when I want to test new *tofu* recipes anyway. (But I never serve *borscht*.)

2 tablespoons peanut, corn, or other oil
2 large sweet red peppers, cut into ½-inch squares
½ pound fresh mushrooms, sliced
1 pound tofu, cut into ½-inch cubes
8 water chestnuts, sliced
¼ cup sweet bean sauce

In a wok or a 10- or 12-inch skillet, heat the oil until it is hot but not yet smoking, 375 degrees F. Stir-fry the sweet red peppers for about a minute, then add the mushrooms and continue to cook, tossing the vegetables around constantly, for another half-minute, until the mushrooms just begin to change color. Gently mix in the *tofu*, then the water chestnuts, and finally blend in the sweet bean sauce. Cook, stirring constantly, just until the ingredients are all heated through.

Spicy Eggplant and Tofu
茄子燒豆腐
Qiezi Shao Dou Fu

Szechwan

Serves 4 to 6

In this recipe, eggplant is cooked until tender, not just crisp (a change from most stir-fried vegetables). The eggplant is stir-fried along with three potent seasonings, and it absorbs those flavors as everything cooks together. The *tofu* helps tone things down a bit, so the total effect is of a richly spiced vegetable combination that doesn't make your eyes water. If you follow the recipe and deep-fry the *tofu* first, there will be a little more substance to the *tofu*. If you prefer to avoid the calories of deep-frying, mix in the uncooked *tofu* cubes when the eggplant is done, and stir gently until the *tofu* is hot and mixed in well.

Oil for deep-frying
½ pound tofu, cut into ½-inch cubes
4 to 6 tablespoons peanut, corn, or other oil
1 pound small Italian eggplants (or 1 regular eggplant), unpeeled, cut into strips 1¼ × ⅜ × ⅜ inches

1 large clove garlic, minced
1½ teaspoons minced ginger root
2 to 3 teaspoons chili paste with garlic, to taste
3 scallions (white and crisp green parts), chopped

In a 2-quart pot, heat 2 inches of oil until it is hot but not yet smoking, 375 degrees F. Carefully drop in half of the *tofu* cubes and fry them until golden. Remove the *tofu* with a slotted spoon and drain well on paper towels. Deep-fry the remaining *tofu.*

In a wok or a clean 10- or 12-inch skillet, heat 4 tablespoons of oil to 350 degrees F. Add the eggplant strips and stir-fry for 2 minutes. Add the minced garlic, ginger, and the chili paste with garlic. Continue to stir-fry until the eggplant is tender. Add more oil as necessary to prevent sticking. When the eggplant is done, mix in the *tofu.* If you will not be serving immediately, cover the pan and keep the vegetables warm over very low heat. Just before serving, transfer the contents of the pan to a serving bowl and sprinkle the vegetables with chopped scallions.

Tofu in Szechwan Sauce

四川辣豆腐

Si Chuan La Dou Fu

Szechwan

Serves 4 to 6

Szechwan Province is poor agriculturally, and there is little meat available to its populace, so the basic food—rice—is seasoned with readily available hot peppers to make it more interesting and palatable. Whereas the restaurant and banquet dishes served in China tend to reflect the more moderate tastes of Peking cooking, in the United States the Szechwan preparations have become very popular as restaurant dishes. Not only are Szechwan and the even spicier Hunan restaurants springing up all over the United States, but struggling Cantonese restaurants sometimes close, reopen, and prosper as Szechwan restaurants.

Rather than indicating that Americans have unsophisticated tastes, our appreciation of Szechwan cooking shows that we are not tied to the negative image of Szechwan cooking as the cuisine of the poor. In fact, when we take another staple, *tofu,* and bathe it in a hot and spicy Szechwan sauce (the sauce is very similar to the Szechwan Sauce that appears in Chapter Two, Condiments), we may discover that we're actually elevating the *tofu* to a new culinary height.

When Tofu in Szechwan Sauce is served within a few hours of preparation, the scallions add their characteristic bite and crisp texture to the soft *tofu*. As the *tofu* marinates in the sauce over a period of time, the scallions lose some of their flavor and their crunch, but the compensation is that the *tofu* absorbs all the delicious flavors of the sauce, and the need for a contrasting texture vanishes. This dish will keep for at least a week if the *tofu* is completely immersed in the sauce and refrigerated.

½ cup "hot" oil, purchased or homemade (see recipe, page 126)
½ cup soy sauce
3 tablespoons red wine vinegar
2 teaspoons sugar
9 large cloves garlic, finely chopped
½ cup minced Chinese hot turnip or hot radish with chili
8 scallions (white and crisp green parts), chopped
1 pound tofu, cut into ½-inch cubes

In a medium-size bowl, combine all ingredients except the *tofu*. When everything is blended together well, stir in the *tofu*. Transfer the *tofu* and sauce to a covered jar and refrigerate. Serve as an accompaniment to rice or noodles.

Vegetarian's Delight

涼拌什錦

Liang Ban Shi Jin

General China influence

Serves 4 to 6

Vegetarian friends of ours introduced us to the idea of a Chinese salad bar lunch—crispy shredded vegetables served with *tofu*, fried noodles, and a selection of enticing dressings. In China, for hygienic reasons vegetables are not served raw, so in this recipe boiling water is poured over the shredded vegetables before they are served. Salad dressings with strong or unusual flavors are recommended to heighten the interest of this salad.

Salad:

4 ounces cellophane noodles
3 cups fresh bean sprouts
1 cup peeled shredded carrots
1 cup unpeeled shredded cucumbers
¼ pound fresh snow peas, tips and strings removed, shredded
8 cups boiling water
1 pound tofu, cut into ½-inch cubes
2 cups Deep-fried Noodles (see page 118)

Dressing:

1 teaspoon minced ginger root
2 scallions (white and crisp green parts), chopped
3 tablespoons soy sauce
2 tablespoons sesame oil
2 tablespoons Oriental rice vinegar or a red wine vinegar
1 tablespoon sugar

or

Salad Dressing II, Salad Dressing III, Sesame Sauce, or Sesame-Peanut Butter Sauce (see Chapter Two, Condiments)

Soak the cellophane noodles in a bowl of hot water for 10 minutes. Drain the noodles, then use scissors to cut them into 1½-inch pieces. In a colander, combine the bean sprouts, carrots, cucumbers, and snow peas, then pour the 8 cups of boiling water over the vegetables. Drain the vegetables thoroughly, rinse with cold water to cool completely, then mix in the cellophane noodles. Toss the salad lightly and transfer to a serving bowl.

Prepare at least two salad dressings. Arrange the dressings along with bowls of *tofu* and fried noodles near the salad bowl. Serve this salad buffet-style or on a lazy Susan.

Stir-fried Vegetables

素燴

Su Hui

General China

Serves 6

When vegetables are stir-fried quickly over high heat, they retain their basic shapes as well as their crispness. Vegetables are added to the pan according to the length of cooking time each requires, so the longest-cooking vegetables are added first (it's not possible to achieve the same kind of fresh flavor and crispness if all the vegetables are cooked at once). One exception I make is to add onions first, even though other ingredients may take longer to cook, as less oil is needed when onions are the first vegetable in the pan.

This recipe uses vegetables that seem to go together just right, with no one item competing for attention. Although julienne strips of celery and carrots may be added for flavor (add them right after the onions because they take longest to cook), they will take away some of the subtlety of the dish. Generally, stir-fried vegetables are enhanced by the addition of a little salt, sugar, and monosodium glutamate, but purists will want to use just the vegetables.

In Chinese cooking the ingredients are usually cut approximately the same size for attractiveness, for ease of handling, and so they will cook evenly. Here, with so many vegetables of different cooking times and shapes, it is appealing to allow the vegetables to retain their individuality. The onions are sliced into rings, the snow peas remain whole, and the spinach is torn into pieces.

2 tablespoons peanut, corn, or other oil
1 medium-size onion, cut into rounds
5 stalks celery cabbage or bok choy, sliced on the diagonal into ½-inch pieces
¼ pound small fresh snow peas, tips and strings removed
4 scallions (white and crisp green parts), sliced
½ pound fresh mushrooms, sliced
¼ pound fresh spinach leaves, cleaned well then torn into bite-size pieces
6 water chestnuts, preferably fresh, sliced
1 cup fresh bean sprouts
Optional: ½ teaspoon salt, ½ teaspoon sugar, ¼ teaspoon monosodium glutamate

It is most convenient in this kind of recipe to have all the ingredients set out in the order in which they are to be used. In a wok or a 10- to 12-inch skillet, heat the oil to 375 degrees F. Stir-fry the onions for 1 minute, then add the cabbage and continue to stir-fry half a minute longer. Toss in the snow peas and cook, stirring constantly for another 30 seconds. Add the scallions, stirring just to mix them in, then add the mushrooms. Raise the heat if necessary. The vegetables should cook rapidly, not simmer or sauté in their own juices. Stir-fry the mushrooms for half a minute, then add the spinach leaves and keep tossing the vegetables around while you add the water chestnuts and finally the bean sprouts. Cook and toss until everything is hot and well mixed, but be careful not to overcook—nothing should be soft. Season the vegetables and serve at once.

Stir-fried Broccoli

炒番芥蘭

Chao Fan Jie Lan

General China

Serves 4 to 6

Although broccoli is not native to China—the Chinese word for it translates to "foreign green vegetable"—the classic Chinese cooking method used in this recipe is a perfect way to prepare it. The broccoli remains a beautiful bright green when parboiled, stir-fried, then cooked just a bit longer in a covered pan. Cauliflower and green beans can also be prepared this way. It may seem like a bit of a fuss to cook broccoli in three stages, but once you've tried this recipe you may agree that it is an excellent way to serve broccoli.

1 large bunch broccoli (1½ pounds)
2 tablespoons peanut, corn, or other oil
½ teaspoon salt
½ teaspoon sugar
Pinch of monosodium glutamate (optional)
½ cup water

Cut the florets off the broccoli; cut the large ones in half so the pieces are about the same size. If you are using the stems as well, peel them first, then cut them into pieces of uniform size, about 1 inch long × ⅜ inch wide.

In a 4-quart pot, bring 3 quarts of water to the boil. Add the broccoli and cook it for 5 minutes. Drain it into a colander and immediately run the broccoli under cold water to stop any further cooking. Drain again. The broccoli can now be set aside or refrigerated until you're ready to continue the cooking.

In a wok or a 10-inch skillet, heat the oil to 375 degrees F. Add the broccoli *carefully*—it may spatter. Stir-fry the broccoli for 2 minutes, then sprinkle on the salt, sugar, and the monosodium glutamate. Add ½ cup of water (up to ½ cup more if the bunch of broccoli is particularly large) and bring the water to the boil. Cover the pan, reduce the heat to a gentle boil and cook for 5 minutes, no longer. Remove the cover and raise the heat to boil away any remaining water. Be careful not to burn the broccoli at this point. It's best to serve this dish immediately, but if you're waiting for something else to be done, leave the broccoli in the uncovered pan on the turned-off burner until you're ready to serve.

Broccoli, Water Chestnuts, and Dried Hot Peppers

辣味芥蘭

La Wei Jie Lan

Hunan

Serves 4

Here, broccoli florets are cooked briefly, just long enough to pick up the spiciness of the hot peppers. The stir-fried broccoli is mixed with water chestnuts then flavored with sesame oil. It can be served hot as a vegetable or chilled as an appetizer or salad.

1 small bunch broccoli (¾ pound)
2 whole dried hot chili peppers
1 tablespoon peanut, corn, or other oil
⅓ cup water chestnuts, sliced in half
1 tablespoon sesame oil, more or less to taste

Break the broccoli into individual florets, cutting the larger florets in half or quarters. Reserve the rest of the broccoli for another use. Remove the seeds from the dried hot peppers, and immediately wash your hands to rid them of the irritating oil which is on the peppers.

In a wok or an 8-inch skillet, heat the peanut, corn, or other oil to 375 degrees F. Carefully drop in the hot peppers, stir them around for 15 seconds, then add the broccoli florets. Stir-fry the broccoli for 5 minutes—it will remain bright green and very crisp. Mix in the water chestnuts, remove the hot peppers, and turn off the heat. Sprinkle the sesame oil over the broccoli, and toss the broccoli around to mix in the oil. Serve immediately, or chill to serve as Cold "Hot" Broccoli.

Stir-fried Miniature Corn With Vegetables

嫩玉米炒番芥蘭

Nen Yu Mi Chao Fan Jie Lan

Peking

Serves 4 to 6

This colorful combination uses three vegetables, each having a very distinctive taste. My friend Monica Yu, who suggested this trio to me, recommends that you cut each vegetable into a different shape, increasing the eye appeal.

6 medium-size dried Chinese mushrooms
Boiling water
1 medium-size bunch broccoli (1 pound)
Half a can (15 ounces) miniature corn ears, drained (reserve the liquid)
2 tablespoons peanut, corn, or other oil
1 tablespoon cornstarch mixed with ¼ cup liquid from the corn

In a small heatproof bowl, pour enough boiling water over the dried Chinese mushrooms to cover them completely. Let the mushrooms soak for 15 minutes, until softened. Cut out and discard the stems, then cut each mushroom cap into quarters.

Meanwhile, cut off the broccoli florets. Cut the large florets in half or quarters so that all the pieces are about the same size. Reserve the stems for another use. In a 4-quart pot, bring 3 quarts of water to the boil. Cook the broccoli florets in the boiling water for 5 minutes, then drain them in a colander.

Slice each miniature ear of corn on the diagonal into 2 or 3 pieces of equal size.

In a wok or a 10- to 12-inch skillet, heat the oil until it is hot but not yet smoking, 375 to 400 degrees F. Add the broccoli and stir-fry for 2 minutes, then stir in the mushroom quarters and the sliced corn. Toss the vegetables until they are heated through. Again stir together the cornstarch and canned corn liquid to make a smooth paste, then stir this mixture into the vegetables. Cook only until the liquid is thickened and glazed, then serve.

Green Beans With Garlic

蒜末四季豆

Suan Mo Si Ji Dou

General China

Serves 4

More than a touch of garlic flavors these fresh green beans, which are stir-fried only for a few minutes to remain at a crunchy, barely cooked stage.

2 tablespoons peanut, corn, or other oil
1 pound fresh green beans, tips removed, sliced on the diagonal into 1-inch pieces
4 cloves garlic, finely chopped
Optional: ½ teaspoon salt, ½ teaspoon sugar, ¼ teaspoon monosodium glutamate, 2 teaspoons sesame oil

In a wok or an 8- to 10-inch skillet, heat the oil to 375 degrees F. Carefully add the sliced green beans, stirring immediately so they do not stick or burn. Sprinkle the garlic over the beans, and stir-fry for 4 minutes. Time yourself—4 minutes of stirring is a lot longer than it seems. Season as desired and serve the green beans hot. If you can't serve them immediately, remove the pan from the heat and leave the beans in the uncovered pan for a few minutes.

Stir-fried Mushrooms, Water Chestnuts, and Fresh Peas

鮮菇豌豆

Xian Gu Wan Dou

General China influence

Serves 6

Fresh peas are usually sweetest when they are eaten right from the shell. The next best thing is to mix them, uncooked, with stir-fried mushrooms and sweet, crisp fresh water chestnuts. I developed this combination to serve cold as a salad, with a touch of sesame oil as a dressing.

2 tablespoons peanut, corn, or other oil
1 pound fresh mushrooms, sliced
2 teaspoons fresh lemon juice
10 fresh water chestnuts, sliced
1 pound fresh green peas, shelled
2 teaspoons sesame oil
Lettuce leaves

In a wok or a 10- to 12-inch skillet, heat the oil to 375 degrees F. Stir-fry the mushrooms until crisp-tender, about 2 minutes. Sprinkle on the lemon juice. Remove the pan from the heat and mix in the water chestnuts and peas. Sprinkle on the sesame oil and toss the vegetables until the sesame oil is blended in. Chill the vegetables, and serve on a bed of lettuce leaves.

Stir-fried Sweet Peppers

炒兩色椒

Chao Liang Se Jiao

General China

Serves 4

Red and green bell peppers are a tasty and colorful addition to many dishes, and they stand well on their own. The brief cooking leaves them crisp but releases their sweet (red) and slightly pungent (green) flavors.

When the peppers are served plain as a vegetable, you may want to add a little salt and sugar as flavor enhancers, and sesame oil to bring an additional smoky taste. When the stir-fried peppers are to be mixed with meat, rice, noodles, or other vegetables, they can be served unseasoned.

2 tablespoons peanut, corn, or other oil
2 large green peppers, cut into thin strips
2 large sweet red peppers, cut into thin strips
Optional: ¼ teaspoon salt, ¼ teaspoon sugar,
1 teaspoon sesame oil (or to taste)

In a wok or a 10- to 12-inch skillet, heat the oil until it just begins to smoke. Add the peppers and stir-fry for about 3 minutes, until slightly cooked. Mix in the optional salt and sugar at this point. Remove the wok or skillet from the heat and sprinkle the sesame oil over the peppers, then stir the peppers to blend in the oil. Transfer the peppers to a serving bowl and serve them hot, or chill and serve cold.

Stir-fried Carrots With Ginger

炒胡蘿蔔

Chao Hu Luo Bo

General China

Serves 4

When stir-fried together, fresh ginger root subtly flavors thin strips of carrots. The carrots, cooked to a crisp-tender stage, are a colorful and tasty addition to any meal.

1 pound carrots
1 tablespoon peanut, corn, or other oil
1 tablespoon minced ginger root

Peel the carrots and discard the ends. Cut the carrots lengthwise into quarters, then slice the thicker pieces lengthwise again. Now slice the strips on the diagonal into 1¼-inch pieces.

In a wok or a 10-inch skillet, heat a tablespoon of oil until the oil is hot but not yet smoking. Add the carrots, stir until they are coated with the oil, then sprinkle the minced ginger root over the carrots. Stir-fry the carrots for 4 to 5 minutes, until barely tender, or until they are cooked to your liking. Serve the carrots immediately, or leave them in an uncovered pan over very low heat until ready to serve

Steamed Carrots With Ginger

清蒸胡蘿蔔

Qing Zheng Hu Luo Bo

General China influence

Serves 4

Here the flavor of fresh ginger root permeates thinly sliced carrot rounds which are steamed until they are soft. Carrots develop an especially sweet taste when steamed, adding to the pleasure of this combination.

1 pound carrots, peeled then sliced on the diagonal into thin rounds
1 tablespoon minced ginger root

Place the carrots on a steamer tray and sprinkle them with the ginger root. Steam the carrots for 10 to 15 minutes, until tender. The carrots should be soft but not mushy, so if you can't serve them right away, remove the lid from the steamer to retard further cooking.

Steamed Vegetables

蒸三色

Zheng San Se

General China

Serves 4 to 6

Broccoli, cauliflower, and carrots all take approximately the same time to steam, and this colorful combination is exceptionally striking. The vegetables can be served plain or with a simple sauce that adds flavor and a lovely glaze.

1 small bunch broccoli
1 small head cauliflower
½ pound carrots
Optional sauce: ½ cup cold seasoned vegetable or chicken broth, 2 teaspoons cornstarch, 2 teaspoons soy sauce

Break the broccoli and cauliflower into small florets of uniform size. Peel the carrots, then slice them into 2-inch pieces on a 45-degree angle. Arrange the vegetables attractively on a large steamer tray, preferably one with holes in it. Steam the vegetables for approximately 15 minutes, until tender.

Meanwhile, in a 1-quart pot combine the cold vegetable or chicken broth, the cornstarch, and the soy sauce. Blend them very well, dissolving the cornstarch. Over medium heat, bring the broth to the boil, stirring constantly. When the mixture boils and thickens, reduce the heat to very low and keep the sauce warm until the vegetables are done.

Transfer the cooked vegetables to a serving bowl or platter. Pour the sauce over the vegetables and serve immediately.

Bok Choy in Cream Sauce

奶油白菜

Nai You Bai Cai

Shanghai

Serves 4

A dish of vegetables in cream sauce is unusual but not unheard of in China. Milk is not easy to come by, so a cream sauce is something of a luxury. This sauce is made with a vegetarian broth and a little milk, in contrast to our typical cream sauces which use all milk or cream. The dark green leaves of the *bok choy* add a colorful touch.

1 tablespoon peanut, corn, or other oil
1 large onion, coarsely chopped
1½ pounds bok choy, shredded
1 cup seasoned vegetable broth
1 tablespoon cornstarch
¼ cup cold milk

In a wok or a 12-inch skillet, heat the oil until it is hot but not yet smoking, about 375 degrees F. Stir-fry the onion for 2 minutes, then add the *bok choy* and continue to stir-fry for another 2 to 3 minutes. Turn off the heat and leave the vegetables in the pan while you prepare the sauce.

In a 1-quart pot, bring the broth to the boil. In a small bowl or cup, mix together the cornstarch and cold milk, stirring until the cornstarch is completely dissolved. Blend the cornstarch and milk into the broth, stirring until the broth is thickened and smooth. Mix the sauce with the vegetables, and serve with noodles.

Vegetarian Stuffed Cabbage

釀洋白菜

Rang Yang Bai Cai

General China influence

Serves 4 to 6

I must admit at the start that this will never replace my mother's old-fashioned stuffed cabbage. However, as a vegetarian dish with a Chinese influence it is a pleasant change from stir-fried vegetables and fried rice. The onion, water chestnuts, and bamboo shoots are more important for texture than taste, while the mushrooms and *hoisin* sauce are essential in contributing flavor.

2 medium-size heads (1½ pounds each) green cabbage (not Chinese cabbage)
1 tablespoon peanut, corn, or other oil
1 small onion, chopped
6 water chestnuts, sliced
¼ cup thinly sliced bamboo shoots
3 cups sliced fresh mushrooms
3 cups cooked brown rice
3 tablespoons hoisin sauce

In an 8-quart pot, bring 6 quarts of water to the boil. Place the two whole cabbages in the pot, turn off the heat, and let the cabbages soften in the water for 5 minutes. Turn them occasionally if they are not completely covered with water. Remove the cabbages from the water, drain, then gently peel off the leaves until there are 18 nice leaves. If the leaves are too stiff to peel, return the cabbages to the pot of hot water until they are soft enough to work with.

In a wok or a 10- or 12-inch skillet, heat the oil until it is moderately hot but not yet smoking, about 375 degrees F. Stir-fry the onion until lightly browned. Turn off the heat. Mix in the water chestnuts, bamboo shoots, and the mushrooms, then add the rice, tossing the ingredients around until well mixed. Blend in the *hoisin* sauce.

Place ¼ cup of filling in the center of each cabbage leaf. Roll the leaf around the filling, tuck in the ends, and secure the cabbage rolls with toothpicks. The stuffed cabbage can be tray-frozen at this point.

Place the cabbage rolls on a steamer tray. Steam the stuffed cabbage for 15 minutes. Allow at least 5 minutes extra steaming time for frozen cabbage rolls.

Egg Dishes

Cantonese Steamed Eggs

蒸蛋

Zheng Dan

Canton

Serves 4

Here is a remarkably simple, tasty, and versatile way to serve eggs. The basic ingredients are beaten eggs and chicken broth, with soy sauce and scallions added for flavor. (To make this preparation *pareve,* substitute a vegetable broth for the chicken broth.) The consistency is custardlike, but the eggs come out light and fluffy, reminiscent of an omelet. A little broth may separate out, making a light sauce.

Bits of fish and ginger root are common additions to this egg dish, but mushrooms, diced cooked chicken, chopped spinach, or whatever you might put into an omelet or a quiche can be used as well. The eggs are commonly served hot, with rice, but they can be cut into squares and served cold if you like. Use a heatproof dish with low sides, such as a one-quart Corningware dish, because the solid ingredients rise to the top and a deep bowl won't allow as even a distribution of the ingredients.

4 eggs (graded large)
1 cup seasoned chicken or vegetable broth
2 teaspoons soy sauce
2 scallions (white and crisp green parts), chopped

In a medium-size mixing bowl, beat the eggs. Mix in the chicken or vegetable broth, soy sauce, and scallions, along with any other ingredients you want to use. Pour the mixture into a 1-quart heatproof dish, and set the dish on a rack in a steamer. The dish should be above the level of the water. Steam the eggs for 15 minutes, starting from when the water begins to boil. The eggs come out puffy, almost like a souffle, but they sink immediately after they are removed from the steamer. If you can't serve them immediately, leave them in the steamer with the cover off until you're ready to serve. Leftovers can be reheated by briefly resteaming.

Baked Peking Custard

烤蛋

Kao Dan

Peking

Serves 4

This is another basic egg custard, but this one is baked, making it more like a quiche than an omelet. The Chinese mushrooms and sesame oil lend an unusual tone, but this remains a home-style dish, not banquet fare. Minced beef or veal is substituted for the ground pork and shrimp that are usually included in recipes for Peking Custard. This custard is served as a luncheon dish or as one of several preparations at a Chinese family meal. Or it can be featured as the main dish at a light dinner.

2 medium-size dried Chinese mushrooms
Boiling water
4 eggs (graded large)
1 cup seasoned chicken broth
½ cup minced uncooked beef or veal
1 tablespoon sesame oil

Place the mushrooms in a heatproof bowl. Pour boiling water over the mushrooms, covering them completely. Soak the mushrooms until softened, about 15 minutes.

While the mushrooms are soaking, preheat the oven to 375 degrees F. Grease or oil a 1-quart baking dish.

In a medium-size mixing bowl, beat the eggs. Mix in the chicken broth and the minced beef or veal. Stir to distribute the meat evenly. Remove the softened mushrooms from the hot water, then dice the mushrooms, discarding the stems. Stir the mushrooms into the egg mixture, then pour the mixture into the baking dish. Bake the custard in the preheated oven for 30 to 35 minutes, until it is set and browned. Remove the custard from the oven, sprinkle the sesame oil on top, and serve.

Mu Shu Eggs

木樨蛋

Mu Xu Dan

Peking

Serves 6

This unusual recipe for scrambled eggs is an adaptation of *mu shu* pork, a very popular restaurant dish in this country. A cooked filling is rolled up inside thin steamed flour-and-water pancakes, and the filled pancakes are eaten as a sandwich. According to one source, the words *mu shu* sound like the Chinese words for tree ears and golden needles, which are essential ingredients in this dish. Other translations indicate that *mu shu* is the word for the yellow cassia flower, and the bits of egg characteristic of *mu shu* dishes are said to resemble this flower. The consistency of *mu shu* dishes is soft but chewy, and while there are no strong flavors, there are definite hints of the exotic.

1 recipe Mu Shu Pancakes (page 309)
2 tablespoons dried tree ears
2 medium-size dried Chinese mushrooms
6 golden needles (tiger lily buds)
Boiling water
2 tablespoons peanut, corn, or other oil
2 teaspoons soy sauce
6 eggs (graded large), beaten
4 water chestnuts, coarsely chopped
¼ cup thinly sliced bamboo shoots
¼ cup scallions rounds (white and crisp green parts)

The *mu shu* pancakes must be ready before the filling is cooked. You can leave the pancakes in the steamer and arrange them on a serving plate just before serving.

In a small pot or heatproof bowl, place the tree ears, dried mushrooms, and golden needles. Pour boiling water over them, covering everything completely with the water. Allow the dried ingredients to soak in the hot water for about 20 minutes, until soft, then drain off the water. Chop the tree ears and mushrooms coarsely, discarding the mushroom stems. Cut the golden needles in thirds. All the other ingredients must be ready and nearby before any cooking begins.

In a 10- or 12-inch skillet, heat the oil to degrees 375 F.—a drop of water carefully sprinkled into the oil will spatter instantly. Stir the soy sauce into the beaten eggs, then pour the eggs into the hot oil. Sprinkle tne tree ears, mushrooms, golden needles, water chestnuts, bamboo shoots, and scallions over the eggs, then scramble the eggs with a large fork, spoon, or chopsticks until they are set. Remove the pan from the heat; or, if using an electric skillet, turn off the heat. Arrange the *mu shu* pancakes attractively on a serving plate, put the filling on another plate, then serve at once.

Each person opens up a pancake, places some filling in the center, wraps the pancake around the filling, and folds over the bottom an inch or two so no filling falls out. The pancakes are eaten as finger food—forks and knives are not used.

Eggs Fu Yung
芙蓉蛋
Fu Rong Dan

Chinese-American

Serves 4

This is a popular luncheon dish in Chinese-American restaurants. Lightly browned egg pancakes made with shreds of meat and vegetables are served with a thickened chicken broth gravy. This dish is more American than Chinese in origin, very much like a Western omelet with Chinese overtones. The title itself is a misnomer, because in China *fu yung* is more correctly used to describe a souffle made with beaten egg whites. It seems likely that the name was borrowed for the omelet pancakes, inaccurately, by restaurateurs anxious to give pronounceable names to menu items. However inappropriate the name may be, the dish is tasty.

4 eggs (graded large)
1 tablespoon soy sauce
½ cup fresh bean sprouts
1 cup shredded cooked chicken or turkey (substitute any meat)
½ cup sliced mushrooms, fresh or canned
4 water chestnuts, sliced
2 scallions (white and crisp green parts), chopped
½ cup seasoned chicken broth
1 teaspoon soy sauce
2 teaspoons cornstarch
1 to 2 tablespoons peanut, corn, or other oil

In a medium-size mixing bowl, beat the eggs. Stir in the tablespoon of soy sauce, then mix in the bean sprouts, chicken or turkey, mushrooms, water chestnuts, and scallions. Set aside while you prepare the sauce.

In a 1-quart pot, combine the chicken broth, 1 teaspoon of soy sauce, and the cornstarch. Bring the mixture to the boil over medium heat, stirring to keep the cornstarch dissolved. The mixture will thicken when it boils. Continue stirring until the broth is smooth, then turn down the heat to very low while you cook the egg pancakes. In a 5- or 6-inch skillet over moderate heat, heat 1 tablespoon of oil until it is hot but not yet smoking (a drop of water will spatter instantly). Give the egg mixture a quick stir, then spoon about ¼ cup of the egg mixture into the skillet. Tilt the pan so the egg covers the bottom evenly. Cook until the pancake is set, browned lightly, and will hold together when it is turned. Turn the pancake with a pancake turner or a large spoon, and cook the other side until lightly browned. Remove the pancake and coat the skillet with a little more oil before cooking the next one. Repeat the procedure until all the egg mixture is used up. Remember to stir the mixture just before ladling it out each time. When all the pancakes are cooked, arrange them on a serving platter and pour the sauce over them.

To keep the cooked pancakes hot while you work, wrap them in foil. If you work slowly, keep them warm in a very low oven.

Meatless Eggs Fu Yung

清炒芙蓉蛋

Qing Chao Fu Rong Dan

Chinese-American

Serves 4

The basic Eggs Fu Yung can be varied by substituting different meats and vegetables for those in the recipe or by omitting the meat and sauce for a nonmeat dish. Here, the eggs are combined with three unusual ingredients—tree ears, golden needles, and dried mushrooms. The cooking procedure is the same, but the chicken broth is replaced with a sprinkling of sesame oil.

¼ cup tree ears
8 to 10 golden needles
4 medium-size dried Chinese mushrooms
Boiling water

6 eggs (graded large)
2 tablespoons soy sauce
2 to 3 tablespoons peanut, corn, or other oil
1 tablespoon sesame oil, approximately

Place the tree ears, golden needles, and Chinese mushrooms in a heat-proof bowl, then pour enough boiling water over them to cover completely. Allow them to soak until soft, about 15 to 20 minutes. Drain off the water. Cut the tree ears into several pieces each, cut the golden needles into 4 or 5 pieces each, and slice the mushrooms thinly, discarding the stems.

In a medium-size mixing bowl, beat the eggs. Stir in the soy sauce, then mix in the tree ears, golden needles, and Chinese mushrooms. In a 5- or 6-inch skillet over moderate heat, heat a tablespoon of oil until it is hot but not yet smoking (a drop of water will spatter instantly). Give the egg mixture a quick stir, then spoon about ¼ cup of the egg mixture into the skillet. Tilt the pan so the egg covers the bottom evenly. Cook until the pancake is set and lightly browned. Turn the pancake with a pancake turner or a large spoon, and cook the other side until lightly browned. Remove the pancake and brush it with a thin coating of sesame oil. Repeat the procedure until all the egg mixture is used up. Remember to stir the mixture just before ladling it out each time. Serve the eggs as soon as they are all cooked. They can be kept warm on an electric warming tray, or wrapped in foil. If you work slowly, keep them warm in a very low oven.

Plain Egg Pancake

煎蛋餅

Jian Dan Bing

General China

Serves 1

This is a very quick way to make an omelet, because the eggs set up almost immediately upon contact with the oil. Eggs cooked in this manner are usually cut into strips and used for garnishes on other dishes, but there is no reason why this technique can't be used to prepare any kind of plain or filled omelet.

1 tablespoon peanut, corn, or other oil
2 eggs (graded large)

In an 8-inch skillet, heat the oil until it is hot but not yet smoking (a drop of water will spatter instantly). In a small mixing bowl, beat the eggs with a fork, then pour them into the pan. Swish the eggs around to cover the bottom of the pan evenly. Gently push cooked egg toward the middle, and allow uncooked egg to flow around the edges. Cook just until all the egg is set. Fill as desired (with jelly, honey, mushrooms, onions) and fold the omelet in half or thirds. Serve at once.

Egg Rolls, Literally
蛋卷
Dan Juan

Shanghai

Makes 10 egg rolls

Eggs are cooked pancake-style then rolled around a stir-fried meat-and-vegetable filling to make real "egg rolls." In the Chinese version the egg rolls are sliced into small pieces which can be handled with chopsticks. Here, they are left whole and served as omelets for a luncheon or light dinner.

1 tablespoon peanut, corn, or other oil
1 small onion, sliced
1 cup shredded Chinese cabbage
1 tablespoon peanut, corn, or other oil
1 cup shredded beef, lamb, veal, or chicken (cut into thin strips about 1 inch long)
1 tablespoon soy sauce
2 to 3 tablespoons peanut, corn, or other oil
10 eggs (graded large)
10 teaspoons soy sauce

Preheat the oven to warm, 200 degrees F., or set up a steamer with hot or simmering water. You will need a place to keep the filled egg rolls warm while you cook the remainder.

For the filling, in a wok or an 8-inch skillet heat 1 tablespoon of oil until moderately hot. Add the sliced onion and stir-fry for 30 seconds. Add the Chinese cabbage, stir-fry for another 30 to 45 seconds, then add another tablespoon of oil to the wok or skillet. Be sure that when the oil is added, it makes first contact with the pan, not the vegetables—it will heat up better this way. When the oil has had a chance to become moderately hot, toss in the meat and stir-fry it until cooked. Mix in the soy sauce, combine everything well, and remove the contents of the pan to a clean bowl.

Cooking the eggs takes a little coordination, but once you get into the rhythm of it you won't find it difficult. Coat a 6- or 7-inch skillet with a scant tablespoon of oil. In a small mixing bowl, beat 1 egg with 1 teaspoon of soy sauce. Heat the skillet until the oil is hot enough for a drop of water to spatter instantly, then add the beaten egg. Swish the egg around the pan to cover the bottom evenly and completely. When the egg is set and the bottom is cooked, spread 2 tablespoons of the cooked filling down the center of the egg, stopping about 1 inch from the top and bottom. Roll or fold the egg around the filling, then carefully transfer the egg roll to a heatproof platter in the warm oven or to a steamer tray set over hot or simmering water. The remaining eggs are cooked the same way, but you won't need to add as much oil to the pan each time. When all the eggs are cooked, serve them over rice or on a bed of shredded lettuce.

Egg Rolls, Literally, With a Vegetarian Filling

捲菜蛋卷

Juan Cai Dan Juan

Shanghai

Makes 10 egg rolls

These egg rolls have an excellent meatless filling, offering a fine combination of soft and crisp textures. The scallions bring a pleasant sharpness to the other bland vegetables. Both this and the previous recipe can be used, as directed, for the egg rolls, or they can be prepared as one or two giant half-moon filled omelet pancakes. Both methods of folding are used in China.

2 to 3 tablespoons peanut, corn, or other oil
¼ cup sliced scallions (white and crisp green parts)
1 cup sliced fresh mushrooms
1 cup diced tofu (¼-inch cubes)
1 tablespoon soy sauce
1 cup fresh bean sprouts
2 to 3 tablespoons peanut, corn, or other oil

→

10 eggs (graded large)
10 teaspoons soy sauce

Preheat the oven to warm, 200 degrees F., or set up a steamer with hot or simmering water. You will need a place to keep the filled egg rolls while you cook the remainder.

For the filling, in a wok or an 8-inch skillet heat 2 tablespoons of oil until moderately hot. Stir in the scallions to coat them with oil, then add the mushrooms and stir-fry for 1 minute.

If the mushrooms stick to the pan or become too dry, add a little more oil. Now add the cubed *tofu,* stirring gently to heat it and mix it in. Sprinkle the soy sauce over the vegetables, and again mix gently to blend in the soy sauce. Toss in the bean sprouts, and as soon as the vegetables are mixed, remove them from the pan

To cook the eggs, coat a 6- or 7-inch skillet with a scant tablespoon of oil. In a small mixing bowl, beat 1 egg with 1 teaspoon of soy sauce. Heat the skillet until the oil is hot enough for a drop of water to spatter instantly, then add the beaten egg. Swish the egg around the pan to cover the bottom evenly and completely. When the egg is set and the bottom is cooked, spread 2 tablespoons of the cooked filling down the center of the egg, stopping about 1 inch from the top and bottom. Roll or fold the egg around the filling, then carefully transfer the egg roll to a heatproof platter in the warm oven or to a steamer tray set over hot or simmering water. The remaining eggs are cooked the same way, but you won't need to add as much oil to the pan each time. When all the eggs are cooked, serve them over rice or on a bed of shredded lettuce.

8

Rice, Noodles, and Breads

Rice and noodles form the backbone of the Chinese diet. They are the foundation of breakfast, lunch, and dinner for most Chinese. Bits of fresh or dried meat or fish, or fresh or preserved vegetables, are sometimes added for interest and nutrition. Many meals consist only of rice enhanced by a salty or spicy tidbit, such as a pickled vegetable. Even when there are vegetable and vegetable-meat combinations set out on the table, each person takes a bit of food from the shared dish and mixes it with rice in his own rice bowl. It is only at a Chinese banquet—where common and inexpensive foods are avoided—that one doesn't see much rice or noodles.

The two major rices of China are a stubby, oval white rice called sweet, glutinous, or sticky rice (three names for the same rice) and unrefined brown rice. Glutinous rice is used for congees, stuffings, and desserts, while brown rice is the everyday "rice bowl" rice of China. The white rice we are accustomed to in the United States, which has the bran covering removed—and with it much of the nutritional value—is a sign of affluence in China. Although it is preferred by the Chinese, it is not available to the majority of people. White rice *is* used in small quantities to refresh the diner between heavier courses at banquets.

The kind of rice you cook to go with Chinese food is largely a matter of personal preference. The nutrition-oriented will want to use brown rice (a generous supplier of the B vitamins), and those trying to duplicate a home-style Chinese meal will use brown rice as well. In the United States, rice is packaged according to the length of the grain—long, medium, or short. Long-grain white rice comes out fluffy and less chewy than brown rice; and the grains of long-grain rice remain separated better than those of short-grain rice when used to make fried rice. Short-grain rice is softer than long-grain, and it is preferred by some people for basic plain rice Medium-grain rice is closer in texture to the short variety. Glutinous rice is a specialty rice, and in the United States it is much more expensive than regular rice. (In China, however, the reverse is true.) Use glutinous rice when it is called for in a recipe, not as a main dish accompaniment.

Noodles, or *mien,* are found in various parts of China, but they are more of a staple in the wheat-growing North. Fresh Chinese flour-and-egg noodles are sold as *lo mien* in Asian groceries, but the term actually means "tossed or mixed noodles." *Lo mien* is used more accurately to describe both a Chinese noodle preparation and the particular kind of noodle used for that preparation. The dish known as *lo mien* consists of boiled noodles which are mixed with stir-fried meat and vegetable combinations then served without further cooking. In *chao mien,* which literally means "stir-fried noodles," boiled noodles are cooled then stir-fried until partially browned before being mixed with the stir-fried meats and vegetables. (The Chinese-American version of this preparation is presented in the recipe Chicken "Chow Mein," page 305.)

The Chinese make noodles from mung beans (cellophane noodles) and rice as well as wheat. Although the noodles come in various thicknesses, they are almost always shaped and served long to symbolize longevity.

Steamed breads and rolls made from wheat flour are found in northern China, where wheat is more important than rice as a staple. They are very bland-tasting when eaten plain, but when they are eaten with pieces of seasoned meat, as in the recipe for Home-style Steamed Crispy Duck (page 232), they are an excellent complement to the meat. They are also good when dipped into some of the spicier sauces. Steamed breads are by no means a staple of the Chinese diet, however, and a meal without them is perfectly normal. Baked loaves of bread such as we use for sandwiches and toast are not part of the Chinese cuisine.

This chapter contains recipes that feature rice and noodles, along with a few steamed and pan-fried breads. Check the Index for other recipes that feature rice and noodles as major ingredients. The congees appear in Chapter Three, Congees and Soups. Recipes for *wontons* and *wonton* wrappers can be found among the appetizers (Chapter One) and soups.

Rice

Plain Boiled White Rice

飯

Fan

General China

Makes about 6 cups

This method of cooking produces a nonsticky rice that is tender and fluffy. The rice is boiled until most of the water is absorbed, then the remainder of cooking takes place over low heat in a covered pot. The rice comes out best when it is rinsed first; it is less likely to boil over than unrinsed rice because excess starch is removed.

The amount of water in which rice should be cooked depends on (1) whether or not you first rinse it—it takes less water to cook if you do rinse first; (2) the shape of the pot—a tall, narrow pot requires less water than a wider one; and (3) how careful you are—I use the four cups of water because I don't have to watch the rice so carefully that way—that is, I can afford to boil off some extra liquid.

2 cups white rice
3½ to 4 cups cold water

Place the rice in a strainer, and rinse it under cold water until the water runs clear. Put the rice in a 2- or 3-quart pot and add the cold water. Bring the water to the boil over high heat; boil uncovered for about 5 minutes, until enough water is absorbed so you can see the surface of the rice. Little "potholes" will appear in the surface of the rice. Turn the heat to low, and without stirring, cover the pot and simmer the rice for about 20 minutes, until it is dry. If using an electric stove, turn the heat down to low a minute or two earlier to allow the burner to cool somewhat before you cover the rice. After the rice has cooked, turn off the heat and leave the rice in the covered pot on the turned-off burner for another 20 minutes, or until you are ready to serve. The rice will stay hot for another 10 to 15 minutes. Fluff the rice with a fork or chopsticks while it is still hot, then serve it immediately, or chill the rice for use in fried rice.

Rice can be cooked in advance and refrigerated or frozen, then steamed over boiling water. If you know in advance that rice is to be reheated, undercook it a bit the first time around.

Quantity Cooking of Rice

大鍋飯

Da Guo Fan

General China

Makes 25 to 30 servings

The first time I tried to cook rice in quantity for a community fair I had a near disaster. Using the 2:1 proportion I usually use for rice, I cooked about 10 pounds of rice. I decided not to rinse the rice first, because I wanted to preserve the nutrients that might be washed out. That was one of several mistakes. I ended up with 100 portions of gummy rice. My partner said to me, "Why didn't you ask me? Don't you know we're experienced at making huge quantities of rice for church dinners?" I subsequently learned that she cooks rice according to the following method and has never had a failure. She sent me these instructions in a letter:

> Fill a large pot with 2 gallons of water and bring to a boil. Add salt and long-grain rice (6–8 cups raw rice) and boil for 16 minutes. Turn the heat down but make sure that the rice and water continue to boil. Then pour into a sieve or colander and rinse. Put 1 or 2 inches of water back in the pot and rest the colander on the pot. Cover with a lid or something else and keep the water in the pot hot. The rice never gets sticky.

If you have your own concept of perfect rice, you'll probably want to stick to your method. The method here is similar to the one used in Plain Boiled White Rice, but proportionately less water is needed when a lot of rice is cooked at once. In addition, the rice is cooked with a little oil, which helps prevent it from becoming pasty.

10 cups white rice
15 cups cold water
2 or 3 tablespoons peanut, corn, or other oil

Place the rice in a strainer, and rinse it well under cold running water. Or, put the rice in a large pot, cover it well with water, swish it around, drain off the water, and repeat the process.

To cook the rice, put the rice in an 8-quart pot with the 15 cups of cold water and the oil. Bring the water to the boil over high heat, and let it boil uncovered, without stirring, until over half the water is absorbed and you can see little "potholes" in the surface of the rice. Turn the heat to very low, then cover the pot and continue cooking for about 20 minutes, until the liquid is absorbed and the rice is cooked. Now turn off the burner but leave the rice exactly where it is for another 30 minutes. It will stay warm but will continue to dry out nicely. Fluff the rice with a large fork or chopsticks before serving. Serve it hot.

Plain Boiled Brown Rice

糙米飯

Cao Mi Fan

General China

Serves 6

Brown rice is more chewy and substantial than white rice, and has a bit more flavor. It cooks to a light brown color, and bits of the bran add texture here and there. Brown rice takes longer to cook than white rice, and it absorbs more water as it cooks. Once cooked, it can be used in any of the recipes calling for rice.

5 cups water
2 cups brown rice

Bring the water to the boil in a 2- or 3-quart pot. Stir in the rice. When the water returns to the boil, reduce the heat to simmer and cover the pot with a tight-fitting lid. Cook the rice for 1 hour, until tender. Fluff the rice with a fork before serving.

Notes on Fried Rice

Fried rice is a very flexible dish, with endless variations. Basically the dish is prepared by stir-frying cold cooked rice (the rice used to prepare fried rice must be cold or the dish will come out sticky) in oil over moderate heat. The stir-frying coats the grains of rice with oil—which helps keep the grains separate—and heats the rice, but it is not meant to brown the rice. The light brown color we associate with fried rice comes from soy sauce that is added. Fried rice can be prepared with white or brown rice, cooked or uncooked meats, vegetables, leftovers, or bits and pieces of just about anything edible.

The four recipes that follow are representative of what you can do with fried rice. The first can be considered the most elegant—if fried rice can be thought of as elegant—because it is full of fresh meats and vegetables and has a good variety of tastes and textures. The second is more of an emergency dish—it uses leftover chicken and has a soft consistency, getting its only textural interest from the scallion garnish. The third is a meatless fried rice for one—it shows what can be assembled for a quick lunch. The fourth, an elaboration on the third, is tasty and nutritious.

In China, bits of pork are used as the meat in fried rice, but it is an easy matter to substitute beef, veal, lamb, poultry, *tofu*, and vegetables in the kosher kitchen.

Special Fried Rice
美味炒飯
Mei Wei Chao Fan

General China

Serves 4 to 6

Fried rice is a dish I often prepare when we have leftover meat or poultry on hand, but it becomes special when prepared with previously uncooked meat. This recipe is for an American-style fried rice: the eggs are scrambled first, removed from the pan, and mixed in at the end, so you see bits and pieces of egg throughout the dish. In the Chinese method, the eggs are beaten lightly and added at the end, and although they cannot be seen, they blend in and add a creamy texture to the rice. Also, this version calls for more meat than a Chinese version would.

2 tablespoons peanut, corn, or other oil
4 eggs (graded large), beaten
1 tablespoon peanut, corn, or other oil
½ to 1 cup diced beef (¼-inch cubes)
½ to 1 cup diced chicken (¼-inch cubes)
¼ cup peanut, corn, or other oil
¼ cup scallion rounds (white and crisp green parts)
1 cup sliced fresh mushrooms
6 cups cold cooked rice (the rice must be cold)
¼ cup soy sauce
1 teaspoon sugar
1 to 2 cups fresh bean sprouts, to taste (optional)

Generously coat a 10- or 12-inch skillet with about 2 tablespoons of oil. Heat the oil until it is hot but not yet smoking. Pour in the eggs, and scramble them over moderately high heat. If the temperature is right, they will set almost immediately. Remove the eggs while they are still moist.

In the same pan, heat another tablespoon of oil to 375 degrees F. Stir-fry the beef and chicken until they are cooked, then remove them from the pan.

In a clean 12-inch skillet or a wok, heat the ¼ cup of oil to 375 degrees F. Add the scallions and stir to coat them with oil, then add the mushrooms and stir-fry them for 1 minute. If all the oil has been absorbed by the mushrooms, you'll need to add more to coat the bottom of the pan so the rice doesn't stick when it is added. Add the cold cooked rice to the mushrooms, and stir quickly to prevent sticking and to keep the grains of rice separated. Sprinkle on the soy sauce and sugar, mix well, then add the cooked meat and the eggs, again mixing everything well. Mix in the bean sprouts, toss everything together, and serve. Pass around extra chopped scallions as garnish. For people who like to add extra seasonings to food, sesame oil, Chinese mustard, soy sauce, and duck sauce can be passed around as well.

Fried rice can be prepared in advance and refrigerated or frozen. In either of those cases, it is best if the scallions and bean sprouts are left out until the rice is reheated. Use any method to reheat—steam, stir-fry, use a microwave, or heat the rice in a covered casserole in a 350-degree F. oven.

Chicken Fried Rice for the Rabbi

鷄絲炒飯

Ji Si Chao Fan

General China

Serves 6

Much of the entertaining I do is casual, so one Monday afternoon when I spontaneously invited the rabbi to have dinner with us that same evening, I had in mind to serve whatever menu I had planned for that evening, which happened to be home-style Chinese food. Steak fried rice was to be one of the dishes, because we had a small piece of steak left from a previous meal. I searched the refrigerator for the foil-wrapped piece of steak, but couldn't find it because it had been eaten as a snack. I found some cooked chicken shreds in the freezer which I'd saved from chicken soup bones some weeks before. You would be surprised at how quickly you can defrost two large packages of chicken shreds when the rabbi's coming any minute!

¼ cup peanut, corn, or other oil
6 cups cold cooked rice
¼ cup soy sauce
1 teaspoon sugar
2 cups cooked chicken shreds
4 scallions (white and crisp green parts), chopped

In a wok or a 12-inch skillet, heat the oil until it is moderately hot, 350 to 375 degrees F. Add the cold cooked rice and stir immediately and rapidly to prevent sticking and to keep the grains of rice separated. Sprinkle on the soy sauce and sugar, mix well, then add the cooked chicken shreds. Mix in the chicken and toss the contents of the pan until everything is hot. Transfer the fried rice to a platter, sprinkle with scallions, and serve.

Vegetarian Brown Rice for One

素炒飯(一人份)

Su Chao Fan (Yi Ren Fen)

General China

Serves 1

Here, a creamy rice-and-egg mixture contrasts with the crunchy *bok choy* and water chestnuts. A touch of *hoisin* sauce adds a wonderful flavor that seems to bring out the best in brown rice.

1 tablespoon peanut, corn, or other oil
1 stalk bok choy, cut on the diagonal into ¼-inch strips
2 water chestnuts
1 cup cold cooked brown rice
1 teaspoon hoisin sauce
1 teaspoon soy sauce
1 egg (graded large or extra large)

Coat a wok or an 8-inch skillet with the oil. When it is moderately hot, add the *bok choy*. Stir-fry for half a minute, mix in the water chestnuts, then add the rice, stirring constantly. Stir-fry the rice until it is hot, then blend in the *hoisin* and soy sauces. Break the egg on top of the rice, and quickly stir in the egg to blend it thoroughly with the rice. Serve immediately.

Vegetarian Brown Rice

素炒飯

Su Chao Fan

Peking

Serves 6

A delightful way to serve fried rice. The chewy Chinese mushrooms elevate it above the mundane fried rice dishes. Separate bowls of marinated *tofu,* crunchy nuts, and crisp, sharp scallions enhance the basic rice in all ways.

4 medium-size dried Chinese mushrooms
Boiling water
½ pound tofu, cut into ½-inch cubes
2 tablespoons soy sauce
1 tablespoon sesame oil
1 to 2 cups salted or unsalted peanuts, cashews, chopped walnuts, or pecans
8 scallions (white and crisp green parts), sliced into rounds
¼ cup peanut, corn, or other oil
6 stalks bok choy or other Chinese cabbage, sliced on the diagonal into ¼-inch strips
½ cup sliced water chestnuts
4 cups cold cooked brown rice
1 tablespoon hoisin sauce
2 tablespoons soy sauce
4 eggs (graded large), slightly beaten
Soy sauce and sesame oil to pass at the table

Place the mushrooms in a small heatproof bowl. Add enough boiling water to cover the mushrooms completely. When they are soft (in about 15 minutes), cut the mushrooms into thin slivers, discarding the stems.

Mix the *tofu* with the soy sauce and sesame oil. Place the *tofu,* nuts, and scallions in separate serving bowls.

In a wok or a 12-inch skillet, heat the ¼ cup of oil until it is moderately hot, 350 to 375 degrees F. Add the *bok choy* and the mushroom slivers, stir constantly for half a minute, then mix in the water chestnuts. Now add the rice, stirring to coat the grains with the oil. When the rice is hot, blend in the *hoisin* and soy sauces. Finally, stir in the slightly beaten eggs, mixing thoroughly. The eggs will coat the rice and will cook quickly from the heat of the rice. Serve the hot rice with its accompaniments.

Vegetarians who do not eat eggs may omit the eggs. The rice will not have the same creamy texture, but it will be tasty nonetheless.

Sesame-Soy Rice
香拌飯
Xiang Ban Fan

Peking

Serves 6

This is a departure from the fried rice dishes. Here, hot rice is fluffed up then mixed with soy sauce, sesame oil, and scallions to make a very tasty side dish that is extremely easy to prepare. The recipe calls for brown rice, but hot cooked white rice can be substituted.

2 cups uncooked brown rice
5 cups water
2 tablespoons sesame oil
2 tablespoons soy sauce
¼ cup chopped scallions (white and crisp green parts)

In a 2- or 3-quart pot, bring the water to the boil. Stir in the rice. When the water returns to the boil, reduce the heat to simmer, cover the pot, and cook the rice for 1 hour, until it is tender. Fluff the hot rice with a fork, sprinkle on the sesame oil and soy sauce, and mix them in. Just before serving, mix in the scallions. Or transfer the sesame-soy rice to a serving platter and garnish with the scallions.

Rice and Leftover Lamb

羊肉飯

Yang Rou Fan

Northern China influence

Serves 4

This meaty version of Sesame-Soy Rice can be turned into a one-dish meal with the addition of cooked vegetables such as peas and carrots. Lamb goes particularly well with rice and sesame oil, but leftover beef, veal, or poultry can be used in its place.

1 scant tablespoon peanut, corn, or other oil
2 cups diced cooked lamb
4 cups hot cooked rice
2 tablespoons sesame oil
¼ cup soy sauce
4 scallions (white and crisp green parts), chopped

In an 8-inch skillet, heat the oil over moderate heat. Add the lamb and stir-fry it briefly just to heat it up. Or steam the lamb until hot.

Fluff the cooked rice with a fork. Stir in the sesame oil and soy sauce; mix well. Mix in the hot lamb. Transfer the rice and lamb to a serving bowl. Garnish with the chopped scallions and serve.

Rice With Stir-fried Lamb

炒羊肉拌飯

Chao Yang Rou Ban Fan

Northern China influence

Serves 4 to 6

Other than in Mongolia, where it is the primary meat, lamb is not known in most parts of China. It is perhaps surprising, then, that lamb adapts well to many Chinese recipes. Always enhanced by the flavors of ginger root and garlic, lamb seems to have a natural affinity for rice as well.

As a rule, Chinese dishes are supposed to be seasoned by the cook and shouldn't need additions at the table. This combination of rice, lamb, and seasonings meets that rule handily.

2 cups uncooked white rice
3½ to 4 cups cold water
2 tablespoons peanut, corn, or other oil
1 teaspoon minced ginger root
2 large cloves garlic, minced
2 cups diced lamb (¼-inch cubes)
2 tablespoons sesame oil
¼ cup soy sauce
½ teaspoon sugar (optional)
¼ cup chopped scallions (white and crisp green parts)

Cook the rice in the water according to the directions for Plain Boiled White Rice (page 285), or use whatever method you choose. A few minutes before the rice is done, in an 8-inch skillet heat the 2 tablespoons of peanut, corn, or other oil to 375 degrees F. Add the ginger root and garlic, and stir for about 30 seconds to release their aromas and flavors. Now add the lamb and stir-fry until cooked. Fluff the cooked rice, then blend in the sesame oil, soy sauce, sugar, and the chopped scallions. Mix in the hot cooked lamb and serve.

Rice With Stir-fried Veal and Diced Peppers

炒小牛肉拌飯

Chao Xiao Niu Rou Ban Fan

General China influence

Serves 4 to 6

This is actually a variation on Rice With Stir-fried Lamb. Either meat will give fine results. Veal, which is even more foreign to Chinese households than lamb, has a delicate taste that is brought out by the peppers, onions, and seasonings used here.

2 cups uncooked white rice
3½ to 4 cups cold water
2 tablespoons peanut, corn, or other oil
½ cup diced onion (¼-inch squares)
½ teaspoon minced ginger root
2 medium-size cloves garlic, minced
½ cup diced green pepper (¼-inch squares)

- **½ cup diced sweet red pepper (¼-inch squares)**
- **2 cups diced veal (¼-inch cubes)**
- **2 tablespoons sesame oil**
- **¼ cup soy sauce**

Cook the rice in the water according to the directions for Plain Boiled White Rice (page 285), or use whatever method you choose. A few minutes before the rice is done, in a wok or a 10-inch skillet heat 1 tablespoon of the peanut, corn, or other oil to 375 degrees F. Add the onions and stir-fry for half a minute, then mix in the ginger root and garlic. Continue to stir-fry for another 30 seconds, then toss in the green and red peppers and stir-fry half a minute longer. Add the remaining tablespoon of cooking oil to the pan, and when it is hot, add the veal. Stir-fry until the veal is cooked, then remove the pan from the heat. Fluff the cooked rice, blend in the sesame oil and soy sauce, then mix in the veal and vegetables.

Rice With Steamed Chicken or Veal

燜肉飯

Men Rou Fan

General China

Serves 4 to 6

In China, it is quite common for small pieces of chicken or pork, bone and all, to be placed over partially cooked rice and in effect steamed while the rice continues cooking. The meat can be marinated first for flavor. In this recipe, either chicken or veal is used, and because Americans are not used to picking meat off the bones in casserole-like dishes, boneless cubes of meat are suggested. If you are not finicky, use one-inch pieces of breast of veal, as the bones will add extra flavor to the rice.

- **1 pound boneless chicken or veal, cut into ½-inch cubes, or 2 pounds breast of veal, cut into 1-inch pieces**
- **1 teaspoon minced ginger root**
- **2 scallions (white and crisp green parts), cut into 1-inch pieces**
- **¼ cup soy sauce**
- **2 tablespoons dry sherry**
- **1 teaspoon sugar**

→

2 cups uncooked white rice
4 cups cold water

In a medium-size bowl, combine the chicken or veal with the ginger root, scallions, soy sauce, sherry, and sugar. Marinate for 1 hour, stirring occasionally.

Rinse the rice under cold water until the water runs clear. Place the rice in a 10-inch top-of-range casserole. Add the water and bring to the boil over high heat. Watch the pot carefully, and when enough water boils off so you can just see the top of the rice, remove the scallions from the chicken or veal and scatter the marinated meat on top of the rice. Pour any remaining sauce over the rice. Reduce the heat to low, cover the casserole, and cook the chicken or veal and rice for about 20 minutes. Turn off the heat, but leave the covered casserole on the burner. The meat and rice will continue to cook and will remain hot.

Noodles

Cellophane Noodles With Beef and Chicken

螞蟻上樹

Ma Yi Shang Shu

General China

Serves 4

The versatile and unusual cellophane noodles become transparent when soaked in water, and in clear chicken broth they all but disappear. In this combination, however, the soft and slippery noodles take on the color of the soy sauce. They offer an intriguing contrast to the meats. Scallions are used as a garnish here, as in so many Chinese dishes, to bring color, a perky sharp taste, and a fresh crispness.

Note: Don't ever try to cook more than eight ounces of cellophane noodles at one time. They are difficult to work with in quantity—they become very sticky.

8 ounces cellophane noodles
2 tablespoons peanut, corn, or other oil

½ pound beef, cut into thin strips 1½ inches long
½ pound chicken, cut into thin strips 1½ inches long
2 tablespoons dry sherry
¼ cup soy sauce
1 teaspoon sugar
¼ cup peanut, corn, or other oil
1 cup water
4 scallions (white and crisp green parts), chopped

Soak the cellophane noodles in a bowl of hot water for 10 minutes or until they are soft enough to cut. Drain the noodles, then cut them with scissors into 2-inch pieces. Set the noodles aside while you cook the meat.

Coat a large wok or a 12-inch skillet with a tablespoon of the oil. Heat the oil to 375 degrees F., then add the chicken and stir-fry until it is just barely cooked. Remove the chicken from the pan, add another tablespoon of oil, and when the oil is hot, stir-fry the beef until it is done. Mix in the cooked chicken, then blend in the sherry, soy sauce, and sugar.

Push the meat to one side of the wok or pan, and add about ¼ cup more oil. When the oil is moderately hot, between 350 and 375 degrees F., add the cellophane noodles. Quickly stir to coat the noodles with oil, and mix the noodles with the meat. Add the cup of water, bring it to the boil, then reduce the heat, cover the wok or pan, and cook the noodles over medium-low heat for about 5 minutes, until the water is absorbed. Transfer the food to a serving platter and sprinkle it with the chopped scallions.

Sesame-Soy Lo Mien

拌麵

Ban Mian

Peking

Serves 4 to 6

So closely related are *lo mien* and spaghetti that there is rivalry between the Chinese and Italians over the origin of these fresh noodles. The Italians say that Marco Polo introduced *pasta* to China during his travels, while the Chinese claim the reverse: they believe that the famous explorer tasted *lo mien* in China and brought his discovery back to Italy. *Lo mien,* spaghetti, Goodman's noodles—regardless of origin, when you mix noodles with soy sauce and sesame oil, they become a Chinese preparation. A little crushed red pepper and a lot of chopped scallions add gusto.

1 pound lo mien
2 tablespoons sesame oil
¼ cup soy sauce
¼ teaspoon crushed dried red pepper (optional)
8 scallions (white and crisp green parts), chopped

Fill a 5- or 6-quart pot about three-fourths full with water, and bring the water to the boil. Drop in the *lo mien,* and stir the noodles immediately to keep them from sticking together. Reduce the heat so the water keeps boiling but doesn't boil over the top. Cook the *lo mien* until tender, about 4 minutes, stirring frequently. Taste for tenderness after 2 or 3 minutes, because different brands of noodles cook differently. Drain the cooked *lo mien,* return it to the pot, and immediately stir in the sesame oil, coating the noodles well. Stir in the soy sauce and toss the noodles with the crushed red pepper. Transfer the *lo mien* to a serving platter and sprinkle lavishly with the scallions.

Rabbi Belzer's Cold Hot Noodles

涼拌麵

Liang Ban Mian

Hunan

Serves 6

This indescribably delicious noodle dish should read HANDLE WITH CARE. It is a very spicy version of Sesame-Soy Lo Mien. Rabbi Belzer always prepared these noodles at our temple fairs in Ridgefield, Connecticut, and his booth always had the longest lines of patrons. Individual portions of chilled noodles which are already flavored with sesame oil are topped with a small amount of a fiery-hot mixture.

1 pound lo mien
4 tablespoons sesame oil
4 scallions (white and crisp green parts), chopped

2 tablespoons minced Chinese hot turnip or radish with chili
1 to 2 tablespoons hot chili paste (or sauce) with garlic
1 large clove garlic, minced
2 tablespoons soy sauce

In a 6-quart pot, bring 4 to 5 quarts of water to the boil. Drop in the noodles, and stir them immediately with a large kitchen fork so they do not stick together. Cook the noodles in the boiling water (reduce the heat enough so the water doesn't boil over) for about 4 minutes, stirring often. Taste for tenderness after 2 or 3 minutes. When the noodles are tender, drain them in a colander and rinse them well under cold water. Return the noodles to the pot or a clean bowl, and mix in the sesame oil. Refrigerate the noodles until you are ready to serve. The noodles can be cooked in advance and frozen, but you may need to add a little more sesame oil if the flavor has dissipated.

For the sauce, combine the scallions, hot turnip or radish, chili paste, garlic, and soy sauce. Mix well. Refrigerate until you are ready to serve. The sauce can be prepared a day ahead and refrigerated, tightly covered, but the scallions are most crisp and fresh-tasting when the sauce is used within a few hours.

To serve the noodles, place a portion (about 1 cup) in a bowl, and put about a tablespoon of the sauce on top. Each person mixes the noodles and sauce—and the daring add more to taste.

Rabbi Belzer's Beef Lo Mien

猶太主教牛肉撈麵

You Tai Zhu Jiao
Niu Rou Lao Mian

General China influence

Serves 6

I suppose I could sit down and formalize a recipe for Rabbi Belzer's Beef Lo Mien, but that would take the fun out of his Jewish-Chinese cooking style. Here's how it looked to me when I watched him prepare *lo mien* at a Chanukah party.

While one group was working on hundreds of the traditional potato *latkes,* the rabbi was cutting thin slices of steak, about one and one-half pounds. He coated his wok with Mazola oil and stir-fried the beef over a gas stove. Now he pushed aside the meat and added a healthy portion of previously diced red and green peppers, frozen chopped broccoli, sliced fresh mushrooms, celery, onions, and scallions, stir-frying these vegetables until they were crunchy. Next he mixed the vegetables with the cooked meat and seasoned the mixture heavily with garlic powder and ground ginger. (He would have used eight cloves of garlic and chopped fresh ginger root had they been available, adding these fresh ingredients to the wok before the vegetables.)

Meanwhile his wife cooked the noodles. She dropped a pound of frozen *lo mien* into a big pot of boiling water, timed it for exactly two minutes, drained the noodles under cold water, then mixed them with sesame oil to keep them from sticking together.

Now Rabbi Belzer mixed the prepared *lo mien* with the meat and vegetables, poured on some sesame oil from a giant can, and added a few tablespoons of thin soy sauce. He confided that instead of using sugar he prefers some sweet wine—Manischewitz, of course. (I didn't catch when this was added or in what quantity.) This deliciousness was mixed well and served at the table with prepared hot sesame oil (sesame oil with chili powder).

He cooked three batches, all measurements by eye, using as much sesame oil in each batch as I'd use in a year. The result was a heavily seasoned *lo mien* that everyone at the party loved. There's nothing like a Chanukah party with *latkes* and *lo mien.*

Beef Lo Mien

牛肉撈麵

Niu Rou Lao Mian

Canton

Serves 4 to 6

Lo, this *mien* dish should serve six, but three of us have been known to finish one pound of noodles with an equal amount of meat. This recipe relies on the contrasting textures of the vegetables playing against the soft noodles, as well as many different flavors. It is tasty but not spicy. A minimum amount of beef would make it more the Chinese noodle dish that it is supposed to be, while the greater amount of beef is usually more to the liking of American tastes.

½ to 1 pound beef, cut into thin strips
¼ × 1½ inches

1 teaspoon peanut, corn, or other oil
1 tablespoon soy sauce
1 tablespoon dry sherry
½ teaspoon sugar
1 pound lo mien
2 tablespoons sesame oil
1 teaspoon salt (optional)
¼ cup peanut, corn, or other oil, approximately
½ cup chopped onion
1 tablespoon minced ginger root
2 large cloves garlic, minced
1 large sweet red pepper, cut in half crosswise then cut into thin strips
1 large green pepper, cut in half crosswise then cut into thin strips
1 cup shredded Chinese cabbage
½ pound fresh mushrooms, sliced
2 cups fresh bean sprouts

Mix the beef strips with the 1 teaspoon of oil, the soy sauce, sherry, and the sugar. In a 6-quart pot filled with 4 quarts of boiling water, cook the *lo mien* until it is just barely tender, usually 3 to 4 minutes. Stir the noodles frequently, and taste them after 2 minutes, as they cook quickly and should not be overdone. Drain the *lo mien* into a colander or a strainer, return the noodles to the pot, and immediately mix them with the sesame oil and the salt.

In a large wok or a 12-inch skillet, heat 2 tablespoons of peanut, corn, or other oil to 375 degrees F. Stir-fry the beef until almost done. If using a pound of beef, stir-fry in two batches. Either remove the beef from the wok or pan or push it aside and add 2 more tablespoons of oil. When the oil is hot again, add the onion, ginger root, and garlic, and stir-fry for 30 seconds. Mix in the red and green peppers, stir-frying for another half-minute, then add the shredded Chinese cabbage and stir-fry half a minute longer. Raise the temperature if necessary to keep the pan hot. If the wok or skillet is too dry, drizzle a bit more oil down the sides. When the oil is hot, add the mushrooms. When the mushrooms are blended in and slightly cooked, mix in the bean sprouts. Toss together the meat and vegetables, then mix in the *lo mien*. When everything is combined and hot, serve the *lo mien*.

A combination such as this should not require additional seasonings, but you may want to have soy sauce and sesame oil available. Or season the dish more heavily yourself while you are tossing everything together

Vegetable Lo Mien

什錦撈麵

Shi Jin Lao Mian

General China influence

Makes 20 samples
or 4 real portions

When I demonstrated Chinese cooking at a Waldbaum's Food Mart in New Haven, Connecticut, during the Chinese New Year, I set up an electric skillet near the produce department and used whatever ingredients were at hand. My partner helped chop and serve, and it didn't seem to matter what we cooked—it always smelled wonderful and tasted as good. If we ran out of one kind of Chinese cabbage, we used another. When there was a surplus of bean sprouts, our *lo mien* became heavily sprouted. We always used *tofu*, explaining to people that it might look like cheese but that it is a high-protein vegetable product. We used a flat, white noodle labeled "cooked steaming noodle," a very confusing name. The noodle required precooking either by steaming or by boiling. Every batch was different, so this recipe represents the essence of what we cooked. I should note that, as delicious as the *lo mien* was, by Friday we bought fresh *challah* from the store's bakery and ate it on the sly.

2 tablespoons peanut, corn, or other oil
1 large Spanish onion, chopped
1 slice ginger root (1 inch thick), minced
4 large cloves garlic, minced
10 fresh snow peas, tips and strings removed, sliced on the diagonal into ¼-inch pieces
2 to 3 cups shredded Chinese cabbage, any kind
1 cup sliced fresh mushrooms
¼ pound tofu, cut into ¼-inch cubes
2 tablespoons soy sauce
½ pound cold cooked *lo mien*, mixed with 1 tablespoon sesame oil
2 cups fresh bean sprouts
2 eggs (graded large)

In a wok or a 12-inch skillet, heat the oil to 375 degrees F. Stir-fry the onion to coat it with oil, then add the minced ginger root and garlic and stir-fry for about 30 seconds. Add the snow peas, Chinese cabbage, and mushrooms in that order, and stir-fry for about half a minute with the addition of each vegetable. Gently mix in the *tofu*, sprinkle on the soy sauce, and mix in the *lo mien.* When the *lo mien* is hot, toss in the bean sprouts, mixing everything around until the ingredients are evenly distributed. Break the eggs on top of the mixture and stir them in rapidly. The eggs will cook from the heat of the other ingredients and add a creamy texture. Serve this wonderful mixture immediately, while the vegetables are still crisp.

Beef Chao Mien

牛肉炒麵

Niu Rou Chao Mian

Canton

Serves 4 to 6

This is the genuine *chao mien* of China. It is different from the "chow mein" served in Chinese-American restaurants in both spelling and preparation. In the authentic Chinese dish, cooled boiled noodles are lightly browned in a thin layer of oil and are then mixed with cooked vegetables and meats. Part of the noodles are crusty and part remain soft. In the restaurant preparation, shredded meat and vegetables are stir-fried, sauced with chicken broth, and topped with the deep-fried, crisp, golden brown noodles we've come to know as "chow mein" noodles. (The term "chow mein noodles" is actually redundant, because "mein" *(mien)* means noodles, so "chow mein noodles" translates roughly to "fried noodles noodles.") Note that in this book the *chao mien* spelling is used for the authentic Chinese preparations, while "chow mein" is used for the Americanized version.

Lo mien (literally "tossed noodles") dishes are also prepared by mixing cooked egg noodles with other cooked ingredients. In *lo mien* preparations, however, unlike *chao mien* ("stir-fried noodles") dishes, the noodles are not fried. In China, *lo mien* also refers to the kind of noodle purchased for the preparation of the same name. A different kind of noodle is used by the Chinese for *chao mien.* The noodles sold as *lo mien* in Asian groceries can be used for all recipes in this book.

1 pound lo mien
8 tablespoons peanut, corn, or other oil
1 cup shredded beef (uniform slices 1½ × ¼ × ¼ inches)
¼ cup soy sauce
1 tablespoon dry sherry
1 teaspoon sugar
½ cup chopped onion

→

2 cups shredded celery cabbage or any Chinese cabbage
1 cup sliced fresh mushrooms

Cook the *lo mien* in 4 quarts of boiling water, stirring often, until the noodles are barely tender, which will take 2 to 3 minutes. Drain the noodles into a colander and run them under cold water. Transfer the noodles to a bowl, mix them with 2 tablespoons of the oil, and set them aside until you're ready to begin cooking. The cooked *lo mien* can be refrigerated or frozen at this point. If the noodles are frozen, they must be thoroughly defrosted before proceeding with the recipe.

In a wok or a 12-inch skillet, heat 4 tablespoons of the oil until hot, about 375 degrees F. Add the cooked noodles all at once, and leave them in the pan until they are lightly browned. Do not stir the *lo mien*. Now turn the noodles to brown the other side, as you would a pancake.

Meanwhile, in a wok or a 10-inch skillet, heat the remaining 2 tablespoons of oil until moderately hot, about 350 degrees F. Add the beef and stir-fry until it is almost cooked. Mix in the soy sauce, sherry, and sugar. Raise the heat to 375 to 400 degrees F. Add the onion and stir-fry for 30 seconds. Toss in the shredded Chinese cabbage and continue to stir-fry half a minute longer, then add the mushrooms and stir-fry until the mushrooms are just barely tender. Mix the cooked meat and vegetables with the partially fried noodles. Serve hot.

Veal Chao Mien

兩面黃炒麵

Liang Mian Huang Chao Mian

Canton

Serves 6

Here is another authentic *chao mien* preparation.

Although ground or shredded pork is the meat used in China, the mildly flavored veal works well in this recipe. The ground veal, enhanced by soy sauce and chicken broth, combines nicely with the stir-fried onions and celery cabbage, both of which add a sweet, fresh crispness to the dish. The focal point of the dish is on the *lo mien*, and the meat and vegetables are meant to complement the noodles, not take over.

1 pound lo mien
6 tablespoons peanut, corn, or other oil

1 cup chopped onion
1 pound celery cabbage, cut on the diagonal into ½-inch pieces
1 pound ground veal
¼ cup soy sauce
1 cup seasoned chicken broth

In a 5- or 6-quart pot, cook the *lo mien* in 4 quarts of boiling water, stirring often, until the noodles are barely tender. Drain into a colander, and run the noodles under cold water until they are cool. This will keep them from sticking. Transfer to a bowl, and mix the *lo mien* with 1 tablespoon of the oil. The cooked *lo mien* can be refrigerated or frozen. Defrost completely before continuing with the recipe.

Heat 1 tablespoon of the oil in a large wok or a 12-inch skillet until the oil just begins to smoke. Add the onion, and stir-fry for 1 minute, then add the celery cabbage and stir-fry for an additional minute. Regulate the heat so the vegetables cook quickly but do not brown. Now add the veal, stirring constantly until the pinkness disappears. Remove the meat and vegetables to a clean bowl.

In the same wok or skillet, heat the remaining 4 tablespoons of oil until it is moderately hot, 350 degrees to 375 degrees F. Add the precooked noodles all at once, and cook them without stirring until they are lightly browned. Turn to brown the other side as you would turn a large pancake. Add the cooked veal and vegetables, tossing everything together well. Sprinkle on the soy sauce and stir in the chicken broth. Heat through and serve hot.

Chicken "Chow Mein"

鷄絲炒麵

Ji Si Chao Mian

Chinese-American

Serves 6

This is "chow mein" the way it is served in Chinese-American restaurants. The dish is typically served over mounds of hot rice. American-style Chicken "Chow Mein" has survived because it tastes good. The dish itself is relatively bland, but the crunch of the noodles against the soft rice is wonderful, and the stir-fried vegetables bring a different kind of crispness to the preparation. It is very inexpensive to prepare, especially since leftover turkey (think about Thanksgiving) can be used in place of uncooked chicken breasts.

2 tablespoons peanut, corn, or other oil
1½ cups thinly sliced onion
1½ cups celery, cut into matchsticks about 1 × ¼ × ¼ inches
1½ cups celery cabbage, cut as above
1 cup sliced fresh mushrooms
2 tablespoons peanut, corn, or other oil
1 pound uncooked chicken breasts, shredded into pieces the size of the celery, or 2 cups shredded cooked turkey
2 cups seasoned chicken broth
¼ cup soy sauce
2 tablespoons cornstarch dissolved in ¼ cup cold water or broth
2 cups fresh bean sprouts
Hot cooked rice
4 cups Deep-fried Noodles (page 118) or packaged "chow mein noodles"

In a large wok or a 12-inch skillet, heat 2 tablespoons of oil until it just begins to smoke. Add the onion and stir-fry for 1 minute. Add the celery and continue to stir-fry for another minute, then toss in the celery cabbage and stir-fry for an additional 45 seconds. Add the mushrooms, and stir continuously for 30 seconds longer, tossing the ingredients around to mix them together. If the cooked turkey is being used, add the turkey at this point, mixing it well with the vegetables.

If uncooked chicken is being used, remove the stir-fried vegetables from the pan. In the same wok or skillet, heat the remaining 2 tablespoons of oil until it is moderately hot, about 350 degrees F. Add the chicken and stir-fry until it is cooked. Return the stir-fried vegetables to the pan and mix them in well. Now stir in the chicken broth and soy sauce. Bring the broth to the boil. Again mix the cornstarch and water together until smooth, then stir the cornstarch paste into the broth. Cook and stir until the liquid is smooth and thickened. Toss in the bean sprouts, and as soon as they are mixed in and warm, turn off the heat. Serve this "chow mein" over plenty of hot rice, and top with crisp fried noodles.

Breads

Steamed Rolls or Bread

饅頭

Man Tou

Peking

Makes 18 rolls

In northern China, where wheat is the staple instead of rice, steamed rolls or bread is served with meals. For breakfast, the rolls or bread is sometimes dipped in a little sugar. For lunch or dinner, pieces of roll or bread are broken off to be eaten with similar size pieces of meat. This recipe for a yeast-risen bread dough is bland and slightly sweet, making it a wonderful implement for mopping up spicy sauces. The dough is almost identical to that used for the filled buns that appear earlier in the book (Chapter One, Appetizers).

1 teaspoon active dry yeast
¼ cup sugar
1 cup unsifted all-purpose flour
1 cup very warm water (120 to 130 degrees F.)
2½ cups additional unsifted flour

In a medium-size mixing bowl, mix the yeast, sugar, and 1 cup of flour. Stir in the very warm water. Beat the mixture with a large spoon for about 2 minutes. Blend in the remaining flour, ½ cup at a time, working it in first with the spoon and then with your fingers.

Turn out the dough onto a clean, lightly floured work surface and knead it for about 5 minutes, until very smooth. Poke a finger into the dough—the hole should not remain. Shape the dough into a ball and place it in a clean bowl that will be large enough to accommodate the ball of dough once it has doubled in volume. Cover the bowl tightly with plastic wrap.

Place the dough in a warm draft-free spot, out of direct sunlight, and let it rise until doubled. In an 85-degree F. room the dough will take 1½ to 2 hours to rise. If the temperature of the room is around 65 degrees F., the dough will take 3 to 5 hours to rise. To hasten the rising, place a large pan of hot water on the bottom shelf of a cold oven, and put the bowl of dough on the shelf above.

To determine if the dough has risen properly, poke a finger into it. The dough should not be sticky, and the hole should remain. After the dough has doubled, punch it down. Knead it for a minute or so, until the dough is smooth again.

To shape the rolls, divide the dough into 18 pieces. Shape each piece into a ball, and flatten each ball with the palm of your hand. Brush each round with oil, and fold the roll in half with the oiled side inside. With a fork, make a crisscross pattern on top (the way you do for peanut butter cookies). Place the rolls on greased steamer trays, leaving an inch between them for expansion.

Let the rolls rise at room temperature for about 30 minutes. Steam them for 15 minutes, until they are puffy and cooked through. If you prefer, shape the dough into a loaf, and steam it for 40 minutes. The steamed rolls or bread can be prepared in advance and frozen. They are best when served warm or hot, and should be resteamed before serving.

Chinese Layered or Crescent Rolls

花捲

Hua Juan

Peking

Makes 24 rolls

This is a Chinese version of fan-tans (steamed, of course), which are old-fashioned many-layered baked rolls. In this recipe, the dough is rolled out thinly, spread with a mixture of chicken fat and sugar, rolled up like a jelly roll, then sliced. The result is a tastier, more interesting roll than the regular *pareve* Steamed Rolls or Bread. The price is in the extra calories and cholesterol. An alternative method of rolling, which is the method I use for *rugelach*, makes crescent-shaped rolls. Incidentally, although the Chinese recipes use lard, chicken fat is not unheard of in China and is not out of place here.

1 recipe Steamed Rolls or Bread (page 307)
½ cup rendered chicken fat, solidified
½ cup sugar

Prepare the recipe for Steamed Rolls up to the point of shaping. Divide the dough into 4 pieces. Working with one piece at a time, roll each piece into a 12-inch square. On each square brush 2 tablespoons of chicken fat, then sprinkle the chicken fat with 2 tablespoons of sugar. Roll up the dough tightly, as you would a jelly roll. Pinch the flap of dough to the roll to seal it Now cut the dough into 2-inch pieces, making 6 pieces from each long piece of dough. Flatten each piece slightly with the palm of your hand

For crescent-shaped rolls, divide the dough into 4 pieces. Roll each piece into a circle about 13 inches in diameter. Brush 2 tablespoons of chicken fat on each circle, then sprinkle the surface with 2 tablespoons of sugar. With a sharp knife or a pastry wheel, cut each circle into 6 wedges, as if cutting a pie. Beginning with the wide end, roll each piece tightly toward the tip, then press the tip into the roll.

Place the shaped rolls on greased steamer trays, leaving an inch between the rolls to allow for expansion. Let them rise at room temperature for 30 minutes, then steam the rolls for 15 minutes. Serve hot.

Mu Shu Pancakes

薄餅

Bao Bing

Peking

Makes 24 pancakes

These flexible, thin flour-and-water pancakes would be tasteless if not for the hint of sesame oil, but they make a good vehicle for *mu shu* dishes and Peking duck. They are rolled out in pairs, cooked on a griddle, then separated and steamed. The pancakes take a while to prepare, but fortunately they can be made ahead of time and frozen.

2 cups unsifted all-purpose flour
¾ cup boiling water
1 tablespoon sesame oil, approximately

Place the flour in a medium-size mixing bowl. Make a well in the center, and pour in the boiling water. Using a wooden spoon, gradually mix together the flour and water until a soft dough is formed. The dough will seem crumbly and won't hold together at first, but soon it will become workable. As the dough cools down, use your hands for easier mixing.

Round the dough into a ball, then knead it on a smooth, lightly floured work surface for 10 minutes, until very smooth. Cover the ball of dough with a bowl or a kitchen towel and let it rest for 15 minutes, which will make rolling easier.

With floured hands, roll the dough into a log 12 inches long. Cut the log into 24 pieces. Flatten each piece with the palm of your hand. Now, with a rolling pin, roll each of the 24 pieces into a 3-inch circle. Place the circles side by side in pairs, and brush each one lightly with sesame oil, covering the surface completely with a thin layer of oil. Now put each pair of circles together, oiled sides together. You should have 12 pairs of circles. Use a rolling pin to roll out each pair into a 5- or 6-inch circle. The oiled surfaces may make the pancakes slippery at first, but they will become more manageable as you continue rolling. Rotate as you roll so the circles keep their shape relatively well and to make sure that they're not sticking to the table. If you work slowly, cover the pancakes with a towel after rolling.

Cook the pairs of pancakes on a moderately hot ungreased griddle. The cooking time is about 1 minute on each side. The pancakes will bubble slightly and get a wet look. It's okay if they brown slightly in spots, but be careful not to burn them. As each set is finished, gently separate the halves and fold each pancake in half, oiled side inside. If it's difficult to separate the pancakes, let them cool a bit, then look for a small opening anywhere on the edge and stick in a knife to get them started.

Place the separated and folded pancakes on an ungreased steamer tray, overlapping them to fit. Steam for 10 minutes. These pancakes can be left in the steamer on a turned-off burner for as long as half an hour. They can be completely prepared in advance and refrigerated or frozen before or after steaming. Resteam immediately before serving.

Pan-fried Scallion Cakes

葱油餅

Cong You Bing

Peking

Makes four 5-inch pancakes

One of my father's favorite snacks is a thick slice of rye bread spread lavishly with *schmaltz,* lightly salted, and topped with raw onion. Now *schmaltz,* for those who grew up in a different generation, is rendered chicken fat. If you are enticed by the very thought of chicken fat smeared on a slab of rye, this recipe is definitely for you.

A piece of dough is rolled very thinly, spread lavishly with *schmaltz* (in China lard is used), lightly salted, and topped with raw scallions. Sound familiar? The dough is rolled in such a way that a multilayered pastry is formed. The pastry is pan-fried for a few minutes, which makes it crisp and delicious. The scallion cakes are a bit reminiscent of onion board.

2 cups unsifted all-purpose flour
⅔ cup water
8 teaspoons rendered chicken fat, solidified
½ cup chopped scallions (white and crisp green parts)
Chicken fat for pan-frying

In a medium-size mixing bowl, place the flour. In a 1-quart pot, bring the water to the boil. As soon as the water boils, pour it gradually into the flour while blending it in with a wooden spoon. The dough will seem very crumbly and won't hold together at first, but keep stirring with the spoon. When the dough becomes cool enough to handle, mix it with your hands until it is workable.

Form the dough into a ball, and turn it out onto a smooth, clean work surface. Knead for 4 or 5 minutes, until smooth. Cover the dough with a towel for 15 minutes. It will relax and will be easier to roll out.

Divide the dough into 4 equal pieces. Working with one piece at a time, with a rolling pin roll the dough into a 10-inch circle. If the circle is too small at first, stretch it gently with the fingers, then continue rolling. With a pastry brush or the fingers, spread 2 teaspoons of chicken fat over the surface of each rolled-out circle of dough. Scatter 2 tablespoons of the chopped scallions over the chicken fat on each circle.

Roll up each pancake into a thin roll that will be approximately 10 × 1½ inches. Press the edges together to seal. Now take one of the 1½-inch ends and roll it up toward the other end like a snail. When you get to the end, press down on the dough; flatten it with your hands and the rolling pin into a 5-inch circle.

To cook the pancakes, heat 1 tablespoon of chicken fat in a 5- or 6-inch skillet over moderate heat. If using a larger pan, you will need more fat. The fat should be almost ⅛ inch deep. Add chicken fat as necessary before cooking each pancake. Cook each pancake for 2 minutes per side, which should be just right to make it golden brown in spots and crisp. Drain the pancakes on paper towels, cut them into small wedges, and serve hot.

Scallion pancakes are best when served immediately after they are fried, but there are times when you will need to make them in advance. Fry the scallion cakes, drain them, and let them cool. Wrap the cooled scallion cakes in foil and refrigerate overnight. To reheat, place the scallion cakes on a baking sheet that has sides, or on a foil-lined pan with the edges turned up. Heat them in a preheated 350-degree F. oven until sizzling hot, 10 to 15 minutes. Cut into wedges and serve hot.

9

Desserts

I predict that Maida Heatter will never write a cookbook on Chinese desserts. For one thing, most Chinese meals do not end with desserts other than fresh fruit. It is true that steamed cakes are served with tea during the day, and Chinese pastries are eaten as between-meal snacks. There are also several banquet dessert dishes, but overall desserts and sweets do not occupy a place of importance in Chinese cuisine.

This chapter presents a sampling of those Chinese desserts and sweet snacks that are most palatable to Western tastes. There are some steamed sweets and snacks that are time-consuming to prepare, have a rubbery consistency we're unused to, and have very little flavor—these were omitted from this chapter. Fruits, steamed cakes, fruit or nut "teas," puddings, and my version of fortune cookies are featured.

Fruit Platter
水果拼盤
Shui Guo Pin Pan

General China

Serves 6

Platters of fresh pineapple wedges surrounded by Chinese fruits are at home either as a dessert or an appetizer. Fresh loquats, lichees, and logans are preferred, but since they are not available in most parts of the United States, the canned fruits are listed in the recipe.

Canned loquats are a bright orange, with a lovely taste, not quite peach or apricot but reminiscent of both. They are about the size of apricots. I'm told that fresh lichees are sweet, juicy, and delicious. In my estimation the canned lichees don't boast of these attributes, but many people like them, and they lend a Chinese character to the fruit platter. Canned lichees are semitransparent, with a bland but slightly tart taste. They are round and a little smaller than loquats. Canned logans, which resemble small lichees, are more pleasant-tasting than the lichees. Fresh strawberries can be added to the platter for color.

1 large ripe pineapple, preferably Hawaiian
1 can (1 pound) loquats
1 can (1 pound) lichees and/or logans

Slice the pineapple in half lengthwise, then slice each half in half again lengthwise. You now have 4 long wedges of pineapple. If the green top is fresh-looking and attractive, leave it on the pineapple sections. With a sharp knife, take a ½-inch slice off the core of each wedge of pineapple. Now cut the pineapple meat in one long section, slicing between the pineapple and the shell, close to the shell. Leave the pineapple meat in the shell. Now slice the pineapple into ½-inch pieces, still leaving the pieces in place in the shell. You should have 4 long wedges of sliced pineapple.

Arrange the pineapple wedges on one or two platters. Strew the Chinese fruits around the pineapple, but make it look attractive, not haphazard. Spear some of the pineapple sections and the other fruits with toothpicks, and have extra toothpicks available when the fruit is served.

The fruit platter can be arranged in advance and refrigerated, but the pineapples will darken in spots after a few hours.

Variation:

An attractive, refreshing side dish or dessert composed of all canned fruits can be used when fresh pineapple is not available. Canned loquats, lichees, logans, pineapple chunks, and mandarin oranges will give the fruit a Chinese look, but you might also consider including sliced peaches and pears, whole apricots, purple plums, and sweet cherries.

Remove all pits from the fruit. Arrange the fruit in layers in a glass bowl or in separate groups on a platter, or mix the fruit together. To serve it more like fresh fruit, serve without any of the canned syrups or juices. To make it more of a compote, mix together some of the juices and pour them over the fruit.

Watermelon Boat or Basket

西瓜舟

Xi Gua Zhou

General China influence

Serves 12

A watermelon boat is an appropriate fresh-fruit dessert for Chinese meals. Cut a watermelon in half lengthwise, scoop out the watermelon with a melon baller, then fill the watermelon with melon balls and attractive pieces of other fresh fruit.

If you carve the watermelon into the shape of a basket, it can be served at a banquet, especially if filled with exotic and expensive melons and other fruits. To carve the watermelon, use a marking pen to outline the area you want to cut away. You'll be making a horizontal slice from each end toward the middle, but don't cut it all the way through or you won't have a handle. Leave a strip about two inches wide for the handle, and cut straight down vertically from the top of the handle to the horizontal cut. Remove the cut sections and even things out so the basket looks attractive. Scoop out all the watermelon with a melon baller. Pick out all the seeds. There should be absolutely no seeds in a banquet dish (although the white watermelon seeds are sometimes used in Eight-treasure Pudding).

Use whatever other melons and unusual fruits are available, as long as they are ripe and of fine quality. Canned loquats and lichees are acceptable if that's the only way to obtain them, but other canned fruits should be avoided, as should frozen fruits. Fresh strawberries, blueberries, raspberries, and wild blackberries (if they are not too sour or seedy) are other good choices.

Glazed Apples

拔絲蘋果

Ba Si Ping Guo

Peking

Serves 6

Glazed yucca is the Chinese precursor of this dessert. Yucca, a root vegetable, is sometimes sold in Spanish groceries. Here, apples are chosen as a substitute because they are readily available and because they work well in the recipe. Firm bananas sliced on the diagonal into one-and-one-half-inch pieces are another common substitute.

Ideally, this dessert provides wonderful contrasts so important in Chinese cooking: the apples are soft and tender on the inside, while a hard coating forms on the outside; the sesame seeds have a distinctive, nutty flavor which balances the sweetness of the syrup. However, this recipe is somewhat difficult to prepare, as it involves coordinating a sequence of last-minute steps. Timing is critical in getting the best results, so follow the directions exactly, doing what you can in advance as suggested. It is particularly important that all ingredients and utensils be at hand before you begin the actual frying.

Because of the length of the instructions, this recipe is given in numbered steps.

2 tablespoons sesame seeds
1 egg (graded large)
⅓ cup water
¼ cup unsifted cornstarch
¼ cup unsifted all-purpose flour
1 cup sugar
¼ cup water
1 tablespoon peanut, corn, or other oil
Oil for deep-frying
A medium-size bowl of ice cubes and water
2 large McIntosh or golden delicious apples

1. First toast the sesame seeds. Place the sesame seeds in a 7-inch ungreased skillet. Turn up the heat to medium, and heat the seeds until they darken slightly. Shake the pan occasionally to prevent burning. Transfer the sesame seeds to a plate or bowl. When cool, store them in a covered container. The sesame seeds can be toasted several days in advance.

2. Mix the batter any time during the day the apples are to be cooked. In a small mixing bowl, beat the egg with a fork, then stir in the ⅓ cup water. Blend in the cornstarch until smooth, then blend in the flour. The batter must be completely smooth. Refrigerate the batter if you do not intend to use it within a few hours, but remove it from the refrigerator an hour before you begin cooking.

3. In an 8-inch skillet, stir together the sugar, ¼ cup of water, and the tablespoon of oil. These ingredients will be used for the syrup. Set the pan aside until you're ready to cook.

4. Before the cooking begins, assemble everything you'll need. Fill a 2- to 4-quart pot or an electric deep fryer with a minimum of 2 inches of oil. Set the bowl of batter on a workspace near the oil, along with a long-handled fork or tongs for handling the apples. Place the pan of syrup on an unlighted burner next to the oil, with a spoon nearby for stirring the syrup. Keep the toasted sesame seeds near the syrup pan. Take out a serving plate, and spread a little peanut oil or sesame oil over the plate to keep the glazed apples from sticking.

Heat the oil for deep-frying to 375 degrees F. A drop of water carefully sprinkled into the oil will spatter instantly, but the oil will not be smoking. While the oil is heating, fill a medium to large mixing bowl with ice and water. Finally, get the apples ready. Peel, core, and slice the apples into 8 to 12 wedges each. This is done at the last minute so the apples don't have time to discolor.

5. Now the actual cooking begins. Heat the syrup over moderate heat until it boils, stirring occasionally. Let the syrup cook until it reaches the hard-crack stage (approximately 300 degrees F. on a candy thermometer). To test for the hard-crack stage, drop a little syrup from a spoon into the bowl of ice water. The syrup will harden immediately on contact with the water. When the syrup has reached this stage, add the toasted sesame seeds and keep it warm over low heat.

If you don't allow the syrup to reach the hard-crack stage, the apples will not have the crunchy glaze associated with this dessert. They will be tasty but sticky and syrupy. If the syrup cools and hardens while you're working, add a little water, stir rapidly to redissolve the sugar, and cook again to the hard-crack stage.

6. This part takes astounding coordination. It is helpful to have two people working on this sweet treat, one to coat the apples with batter and fry, and one to coat with syrup and cool. It's best if the oil and syrup are ready at the same time. When they are, put the apple slices into the batter, coating them completely. Place several apple slices at a time in the hot oil, and fry them for about 1 minute, until lightly browned all over. With a fork, tongs, or chopsticks if you're talented, remove the fried apples from the oil. Drop them into the syrup, then turn the apples with a fork or spoon to coat them completely.* Pick up the glazed apples one at a time with the fork, tongs, or chopsticks and plunge them into the bowl of ice water. The syrup should immediately harden around the apples. Place the apples on the oiled plate. Continue frying, coating, and cooling the apples. Serve as soon as possible because the coating softens rapidly.

---

*If your timing is off and the syrup isn't ready, set the fried apples on paper towels to drain until the syrup is hot

Almond Float
杏仁豆腐
Xing Ren Dou Fu

Two recipes for this custardlike almond gelatin dessert are presented. The authentic Chinese recipe uses agar-agar, a kind of seaweed which is used as the gelatin of China, and almond "milk" made from almonds and water. This version is pure white and mildly flavored, and it literally melts in your mouth. The second version is a modern recipe that looks and tastes much like the real almond float, but it substitutes kosher gelatin and milk flavored with almond extract for the almond milk. This dessert, which resembles *tofu*, is a little firmer than the agar-agar and almond recipe. In both recipes, after the mixture sets, it is cut into small diamond-shaped pieces or cubes, and enough sweetened water is poured into the serving dish to make the small pieces float. The dessert is garnished with fruit.

Almond Float I

Canton

Serves 4 to 6

Agar-agar is clear and comes in long strands, so it looks a little like cellophane noodles. It can be softened slightly in cold water and used as a vegetable in salads. When heated in water, it dissolves, but when it cools again, it acts like gelatin. Gelatin can be substituted for the agar-agar (which is tasteless), and the directions for the substitution are included in this recipe.

Almond "milk" is made by grinding uncooked almonds with water, then extracting all the liquid from the mixture. The liquid looks like milk but tastes like almonds.

½ pound sliced blanched almonds
2 cups water
¼ cup agar-agar, cut into 1-inch pieces before measuring, or 1 envelope (1 tablespoon) unflavored kosher gelatin
½ cup water
1 tablespoon sugar
Sweetened water: 1 cup water mixed with ¼ cup sugar
Garnishes: fresh strawberries, pitted orange sections, peeled apricots; drained canned loquats, mandarin oranges, or other fruits; slivered or halved almonds

In a food processor fitted with the metal chopping blade, or in a blender, place the almonds. Turn on the processor and gradually add the 2 cups of water. Process until the almonds are ground as finely as possible, preferably to a paste. Strain through cheesecloth over a medium-size mixing bowl, squeezing out every bit of liquid you can. (In a pinch, you can strain the almond water through a fine strainer. Press the almonds with the back of a spoon to extract all the liquid.) Pour the "milk" into a 2-cup glass measure. You should have almost 2 cups of liquid—add enough water to make 2 cups.

In a 1-quart pot over high heat, bring the ¼ cup agar-agar and the ½ cup water to the boil, stirring frequently. When the agar-agar is completely dissolved, reduce the heat to medium and pour in the almond "milk." Stir in the sugar. Heat until the mixture comes to the boil, stirring often, then pour it into a 7- or 8-inch square pan. To substitute unflavored gelatin, sprinkle 1 envelope gelatin over ¼ cup cold water in a small mixing bowl. In a 2-quart pot over low heat, heat the 2 cups of almond "milk" with the tablespoon of sugar. When it is warm, add the softened gelatin and water, scraping in all the gelatin. Continue to cook until the mixture comes to the boil, stirring often. Pour the mixture into a 7- or 8-inch square pan.

The recipe is now the same for either agar-agar or gelatin. Chill the almond "milk" for about 3 hours, until it is set. Meanwhile, in a 1- or 2-quart pot, heat the cup of water and ¼ cup of sugar to boiling, stirring to dissolve the sugar. Cool the sugar syrup, then refrigerate it until it is time to serve the dessert. The almond "milk" and syrup can be prepared in advance and refrigerated overnight.

When the gelatin is set, cut it into small cube or diamond shapes. At serving time, with a flat metal spatula carefully transfer the cubes or diamonds to a flat-bottomed serving dish at least 2 inches deep. Some kind of casserole is usually appropriate. Don't overcrowd the pieces or they will be difficult to serve. Pour enough syrup into the dish so the almond gelatin floats. Garnish the Almond Float attractively with colorful fresh or canned fruits, and almonds if you like. Each serving consists of gelatin, syrup, fruit, and nuts.

Almond Float II

Canton influence

Serves 8 to 12

This simplified version of Almond Float saves time and produces a refreshing, light dessert. Milk and almond extract give it a creamy white color and a mild almond flavor. Evaporated milk makes a richer dessert than regular milk.

If you want the Almond Float to be *pareve,* for the milk and water substitute approximately 3½ cups of almond "milk" made from 1 pound of almonds processed in two batches with 2 cups of water in each batch. See the directions for almond "milk" in Almond Float I.

½ cup cold water
2 envelopes (1 tablespoon each) unflavored kosher gelatin
1 large can (13 ounces) evaporated milk
Water
1 can (16 ounces) loquats or mandarin oranges
2 tablespoons sugar
2 tablespoons almond extract
Sweetened water: 2 cups water mixed with ½ cup sugar, or 1 cup water mixed with ¼ cup sugar and 1 cup syrup from canned fruit
Garnishes: fresh strawberries and drained canned loquats, mandarin oranges, or other fruits; slivered or halved almonds

Into a medium-size or large mixing bowl, pour the ½ cup cold water. Sprinkle the gelatin on top and set it aside to soften.

Into a 2-cup glass measure, pour the evaporated milk. Add water to make 2 cups, then pour this into a 2-quart pot. Open the canned fruit, and drain the liquid into the 2-cup measure. Add enough water to make 1½ cups, then add this to the 2-quart pot as well. Stir in the 2 tablespoons of sugar. Heat the milk mixture over moderate heat, stirring occasionally. When the mixture is hot but not boiling, pour it slowly into the softened gelatin, stirring constantly. Stir until the gelatin is completely dissolved. When the mixture has cooled for 15 minutes, blend in the almond extract. Pour the almond milk into an oblong 2-quart baking dish (approximately 12 × 7 × 2 inches). Chill the almond gelatin for about 3 hours, until it is set.

Meanwhile, in a 2-quart pot heat the 2 cups water mixed with the ½ cup sugar (or the alternative sweetened water mixture) to boiling. Stir to dissolve the sugar. Set aside and cool the sugar syrup completely.

When the gelatin is set, cut it into small cube or diamond shapes. To serve, with a flat metal spatula carefully transfer the cubes or diamonds to an attractive flat-bottomed serving dish at least 2 inches deep. Some kind of casserole dish is usually good. Pour enough syrup into the dish so the almond gelatin floats. Garnish the Almond Float attractively with the fruit. Each serving consists of gelatin, syrup, fruit, and nuts.

Steamed Cake
發糕
Fa Gao

General China

Makes one 8-inch square cake

This home-style cake would be served in China with tea as a daytime snack. Moist and sweet, with a nice flavor from the brown sugar, it is very much like a baked cottage pudding, but it does not get topped with any of the rich sauces usually associated with cottage puddings. The cake is light and soft when served hot, and I think it is at its best served right from the steamer.

4 eggs (graded large)
½ cup firmly packed dark brown sugar
¼ cup white sugar
1½ cups unsifted all-purpose flour
1 teaspoon double-acting baking powder
1 teaspoon vanilla extract
½ cup sliced blanched almonds

Grease an 8-inch square pan with 2-inch sides. Be sure the pan will fit into your steamer.

In the large bowl of an electric mixer, beat the eggs until frothy. Add the brown and white sugars and beat until smooth. On low speed, blend in the flour, baking powder, and vanilla extract, then stir in the almonds. Pour the batter into the prepared pan. Place the pan in a steamer with 1 to 1½ inches of water. Cover the steamer, and bring the water to the boil. Steam the cake for 20 minutes. Cut the hot cake into squares, and serve hot with tea. Leftovers, which will keep for a day or two if wrapped well and stored at room temperature, can be served cool.

Steamed Layered Nut Cake

千層糕

Qian Ceng Gao

General China

Makes one 8 × 12-inch cake

This many-layered cake is similar to a very fancy sweet roll. Like other Chinese cakes made by the home cook, this one is steamed. The Chinese version is layered with lard, which supplies the major flavoring. The vegetable shortening substituted here works well in creating the layers, but it adds no flavor. You may wish to compensate by serving the cake with a sugar syrup flavored with vanilla extract. Chopped nuts add some taste and contribute an important crunchy texture.

This cake relies much more on the phenomenon of the 81 layers than on the taste for its appeal. It can be served during the day with tea or as a bland snack between courses at a big meal. If you serve it for dessert, serve some colorful fruit alongside.

1 package (1 tablespoon) active dry yeast
¾ cup sugar
6 cups unsifted all-purpose flour, approximately
1½ cups very warm water (120 to 130 degrees F.)
½ cup vegetable shortening
½ cup finely chopped pecans or other nuts
Optional sugar syrup: 1 cup water, ½ cup sugar, 1 teaspoon vanilla extract

In a large mixing bowl, combine the yeast, sugar, and 3 cups of the flour, mixing well. Stir in the warm water, and with a spoon beat the mixture for 2 minutes. Gradually, a cup at a time, blend in the remaining flour. You will need to mix in the last cup of flour with your hands—the dough will be too stiff to mix with the spoon. Use enough flour to make a stiff dough that is no longer sticky.

On a clean work surface, knead the dough for 4 or 5 minutes, until smooth. Transfer the dough to a clean mixing bowl that will be large enough to accommodate the dough once it has doubled in size. Cover the bowl with plastic wrap, place in a warm draft-free spot, and let the dough rise until it has doubled. This will take about 2 hours at 85 degrees F. To speed up the rising, fill a smaller mixing bowl partway with hot water, and set the bowl of dough into the smaller bowl. The water should not touch the bottom of the bowl of dough.

Punch down the dough after it has doubled, knead it briefly until smooth and workable, then divide the dough into 3 pieces of uniform size. Use a rolling pin to roll out each piece of dough to a rectangle measuring 8 × 12 inches. If the dough seems difficult to roll, let it rest for a few minutes, then continue.

Spread 1 tablespoon of shortening on one layer, and sprinkle it with 1 tablespoon of chopped nuts. Cover that with another layer, and spread the second layer with a tablespoon of shortening and a tablespoon of chopped nuts. Top with the third layer but don't spread with shortening and nuts. You now have 3 layers of dough in one 8 × 12-inch rectangle.

With the narrow side of the dough facing you, roll out the rectangle to a long rectangle measuring 12 × 24 inches. Cut the new rectangle into thirds, making 3 rectangles, each 8 × 12 inches. Fill and stack the layers as you did the first time. Repeat the rolling and filling two more times. You will end up with an 8 × 12-inch rectangle having 81 thin layers of dough with shortening and nuts sandwiched between.

Place the layer cake on a greased steamer tray, preferably one with holes, and let the cake rise for 30 minutes. Steam the cake for 1 hour. Check the pot from time to time to make sure all the water has not evaporated.

A few minutes before the cake is ready, prepare the optional sugar syrup. In a 1-quart pot, bring the water and sugar to the boil over moderately high heat, stirring frequently. Continue to cook and stir for 30 seconds after the water has come to the boil, then remove the pot from the heat. Stir in the vanilla. Set aside.

With a very sharp knife, cut the steamed cake into small square or diamond-shaped pieces. Serve warm or cool. If desired, pour a tablespoon or two of hot sugar syrup over each serving.

Eight-treasure Pudding

八寶飯

Ba Bao Fan

General China

Serves 6

This classic steamed rice pudding, also called Eight-precious Pudding, is considered a banquet dish because it takes great artistry to arrange the fruits into a beautiful design at the bottom of the bowl, and it requires no small talent to turn out the pudding in one piece without disrupting the pattern. In China, eight dried ingredients are used (hence the name of the dish), including such things as white watermelon seeds, lotus seeds, and dried red and green plums. A center of red bean paste is considered attractive and desirable, and glutinous rice is a must for the sticky consistency. But the fruits, and nuts if you like, are open to choice. I've selected dried fruits that you may well associate with a Passover compote or a *tsimmes*—they are colorful and tasty.

Glutinous rice gets one of its alternate names, sweet rice, from dishes such as this. The rice itself is not sweet, but here it is combined with sugar in the pudding, and a sugar syrup is poured over the dish at serving time. The pudding has the consistency of very firm rice pudding. The rice itself is on the chewy side.

2 cups uncooked glutinous rice
4 cups cold water
1 cup mixed dried fruits (prunes, apricots, peaches, pears)
Hot water to soak the fruit
½ cup sugar
½ cup sweetened red bean paste, preferably homemade (page 139)
Sweetened water: 1 cup water, ½ cup sugar, 1 tablespoon cornstarch dissolved in ¼ cup water

In a 2-quart pot, place the rice and water. Bring the water to the boil over high heat. Reduce the heat, cover the pot, and cook the rice over moderately low heat until it is tender and all the water is absorbed. This will take about 30 minutes.

Meanwhile, soak the dried fruit in very hot water until it is plump. The fruit should be completely covered by the hot water. Drain off the water, and cut the fruit into attractive pieces.

Grease a shallow heatproof bowl that will be large enough to hold the rice and fruit—a 6-cup (1½-quart) bowl is about right. Arrange the pieces of plumped fruit attractively in the bottom of the greased bowl. Create an interesting pattern if possible. Fluff the hot cooked rice with a fork, and mix it with the ½ cup sugar. Using about half the rice, press a layer of rice over the fruit, being careful not to disturb the fruit. Put the red bean paste in the center of the rice, and gently spread it out with the back of a spoon. Be careful not to disturb the rice or the fruit. Now completely cover the red bean paste with the remaining rice, and pat the rice down evenly. Cover the bowl with foil. The pudding can be refrigerated or frozen at this point.

To cook, place the covered bowl of rice pudding on a rack in a steamer. Steam the pudding for 1 hour, quickly adding hot water to the pot from time to time if necessary. Allow a few extra minutes of steaming time if the pudding is frozen.

While the pudding is steaming, prepare the sweetened water. In a 1-quart pot, combine the cup of water and ½ cup of sugar. Bring it to the boil, then stir in the cornstarch-and-water paste. As soon as the liquid is thickened and smooth, turn the heat down to low.

To unmold the hot pudding, place a flat serving plate over the top of the bowl. Invert the bowl and the plate so the plate is on the bottom and the bowl is on top. Do this quickly and with a forceful motion, so that as you flip the bowl, the rapid downward motion will help release the pudding in one piece. Top individual servings of the pudding with the sugar syrup.

Peking Dust

栗子泥

Lizi Ni

Peking

Serves 4 to 6

This exceedingly rich dessert is most definitely a banquet dish. The use of heavy cream is one indication that it is out of reach for most families in China. And the length of time required just to shell the chestnuts is further evidence that this is a specialty dessert.

The dessert consists of a puree of sweetened chestnuts covered with a mound of whipped cream. This, in turn, is topped with more whipped cream, making it look like a snowcapped mountain. It can be decorated with sugared or spiced nuts, which will make it even more pleasing. In my heart of hearts I would love to pour hot fudge sauce over it all, but even without the sauce this is a fine dessert.

1 pound fresh chestnuts
¼ cup white or firmly packed light brown sugar
1 cup heavy cream, chilled
2 tablespoons confectioners' sugar
Optional garnish: 1 cup Crispy Sweet Walnuts (page 113) or Crisp Spiced Sugar Pecans (page 114)

Before you begin, chill a small mixing bowl and beaters to be used later for whipping the cream.

With a sharp paring knife, cut a deep X in the top of each of the chestnuts. Place the chestnuts in a 2-quart pot and cover them generously with water—the water should cover the chestnuts by an inch. Cover the pot and cook the chestnuts over moderate heat for about 45 minutes. Drain off the water. With a small sharp knife, peel off the shells and inside skins of the chestnuts.

Puree the chestnuts in a food processor or run them through a food mill. They should be slightly grainy, not pureed into a paste. Mix the chestnuts with the ¼ cup of sugar.

In the chilled mixing bowl, stir together the chilled heavy cream and the confectioners' sugar. Whip the cream until it holds stiff peaks. In the center of a small attractive serving plate, make a mound of half the whipped cream. Gently pat the chestnut puree around it, making a small mountain. Refrigerate the dessert at this point, and refrigerate the remaining whipped cream.

Just before serving, press the crisp pecan garnish around the chestnut puree at the base. Top the mountain with the remaining whipped cream, allowing it to drizzle down the sides attractively.

Sesame-Seed Red-Bean-Paste Dim Sum

豆沙包

Dou Sha Bao

Canton

Makes 24 small pastries

Here is an example of a filled pastry that can be served as a daytime snack or as a slightly sweet refreshment at a multicourse meal. Red bean paste is selected as the filling to illustrate how it can be used in Chinese cooking, but chopped or ground dates make a tasty substitute. The sesame seeds are used for flavor and a contrasting texture. The filling is on the bland side, and its attractiveness comes from its color, which shows through when Wheat Starch Dim Sum Wrappers are steamed.

This pastry can also be fried, producing a very crisp outside layer and a chewy filling. The red color of the filling will not show through, but the unusual textures will compensate. Serve the fried *dim sum* immediately, because the dough softens within a very short time.

½ recipe Wheat Starch Dim Sum Wrappers (page 82)
½ cup sweetened red bean paste, homemade if possible (page 139)
2 tablespoons sesame seeds

Prepare the wheat starch wrappers according to the recipe. Mix together the red bean paste and sesame seeds for use as the filling. Roll and fill the dough as directed in the recipe for Wheat Starch Dim Sum Wrappers. Place the *dim sum* on a greased tray and steam them for 5 to 7 minutes, until the dough is semitransparent. Serve the *dim sum* hot or at room temperature. They can be frozen and later served at room temperature or resteamed and served hot.

Date and Red-Bean-Paste Buns

枣泥豆沙包

Zao Ni Dou Sha Bao

Peking

Makes 12 buns

In China, steamed buns filled with sweetened red bean paste are eaten as snacks and sweet treats. Here, chopped dates and sesame seeds are added to the more basic red bean paste buns to make them tastier. The rich, dark filling contrasts with the puffy white dough.

½ recipe Steamed or Baked Buns (page 84)
8 ounces pitted dates, minced
2 tablespoons sesame seeds
½ cup sweetened red bean paste, preferably homemade (page 139)

Prepare the dough according to the directions on page 85. While the dough is rising, prepare the filling. In a small mixing bowl, using a fork or spoon, mix together the minced dates, sesame seeds, and sweetened red bean paste.

When the dough has risen sufficiently, fill, wrap, and steam the buns according to the directions beginning on page 86, making 12 buns in all. Serve the buns hot or warm, or tray-freeze the steamed buns and resteam them before serving.

Fortune Cookies

百福餅

Bai Fu Bing

Chinese-American influence

Makes 16

Although the fortune cookie is said to have originated in the United States, it is not without Chinese antecedents. Various accountings describe how secret wartime messages, birth announcements, and jokes have been found in Chinese pastries.

In the United States, commercially produced fortune cookies are made from a flour-sugar-water dough. From this dough, wafers are baked on a hot griddle; and while the wafers are still warm, fortunes printed on paper are placed inside and the wafers are folded in the familiar shape of fortune cookies. The cookies harden as they cool. At least one brand of fortune cookies contains fortunes with a Jewish bias.

Homemade fortune cookies are most easily prepared using egg roll or *wonton* wrappers. Typed messages are folded into the wrappers, which are then fried. The fortunes can be inspirational or amusing Of course, you can write fortunes specifically for your guests. When one of our friends was running for School Board, we had a fortune in that evening's selection which said, "Vote for Greg La Pointe for School Board." (He won.)

16 fortunes
4 egg roll skins or 16 wonton wrappers
Oil for deep-frying
Confectioners' sugar, about 2 tablespoons

Type the fortunes so they are not more than 3½ inches wide or more than two single-spaced lines. Cut out the fortunes. Fold them in half or thirds so they won't stick out of the wrappers.

Cut the egg roll skins into 4 squares each. The *wonton* wrappers are already the right size. Place a fortune a little above the center of each wrapper. Moisten the edges of the wrappers, and fold the *wontons* according to the illustrations and directions on page 77.

In a large electric skillet or a pot at least 3 inches deep, heat a minimum of ½ inch of oil to 375 degrees F. Fry the fortune cookies until they are golden brown all over. Remove them from the oil, and drain them very well on paper towels. While they are still warm (but not hot), sprinkle them with confectioners' sugar

When the fortune cookies have cooled completely, transfer them to plastic bags or plastic containers. Store them for a few days at room temperature, or freeze them for many weeks.

Walnut "Tea"

核桃羹

He Tao Geng

General China

Serves 6

Walnut "tea" is made from fried chopped walnuts and sugared water. It is particularly important to serve this souplike dessert-beverage attractively, because the taste at first is reminiscent of Wheatena, and it will have to look pretty if you're going to get people to venture beyond that first sip. As it is sipped, the beverage becomes refreshing—light and sweet, but satisfying. Small colorful Chinese teacups are ideal vessels in which to serve and drink this "tea."

2 cups water
1 cup walnut meats
1 cup peanut, corn, or other oil for deep-frying
4 cups water
⅔ cup sugar
3 tablespoons cornstarch dissolved in ¼ cup cold water

In a 1- or 2-quart pot, bring 2 cups of water to the boil. Add the walnuts, boil them for half a minute, then drain them in a colander or strainer. Set the walnuts out on paper towels, and pat them dry.

In a clean, dry 2-quart pot, heat the oil until it just barely begins to smoke. Add the walnuts carefully, and fry them until golden, stirring occasionally with a clean, dry spoon. Be careful not to burn the walnuts—regulate the heat as necessary. Drain the nuts on paper towels. When they cool down to room temperature, chop the nuts finely in a wooden chopping bowl or on a chopping block. Store the walnuts in a covered jar until you're ready to make the "tea."

In a 2-quart pot, bring the 4 cups of water to the boil. Add the sugar and cook until the sugar dissolves. Stir in the walnuts. Again stir together the cornstarch and the cold water until a very thick, smooth paste is formed.

Stir the cornstarch paste into the boiling sweetened water, and cook and stir until the dessert-beverage is thickened and smooth. Remove the pan from the heat and serve.

Sweet Orange "Tea"

橘子羹

Juzi Geng

General China

Serves 6

Fresh oranges steep in a sugar syrup to produce this refreshing "tea." The Chinese serve this sweet beverage from small teacups as a snack during the day, between courses at a meal, or at the conclusion of a meal.

2 large juice oranges
2 cups water
¼ cup sugar
4 teaspoons cornstarch

Cut the oranges in half and section them the way you do for grapefruit. Remove all the pits. Squeeze the oranges into a 2-quart pot. All the sections should come out, as well as the juice and extra pulp. Discard the rinds. Stir in the remaining ingredients. Bring the mixture to the boil over medium heat, stirring occasionally. When it comes to the boil, continue to cook for half a minute, stirring constantly. Turn off the heat, cover the pot, and let this orange beverage sit for 5 minutes before serving. Leftovers can be reheated over low heat.

Tea

茶

Cha

General China

If I tell you that tea is to the Chinese dinner what the *afikomon* is to the Passover *Seder*, you will know why tea is the very last recipe in this book. Tea is consumed all day long in China, and it is served to guests (unexpected as well as invited) upon their arrival. In most parts of China tea is not drunk during the meal, but tea is always the last item served at a Chinese meal.

There are books devoted exclusively to tea, but it is possible to introduce you to some major facts about tea in a short space. All tea comes from the leaves of a particular kind of plant, a shrub called *Thea sinensis* or *Camellia sinensis*. The conditions under which that plant grows (wild, cultivated, the altitude, rainfall, temperature, and other climatic factors); which of its leaves and the time of year in which those leaves are harvested; how the harvested tea leaves are processed—all these affect the color, flavor, and quality of the beverage made from the plant.

There are three very basic categories of tea (although some authorities treat the third as a subset of the other two). "Unfermented" tea, which we know as "green" tea, produces a light colored brew with a naturally sweet fragrance and subtle taste. "Fermented" or "black" tea is a rich red color with a robust flavor. Unfermented tea is sun- or air-dried, rolled, then roasted. Fermented tea is also dried and rolled, but then it is left to stand in a damp room before being roasted. "Semifermented" tea, known as *oolong* tea, combines the delicate aroma of green tea with the darker color and stronger taste of the black. Scented teas, such as jasmine, usually combine dried flowers or fruit blossoms with semifermented tea, although green or black tea can be used. The most famous smoky tea, *Lapsang Souchong,* is a dark, pungent black tea. The terms "orange pekoe" and "pekoe" that we see on boxes of tea in this country refer to the size and appearance of the leaf and where it grows on the plant.

No matter what the kind of tea, pour freshly boiled water directly over tea leaves to produce a cup or pot of tea. When making tea in quantity, steep the tea leaves for 3 to 5 minutes, then strain the brew through coffee filters or white paper towels. If using paper towels, fasten them with a rubber band around the rim of the pot or pitcher into which the tea is being strained. The amount of tea leaves to use in making tea varies with the kind of tea (and there may be as many as 300 kinds of tea), but in general ½ to 1 teaspoon of tea leaves per 8-ounce cup is recommended.

When individual guests are served during daytime hours in China, the tea leaves are placed in the individual cups, and the tea brews right in the cups. That way the guest knows that the tea is freshly made. The guest's second cup of tea is made by pouring fresh water over the same leaves, and this cup of tea is considered better than the first because, say tea connoisseurs, the full flavor and aroma of the leaves do not come through until the second steeping. Sugar and lemon or cream are not served with tea in China, although preserved ginger is occasionally used.

To brew tea in cups for individual servings, place about ½ teaspoon of tea leaves in each 6-ounce cup, and pour a small amount of freshly boiled water (a tablespoon will do) over the leaves, enough to moisten them. Cover the cup for a minute, then fill it with freshly boiled water

Selected Bibliography

American Heritage Dictionary. Second College Edition. Boston: Houghton Mifflin Company, 1982.

Chang, Irving B. and Wonona W., and Kutscher, Austin H. and Helene W. *An Encyclopedia of Chinese Food and Cooking*. New York: Crown Publishers, Inc., 1970.

Chu, Grace Zia. *Madame Chu's Chinese Cooking School*. New York: Simon and Schuster, 1975.

Chu, Grace Zia. *The Pleasures of Chinese Cooking*. New York: Simon and Schuster, 1962.

Hahn, Emily. *The Cooking of China*. New York: Time-Life Books, 1968.

Ho, Lucy. *Authentic Chinese Cooking*. New York: Dover Publications, Inc., 1973.

Lom, Arthur, and Morris, Dan. *The Hong Kong Cookbook*. New York: Funk & Wagnalls, 1970.

Miller, Gloria Bley. *The Thousand Recipe Chinese Cookbook*. New York: Grosset & Dunlap, 1979.

Nix, Janeth Johnson. *Sunset Chinese Cook Book*. Menlo Park, California: Lane Publishing Co., 1979.

Pei Mei, Fu. *Pei Mei's Chinese Cook Book*. Volume I. Taiwan: T & S Industrial Co., Ltd., 1969.

Yee, Rhoda. *Dim Sum*. San Francisco: Taylor & Ng. 1977.

Index

Notes